Guyana

the Bradt Travel Guide

Kirk Smock

edition
2

www.bradtguides.com

Bradt Travel Guides Ltd, UK
The Globe Pequot Press Inc, USA

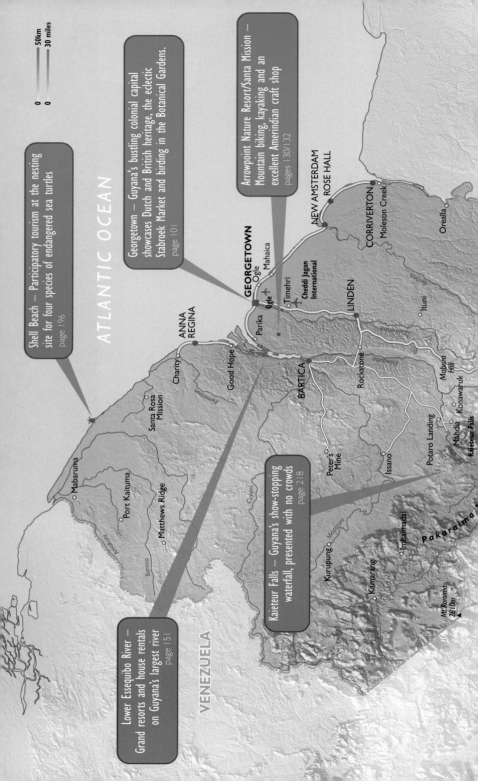

Shell Beach – Participatory tourism at the nesting site for four species of endangered sea turtles
page 196

Georgetown – Guyana's bustling colonial capital showcases Dutch and British heritage, the eclectic Stabroek Market and birding in the Botanical Gardens.
page 101

Arrowpoint Nature Resort/Santa Mission – Mountain biking, kayaking and an excellent Amerindian craft shop
pages 130/132

Kaieteur Falls – Guyana's show-stopping waterfall, presented with no crowds
page 218

Lower Essequibo River – Grand resorts and house rentals on Guyana's largest river
page 151

ATLANTIC OCEAN

VENEZUELA

GEORGETOWN
Ogle
Mahaica
Timehri
Cheddi Jagan International
NEW AMSTERDAM
ROSE HALL
CORRIVERTON
Moleson Creek
Orealla
LINDEN
Ituni
Parika
ANNA REGINA
Charity
Good Hope
BARTICA
Rockstone
Santa Rosa Mission
Mabaruma
Port Kaituma
Matthews Ridge
Peter's Mine
Issano
Potaro Landing
Mahdia
Konawaruk
Kaieteur Falls
Mabura Hill
Kurupung
Imbaimadai
Kamarang
Mt Roraima 2810m
Pakaraima

0   50km
0   30 miles

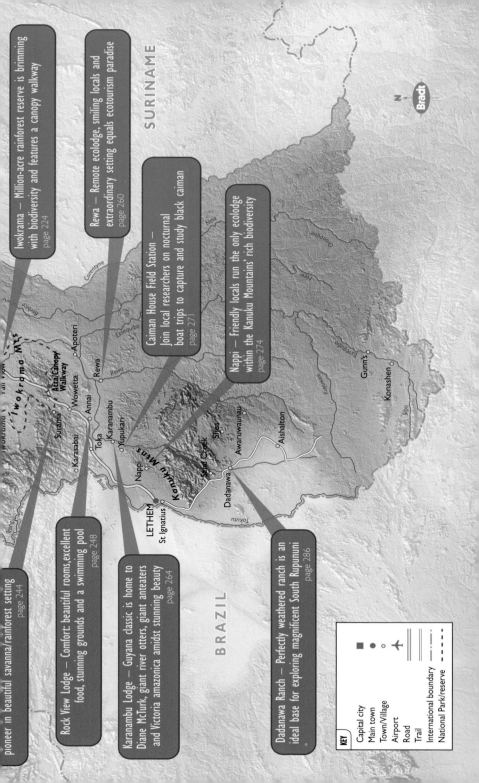

Iwokrama — Million-acre rainforest reserve is brimming with biodiversity and features a canopy walkway
page 224

Rewa — Remote ecolodge, smiling locals and extraordinary setting equals ecotourism paradise
page 260

Caiman House Field Station — Join local researchers on nocturnal boat trips to capture and study black caiman
page 271

Nappi — Friendly locals run the only ecolodge within the Kanuku Mountains' rich biodiversity
page 274

SURINAME

pioneer in beautiful savanna/rainforest setting
page 244

Rock View Lodge — Comfort: beautiful rooms, excellent food, stunning grounds and a swimming pool
page 248

Karanambu Lodge — Guyana classic is home to Diane McTurk, giant river otters, giant anteaters and Victoria amazonica amidst stunning beauty
page 264

Dadanawa Ranch — Perfectly weathered ranch is an ideal base for exploring magnificent South Rupununi
page 286

BRAZIL

Iwokrama Mts

Atta Canopy Walkway
Surama
Karasabai
Toka
Annai
Yupukari
Karanambu
Woweta
Rewa
Apoteri
Essequibo
Corentyne
Berbice
New
Canje

LETHEM
St Ignatius
Nappi
Kanuku Mts
Sand Creek
Sena
Awaruwaunau
Dadanawa
Takutu
Aishalton
Kwitaro
Rupununi
Gunn's
Konashen
Sipu
Kassikaityu

Bradt

N

KEY
■ Capital city
● Main town
○ Town/Village
✈ Airport
═ Road
┄ Trail
━ International boundary
┅ National Park/reserve

Guyana
Don't
miss...

Birds
Guyana's diverse habitat is home to more than 815 species of bird from 72 different families, including the Guianan cock-of-the-rock (BT) page 41

Rainforest
Approximately 80% of Guyana's landmass is covered by tropical rainforest, and much of it is still intact (DF) page 29

Wildlife
Jaguars are usually spotted along trails or gaps along the forest edge where roads or rivers run
(SAT/FN/MP/FLPA) page 30

The Rupununi Savannas
The Rupununi Savannas encompass roughly 5,000 square miles and cover a significant portion of southern Guyana and parts of northern Brazil
(CH) page 239

Community tourism
Community tourism efforts in Guyana not only provide villages with much needed income, they also teach them the importance of conservation and sustainable land-use issues (CH) page 250

above left Many Amerindian communities produce necessities of their daily life with an amazing amount of artistry, including intricately woven basketry (CH) page 23

above Woman grating cassava; during Amerindian Heritage Month competitions to find the fastest cassava grater are held (KN) page 25

left Culture show by the Makushi Amerindians in Surama (EL) page 244

below At 143ft, St George's Cathedral in Georgetown is one of the world's tallest free-standing wooden buildings (EL) page 121

above The best market for admiring and buying the wide array of fresh fruits and vegetables grown in Guyana is Bourda Market in Georgetown, a daily, permanent market dating back to 1880 (i/A) page 122

right Children in Rewa, a small community of roughly 250 inhabitants located at the confluence of the Rewa and Rupununi rivers (CH) page 260

below Every Easter weekend travellers from throughout Guyana and northern Brazil flock to Lethem for the Rupunini Rodeo (DF) page 285

Iwokrama Forest
The Experience of a Lifetime

"Globally Unique"

The Iwokrama Forest and surrounding North Rupununi Wetlands act as a convergence point for the three diverse ecosystems: the Pantanal, The Amazonian and the Guiana Shield ecosystems.

The resulting diversity of flora and fauna is unmatched anywhere in the world with:
- *highest recorded densities of fishes and bats for any area of its size worldwide.
- *healthy population of endangered giants such as Jaguars, Black Caiman, Arapaima, Giant River Otters, Giant Ant Eaters and Giant River Turtles.

Step into the Iwokrama Forest in central Guyana... one of the world's last frontier forests... waiting for adventurers seeking a truly **unique experience.**

Exotically designed cabin accommodations with bathroom facilities. Dining Area, Bar, Visitor Centre, Small Shop, & Business Centre.

Experience: The Iwokrama Canopy Walkway which offers a unique experience. The 154 metre (505 ft.) mid-level canopy, a series of suspension bridges and decks, envelopes you in from heights of up to 30 metres (98 ft.), The Early Morning Boat ride round Indian Island, The Trip to see the Petroglyphs and Fair View Village, The Guided Nocturnal Tour of the Rain Forest trail with Torches, Canoe Rides, The Butterfly Farm, The Bird Sanctuary, The People, The Culture ...*and so much more!*

Learn more at www.iwokrama.org

IW**O**KRAMA

International Centre
77 High Street, Kingston, Georgetow
Guyana, PO Box 10630, Tel: 225-150

AUTHOR

Kirk Smock (*www.kirksmock.com*) is a freelance writer and tourism consultant from the US. He lived in Guyana with his wife for 2½ years while she fulfilled a public health fellowship in Georgetown. Since Kirk left Guyana in late 2007, he has remained actively involved with tourism development in the country while working on the Guyana Sustainable Tourism Initiative, a USAID-funded project. Kirk currently lives in Baltimore with his wife, their son and two cats – one of which is Guyanese. His work has appeared in several publications.

AUTHOR'S STORY

When my wife and I moved to Guyana in 2005, we knew very little about the country. Before packing our bags and boxes we paged through guidebooks and searched the internet for any information that would provide a clue about what life would hold. Websites of local newspapers seemed obsessed with bad news and some guidebooks were less than encouraging. But we did come across some stunningly beautiful photographs and heard enough positive accounts to eventually decide we'd have to come to our own conclusions.

Shortly after moving to Guyana it was easy to see that the typical economic hardships and social ills experienced by developing countries were offset by a rich natural history and vibrant culture. Viewing the country through the eyes of a freelance writer, I couldn't understand why more magazine articles weren't written about Guyana, and why there didn't seem to be any tourists.

During my early travels through Guyana – whether it was trekking through claustrophobic jungles or exploring the seemingly never-ending savannas by 4x4 – I was awe-struck by the beauty and pristine nature of the country.

I scribbled notes about boating through pretend lands and wrote about rainforests that were surely too archetypal to be real. I quickly recognised that information on Guyana as a tourism destination was extremely limited.

After living in Guyana for more than a year, my job took me to the British Birdwatching Fair to market Guyana as an emerging destination for birdwatchers. While trying to drum up interest within the media, I spoke with Hilary Bradt. Magazines didn't seem ready for an unknown destination, so I thought a book publisher was a real long shot. I couldn't believe it when she told me they had long been looking for an author to write a Guyana guidebook. I immediately recognised that Bradt is truly a company that understands travel and the rewards of getting off the beaten path. And they are willing to take risks to help promote tourism in countries with very low tourism numbers.

When preparing to move to Guyana, I never would have imagined having the opportunity to write a guide on this overlooked land. Since the first edition was published in late 2007, I have had the honour of working closely with Bradt to promote Guyana, and I have seen the positive impact a Bradt title has had on Guyana's tourism development. I can only hope that this book continues to do its part in bringing Guyana more recognition as a tourism destination, and in some form benefits those who work so hard to make tourism in Guyana a reality.

PUBLISHER'S FOREWORD   *Donald Greig, Managing Director*

Guyana typifies for me the sort of emerging destination that Bradt has supported in its guidebooks since Hilary Bradt first founded the company almost 40 years ago. Vast tracts of rainforest form one of the most pristine environments on the planet, home to a world-class array of wildlife: I have never seen a creature so other-worldly as a giant anteater racing across the savanna, nor witnessed a group of people so intensely excited as when a jaguar appeared on the banks of the Rupununi River. Real eco-tourism, the sort where the locals own, staff and reap the benefits from the village lodges, is developing at a pace which is as sustainable as it is welcoming. Things may not always run exactly according to plan, but any frustrations with infrastructure are far outweighed by the delights of discovering somewhere so rich in natural wonders. Imagine lying on your stomach and peering over the edge of a waterfall five times the size of Niagara. In fact, don't just imagine it. Get yourself to Guyana, to Kaieteur Falls and try it for yourself!

Second edition published July 2011. First edition published January 2008

Bradt Travel Guides Ltd, IDC House, The Vale, Chalfont St Peter, Bucks SL9 9RZ, England;
www.bradtguides.com
Published in the USA by The Globe Pequot Press Inc, PO Box 480, Guilford, Connecticut 06437-0480

Text copyright © 2011 Kirk Smock
Maps copyright © 2011 Bradt Travel Guides Ltd
Illustrations copyright © 2011 Individual photographers and artists
Editorial project manager: Emma Thomson/Rachel Fielding

ISBN-13: 978 1 84162 358 0
British Library Cataloguing in Publication Data
A catalogue record for this book is available from the British Library

Photographers Bill Thompson (BT), Cheryl Hart (CH), Duane de Freitas (DF), Eric Lindberg (EL), Flip De Nooyer/FN/Minden/FLPA (FDN/FN/M/FLPA), imagebroker/Alamy (i/A), Karen Straus (KSt), Kirk Smock (KS), Kristina Nemeth (KN), Pete Oxford/Minden Pictures/FLPA (PO/MP/FLPA), Photoshot (P), SA Team/FN/Minden/FLPA (SAT/FN/M/FLPA), SuperStock (SS)
Front cover Collared anteater (P)
Back cover Kaieteur Falls (SS), Jaguar (SS)
Title page Spider monkey (FDN/FN/M/FLPA), Queen's wreath purple flower (PO/MP/FLPA), Boy at Amerindian Heritage Month celebrations (CH)

Illustrations Fiona Reid, Carole Vincer
Maps David McCutcheon, based on source material from ITMB and Guyana Lands and Surveys Commission
Colour map Relief map bases by Nick Rowland RGS

Typeset from the author's disc by Wakewing
Production managed by Jellyfish Print Solutions and manufactured in the UK

Acknowledgements

There were countless people who had a hand in making the first and second editions of this guidebook possible. Many helped by providing advice, snippets of information, insights and encouragement (all directly or indirectly), and while I can't list everybody's names here, I do extend my sincere gratitude to each of you.

Those who contributed directly to the book also deserve particular recognition. Special thanks go to Kathryn Boryc, for writing the health section, being my unofficial editor throughout, and for providing me with the unfaltering support that saw two editions of this book through to completion. To Bruce and Julia Roberts, for writing the section on fishing, welcoming us to Guyana as family and introducing me to the South Rupununi. Other contributors include Michelle Kalamandeen who provided the scientific information on sea turtles and Shell Beach, and many people at Iwokrama, including Mark Engstrom and Burton Lim for providing information on Guyana's mammals. For maps, thanks to ITMB and Naseem Nasir and the Guyana Lands and Surveys Commission. The wonderful illustrations come from Fiona Reid and Carole Vincer and huge thanks go out to all of the talented photographers who contributed their images to this edition.

My sincere gratitude to all of my friends and colleagues in Guyana whose impressions, opinions and knowledge of Guyana helped form this guidebook. There are many of you who have helped in countless ways, and I am more than grateful. Special thanks go to everybody at the USAID/GTIS project for professional and personal support, and to the tremendous staff at Bradt for believing in Guyana as a destination and me as a writer.

And finally, to my mother and family for supporting my wanderlust and raising me to believe anything is within reach, including the completion of a book. Kathryn, thank you for joining me on the journey; there is no-one better. Noah, for bringing us such joy and inspiration, this book is for you; I hope you find the pictures (and someday soon, the words) in this edition as enjoyable as the first.

FROM THE PUBLISHER Kirk Smock has done a superb job of capturing and documenting Guyana in his guide and we salute his tireless endeavours. We also say thank you to John Gimlette for providing the foreword to this edition. His book, *Wild Coast*, about his travels through the three Guianas, is a splendid and fascinating work and I'd thoroughly recommend reading it before you go.

Contents

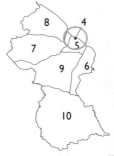

UPDATES WEBSITE AND FEEDBACK REQUEST

If you have any comments, queries or grumbles, insights, news or other feedback please contact us on ✆ 01753 893444; or e info@bradtguides.com. Alternatively you can add a review of the book to www.bradtguides.com or Amazon.

Periodically our authors post travel updates and reader feedback on the website. Check www.bradtguides.com/guidebook-updates for any news.

Foreword

High up, on the northeast shoulder of South America, lies Guyana, a fabulous forested nation, barely explored. With jungle covering most of it, much of this land seldom sees sunlight, and new species are always tumbling out of the dark. It's not an easy place to compass, and was shunned by the conquistadors, and left to others to carve into colonies. It's been a long struggle but what has emerged is a beautiful and mysterious country.

Thanks to this book, visitors to Guyana are now able to understand it probably better than ever before. A few years ago, I had set off on a two-month journey along its coast and up its rivers, clutching a copy of Kirk Smock's work. At the time, I was writing my own book, *Wild Coast,* and, before leaving, I'd spent months researching the country's history, flora, fauna, anthropology, politics and culture. So, even before I arrived, I'd realised that Kirk's research was not only wide-ranging but impeccably accurate. What I'd yet to realise was the lengths he'd gone to identify and list the country's precious and well-dispersed facilities for travellers. If there was a hotel or eatery to be found, then Kirk Smock found it, evaluated it, and brought it to his reader. For me, his guide was in every sense a godsend.

Now, in this eagerly anticipated new edition, Kirk brings us, once again, the bare bones of a great adventure. Whatever it is you're after, this is how to find it: the ranches, the forest camps, the great waterfalls, the breezy coastal towns, the 'African' markets, the long-lost forts of the Dutch; a week with the Amerindians, or perhaps a night in an alligator-lovers' boutique hotel.

So, thank you Kirk, and thank you Bradt. Without this book, I would have still loved Guyana but much of the detail would have been lost in the struggle to get around, well-watered and fed.

As it was, Guyana proved a remarkable experience. I don't suppose I shall ever see such dramatic rivers again, gnashing along with fury, or sliding along like a land in the mirror. And I love the idea that much of this land isn't even known to those that live here, and that its creatures – mad, gaudy, toxic and exotic – are probably safer here than anywhere else in the world. Other places may feel more magnificent than Guyana, or perhaps emptier, but nowhere feels quite so unconquered.

John Gimlette
Author of *Wild Coast: Travels on South America's Untamed Edge*

Introduction

Guyana is South America's little-known curiosity that lies far off the well-trodden tourist path. It's bordered by Venezuela, Brazil, Suriname and the Atlantic Ocean, but is a continental anomaly. The lively English-speaking locals – a melting pot of East Indian and African descendants, peppered with indigenous Amerindians, Europeans and Chinese – and a history of British colonialism create a culture decidedly more Caribbean than Latin.

With 215,000km² (83,000 square miles), Guyana has plenty of space, but 90% of the roughly 750,000 inhabitants live along the developed coastlands, which is only about 5% of the total landmass. The remaining 95% is relatively unpopulated outside of small interior villages, Amerindian communities and migrant mining and forestry camps. Some 80% of Guyana is still covered in rainforests.

A lack of interior development (the main road running north–south through Guyana remains unpaved) has allowed Guyana's unique geography – coastal waters, mangroves, marshes, savannas, mountains and tropical rainforests – to support a range of ecosystems that widely remain in a pristine natural state. Within the interior, the Guiana Shield (one of four largely intact pristine tropical rainforests left in the world) converges with the Amazon Basin, providing a home to a dizzying array and number of flora and fauna.

To date, research in Guyana has identified more than 225 species of mammals, over 300 species of reptiles and amphibians, more than 810 species of birds and some 6,500 species of plants. Within these numbers are some of South America's, and the world's largest species, including black caiman (alligator), capybara (rodent), arapaima (scaled freshwater fish), green anaconda (snake), giant anteater, giant river otter, giant river turtle, false vampire bat, harpy eagle and jaguar. The research is far from conclusive.

Guyana's tourism offerings are largely nature-based and ideal for discerning visitors who like a sense of adventure with their travels. Northwestern Guyana offers miles of undeveloped coast, nesting sea turtles, dense forests and meandering rivers that double as the area's main roads; the easily accessible lower Essequibo River has several resorts and private house rentals from which to experience the many moods of South America's third-largest river.

Georgetown, the capital city, is home to more than 200 species of birds and beautiful colonial architecture; Berbice, in the northeastern part of the country, is covered in sugarcane fields and fruit and vegetable farms. Within the central rainforests you'll find one of the world's most powerful waterfalls and a million-acre rainforest reserve; in the Rupununi savannas of southwestern Guyana you can visit welcoming Amerindian communities, functioning cattle ranches and a handful of lodges that provide plenty of opportunities to immerse yourself in the natural surroundings.

The options for visitors are as varied as the terrain (for an overview see *Highlights*, page 52) and throughout Guyana tourism is still developing. Because Guyana has never experienced the droves of tourists common to other South American countries, everything is done on a smaller, and more intimate scale here.

Most lodges are small, family- or community-run affairs that welcome visitors as old friends. Expect to be called by your first name, often upon arrival, and to be remembered should you ever return. Tourism in Guyana is different from most places; it's far from polished and can entail hiccups. Guyana is not for the fussy. But it's exactly this unpolished and unpretentious tourism that creates a unique experience that often leaves visitors feeling as though they have stumbled upon a rare, nearly undiscovered tourism gem.

Since writing the first edition of this guidebook, Guyana's tourism industry has seen some welcome developments. Birders and nature enthusiasts are starting to come in greater numbers and lodges have upgraded their facilities and added new rooms, guides have received additional training, new communities have developed products and tourism is being regarded as a feasible means of conserving and preserving the country's natural riches.

However, an increase in visitors to Guyana is relative and you'll likely only feel crowded by the forest. I still recall a trip towards the end of my own travels researching the first edition of this book. I visited Shell Beach, and during one afternoon I walked the endless beach alone for an hour before sitting down to write. I noted that I was on the northern coast of South America, waves of the Atlantic lapping at my feet, a wall of coconut palms to my back and the tracks left from a nesting green sea turtle on my right. There was no sign of civilisation in any direction and for the umpteenth time during my travels in Guyana I felt as though I had stepped into something larger than the present, something that diminishes all that mankind has created in this world, both good and bad. It was nature, in a raw, unaltered, almost timeless state that made me feel insignificant. It was a welcome and humbling feeling.

It's this sense of experiencing a rare natural world that I still associate with travelling in Guyana today. Every trip I take into the interior involves my feeling astonished and entirely lucky to be where I am, whether it's on a quiet river, a mountaintop, or sharing a dinner with a family.

The pristine nature, the rich biodiversity, the endangered species, the incredibly varied ecosystems are all here, and thankfully the welcoming locals see the benefits of marrying conservation with development.

Many Amerindian communities are turning away from the wildlife trade, mining and forestry and looking at tourism as a means of bringing income to their villages while preserving their resources for future generations. Lodges are built, trails are cut and guides are trained, but visitors do not magically show up.

Guyana remains a virtual unknown. Villages and people can't depend on tourism without enough visitors to make it possible. I hope that this book will generate interest in Guyana and encourage travellers to take a chance and veer off the beaten path on their next holiday. You are welcome to email me at e kirksmock@gmail. com with any trip-planning queries.

Part One

GENERAL INFORMATION

Location North Atlantic coast of South America, between latitudes 1 and 9 and longitudes 57 and 61.

Neighbouring countries Suriname to the east, Brazil to the south and southwest, and Venezuela to the west

Size/Area 214,969km^2

Climate Tropical. Coast wet season mid-November to mid-January and May to mid-July; interior wet season May to end of August; short rains December; rest of year generally dry. Average temperature 27.5°C; coastland ranges from 18 to 34°C; interior ranges from 18 to 40°C

Status Republic within the Commonwealth

Population 769,141 (2010 est.)

Life expectancy 67

Capital Georgetown, population 170,000

Other main towns/villages Linden, New Amsterdam, Rose Hall, Anna Regina, Bartica, Lethem

Economy Agriculture, timber, fishing, mining

GDP US$6,500 (2009 est.)

Languages English (official), Creole, Amerindian dialects, Hindi, Urdu

Religion Christian, Hindu, Muslim

Currency Guyana dollar (G$)

Exchange rate US$1 = G$205 (July 2011)

National airport Cheddi Jagan International Airport

International telephone code +592

Time GMT −4

Electrical voltage 110V in Georgetown and lodges; 220V in most other places; three-pin 'American-style' plugs (see page 81)

Weights and measures Metric

Flag Green background with red isosceles triangle with left border on left side superimposed on a long, yellow arrowhead with white border

National anthem *Dear Land of Guyana*

National flower *Victoria amazonica*

National bird/animal Hoatzin/Jaguar

National sport Cricket

Public holidays 1 January, 23 February (Republic Day and Mashramani), Good Friday, Easter Monday, 1 May (Labour Day), 5 May (Indian Arrival Day), 26 May (Independence Day), first Monday in July (Caricom Day), 1 August (Emancipation Day), 25 December, 26 December (see also page 91)

Background Information

GEOGRAPHY

Guyana covers an area of 83,000 square miles (214,969km²) on the northeastern coast of South America. Guyana borders the Atlantic for 270 miles and moves southwards into South America for a distance of 450 miles. Suriname borders Guyana to the east, Brazil to the south and southwest and Venezuela to the west.

Guyana is composed of three distinct geographical zones: the coastal belt, the forested and mountainous interior and the savannas.

With a varying width of ten to 40 miles, the coastal belt accounts for only 5% of Guyana's total land area, yet it is where 90% of the country's population is found. Much of the coastal belt, which actually lies several feet below sea level at high tide, has been reclaimed through a series of sea walls, dams and *kokers* (sluice gates). This offers a degree of protection for the highly cultivated lands, but the susceptibility to flooding remains.

From the coast, the landscape rises dramatically to a series of mountain ranges and high plateaux covered in dense equatorial rainforests. This area is rich in minerals that spawned the age-old belief that Guyana is the site of El Dorado, the lost city of gold. Most of the mining that occurs here is for gold, diamonds and bauxite.

Further south are the savanna lands known as the Rupununi. This area in southwestern Guyana changes dramatically with the seasons, being mostly floodland in the wet season (May–August) and experiencing drought conditions in the dry season.

Guyana, whose name is derived from an Amerindian word meaning 'Land of Many Waters', has numerous large rivers and waterways, but three dominate in terms of size and importance. The Essequibo River is South America's third-largest river and runs the entire length of the country, its mouth 20 miles wide where it spills into the Atlantic just west of Georgetown. The Demerara River creates the western border of the capital city and is the site of the main port, and the Berbice River is to the east of Georgetown and runs deep into the south of Guyana.

CLIMATE

The climate in Guyana is equatorial, meaning hot all year round, with an average temperature of 27.5°C and an average annual rainfall of 91ins. Humidity is generally high all year round but is noticeably more uncomfortable during the rainy seasons when saturation levels are often above 90%. There are, however, distinct climatic differences between the coastal belt and the interior.

The coast is cooled by sea breezes and has a temperature range of 18–34°C. The wet season is from mid-November to mid-January and then May to mid-July.

In the interior, the average temperature ranges from 18 to 40°C with a wet season from May to September and a period of short rains in December called the 'cashew rains'. The wet season turns normally dry savanna lands into flooded wetlands. Average rainfall in the interior is roughly 70 inches per year.

HISTORY

According to archaeological evidence, Guyana's indigenous peoples have been living in the area for roughly 11,000 years. The first Europeans came to the area in the late 15th century when Christopher Columbus and crew sailed along the shores of Guiana. In 1595, Sir Walter Raleigh explored the area and returned with tales of finding the lost city of gold, El Dorado.

By the 17th century, Dutch settlers began arriving and by the late 1600s had colonised much of the area along the coast and established several sugar plantations. The good times ended, and a long history of turbulence began in 1665 when the second Anglo–Dutch war broke out and the English attacked the Dutch colonies. In 1689 and again in 1708 and 1712 the French attacked the Dutch settlements.

The Dutch recovered, however, and throughout much of the 18th century were able to expand their sugar, coffee and cotton estates. It wasn't long before the British became envious of their success and in 1781 captured the Dutch colonies. For the next two decades control of the area frequently changed hands between the British, French and Dutch, until 1803 when the British finally conquered for the last time.

In 1831, the colonies were named 'British Guiana' and remained as such until 1966 when the British granted independence, and the colony became the Cooperative Republic of Guyana in 1970.

GUYANA'S ORIGINAL INHABITANTS Archaeological studies have shown that Guyana's indigenous peoples, or Amerindians, have been living in the area that is now Guyana since around 9000BC. It's widely believed that they arrived from Asia, via a land bridge, in pursuit of the herds of animals they relied on for food.

It appears they first settled in the northwest region of Guyana where they maintained their hunting ways. About 7,000 years ago, they began to adapt to their new environment by gathering fruits and nuts to supplement their diets. Some groups kept up their nomadic ways and moved throughout the region while hunting wild animals, while others, such as those that settled in the northwest, set up more permanent camps as they gathered fish, turtles and crabs.

Beginning about 4,000 years ago Amerindian groups began supplementing their food more and more by cultivating the land. Archaeologists have found evidence of agricultural communities centred on the growing of cassava roots that date back some 3,000 years.

The Amerindians also became proficient in the art of weaving baskets, creating clay pots and constructing dugout canoes. (These are skills for which the Amerindians are still renowned today.) There are also many petroglyphs throughout Guyana that capture scenes of the hunter-gatherer lifestyle and attest to their fondness for carvings and paintings.

As the Amerindian groups spread from the coastal areas to the interior, there were many tribal wars fought, but for the most part they thrived in Guyana for thousands of years, until Europeans began arriving.

EARLY EUROPEAN VISITORS Christopher Columbus is credited with discovering the Caribbean region when, in 1492, he landed in the Bahamas. His discovery encouraged other explorers and in 1499 Alonzo de Ojeda and Amerigo Vespucci sailed along the coast of South America, including what is now Guyana. The voyagers apparently saw little potential in the dense mangroves and made only one botched landing attempt near the Amazon.

The early part of the 16th century saw an increase in ships and colonisers coming to the area but little interest was shown in the tropical disease-ridden forests of Guiana, the name given to the area between the Amazon and Orinoco rivers. But after gold was discovered in Peru and Colombia word spread of the legendary King El Dorado and his city of gold, Manoa.

Most expeditions made to Guiana throughout the 16th century were in search of the lost city of gold that had captivated much of Europe. However, many of the Spanish expeditions suffered great hardships through war with the Amerindians, disease and famine, which could be why no permanent settlements were made during this time of exploration.

Perhaps the most famous explorer of the time was Sir Walter Raleigh. In 1595, one year after sending an expedition to Guiana to gather more information on the myth of El Dorado, he led his own expedition to the New World. Raleigh was perhaps the first European to become truly enchanted by Guiana. He found no sign of the golden city but left more confident of its existence than when he arrived.

Back in England, he encouraged more exploration in the area, even going so far as suggesting a British colony be established. In 1595, to further his cause, he published a book on his travels called *The Discoverie of the Large, Rich and Bewtiful Empyre of Guiana*. He praised Guiana, saying that, 'Whatever prince shall possess it, that prince shall be lord of more gold, and of more cities and people than either the King of Spain or the great Turk.' The book spread through Europe and new expeditions were quickly launched from England, Spain, France and Holland.

FIRST DUTCH SETTLERS Again, the fog of history has settled over exact dates, but it is believed that in 1598 the Dutch made their first voyage to Guiana, although some histories claim the first Dutch settlement was made along the Pomeroon River in 1596.

At any rate, during the first decade of the 17th century, more Dutch settlers arrived in Guiana and began forming small settlements. These early Dutch settlers established good relationships with the native inhabitants and used their camps as trading posts. The Dutch offered items like knives, axes, alcohol and cloths, for which the Amerindians gladly traded cotton, tobacco and hammocks. (Unfortunately the Amerindians were also being introduced to new diseases that caused countless deaths within their tribes.)

In 1613, the Dutch decided it was time to make a more permanent and secure home, moved inland, and eventually established Fort Kyk-over-al (meaning 'see over all') at the confluence of the Essequibo, Mazaruni and Cuyuni rivers. They continued trading with the Amerindians and also with English colonisers from the West Indies. To boost their items of trade, the Dutch began cultivating the land in a more organised manner. Their settlement prospered and in 1621, on the heels of this success, the Dutch West India Company was established, the colony they had settled was named Essequibo and colonisation began under their governance.

DUTCH COLONISATION As colonisers will, the Dutch soon looked to expand beyond the Essequibo colony. In 1627, the Dutch West India Company granted Abraham Van Pere permission to colonise the area of Berbice. Van Pere, along with other willing Dutch merchants, created the small settlement of Fort Nassau some 75 miles up the Berbice River.

The settlements were being used as trading posts with the Amerindians but the Dutch were also cultivating their own sugarcane, cotton, tobacco and coffee on small plantations. To ensure the success of these plantations, the Dutch needed labourers, so as colonisers are also wont to do, they set up a system of slavery.

The Dutch West India Company eventually brought in African slaves, but the first slaves used in Essequibo and Berbice were Amerindians. Under their new colonial laws, the Dutch granted 'free nation' status to some Amerindian groups while designating others as slaves. The Arawaks, Akawaios, Caribs and Warraus were deemed free and then encouraged to help round up members of the other enslaved groups.

The first African slaves began arriving in the mid 16th century and soon replaced Amerindians as the preferred labour on the plantations. Amerindians continued working with the Dutch by helping to control African slave uprisings and capture any runaways.

With the influx of manual labour provided by the slaves, plantation agriculture was able to flourish and more and more land was being cultivated in Berbice and Essequibo. In the 1650s the Dutch West India Company began allowing private individuals to establish settlements in Essequibo, which brought a new wave of Dutch settlers to the area. With the rapid growth of people and plantations came the opportunity to begin producing sugarcane for export, a prosperous venture that began laying its own historical groundwork.

The success of the colonies didn't go unnoticed by other imperialistic countries, especially after the onset of wars in Europe. In 1665 the English attacked Essequibo and Berbice, and then in 1689 and 1708 the French followed suit. In 1712, the French attacked again and held Fort Nassau until a ransom was paid, which caused a period of economic decline for the Berbice colony.

The Dutch quickly recovered from the attacks and, thanks mainly to the efforts of African slaves, their settlements and plantations expanded throughout the first half of the 18th century. In 1720, in an effort to provide more protection to plantations in Essequibo, a fort was constructed on Flag Island (later called Fort Island) near the mouth of the Essequibo River. The fort, named Zeelandia, was greatly improved in 1743 and the seat of the government was moved to this location. The security it provided also encouraged more settlements along the coast and upper part of the river, including by English farmers from the West Indies.

In 1742, Laurens Storm Van Gravensande, the man responsible for improving Zeelandia, was appointed Commander of Essequibo. He suggested that the area along the Demerara River needed further exploration and used his new status to get permission to recruit new settlers to help with his plan. Groups of English, German, Spanish, French, Swedish and Danish pioneers joined the commander on his mission. Their efforts resulted in the third colony, Demerara.

The European settlers chose an island on the Demerara River, about 50km from the coast, as the capital of their new colony; they called it Borselen. Settlements were encouraged along the lands near the island, but many of the English preferred the more fertile lands closer to the coast and slowly spread northward.

Development was rapid in Demerara, partially thanks to the English settlers who, by 1763, accounted for one-third of the population. Demerara quickly outpaced Essequibo and by 1769 there were 206 plantations and roughly 6,000 slaves in the colony, compared with 92 plantations and some 4,000 slaves in Essequibo.

The Berbice revolt African slaves played a major role in the development of the colonies, but they were certainly not appreciated for their efforts. Their living and working conditions were harsh and their masters treated them cruelly. Extreme measures were taken by plantation owners to prevent uprisings, but they were outnumbered, and in 1763 Berbice was overcome by Guiana's first major slave rebellion.

The revolt began on 23 February 1763, when slaves from the Magdalenenburg and Providence plantations on the Canje River rebelled, killed the African foreman and two whites, looted the estates, took up arms and headed towards the Corentyne River on the border with Suriname.

News of the revolt spread to the Berbice River, and on 27 February, rebelling slaves overtook several plantations. On 1 March, the original Canje insurgents, who had remained out of sight for the week, attacked plantations along the Corentyne River. Meanwhile, more and more slaves from plantations along the Canje River were also joining the revolt.

Berbice was being controlled by two different groups of insurgents and the white colonisers were quickly being run off their plantations. By the end of March the revolting slaves had captured most plantations in Berbice. This feat was aided by the fact that at some point the two factions joined forces and swiftly organised themselves against the colonists.

The main leader of the rebels was Cuffy, a slave who had spent most of his life on the Lilienburg plantation on the Berbice River. Two other slaves, Akara and Atta, helped with leadership roles, but it was Cuffy who was given the title of Governor of the Negroes of Berbice.

Cuffy based his organisational plan on what he knew of the European military, and with a stockpile of weapons that were looted from the estates, they went to war. The rebels made their way up the Berbice River towards Fort Nassau, burning, looting and killing along the way.

Governor Van Hoogenheim, along with his small army and some displaced plantation owners, had sought refuge at Fort Nassau while trying to figure out if they should defend their colony or retreat. They likely did the maths (at the time Berbice had a population of roughly 350 whites and 3,800 African slaves) and decided that their only hope was by retreating towards the coast.

A few brave colonists formed militias in an effort to keep control of what few plantations they had left, but many of the Europeans turned their backs on their home and fled for safety. Van Hoogenheim wasn't prepared to lose his colony so quickly and he set about requesting assistance from anyone he could – Demerara, Essequibo, Suriname, the Netherlands. But the neighbouring colonies were too worried about possible revolts of their own and sent few reinforcements at the beginning.

The governor and the colonists based themselves at Dageraad plantation and set about refortifying the area around it to be better prepared for imminent attack. Throughout March and April there was correspondence between Van Hoogenheim and Cuffy; the latter insisted that they would never become slaves again and suggested that they partition Berbice – the Europeans could inhabit the coastal areas and the freed slaves would occupy the interior. Cuffy was looking for a solution other than war, but no agreements were made.

On 2 April the Africans attacked Dageraad, but it seemed an unorganised affair and little damage was done or progress made. On 13 May, however, they attacked Dageraad again, and this time they had roughly 2,000–2,500 men. Unfortunately for them, a few days before they launched their attack, 146 armed soldiers had arrived at the plantation. The battle lasted about five hours before the Africans retreated after losing some 50 men (the soldiers reportedly lost eight).

This was the last major battle for the coming five months, during which time, outside of a few small clashes, the two sides mainly held their ground and dealt with internal issues. For the colonists, their victory at Dageraad was a much-needed morale booster. But their positive spirits were quickly dampened when several of their soldiers were hit with dysentery. And there was still no sign of reinforcements from the Netherlands.

Relations had begun to crumble in the African camps as well. The defeat at Dageraad rattled their fortitude and caused unrest within the group. They slowly ran out of food and ammunition and ethnic troubles amongst the different African tribes began to arise on the heels of power struggles between those in charge.

After their defeat, Cuffy continued his written communications with Van Hoogenheim regarding a resolution to the situation other than another war; Atta seemed to feel there was no room for compromise and that they should overtake them with force. At some point between August and October, Cuffy and Atta went to blows over the leadership role. Cuffy ended up losing the battle and his role as governor; sadly he dealt with the defeat by taking his own life.

By October, disease had whittled down the white ranks to 40-odd men that were fit for battle. Had the insurgents known this weakness existed then perhaps they would have attacked and changed the final outcome of the revolt, but they did not know and they continued to deal with interior conflicts.

Thanks to escaped prisoners who managed to flee from the Africans, the Europeans were frequently hearing tales of disunity, starvation, lack of ammunition and low morale. In December military reinforcements from Europe finally arrived and this knowledge was used to their advantage. The whites now had hundreds of men and several ships to help them reclaim control of their colony.

In December the troops slowly regained control of plantations along the Canje and Berbice rivers. Many slaves reacted by setting fire to the estates before retreating further inland, while many more surrendered willingly to the European troops. The two remaining main African leaders didn't give up so easily and set up interior camps. Accabre was joined by 600, while roughly 1,200 followed Atta into the jungle.

In January 1764 troops swept through the colony in an effort to capture the last of the rebel slaves. Accabre and those at his camp were forcefully overcome but Atta and his group were able to hold off three expeditions. They were not captured until April 1764; 14 months had passed since the revolt began.

Punishment was swift and severe; around 125 slaves were publicly executed and the others were re-enslaved.

In the end, the slaves did not get the freedom they fought for, but they permanently wounded colonial life in the plantations, and today the participants are regarded as heroes for taking a stand against the inhumane conditions and oppression they were forced to live under.

THE BRITISH ARE COMING: THE BACK AND FORTH YEARS In 1776 the American War of Independence began, and so did a long period of change amongst the controlling powers of Guiana. During the war, France allied with America as they battled Britain, but the Dutch remained neutral. And while the Dutch weren't supplying America with any troops, they were providing necessary goods, and this, in the eyes of the British, was just as bad. In an effort to stop the Dutch from shipping supplies to America, the British attacked their colonies. In 1781 the British took control of Berbice, Demerara and Essequibo with little or no resistance.

The British wasted no time in setting up a fort to protect their new lands, and at the mouth of the Demerara River they built Fort St George. New land grants were also offered and British settlers from Barbados rushed at the opportunity to start profitable sugar plantations of their own. Meanwhile, the British set about building government buildings around Fort St George and the rough workings of a town began to develop in the area.

However their reign was short-lived: in January 1782 French troops, who were allies of the Dutch, arrived and gained control of the three colonies. The French continued the efforts of the British and set about building a more established city at the mouth of the Demerara. With the help of slaves, a couple of canals were dug, lots of land grants were issued and two new forts were constructed. The French called their city Longchamps.

In 1783 the war ended and the French graciously handed the colonies back to the Dutch. The Dutch, pleased with the new developments along the Demerara, decided to move their old capital, Borselen, to Longchamps and renamed it Stabroek.

The coastlands, however, were highly susceptible to floods and still mostly uninhabitable, but the Dutch settlers, using their forefathers' knowledge and the efforts of African slaves, built extensive canals, dykes and *kokers* (sluice gates) to conquer the unruly waters. Streets were laid out and houses began to pop up. In about five years, some 90 houses had been built and nearly 800 residents called Stabroek home.

Around this same time, in 1784, the government of Berbice also decided to move their capital closer to the Atlantic coast. There was a small settlement on the confluence of the Berbice and Canje rivers that was deemed most appropriate. It took several years of planning, clearing and building but by 1791, New Amsterdam was the new official capital of Berbice.

Dutch progress was once again halted in April 1796 when, during the French Revolution, the British attacked and took control of the colonies. This saw another influx of British settlers from Barbados, who set up many sugar plantations along the Atlantic coast. This was also a period of rapid growth around Stabroek as the British focused their efforts on constructing roads amongst the canals built by the Dutch, and many small towns began to form.

At the end of the French Revolution in March 1802 the British ceded control of the colonies to the Dutch once again. But they had no intention of turning their back on the progress of those six years – the number of sugar plantations increased greatly, as did their output: sugar production went from 4 million pounds to more than 17 million; coffee rose from nearly 5 million pounds to 7.5 million; and the beloved rum of the area spiked from 86,000 gallons to 475,000 gallons.

Indeed, the British weren't gone for long. Another war broke out in Europe in 1803 and in September the stubborn British re-seized the colonies they regarded as theirs. It wasn't until the Treaty of Paris was signed in 1814 that the colonies were formally ceded to the British. At this time Stabroek was officially renamed Georgetown, the capital of the colony of British Guiana.

BRITISH COLONIALISM One of the first major changes the British implemented was the abolition of the slave trade in 1806. Under this new law, slaves could no longer be traded from one colony to another, although some were still being brought in from the Caribbean along with new plantation owners from the area.

The Demerara revolt Of course this new law did nothing to improve the horrible conditions under which the majority of slaves lived and in 1823 there was another large slave revolt, this time in Demerara. Rumours had been spreading through the slaves; word was that the king had granted them freedom, the news of which was being withheld by plantation owners. The uprising started on 18 August 1823 when a group of slaves banded together to fight for their freedom.

After hearing of the revolt, the governor sent troops to ask the rebels what it was they were demanding. The soldiers refused to entertain the slaves' demands for freedom and told them to lay down their arms, which were mostly just machetes. The slaves also refused.

On Monday afternoon, the governor declared martial law. For the next day and a half, the number of rebelling slaves grew and they took control of many plantations without violence. Upon locking the estate owners up in their own houses they insisted they were not revolting, but were on strike.

By Wednesday the governor had lost patience and sent in troops to confront the slaves at Bachelor's Paradise plantation. The troops were greatly outnumbered by the 2,000 slaves on hand, but the slaves were no match for the weapons of the troops. An attack ensued and some 250 slaves were killed. Slaves who had escaped were quickly hunted down by Amerindian slave catchers and killed.

Many that participated in the uprising were swiftly tried, found guilty and publicly executed in Georgetown. Lifeless bodies and decapitated heads were displayed throughout the town; it was both a warning to other slaves and a pompous form of celebration by the troops.

News of the uprising and obscene celebrations that followed reached London and caused uproar. The Demerara revolt didn't result in freedom for the slaves, but it caused a lot of dialogue about the abolition of slavery.

Abolition of slavery (sort of) On 1 August 1834 the Emancipation Bill went into effect. It stated that immediate measures would be taken to abolish slavery in all British colonies. The news of the Act, as expected, quickly spread from plantation to plantation and sparked excited talk amongst the slaves about life after slavery.

It was decided that 1 August should be a national holiday. Most freed slaves spent the day celebrating, thinking that the days of horrible living conditions and forced manual labour were behind them. The next morning they were awakened and told to get to work in the fields. They weren't completely free just yet.

Many of the slaves missed or didn't understand the apprenticeship stipulation that came along with the Emancipation Bill. This ruling said that all slaves over the age of six were required to serve a period of apprenticeship: six years for field slaves and four years for house slaves. The fact that they were required to work only 45 hours per week (as opposed to the previous 60 or 70 hours) and be provided with food, clothing and education by their masters was supposed to make the six years seem like a small sacrifice to pay.

Plantation owners used the situation as an extension of their supposed rights to forced manual labour that they paid for in buying the African slaves. Even though they were well compensated for each slave they lost (slaves received nothing), plantation owners were upset and reacted harshly to the bewilderment and anger shown by the freed slaves upon learning of the stipulation to their freedom.

There was confusion throughout the colonies and many slaves refused to head back into the fields. As law bound them to work, punishments were harsh for those showing resistance, and order was quickly restored in most places. One such instance took place on 9 August in Essequibo when some 700 ex-slaves quit working and gathered at a local church under their own flag representing their free status. Troops arrived, followed by the governor, who explained the new ruling and ordered everybody back to work. No violence was ever threatened and no harm was done by any of the workers, but the so-called leaders were taken to Georgetown, tried and punished. A worker named Damon was seen as the instigator and was sentenced to death. Times, it seemed, had changed very little.

For fear of further uprising that may be caused by freeing ex-house slaves but not ex-field slaves, after four years of extended free labour for plantation owners, and harsh living and working conditions for the apprentices, total freedom was granted to all workers on 1 August 1838.

Life after slavery Having long ago lost the desire to toil away for long hours in the sugarcane fields, very few ex-slaves continued to work on a daily basis at the plantations after complete freedom was granted them. Many gained sustenance from harvesting fruit trees, rearing animals such as pigs and fishing in the canals. Many plantation owners did what they could to get their past workers to return to work, and many of the freed slaves who continued to live on the plantations saw their animals slaughtered (those darn pigs were ruining the cane fields) and fruit trees cut down. Some owners even went so far as to outlaw fishing in their canals.

However this still didn't cause the labourers to return to work, as the plantation owners had hoped. Instead, when the Africans needed money, they would get together in a group and sell their labour to the employers for a certain number of hours or days. They would work, earn the money they needed and return to their easier life. Whether or not the plantations were making money was of no concern to them and they finally had a bit of upper hand over the owners that treated them so poorly for so long.

Another plan the plantation owners adopted initially to depress further the Africans was to deny sale of land to them. Luckily for the freed slaves, the financial situations of many plantation owners became so dire so quickly that this ruling didn't last even a year. Due to the cheaper cotton that was being produced in the United States, cotton plantations in Guiana were forced to begin selling off their land. Once again, the Africans banded together, pooled the money that they had been saving over the years, and began buying up large plots of land and turning them into villages.

As sugar prices dropped, more landowners suffered economic setbacks, and therefore reduced wages and benefits for African labourers. The workers were alienated. They went on strike. More realised they needed to remove themselves further from their pasts and began moving off the estates. By 1852, roughly half of Guiana's 82,000 working-age Africans had moved from estates to villages, 25 of which they had recently established. They were free to grow their own crops, raise their own livestock, fish the waters and work on the estates when they pleased.

Indentured labourers Plantation owners knew that they would be facing labour shortages once the apprenticeship period ended for ex-slaves, and they also knew that having to pay normal wages to workers would drastically cut into the profits they had been enjoying in the years of free labour. It was decided that their best alternative was to bring indentured labourers to British Guiana.

The cunning colonisers also saw the diminishing number of white residents in British Guiana as a threat and so they looked to Europe when recruiting indentured labourers. Their recruiters settled on the poor, Portuguese-owned island of Madeira, whose inhabitants relied on agriculture for their survival.

In 1834, the first group of Portuguese arrived and set about serving their two- to four-year period of indenture in Demerara. In 1835, groups of plantation owners brought in some 600 more workers from Madeira. Also in 1835–36, labourers were brought from other European countries, including Germany, England, Scotland and Ireland.

Portuguese labourers didn't begin arriving again in any sizable numbers until 1841, when more than 4,000 came to Guiana. Due to the high mortality rates and health problems experienced by many of the Portuguese, these numbers dropped until 1846 when 6,000 arrived after a famine hit Madeira. The year 1848 saw another 4,000 Portuguese labourers arrive, and they continued to trickle in throughout the subsequent years. In total, approximately 30,000 Portuguese labourers arrived in British Guiana.

In 1838, the first indentured labourers arrived from India. Two ships docked in May with nearly 400 Indians who were put to work on sugar plantations to serve their five years of indentured labour. But some plantation owners treated the Indians as little more than slaves who earned a meagre pay. Word of the inhumane attitude towards the Indians spread to England, and then to India; British officials were so upset that they placed a ban on all future emigration to British Guiana.

With government assistance, in 1845 immigration from India was able to resume and roughly 800 more labourers arrived that year. The following three years saw a surge as some 11,000 Indians were brought to British Guiana. Due to unreasonably high death rates within this group of immigrants, in late 1848 the

BORDER DISPUTES

While most international maps accept Guyana's boundaries as defined by Guyana, Venezuela and Suriname have different ideas. Guyana has been dealing with land claims from its neighbours for centuries, and while neither has been officially resolved as yet, they currently aren't causing any major skirmishes either.

VENEZUELA The dispute from Venezuela dates back to the mid-1800s when the British government commissioned the German explorer Robert Schomburgk to formally map British Guiana's boundaries. Schomburgk set out on foot, and with the aid of many Amerindian guides, eventually travelled through the majority of Guyana.

His mapping marked the beginning of the western boundary of British Guiana with Venezuela at the mouth of the Orinoco River. Once the map was published in the 1840s, Venezuela protested saying that the entire area west of the Essequibo River belonged to them. Negotiations led nowhere and in 1850 it was decided that neither country would occupy the area.

This changed when gold was discovered in the region in the 1850s. British settlers and a mining company moved in and Venezuela once again protested. British Guiana ignored their neighbours and in 1887 Venezuela appealed to the US for assistance. In 1897, an international tribunal was formed to arbitrate the boundary; two years later it was decided that 94% of the territory belonged to British Guiana; Venezuela was given the mouth of the Orinoco River and a small piece of land to the east. Both sides accepted the new boundary in 1905.

In the 1960s, Venezuela once again decided to reclaim the land west of the Essequibo River and occupied Guyana's half of Ankoko Island on the Cuyuni River. Minor military skirmishes took place, but Venezuela remained put.

On 18 June 1970, the two countries signed the Protocol of Port of Spain, which placed a 12-year moratorium on the dispute. After the 12 years, Venezuela declined to resign. The two countries have continued to disagree over the area ever since. Projects proposed by Guyana, including hydro-electric plants and a rocket launching pad, were resisted by Venezuela and never materialised. The

Indian government once again instilled a ban on emigration to British Guiana. The practice didn't resume until 1851.

At this time, another push to boost available labour in Guiana was under way through the encouragement of Chinese immigration as indentured labourers. In 1853, about 80 labourers arrived from China, and through the early 20th-century decades, some 15,000 Chinese came to work in Guiana.

In the meantime, East Indian immigration continued to grow, and by the early 20th century, almost 240,000 immigrants had arrived in Guiana. It was thanks to this large number of East Indians that Guiana's plantations didn't completely crumble in the latter half of the 19th century.

Labour shortage and the decline of British Guiana's plantations Even with the relatively large numbers of indentured labourers being brought in, British Guiana was experiencing a labour shortage crisis. Supplemental contract labour was brought in from neighbouring West Indies' islands where local plantation owners promised freed slaves higher wages. From 1835 to 1841, roughly 8,000 workers were brought from the islands, but a shortage still persisted. Plantation owners then

issue was raised at the Geneva Convention, and many treaties have been proposed, but the matter remains unsolved.

SURINAME Guyana's boundary dispute with Suriname dates back even further, as British Guiana and the Netherlands never came to an official agreement on the boundary between the two countries. Guyana bases the current boundary on maps printed by British Guiana in the early 1900s. The boundary was placed along the *thalweg* (deepest channel) of the Corentyne River, as is the norm for rivers that create the boundaries between countries.

The Netherlands initially agreed to the boundary, but the government of Suriname later protested, stating that the entire Corentyne River was part of their territory, and the west bank marked the actual boundary. Suriname based their claim on a treaty signed in 1799 by the governors of Suriname and the then colony Berbice.

The matter was further complicated by additional rivers. During Schomburgk's mapping of British Guiana's boundaries, he found that the Kutari and Curuni rivers joined and formed the source of the Corentyne, and part of the boundary. Schomburgk's map was accepted by both countries.

In 1871, the geologist/explorer Barrington Brown discovered an additional river west of the Kutari and named it New River. New River was found to be wider than the Kutari, and was later declared to be the actual source of Corentyne, and thus the actual boundary.

These two issues have been the source of disagreements ever since. In the 1920s, geologists studying the area along the Corentyne and in the 'New River Triangle', as the disputed area was called, declared that the region likely held oil deposits. This gave both sides more reason to fight for what they believed to be theirs.

There have been some minor skirmishes between the countries, but for the past several decades Guyana and Suriname have agreed not to occupy the New River Triangle area and drilling for oil has largely been delayed while the matter is settled in UN courts.

looked to the source of their ex-slaves: Africa. A similar system of contract labour had been set up there and from 1838 to 1861 more than 13,000 Africans arrived in Guiana under these new labour agreements.

But even with all of the workers that were being imported and put to work for relatively low wages, Guiana's plantations struggled. Many weren't able to withstand the changes to their finances. The 1840s saw many plantations cease operations. In 1846 a further blow was delivered when the Sugar Duties Act was passed and Guiana lost its monopoly on the British market.

In 1829, the heyday of British Guiana's plantations, there were some 230 sugar estates and 175 plantations producing coffee and sugar. Twenty years later, the numbers had been reduced to 180 sugar and just 16 coffee plantations. Thanks to the cheaper cotton continuing to come from the United States (slave-labour was still legal), Guiana's cotton plantations could no longer compete.

Areas of Guiana that had been settled and farmed for decades were being abandoned, given back to the bush from which they were originally claimed. The local economy was in a state of decline and suddenly the population of Guiana was mainly composed of mixed races of indentured labourers and freed slaves living in a foreign land not of their choosing. The roots of Guyana's often turbulent and racially divided political situation can be traced back to these early days.

Adapting The Portuguese never really adapted or embraced their work in the fields. Working with sugarcane was difficult and they associated it with slave labour. They also felt that as whites they shouldn't have to work side by side with Africans and Indians. In colonial life they were low in the pecking order, but many set about changing this immediately after their time of indenture was completed. Very few returned to work in the fields.

They used their savings to buy plots of land and set about finding jobs from white shopkeepers. In many cases the colour of their skin allowed them to take jobs away from Africans working in the retail shops. Before long, the Portuguese rose from employees to entrepreneurs, opening their own shops, many of which are still prominent in Guyana today.

By the 1850s, some 16 years after their arrival, Portuguese owned more than half the 300 shops in Georgetown. The same was true for the 50-odd shops in New Amsterdam and more than 400 shops that were scattered throughout the villages. An important part of the Guianese economy suddenly hinged on the Portuguese immigrants that were still considered to be of a lower class than other European expatriates in Guiana.

MOVING TOWARDS INDEPENDENCE The 1870s brought two great discoveries to Guiana: Charles Barrington Brown was the first European to find Kaieteur Falls and large gold deposits were finally found in Guyana's interior. Both brought the colony a certain amount of fame, but it was the discovery of gold that garnered the most interest from the outside. When Venezuela got word of the gold being mined in western Guiana they claimed that the set boundaries were inaccurate, and that everything west of the Essequibo River actually belonged to them (see box above).

The latter part of the 19th century also saw many improvements to the sugarcane cultivation and manufacturing industries, and soon British Guiana was seen as being the most technologically advanced nation in the region.

In the 1890s, many of the Indian labourers began moving off the plantations and onto their own lands along the coast. Many new settlements grew and this movement of labour also helped give rise to an emerging rice industry.

The first half of the 20th century was a period of social growth for the colony. Unhappy labourers formed unions, political parties dabbled with socialist experiments and a national pride led to a desire to be free from British control.

On 26 May 1966 British Guiana was granted independence from Britain. No longer a colony, the country became known as Guyana and in 1970 it was declared a cooperative republic.

GOVERNMENT

Guyana has three main branches of democratic power: parliament, the president, and the cabinet.

Parliament is a collective part of the government representing the interests of the whole population. In Guyana, the unicameral parliament consists of the president and the National Assembly, and has all legislative power.

The National Assembly has 72 members, including an elected Speaker; 40 members elected on the basis of proportional representation from national lists drawn up by the political parties; 25 members elected by regional councils; four non-elected ministers; and two non-elected parliamentary secretaries.

The president may dissolve the assembly and call for new elections at any time, but it must be no later than five years from its first sitting.

The Cabinet consists of the president, prime minister and other ministers appointed by the president.

The president is the head of state, the supreme executive authority and commander-in-chief of the armed forces. Political parties participating in the general election choose a presidential candidate to represent their party; whichever party, or presidential candidate, secures the most votes is declared the elected president.

The highest judicial body is the Court of Appeal, while the second highest is the High Court; the chancellor and the chief justice who preside over them are appointed by the president.

On the local level, Guyana is divided into ten administrative regions; a Regional Democratic Council comprising 12 to 36 elected members administers each.

POLITICS

Guyanese politics has had its share of ups and downs. Guyana's first modern political party was formed in 1950, when Cheddi Jagan, an Indo-Guyanese and US-educated dentist teamed up with Forbes Burnham, an Afro-Guyanese and British-educated barrister to form the People's Progressive Party (PPP). Burnham was the chairman, Jagan was the second vice-chairman and Jagan's wife, US-born Janet Jagan, was secretary general.

In 1953 popular elections were held under a new constitution and the PPP won 18 out of 24 seats. Just five months later, however, the British suspended the constitution, brought troops to Guiana and declared a state of emergency. They believed the PPP had plans of making Guiana a communist state.

In 1955, due to 'ideological, racial and personal factors', the PPP was split into two parties and Burnham left to found what would eventually become the People's National Congress (PNC). This split effectively caused a racial political divide in the country that still survives today. It was the beginning of a political environment that is largely based more on race than ideology.

In 1957 elections were once again permitted and Jagan's PPP won with 48% of the vote; the PPP won again in 1961 with 43% of the vote. Jagan was the first Premier of

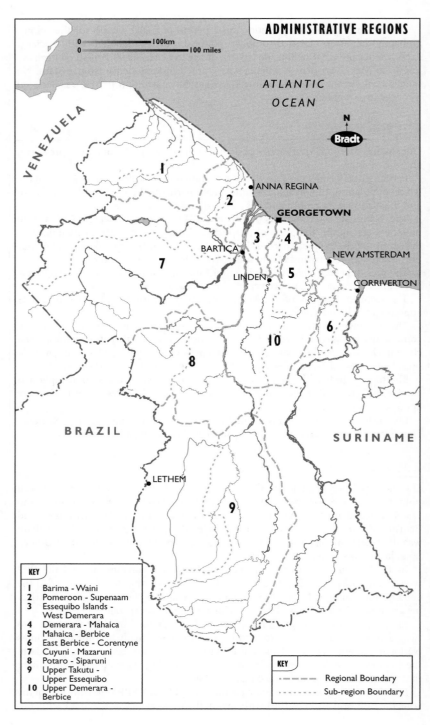

ADMINISTRATIVE REGIONS

ATLANTIC
OCEAN

N

Bradt

VENEZUELA

ANNA REGINA

GEORGETOWN

1

2

3   4

BARTICA

NEW AMSTERDAM

7

LINDEN

5

CORRIVERTON

6

10

8

BRAZIL

SURINAME

LETHEM

9

KEY

1 Barima - Waini
2 Pomeroon - Supenaam
3 Essequibo Islands -
   West Demerara
4 Demerara - Mahaica
5 Mahaica - Berbice
6 East Berbice - Corentyne
7 Cuyuni - Mazaruni
8 Potaro - Siparuni
9 Upper Takutu -
   Upper Essequibo
10 Upper Demerara -
   Berbice

KEY

- - - - Regional Boundary
······· Sub-region Boundary

Each of Guyana's ten administrative regions draws its boundaries and name from Guyana's major rivers. They are: Barima-Waini (Region 1); Pomeroon-Supenaam (Region 2); Essequibo Islands-West Demerara (Region 3); Demerara-Mahaica (Region 4); Mahaica-Berbice (Region 5); East Berbice-Corentyne (Region 6); Cuyuni-Mazaruni (Region 7); Potaro-Siparuni (Region 8); Upper Takatu-Upper Essequibo (Region 9); Upper Demerara-Upper Berbice (Region 10). See map opposite.

British Guiana and in 1963 the UK agreed to grant independence to the colony, but not before an election was held under a new system of proportional representation.

In the elections of 1964 the PPP won 46% of the seats, the PNC won 41% and the United Force (TUF) won 12%. No party had enough to claim a majority so the PNC and TUF entered into a coalition that gave Burnham the majority.

On 26 May 1966 British Guiana gained political independence and thereafter became known as Guyana. On 23 February 1970, the anniversary of the Berbice slave revolt, it was declared a Cooperative Republic.

Burnham ruled Guyana as prime minister until 1980 when a controversial new constitution named him executive president. Burnham then ruled Guyana until his death in 1985 and over those 21 years he became increasingly autocratic. Burnham's attempts to build a socialist society were often regarded as a way of preserving his own political power.

Outside imports were banned, Guyana's national railway was ripped up and sold to countries in Africa and Guyana fell into a period of serious economic decline. Production in the sugar, rice and bauxite industries fell, reserves of foreign currency and raw materials were becoming depleted and foreign debt skyrocketed. As standards of living fell, migration to neighbouring countries, the Caribbean, North America and the UK rose drastically. Ongoing elections were largely regarded as fraudulent, while human rights and civil liberties were suppressed.

After Burnham died, Prime Minister Hugh Desmond Hoyte acceded to presidency and was officially elected in national elections at the end of 1985. Recognising the dire condition of Guyana's economy, Hoyte launched an Economic Recovery Programme that slowly moved the party policies from state socialism and one-party control to a market-based economy. Freedom of the press was also granted.

In 1992, in what were the first elections to be internationally recognised as free and fair since 1964, Cheddi Jagan and the PPP returned to power.

In 1997, Cheddi Jagan died and was succeeded by Samuel Hinds, his prime minister. Hinds then appointed the late Jagan's wife, Janet, as his prime minister and when elections were held in 1997, Janet Jagan was elected the first female president of Guyana, just after holding the role of Guyana's first female prime minister.

Janet Jagan remained president until 1999 when she resigned due to health problems. Bharrat Jagdeo succeeded her. In 2001, the PPP/Civic remained in power with Jagdeo at the helm. The 2001 elections were marred by violence, which was to sweep over Guyana in 2002, the same year Desmond Hoyte died.

Robert Corbin replaced Hoyte as the leader of the PNC/Reform. In the national elections of 2006, with 54.6% of the vote, the PPP/Civic and Jagdeo were once again victorious, and while the country was prepared to endure the same violent uprisings that shadowed the previous election, the entire process went off peacefully.

Background Information POLITICS

There were many great explorers and researchers who underwent expeditions in British Guiana, but perhaps one of the most influential was Robert Schomburgk. Besides mapping out Guyana's current boundaries, he was also noted for being a scientist with the heart of a pioneer.

Schomburgk first came to British Guiana in 1835 under a commission from the Royal Geographical Society (RGS), who asked him to explore the country. His first expedition for RGS took him to the Rupununi and through the Kanuku Mountains. On this trip he catalogued many species of plants, animals and birds. He also learned how to prepare *curare*, a poison used by Amerindians in hunting that became an essential component of modern anaesthesiology.

His second trip was up the Corentyne and Berbice rivers, and this is when he first came across the *Victoria regia* (now *Victoria amazonica*) water lily. His final journey for the RGS, taking him to the source of the Essequibo River, to Mount Roraima and the upper Orinoco River, was perhaps Schomburgk's most epic.

Based on the successes of earlier explorations, in the 1840s the British government commissioned him to map the boundaries of British Guiana. He did so in four expeditions, during which he was joined by his younger brother, Richard, a botanist. Their travels took them to all corners of British Guiana, but the maps that resulted have remained controversial to this day (see box, *Border disputes*, page 12). Nonetheless, when Schomburgk returned to England in 1944 he was knighted by Queen Victoria.

The 2011 elections are expected to take place no later than September, and new presidential candidates will be representing both major parties, the PNC/Reform and PPP/Civic. With two terms served, Jagdeo is not constitutionally allowed to run again, and PNC/Reform leader Corbin has publicly declared that he will not run for president again.

ECONOMY

When Guyana was granted independence in 1966, it was one of the least-developed countries in the Western Hemisphere, and with the government commanding control of almost all economic activities through the 1980s, the state of Guyana's economy only worsened. Foreign-owned companies were nationalised and all outside investment was discouraged.

In 1990, one year after Hoyte had launched his Economic Recovery Programme, Guyana's GDP was at US$369 per capita, one of the lowest in the Western Hemisphere. Indeed, the current GDP of US$4,700 still makes Guyana one of the hemisphere's poorest countries but conditions have only been improving since the 1990s.

In recent times the government has reduced its involvement in the economy, sold many of the government-owned businesses, including the telephone company and business within the timber, seafood and rice industries. Foreign investment has been encouraged and large international companies have invested in the local mining, timber and agricultural activities.

Guyana's economy largely revolves around the main agriculture and mining activities of sugar, bauxite, rice and gold, which account for 70% of the country's export earnings. Timber, shrimp, fish, diamonds, rum and other agriculture products account for the majority of Guyana's remaining exports. While Guyana may not have the turquoise waters, the country does have the powdery white sand, much of which is exported to the Caribbean islands to the north.

Guyana is also pursuing foreign investment as a way of creating jobs, enhancing technical capabilities and creating more exportable goods. It's hoped that by improving the local economy it will lessen the devastating impact that the emigration of skilled and professional workers has on Guyana.

Guyana's forests, which encompass an area larger than England, provide critical environmental services to the world in the fight against climate change, a threat that is particularly acute for the country itself: 90% of Guyana's productive land is at risk from changing weather patterns, and flooding in 2005 resulted in widespread destruction. The Government of Guyana has responded to this situation by promoting a Low-Carbon Development Strategy (LCDS; see box, page 20) for economic growth. Designed to 'transform Guyana's economy while combating climate change', the LCDS is pioneering ways to extract value from standing forests while preserving the biodiversity that they harbour and the ecosystem services that they provide.

The government is also putting more emphasis on tourism as an industry that has the potential of improving Guyana's economy, especially for many hinterland communities. If the forests survive, so do the multitude of species that create one of the world's most biodiverse areas.

PEOPLE

In 2010, Guyana's estimated population was 769,141, with an estimated growth rate of -0.55%. A national census was completed in 2010 and many experts expect the actual population to be much lower than previously estimated. About 90% of Guyana's population lives along the coastal belt, mainly from the Pomeroon River in the west to the Corentyne River in the east. Roughly one-third of the population, or about 250,000 people, live in and directly around Georgetown. Other main towns and villages include Linden (30,000), New Amsterdam (20,000), Rose Hall (8,000), Anna Regina (12,000), Bartica (11,000) and Lethem (3,000).

The ethnic groups of Guyana include East Indian (50%) or Indo-Guyanese; African (36%) or Afro-Guyanese; Amerindian (7%) along with white, Chinese, Brazilian and mixed (7%). For cultural information see *Culture* on page 21.

LANGUAGE

English is the official language of Guyana, although it is commonly spoken in a Creolese dialect. When listening to locals speak rapidly to each other in Creolese it can often seem as though they're speaking a foreign tongue lightly peppered with English words. It can take some time to gain an ear for it. Don't feel bad about asking locals to repeat themselves or slow down a bit. It can often lead to a good cultural ice breaker.

Other languages spoken in Guyana include several different Amerindian dialects. While many Amerindians speak English, it is probably their second language and in their homes and communities they often speak their native tongues.

With the influence of Brazil becoming ever-more present, Portuguese can also be heard with a growing frequency. This is also true in parts of Guyana where mining is common and in the Rupununi, where being able to speak Portuguese is commonly becoming more of an asset.

Other languages spoken include Chinese, Hindi and Urdu.

RELIGION

The major religions in Guyana are Christianity (50%), Hindu (35%) and Muslim (10%). Most Indo-Guyanese are Hindu and the majority of Afro-Guyanese are Christian. Within Christianity, which is a mix of all races, the strongest group is Protestants, followed by Catholics.

Missionary activity has been concentrated mostly within Amerindian communities. The majority of the Amerindian population is Christian as a result, and many traditional beliefs and practices are quickly fading.

EDUCATION

The government of Guyana, through the Ministry of Education, is responsible for providing most of the education in Guyana: in schools, curricula, standards and policies are set by the government and implemented by the education system (overseen by the Ministry), which is divided into 11 districts, ten for each administrative region of Guyana and one for Georgetown. Education in Guyana is aligned with the Caribbean Examinations Council (CXC), which regulates and sets standards for exams and qualifications required for each level of education in member countries.

Roughly 6% of Guyana's GDP is spent on education, making it one of the world's top countries for education spending. It's compulsory for children to attend school

LOW CARBON DEVELOPMENT STRATEGY (LCDS)

From government policies to the work of organisations like Iwokrama International Centre and Conservation International, there is a longstanding conservation ethic that exists within Guyana that has allowed the country to retain most of its pristine rainforest, which covers an area larger than the size of England. In recent years, Guyana has been looking to use its forests as the backbone to benefit the local population and the country is now working hard to preserve its forests forever.

Guyana's standing forest covers nearly 80% of the country's landmass and, according to a recent study commissioned by Guyana's Office of the President, the trees and land are worth US$5.8 billion. That's if all timber is harvested, minerals extracted, and land used for commercial agriculture, plantation forestry, and ranching. Thankfully, Guyana has no plans to destroy its rainforests for money.

In addition to storing the harmful carbon dioxide emissions that contribute to global warming, rainforests provide a suite of 'ecosystem services' to the world that include generating rainfall, cooling the atmosphere, moderating weather conditions and sustaining biodiversity. Recognising the importance of his country's trees, in 2007 President Jagdeo offered to protect most of the Guyana's standing tropical rainforest to help address the issue of climate change. Over time, the President's offer morphed into a more formal plan for Guyana: the Low Carbon Development Strategy (LCDS).

Key goals of the LCDS include an overhaul of existing forest-dependent sectors (mining and forestry), investment in a low carbon economic infrastructure (eg: hydro-electricity), creation of new economic opportunities for Amerindian communities and the broader Guyana citizenry, and investment in high-potential, low-carbon sectors, such as aquaculture, select agriculture and ecotourism.

from the age of five years and nine months until 16. Most students attend state schools, but there are a handful of private schools in Guyana, mainly in Georgetown. Within the interior villages, many children are required to travel several miles to get to the nearest school; for secondary school, many students board.

On the Education Index of the United Nations Human Development Report, Guyana ranks 37, making it one of the highest ranked developing countries. In the Caribbean it is third after Cuba and Barbados, and in South America it is second to Argentina. Guyana is said to have met the Millennium Development Goal of universal primary education but lagging in providing satisfactory access to secondary education.

That said, Guyana remains a poor country and this can be seen in the infrastructure of state schools. Modern instructional and multimedia tools are nearly nonexistent and basic resources are often lacking. While Guyana enjoys a 92% literacy rate (defined as those over age 15 that have ever attended school), significant portions of the population have functional literacy difficulties that cause socio-economic disadvantages, particularly when compared to regional counterparts.

CULTURE

Guyana's cultural diversity earned it the name of the Land of Six Peoples. Citizens of East Indian and African descent make up the majority of the population. The other ethnic groups are Amerindians, Chinese, Europeans (mostly Portuguese) and more

Essentially, the LCDS seeks to help reduce greenhouse gas emissions and global warming by protecting Guyana's rainforests, while creating a model green economy for rainforest-rich developing countries.

Guyana is now aligned with the United Nations Framework Convention for Climate Change, which is set to replace the Kyoto Protocol when it expires in 2012, and their Reducing Emissions from Deforestation and Forest Degradation (REDD+) programme. Deforestation is responsible for releasing nearly 20% of global greenhouse gas emissions – more than the world's entire transportation sector – and REDD+ seeks to reduce drastically this number.

Guyana has made it known to the world that in order to preserve its standing forests, the country needs funding to create a new low-carbon economy. In November 2009, Guyana and Norway signed an agreement that has Norway providing up to US$250 million until 2015 to help protect and pay for the ecosystem services of Guyana's forests. At the time it was the largest national-scale agreement of its kind in the world, and next to Brazil's Amazon Fund, the second-largest forestry protection scheme. With this new support and focus, Guyana is moving forward with creating what is billed as a 'working example of what it takes to forge a low-deforestation, low-carbon, climate-resilient economy'.

Guyana's plan is evolving along with global strategies to combat climate change, but the importance of the world's remaining rainforest is not in question. Global discussions are in a constant flux, and Guyana's LCDS as briefly outlined above is constantly evolving along with the latest research and economic policies. Hopefully it won't take long for this information to become outdated as Guyana truly becomes a successful model for avoiding deforestation in rainforest-rich developing countries.

Guyana is currently home to nine Amerindian nations. In the days prior to the arrival of Europeans, there were many more indigenous groups in the area but populations dwindled for a variety of reasons that caused them to flee or become extinct. Among these were tribal wars, Western diseases and Amerindian slavery.

In the early days of European settlers, before the days of African slaves, many Amerindians were enslaved and forced to work on plantations, but certain groups (Arawaks, Akawaios, Caribs and Warraus) were declared a 'free nation', and encouraged to capture members of other groups.

After Africans arrived, Amerindians continued to work with the plantation owners, mainly by capturing slaves who tried escaping into the forests, lands the Amerindians knew well. And as adventurous Europeans began to arrive to explore more of the interior regions they relied on Amerindians as their guides.

Today, the nine different groups of Amerindians in Guyana are scattered throughout the country in distinct geographical locations that largely dictate their different lifestyles. The Arawak, Carib and Warrau are coastal; the Akawaio, Patamuna and Arekuna are highland rainforest dwellers; the Makushi and Wapishana are largely savanna peoples; and the Wai Wai are lowland forest peoples.

Some 15,500 Arawak people are settled in Region I, mainly around the Santa Rosa/Moruca area, while roughly 4,000 Carib peoples live mainly along the coastal wetland forest areas of the northwest and about 5,000 Warrau live in the area's coastal swamps.

The Akawaio, who number around 6,000, can be found in the upland forests and Mazaruni River basin while the 5,000 Patamuna are located in the upland savannas of the Pakaraima Mountains and the Arekuna people live in the highland forests of the upper Mazaruni district.

The nearly 8,000 Makushi inhabit the north Rupununi savannas and the 7,000 Wapishana live mainly in the south Rupununi savannas.

The Wai Wai live in the tropical forests of the upper Essequibo River, in the far south of Guyana. Their two main villages have a population of only 200.

For the most part, present-day Amerindians are no longer nomadic. They live semi-traditional lifestyles in politically defined territories. A village *tuschao*, or captain, and a group of councillors that are elected by the villagers for a period of five years, govern each community. Many rely on subsistence farming for food, planting mostly cassava, plantain, bananas, sweet potatoes, eddoes and yams.

Guyana's Amerindian population is largely traditional peoples that have adapted to changes brought on by many outsiders over the years. Their cultures continue to adapt to the ever-expanding influences of an encroaching modern world and they will certainly continue to influence an important part of Guyana's culture.

recently Brazilian. It is estimated that some 50,000 Brazilians are currently living in Guyana, many of whom come for the mining prospects in the interior. All of the cultures hold on to their distinct cultural roots while also embracing what it is to be Guyanese, and the result is a vibrant culture.

Guyana's culture is unique because it isn't typically South American. There is no Latin heritage in the country, resulting in a culture that closely resembles other English-speaking Caribbean nations to the north. In fact, Guyana is regarded as a Caribbean nation and people are more apt to claim a mutual identity with their northern neighbours than any other.

But what Guyana has that many Caribbean islands lack is a strong indigenous population, with a culture all its own. And the fact that Guyana isn't an isolated island means that the influence of other South American cultures is slowly seeping in. The influence of Brazil is strongest in the south, but it is rapidly spreading northwards; Georgetown contains neighbourhoods, which are largely populated by Brazilians. A lesser influence of Venezuela is found in the northwest.

ARTS AND CRAFTS The arts of Guyana are influenced by many varied ethnic and cultural backgrounds, including the indigenous Amerindians, Indians, Africans and Europeans. Popular mediums run the gamut from woodworking, painting and ceramics to sculpture, basketry and jewellery.

Many Amerindian communities produce necessities of their daily life with an amazing amount of artistry, including Akawaio and Wai Wai intricately designed basketry, Wapishana and Makushi weaving and a variety of paddles, fishing traps, tools and the like that stem from Amerindian cultures.

Guyana has also given rise to a great many painters, including Stanley Greaves, Philip Moore, Aubrey Williams, Ronald Savory, Patrick Barrington, Hubert Moshett, George Simon, Winslow Craig and ER Burrowes that all draw from a host of influences that reflect Guyana, including Amerindian heritage, ethnic diversity and the country's physical beauty. Oswald Hussein draws on many of the same influences in his fantastic sculptures.

Excellent displays of local artwork can be found at the Walter Roth Museum of Anthropology and Castellani House (see page 120).

LITERATURE Besides the countless pieces of literature that have been inspired by Guyana, the country has also produced some famous authors. Among them are Wilson Harris, Jan Carew, Denis Williams, Pauline Melville and ER Braithwaite, who wrote the famous *To Sir With Love*, which was actually based on his experiences in London. Edgar Mittelholzer also gained recognition for *Corentyne Thunder* and the *Kaywana* trilogy, which traced 350 years of Guyana's history through the eyes of one family.

MUSIC Music plays an important role in Guyana's culture and it seems that along the coast you're never far from some style of music blaring forth from a set of speakers. Music emanating from Guyana is as varied as the culture, with Indian, African, European, Amerindian and Caribbean elements influencing it. In today's popular culture soca, chutney, Brazilian, reggae and popular American music, both present and past, dominate.

Guyana has produced several internationally known musicians but none shared the popularity gained by Eddie Grant and his group the Equals. Eddie was born in Guyana but migrated to England in 1960 where he went on to gain international success with songs including 'Baby Come Back' and 'Electric Avenue'.

Calypso This Afro-Caribbean music originated in Trinidad in the early 1900s. Calypso quickly grew in popularity throughout the Caribbean where it was used as a means of spreading news. The singers often pushed the boundaries of free speech by using their music to provoke conversations on such issues as political corruption. Its popularity never really faded, with calypso having long been associated with celebrations and carnival, which in Trinidad is still a time to showcase new music. In Guyana calypso is common during festivities, especially during Mashramani.

Soca Soul calypso is a calypso infected with heavy, often electronic, dance beats. Like calypso, soca began in Trinidad in the 1960s, but it has grown in popularity in recent years, taking over from Caribbean music.

Soca was originally used to express social commentary but by the 1980s soca lyrics grew increasingly sexual. Today, soca is mainly a way to express Caribbean views of sexuality, often in graphic language. Just as graphic are the popular dances that accompany the songs.

Chutney This is a relatively new form of party music that combines traditional Indian folk songs with calypso and soca beats.

FESTIVALS

Guyana's melting pot of a population provides numerous festivals and reasons to celebrate throughout the year. Many of the religion- or culture-specific holidays have grown into national celebrations enjoyed by all Guyanese, and they often combine the best of Guyana's arts, music and food. At the time of writing a new jazz festival was announced. While details for the planned annual Guyana Jazz Festival were still limited, the three-day event was scheduled for August 2012 at the Providence Stadium; updated information can be found by visiting www.guyanajazz.com. The list of festivals below is by no means exhaustive; see page 91 for a list of Guyana's public holidays.

MASHRAMANI Guyana's answer to Carnival comes through Mashramani. On the 23 February, people from all over Guyana gather in Georgetown to celebrate Republic Day, the day Guyana received independence from Britain. All races, ages, shapes and sizes line the streets to dance, eat, drink and watch the parade of costumed revellers and lavishly decorated floats.

Mash, as it is commonly known, had its beginning in the bauxite mining town of Linden in 1970. Using the nearby Carnival celebrations in Trinidad, the local branch of the international leadership and development training group, the Jaycees, planned a party to celebrate Guyana's independence. But, not wanting to appear as though they copied Carnival, they chose a new name. The group decided an Amerindian word should be used; Mashramani is derived from an Arawak word for a celebration after a successful cooperative effort.

As with most events involving music, dancing and alcohol, the festival was a huge success. Mash celebrations were eventually moved to Georgetown and the festival was officially recognised by President Burnham as the national celebration for Republic Day.

Today several towns in Guyana host Mash celebrations (often after Republic Day so as to not compete with the main party), but Georgetown's is the largest.

There are dances, concerts, parties and costume competitions in the days preceding Republic Day, but it's on 23 February when it culminates with a national party that lasts all day and well through the night.

Most of the activities revolve around the parade of costumed participants, elegantly decorated floats and towering stacks of speakers that line the streets.

Under an invisible cover of loud music and a fog of too much food and drink, Guyana's population comes together and celebrates as one.

In recent years a heavy corporate presence has seeped into Mash, mainly through sponsorship of the floats, but there are also many that represent Guyana's administrative regions, government ministries and other enthusiastic groups.

The main parade route begins at the intersection of Church and Camp streets. From there the parade heads east on Church Street to Irving Road where it turns north at Thomas Road and makes its way west to National Park. The floats then wind through the stadium for judging.

The parade usually starts around 10.00, but people begin lining the streets much earlier. End time varies as judging often gets backed up at National Park, causing much stop and go within the parade. Parties along the main parade route and throughout the city last well into the early morning hours, causing an unofficial public holiday the following day (although all stores are open).

AMERINDIAN HERITAGE MONTH To honour Guyana's indigenous population, every September is recognised as Amerindian Heritage Month. It is a month that is meant to focus on the development of the Amerindian people and celebrate the contributions they have made to society.

Amerindian Heritage Month grew from the day when many Amerindian villages would commemorate the momentous date of 10 September 1957, the date Stephen Campbell was sworn in as Guyana's first Amerindian parliamentarian.

Within the month, this date still holds significance, as 10 September is recognised as Heritage Day. Every year a 'Heritage Village' is declared and they host a wide array of celebrations in honour of Amerindian Heritage Month. Recently, Heritage Day celebrations were expanded to an entire week.

During the week Amerindians from villages throughout Guyana gather together to showcase all aspects of Amerindian daily life. There are cultural presentations, competitions (fastest cassava grater, fastest fire starter, best archery, best craft, etc), dances, traditional crafts and foods for sale and a Miss Amerindian Heritage Pageant. All events are open to visitors.

Unfortunately in Georgetown the month passes highly unrecognised. The official 'launching' of the month takes place at Umana Yana, when government representatives speak kind words about Guyana's original inhabitants. On weekends, Umana Yana also hosts an excellent art exhibition that showcases a range of Amerindian handicrafts.

PHAGWAH The 'Festival of Colours' is the Hindu celebration of spring, commemorating the triumph of good over evil. The highlight of this festival comes when Hindus, who traditionally wear white for Phagwah, move from house to house or gather together and cover each other with powders and water coloured red, green, blue, yellow, pink, purple and orange.

In Guyana, Phagwah is a national holiday that all races and religions participate in. In Georgetown, the central celebration takes place at the Mandir in Prashad Nagar, but you're likely to get covered in dye anywhere in the city.

Phagwah normally takes place in March or April, but varies according to the lunar cycle.

DIVALI (DEEPAVALI) The Hindu Festival of Lights is usually observed in November (actual date depends on the lunar cycle). On this day, Hindu families light thousands of *diyas* to symbolise the triumph of good over evil. Georgetown is the site of an extensive lighted vehicle parade consisting of characters from holy scriptures.

EASTER Easter Sunday is celebrated in the traditional manner in Guyana, but on Easter Monday much of the country's population heads outside to fly kites, a symbolic act representing Christ's Resurrection. While kite flying is part of tradition throughout Guyana, perhaps the greatest concentration of homemade kites is along Georgetown's sea wall, where strong winds provide the perfect flying conditions.

MUSLIM FESTIVALS Eid-ul-Fitr (end of Ramadan), **Eid-ul-Adhah** (festival of sacrifices), and **Youman Nabi** (birth of the Prophet Mohammed), are also celebrated in Guyana with feasts that change dates depending on the lunar calendar.

INDIAN ARRIVAL DAY On 5 May the Indian population of Guyana celebrate their history and culture that began on the day when the first group of indentured labourers arrived from India in 1838. There are celebrations that take place in many of the villages lining Guyana's coast; there is also a Festival of India that occurs around this date. The festival, which takes place in Georgetown, is essentially a trade fair and exposition with an array of goods, including furniture, handicrafts, clothing and jewellery produced in India. The festival also includes excellent traditional Indian cuisine.

EMANCIPATION DAY This celebration is in recognition of the abolition of slavery in 1834. Celebrated on 1 August, this commemoration day features an African Festival in National Park. Traditional foods and crafts are on sale throughout the day and in the evening there is a grand cultural event in the stadium, with music, drama and dance.

SPORT

CRICKET The main sport in Guyana is cricket. Nothing else comes even close to generating as much passion as does cricket. It's played in the streets, in the parks, on the beaches and just about anywhere else that has enough space. The entire country of Guyana comes together around their beloved sport.

Guyana is part of the West Indies in terms of team selection, to which they have contributed several captains, many of whom got their start at the local holy shrine to cricket in Guyana, Georgetown Cricket Club, known better as the Bourda Cricket Ground. Dating back to 1865, Bourda is the oldest cricket ground in the Caribbean and the only international cricket club beneath sea level. Cricket matches played at Bourda have always been revered for the lively crowds that pack the old wooden stands and the Test and other international matches that were played here over the years showcased the talents of some of Guyana's best-known players, including Clive Lloyd, Lance Gibbs, Rohan Kanhai, Roy Fredericks, Alvin Kallicharan, Basil Butcher, Joe Solomon, Colin Croft and Shivnarine Chanderpaul.

But the days of Bourda hosting international matches are in the past, as a new stadium was completed in 2007, just in time for Guyana to host the Super Eight matches of the ICC Cricket World Cup. The Guyana National Stadium at Providence is quite an improvement over Bourda. It has room for 15,000 cricket fans, six pitches and four practice nets and warm-up pitches. But it has a long way to go before garnering the history of Bourda.

Other competitive-level sports in Guyana include boxing (which is the only sport that has ever produced an Olympic medallist (bronze) from Guyana), squash, football, basketball, rugby, volleyball, table tennis, lawn tennis and hockey. Horseracing and car racing also have long histories of popularity in Guyana.

FISHING (*Bruce and Julia Roberts*) If you're interested in saltwater sport fishing, Guyana is not your destination unless you know that 'sea bob' and 'white belly' are not cartoon characters and 'gillbacker' is not a creature in a JRR Tolkien novel. The first two are commercial shrimp and the last is a bright yellow catfish that's a highly sought after local delicacy and all are products of Guyana's thriving commercial offshore fishing that specialises in shrimp and onshore fish species that abound in the nutrient-rich waters.

The coastline of Guyana is lapped by more than 200 miles of café-mocha waters pumped out by the Orinoco and Essequibo rivers; during the rainy season they can push their muddy waters out as much as 20 miles into the blue Atlantic. Rich in nutrients and teeming with a varied collection of fish species, this is a bonanza for commercial net and trawler fisherman. Slim pickings, however, for the rod-and-reel angler.

Sport fishing In the brackish waters of the many small, mosquito-infested coastal rivers and mangrove swamps (with names as poetic as Maihcony, Abary, Mahaica and Canje) the right tides, the right season, and the right water can yield fly fishing for small to medium migratory tarpon. There is however only a small window of opportunity for success, and it's as much luck as destiny.

Now, fresh water is where it gets interesting, and there's plenty of it, as the name Guyana itself will attest, having been derived from an Amerindian word meaning 'Land of Many Waters'. The Guiana Shield in the southwest of the country, which is crowned by 9,000ft Mount Roraima, sources the journey of many rivers that drain the Amazonian rainforest. This begins with clear, raging white water cascading over rapids and waterfalls before turning to slower-moving, tannin-stained rivers that meander their way north through lush, untouched rainforest and eventually build up to silty roiling torrents that enter the Atlantic at sea level. See page 49 for a list of freshwater fish species.

Seasons All the fishing, except bottom fishing for catfish, is strictly seasonal as the rivers in Amazonia routinely rise and fall between wet and dry seasons as much as 40ft. The fish species follow the rising waters into the rainforest and are largely inaccessible from May to around the first week October. The best time for fishing is between the middle of October and the middle of February (November, December and January being the peak). From the middle of February to the end of March, conditions will be variable at best, as the water could be too low or rising swiftly as the rains begin to fall once again.

Tackle There are only very limited tackle stores in Guyana, so if you do plan to fish, bring your own equipment.

Spin fishing There are many internet sites that offer information on lure types for these species, but remember that the large 'wood chopper'-type baits and lures are meant for the *Cichla temenisis* of northern Brazil and do not work well in Guyana. Your best option is with regular, large-mouth bass lures; the Johnson silver minnow in ½ or ¾ ounce is your best all-round player.

Open-faced spinning reels and medium-action 6–7ft spinning rods are favoured. Be prepared to fish a little heavier line weight than normal, between 12 and 15 monofilament works best.

Bottom fishing A stouter rod of about 6½–7ft with heavy to medium action is ideal with preference for braided, non-stretch line with weight between 15 and 20lb. Rigging should consist of your basic Carolina rig, using 1–2oz lead weights, and live bait hooks.

Fly-fishing You will want a 9ft, six- or seven-weight rod. There's no drift fishing here so come prepared to cast until your arm falls off. Flies should resemble baitfish with the 'Lefty's Deceiver', tied to about three to five inches long, being the best. Fast stripping and a fast retrieve works best.

Access None of the best fishing places are easily accessible; remember that these are remote areas where no organised ecotourism has penetrated. All fishing in Guyana has to be with the aid of a boat, because with heavy jungle cover in most places, there are *very* few areas where bank fishing is feasible.

Excellent options for sport fishing in Guyana include Rewa Village (see page 260), Karanambu Lodge (see page 264), Iwokrama (see page 224) and Surama Village (see page 244).

Another option is by enquiring when visiting any of the local Amerindian communities of Guyana, especially those in the Rupununi. The locals have long depended on fish as a main component of their diet and they make great guides.

Guide service At the time of writing, Guyana had no officially recognised fishing guide services (progress is being made in this regard), but there are a handful of people who will organise fishing trips to some of Guyana's best fishing holes. One of Guyana's best river guides for fishing trips is Ashley Holland (see page 58) who combines fishing excursions with an exploratory spirit in the Rupununi, mainly on the Rewa and Rupununi rivers. Duane de Freitas of Dadanawa Ranch and Rupununi Trails (see page 59) is also renowned for his equally legendary river trips that take guests to remote areas of Guyana. Both will work with clients to specifically cater a trip to certain species of fish.

At the time of publication, a project to develop a catch-and-release sport fishing industry in Guyana was in its early stages. Early plans called for using the Rewa Eco-Lodge (see page 262) as the base from which to develop the industry. The project will involve proper fishing guide training and introducing much better fishing equipment for use by visitors. If you're interested in the developments, enquire with the guides listed above, ask a local tour operator or visit www.guyana.travel.

2

Natural History

The Smithsonian Institution has been conducting biodiversity inventories for Guyana since 1983, and in these 25 years thousands of species have been identified, including more than 225 species of mammals, over 300 species of reptiles and amphibians, 815 (and counting) species of birds and more than 6,500 species of plants. And the research is still not conclusive, with most researchers and scientists believing that hundreds more species remain unidentified.

This section provides the reader with only a brief overview of Guyana's rich biodiversity; for a list of sources that provide more thorough information see *Further information*, page 295.

FLORA

Approximately 80% of Guyana's landmass is covered by tropical rainforest, and much of it is still intact. Some 6,500 species of plants have so far been identified in Guyana. And of those species, hundreds are put to use as food, medicine or other requirements.

Guyana is tropical, and almost everything seems to flourish here. Many orchids, helliconias and flowering trees that are so coveted in other parts of the world abound, but perhaps the most celebrated of Guyana's species is its national flower, the *Victoria amazonica*. The largest of the giant water lilies, its leaves can grow up to 3m in diameter and support the weight of a baby. Their stalks can reach lengths of 7–8m.

At dusk the lily's flowers slowly open, eventually blooming a brilliant white. At the same time they also emit a strong odour and increase their temperature to attract a beetle that pollinates them. Roughly 24 hours later, when the flower blooms again, it is a pinkish-red colour.

MEDICINAL USES Many of the plant species found in Guyana's tropical forests have been used in the making of medicines, both by large pharmaceutical companies and by locals in need of bush medicine. If you suffer an ailment while in the forest and are with a local guide, chances are they'll know of a local remedy that will alleviate pain, cure you of the malady or, in worst-case scenarios, greatly increase your chances of making it to mainstream medical care.

One of the many local contributions to modern-day science comes from curare, a paralytic, plant-derived poison that Amerindians have used for centuries in fishing and hunting. It's produced through a varying combination of plants, barks and leaves, and in strong enough quantities it will cause death by asphyxiation, by paralysing muscles needed to breathe.

It was first recorded by early explorers to Guyana, who also brought samples back to Western medicine, where it eventually became used in muscle relaxants and anaesthesias.

FOOD PLANTS Guyana has long been regarded as the breadbasket of the Caribbean. Some of the main crops grown include sugarcane, rice, cassava, banana, plantain, pineapple, pumpkin, coconuts, limes, mangoes, eddoes and papayas.

LOGGING There are about 1,000 tree species in Guyana and many of these are highly coveted species of hardwoods with exotic names like greenheart, purpleheart, bulletwood, crabwood, iteballi, locust, mora, wallaba, wamara and tonka bean. Many of Guyana's hardwood species are in demand from countries overseas and the timber industry is growing. Thankfully, Guyana has a good system in place that oversees the forestry sector in an attempt to ensure that forests are managed sustainably through a process of selective logging, directional felling and reduced impact logging.

The country's Low Carbon Development Strategy (see pages 20–1), and the rigorous supervision it requires, will help enforce stricter rules, but if sustainable forestry practices aren't followed (and they not always are), Guyana's forests could suffer the same fate as much of the world's other rainforests. Roughly 13.6 million hectares of Guyana's 16.5 million hectares of rainforests have been declared State Forest; of this just more than half has been set aside for selective timber harvesting. But even with almost half of Guyana's rainforests allocated for possible timber harvesting, mining is the cause for most of Guyana's deforestation. Any signs of clear cutting found in Guyana are a result of mining, as one of the biggest threats to Guyana's biodiversity remains the elusive El Dorado that attracted the first Western explorers centuries ago.

MAMMALS

(*Information provided by the Iwokrama International Centre for Rainforest Conservation and Development*) Amongst the more than 225 species of mammals that have been documented in Guyana are some of the world's largest, including capybara (rodent), giant anteater, giant river otter, false vampire bat (largest bat in Central and South America) and jaguar (largest cat in the Western Hemisphere).

Many of Guyana's mammals that don't get to claim a world record are still much sought after, including five additional species of big cats, manatee, tapir, capybara and eight species of primates.

Information on some of Guyana's key mammal species is provided below. Average statistics are given in parentheses as body length/tail length/weight or body size/weight.

CARNIVORES Even though these mammals are often associated with large canines perfect for tearing flesh, many will still supplement their diet with fruits, nuts or other vegetable matter.

Jaguar (*Panthera onca*) Locals call this big cat 'tiger' (1.25m/55cm/70kg), which outside of its girth can be identified by its beautiful markings of black spots forming broken circles around a small central spot. Also look for a large head and short, stocky legs. Jaguars are both nocturnal and diurnal, and while they are mainly terrestrial they climb low trees and are excellent swimmers.

The solitary creatures are usually spotted along trails or gaps along the forest edge, where roads or rivers run. Their size is used to take down large prey, including peccaries, capybara and deer, but jaguars are also known to attack livestock, dogs and horses. Chances are you'll see one before hearing one, but you may hear a roar or series of loud grunts.

The preferred habitat is primary forest. Adult jaguar tracks, which you are much more likely to see on your visit, are 120mm wide on the front paw and 95mm wide on the rear. They have four toes with rounded pads; there are no claw marks. The footpad is also wide and has a rounded top.

Puma (*Puma concolor*) Locally called the 'deer tiger', the puma is slightly smaller, and much slimmer, than a jaguar (1m/60cm/45kg). Its body is outfitted with a small head flanked with large pointed ears, long legs and long black-tipped tail; colours are sandy to reddish brown on the top and cream or white on the under parts. Only young pumas have brown spots.

Pumas are nocturnal and diurnal and mainly stick to the ground but are good climbers and rarely enter water. Sightings of the solitary animals are rare, and while they're found in all types of forest and savannas they prefer higher-level rocky terrain to wetlands. The puma's main prey is deer, paca and agouti, but they also attack livestock.

Tracks are about 80mm wide with four toe pads that are more pointed than rounded. The top of the footpad has a small indentation (which the jaguar lacks).

Jaguarundi (*Herpailurus yaguarondi*) This medium-sized cat has a long body (75cm/50cm/7kg) with shorter legs and a long narrow tail, which distinguishes it from the similar-looking, but bushy-tailed tayra (see page 34). They have no spots and their colours can be dark grey (more common) or reddish.

Jaguarundis are mainly diurnal and are good climbers. They favour dense brush near water but are found in forests, savannas and cultivated areas; look for them crossing roads. Their diet consists mainly of small rodents, birds and occasional lizards.

Their tracks are roughly 40mm wide, with the front toe and footpads being more spread out.

Ocelot (*Leopardus pardalis*) Ocelots are medium-sized (75cm/35cm/10kg) spotted cats. They are much smaller and not as stocky as jaguars and their spots typically form rows. Ocelots have a heavier build than the other two smaller spotted cats (margay and oncilla).

Ocelots are mainly nocturnal and usually terrestrial, climbing and swimming only occasionally. They can be found in all forest types and are solitary cats that travel at night; during the day they rest in trees or amongst buttresses or tree fall. Their diet consists of small terrestrial mammals, iguanas, land crabs and birds.

Tracks have four toe pads and the front tracks (60mm) are noticeably wider than the hind tracks (50mm).

Oncilla (*Leopardus tigrinus*) Roughly the size of a domestic cat, this is the smallest of the spotted cats (50cm/30cm/2.25kg). Its slim body, with long bushy tail, is yellowish brown with black spots that form stripes on the neck.

Usually found in mature forest, it's a nocturnal animal that feeds on mice and small birds.

Front tracks (27mm) are broader than the hind (22mm) and there is a large gap between front footpad and toe pad.

ANIMAL TRACKS

Tayra

Front 55mm

Hind 55mm

Giant anteater

Front 100mm

Hind 80mm

Brazilian tapir

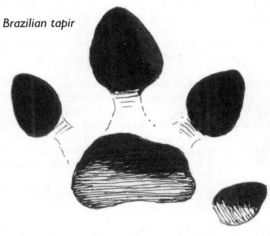

Front 175mm

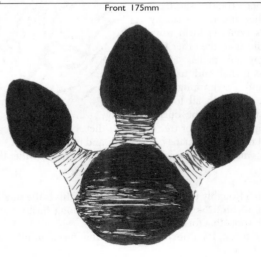

Hind 170mm

White-lipped peccary

Front or Hind 55mm

Puma

Front 85mm

Hind 80mm

Giant otter

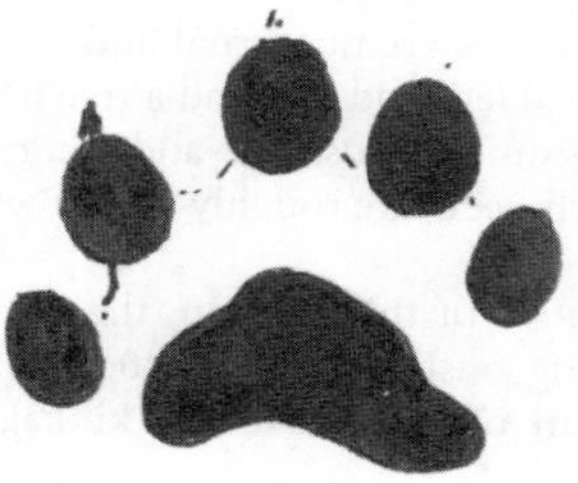

Front 95mm

Hind 105mm

Capybara

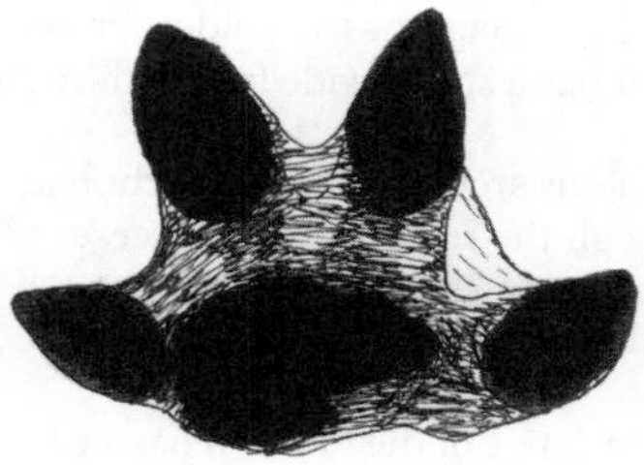

Front 110mm

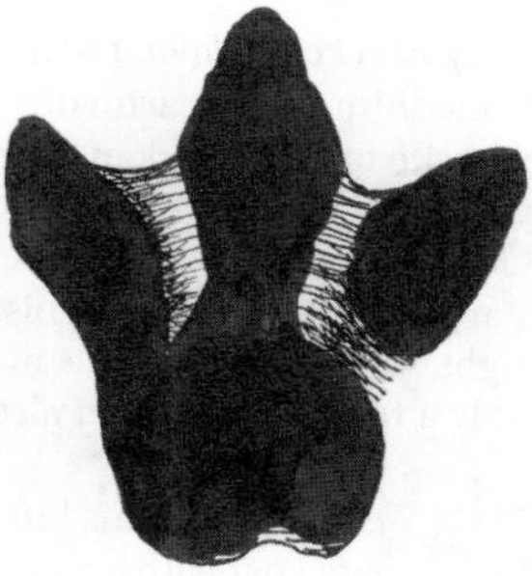

Hind 105mm

Jaguar

Front 120mm

Hind 95mm

Agouti

Front 25mm

Hind 30mm

Paca

Front 40mm

Hind 45mm

Margay (*Leopardus wiedii*) Margays are small and slim spotted cats (60cm/40cm/3.5kg) with long bushy tails and long legs with large feet. Typically found in mature forest, margays are nocturnal and arboreal, hunting mostly in trees (they can rotate their hind legs and descend a tree head first). They eat small arboreal mammals, including mice, opossums and squirrels, as well as occasional birds. Tracks, which are rarely seen, are roughly 35mm wide.

Olingo (*Bassaricyon beddardi*) A relative of the raccoon, the small and catlike olingo has a grey-brown body with a long, bushy tail (40cm/40cm/1.5kg). With the same short and rounded ears, olingos are often mistaken for kinkajous, which are longer and have prehensile tails.

Usually found in undisturbed evergreen forest, olingos are nocturnal and arboreal and typically solitary. They eat fruits, nectar, invertebrates and small vertebrates.

Kinkajou (*Potos flavus*) Sometimes called honey bear or night monkey by locals, this medium-sized carnivore (55cm/50cm/3kg) has a golden-brown body and prehensile tail that darkens at the tip. It has a short, wide face with round ears and large eyes.

Common in all types of forest, kinkajous are nocturnal and arboreal and usually solitary. Because it moves noisily through the trees and often freezes when caught in light, this is one of the most commonly seen nocturnal arboreal mammals. Mainly a fruit eater, its diet also includes nectar, insects, mice and bats.

Coati (*Nasua nasua*) This long-nosed relative of the raccoon has an orange-brown to dark brown coat with a pale yellow belly, and a bushy and banded tail that is often standing straight up. The short legs have long claws on the front feet and the brown face has white spots.

Seen in all forest types and scrub, the diurnal coatis are both terrestrial and arboreal. Females live with their young in large groups, while the males are solitary outside of breeding season. They eat fruits, worms, insects and small rodents.

The roughly 45mm-wide tracks are five-toed with large foodpads and long claw markings.

Tayra (*Eira barbara*) These are long-legged and weasel-like animals (75cm/40cm/4kg). The body is typically black with pale yellow or grey-brown head and neck; tails are long and bushy. Their arched backs are long and their large feet are tipped with strong claws.

Most common in evergreen and deciduous forest and second growth, they are mainly diurnal and semi-arboreal, often moving rapidly through the trees or on the ground. Tayras eat insects, fruit and vertebrates, including lizards, monkeys and agoutis.

Tracks are five-toed and wide (55mm) with noticeable claw marks.

Bush dog (*Speothos venaticus*) This rarely seen, strange dog has a short and squat body (65cm/12cm/6kg) with a stubby tail and light brown to dark brown colourings. Prefers swampy areas of mature forests and feeds on agouti, paca and fish. It sounds much like common dogs.

Tracks have small footpads and four toe pads with claw marks; front is 45mm wide and at 42mm the rear is narrower and longer.

River otter (*Lontra longicaudis*) Locally called small water dog, river otters have low streamlined bodies (65cm/40cm/6.5kg). Upper colourings are brown and the underbody is pale grey and whitish. Its feet are webbed and the thick tail tapers towards the tip.

Diurnal river otters are terrestrial and semi-aquatic, moving with agility in the water and awkwardness on land.

They are found along typically larger forested rivers, streams and lagoons and eat fish and aquatic invertebrates. Their burrows can be seen on banks along rivers or streams.

Tracks, often found on sandy banks, are fairly broad (60–80mm) with visible webbing between toes; the tail also leaves drag marks between them.

Giant river otter (*Pteronura brasiliensis*) Most often called water dogs in Guyana, their low, streamlined bodies (1m/60cm/30kg) are larger than those of river otters. They are mainly a rich brown colour with white markings on their throats and chins, their feet are webbed and they have a thick tail that flattens into a paddle at the tip.

Diurnal and semi-aquatic, they are often seen in groups of five or more along mostly remote large rivers, lakes and flooded areas. Groups sleep in burrows on the riverbank and eat fish and caiman. Their social lifestyle and diurnal habits have made them easy prey for hunters, who kill them for their fur.

Tracks are larger and wider (95–105mm) than river otters', with the same drag marks.

PRIMATES With their dextrous, grasping hands and feet these mammals are often seen climbing through trees. Their long tails are prehensile (grabbing) in some larger species.

Squirrel monkey (*Saimiri sciureus*) This small and slender monkey (30cm/40cm/800g) has beautiful colouration. The sides, shoulders and rump are pale grey with an olive tinge; the mid-back is a dark, rusty hue; the forelimbs, hands and feet are a bright golden orange; and it has a white mask around the eyes and forehead.

The diurnal and arboreal monkeys are commonly found in primary and secondary forest and along the river's edge. Very social, they are often in groups of 15 to more than 100 foraging in the sub-canopy for food. They are mainly insectivorous, but also eat ripe fruits and small vertebrates.

Wedge-capped capuchin monkey (*Cebus olivaceus*) Medium-sized (45cm/50cm/3kg) with a mostly brown body with a long, prehensile tail. The top of its head has a wedge-shaped black cap that comes to a point on the forehead. Pink around its mouth, nose and eyes, the rest of its head is a greyish white.

Common in primary or secondary forest, they are social and usually in groups of ten to 40. They are omnivorous, feeding on fruits, seeds and insects.

Brown capuchin (*Cebus apella*) Also medium-sized (45cm/50cm/3kg) and with a cap of black hairs on its head and black sideburns. The hands and feet are black and the prehensile tail is black at the tip.

They are diurnal and arboreal, live in groups of eight to 14 and are very curious. Found in primary or secondary forest, they mainly eat fruit, but will also dine on insects, eggs, reptiles and small mammals.

Golden-handed tamarin (*Saguinus midas*) Guyana's smallest primate (25cm/35cm/450g) is entirely black except for yellow markings on the back and bright orange-yellow hands and feet.

Diurnal and arboreal, they are found in primary and secondary forest, especially along roadsides and streams. Usually seen in groups of two to six, feeding on insects and fruits about 5m or more above ground.

White-faced saki monkey (*Pithecia pithecia*) These shaggy monkeys are medium-sized (40cm/40cm/2kg) with long hair covering their entire bodies, including their tails. Males are all black except for pale white hair circling the dark nose, mouth and eyes. Females are dirty grey, with sparsely haired belly and throat a rusty colour.

The diurnal and arboreal monkeys are most common in primary forest and typically seen in the sub-canopy or lower feeding on fruits, seeds, leaves and insects.

Brown-bearded saki (*Chiropotes satanas*) Closely resembling the white-faced in size (40cm/40cm/3kg) and shagginess, these don't have the white hair on the face but do have long beard extending from the jaw down to the top of the chest.

They are diurnal and arboreal, live in family groups of 18 to 30 and can sometimes be seen in the sub-canopy with other primates, including squirrel and capuchin monkeys.

Red howler monkey (*Alouatta seniculus*) Because of their large size (55cm/55cm/7kg) and dark reddish and orangish fur, they are locally called baboons. They have large heads and prehensile tails. On their chins they have furry beards, which are longer in males.

They are diurnal and strictly arboreal and are often found in the forest near tree gaps or along rivers. They feed on leaves and fruits and live in troops of three to nine; they are almost always heard before seen. Their prehistoric-sounding loud calls are a series of snorts, grunts, roars and howls that can be heard from several kilometres away. They are heard most often at dusk and dawn but also through the night.

Black spider monkey (*Ateles paniscus*) Guyana's largest monkey (50cm/75cm/10kg) has a small head, long gangly limbs and a prehensile tail used as a fifth appendage. Its entire body is covered in longer black hair except for a bare pink face.

Common in primary or secondary forest, they live in troops but are often seen in groups of two to five. They feed on fruits, flowers and leaves and can be curious about observers. They make a series of low grunts, barks, whistles and loud screams and will often threaten those watching them by shaking branches, calling or dropping items.

UNGULATES The animals in this group are large herbivores that walk on their toes tipped with one, two or three hooves.

Tapir (*Tapirus terrestris*) South America's largest native mammal (2m/250kg) is commonly called the bush cow in Guyana. These peculiar-looking creatures have short grey hair and elongated, trunk-like snouts that curve downwards. They also have a dark crest of hair that runs from the forehead and along the neck.

Tapirs are nocturnal and diurnal and have a wide range of habitat in the forest, but they are good swimmers and are typically seen near streams, creek beds and swamps. They are shy and quiet solitary creatures but can make a racket when travelling through the bush. They communicate using a loud, long whistle.

Their tracks are three-toed, with a fourth toe sometimes showing on the front foot, and are 170–175mm in width.

White-lipped peccary (*Tayassu pecari*) These bush hogs are medium-sized (1.2m/35kg) pig-like beasts, have stocky bodies and slim legs and are all black or dark brown except for a white patch on their lower jaw and throat.

Mostly found in mature evergreen forests that have little human disturbance, they are very social and live in herds of 40 to more than 200. They travel walking single file on forest paths, turning up the soil for fruit, roots, vegetation, invertebrates and palm nuts along the way. They are very aggressive and are one of the more dangerous mammals in the forest. They often make a clicking sound with their canine teeth when surprised, although you are likely to smell them before you see them. A foul musty odour is a good sign of their presence. If you come across a herd, climb the nearest tree.

Their tracks have two triangular hooves with a slightly rounded tip, about 55mm wide.

Collared peccary (*Pecari tajacu*) Small and very pig-like (90cm/20kg), they have stocky bodies and slim legs. They are grey-brown in colour with a pale collar along their shoulders and chest and their heads are large and triangular.

These social animals are usually seen in groups of five to 15 in all forest types, savanna and agricultural areas. They dine mostly on palm nuts and other fruits, with the occasional vegetables, roots and invertebrates. They have the same dirty sock odour as white-lipped peccaries.

Tracks are two triangular hooves with slightly rounded tip, about 35mm wide.

Red brocket deer (*Mazama americana*) Commonly called bush deer, they are medium-sized (90cm/22kg) with rounded bodies and arched backs; the rump is higher than the shoulders or head. They are reddish brown with white along the throat, chest and underneath their small tails. Males have short, straight antlers and young have white spots.

They are common in primary and secondary forest, and usually seen alone in the morning, at dusk or at night while foraging for fungi, fruits, flowers and vegetation.

Tracks are 25mm wide and are split hoof prints that taper to narrow tips; together they form a triangle.

Grey brocket deer (*Mazama gouazoupira*) Besides being shorter, more slim (80cm/15kg) and a greyish-brown colour, their bodies are similar to red brocket deer. Their ears and legs are also longer. Young also have white spots.

They are mainly diurnal and usually seen alone near streams in primary and secondary forest feeding mainly on fruit.

Tracks are similar to, but slightly smaller than, red brocket deer.

LARGE RODENTS These mammals are important to the forest as they use their chisel teeth to crack hard nuts and feed on seeds, dispersing them throughout the forest.

Capybara (*Hydrochaeris hydrochaeris*) The world's largest (90cm/30kg), and certainly strangest-looking, rodent. It's stocky with a large, rectangular head and an arched, rounded rear. The fur is dark reddish-brown and they have large webbed feet.

Always seen near water in lowland forest, swamp, gallery forest and flooded savanna. They are diurnal or nocturnal and semi aquatic, usually found in family groups of two to six feeding mainly on grass and aquatic vegetation.

Webbed tracks are very broad (105–110mm) with four toes visible on the front foot and three on the hind foot.

Paca (*Agouti paca*) In Guyana, these are most often called *labba* and are often hunted for their meat (the saying goes that if you eat labba and drink creek water, you'll always come back to Guyana). They have large, stocky bodies (70cm/8kg) with reddish-brown fur and four stripes of white spots on each side.

Found in forest and secondary brush, they are terrestrial, nocturnal and usually solitary or in male–female pairs. They eat fruit and nuts and are often seen along creeks, streams and rivers.

Their broad tracks (40–45mm) have four toes on the front and three on the hind.

Red-rumped agouti (*Dasyprocta leporina*) Commonly referred to as *akuri*, this is a medium-sized (50cm/3.5kg) rodent with long legs and a large rectangular head; it's said to look like a short-eared rabbit on stilts. Its head, back and shoulders are grey-black while the rump is an orangish red.

They are commonly found throughout primary or secondary forest and are diurnal and terrestrial. They feed on nuts, seeds and fruit and are most commonly seen at dawn or dusk.

Their forefront tracks are 25mm wide in front and the hind is 30mm wide. The hind foot has three elongated toes and pointed claws while the front foot shows three or four toes.

ANTEATERS This group of mammals have long snouts and no teeth. They tear open ant and termite nests with their powerful front legs and long claws and then use their long, sticky tongues to feast on the bugs. When on the ground, anteaters twist their feet and walk on the sides, or the knuckles.

Giant anteater (*Myrmecophaga tridactyla*) These large, creatures are unmistakable when seen. Their lengthy nose and bushy tail make this creature appear incredibly long (1.2m/75cm/30kg). It is mostly black with white forelegs and a distinct white stripe running from its ears to mid-back. They are found in forest and savanna, especially in open areas with large termite mounds (in the Rupununi). They are terrestrial and active day or night. Outside of breeding they are solitary, but the female also carries the young on her back for up to nine months. It moves with a shuffling gait or rolling gallop and will rear up and slash at predators when cornered.

Tracks have front claws pointing backwards or sideways and are 100mm wide in front and 80mm wide at the back.

Tamandua (*Tamandua tetradactyla*) Medium-sized (60cm/50cm/6kg) with a long prehensile tail. Usual colourings are blonde on head, upper back legs with a black vest but can also appear as entirely blonde.

They are semi-arboreal, nocturnal or diurnal and are found in primary and secondary forest and savanna. They are solitary creatures that feed on ants, termites and bees.

Tracks have front claws pointing backward and are 55mm wide in front and 40mm wide in the rear.

Pygmy anteater (*Cyclopes didactylus*) This tiny anteater (15cm/20cm/225g) is golden brown with black stripes down the middle of the back and belly. The furry tail is prehensile and there are two large claws on the front foot and four on the hind foot.

They live in mature forest and tall secondary forest, are nocturnal and strictly arboreal. They are solitary and feed on ants in hollow stems of trees.

SLOTHS These sedentary creatures spend most of their lives in trees, hanging upside down from hooked claws and eating leaves. Only rarely do they descend to the ground.

Three-toed sloth (*Bradypus tridactylus*) The more striking of the two sloths, it has a mostly yellow head with a dark nose and crown. Its furry body (60cm/6kg) is dark grey-brown with off-white blotches. Its forelegs are longer than the hind legs with three long claws on each foot.

Found in mature and secondary forest they are nocturnal, diurnal and arboreal. They descend to the ground roughly once a week to dig a hole with their stubby tail and defecate. On the ground it moves by dragging itself, but is a good swimmer.

They are solitary, silent and very easily overlooked. To spot them look for a furry grey ball on or under a branch.

Two-toed sloth (*Choloepus didactylus*) Similar habits and body size and shape as three-toed. This has long brownish fur that is darker on the limbs. There are two claws on the front foot and three on the hind foot. This sloth has no tail, and a pig-like snout.

These are mainly nocturnal and arboreal. Like the three-toed it comes down once a week to do its business and is also a good swimmer.

ARMADILLOS Armadillos are easily identified by their protective bony shell.

Giant armadillo (*Priodontes maximus*) Another unmistakable creature, their large bodies (90cm/50cm/30kg) are covered in a greyish shell that has yellow edges. Their pink underbelly is not covered. They have large feet, with massive claws on the front ones. Their tails are covered in scales.

Found in rainforest and savanna, they are nocturnal, terrestrial, subterranean and solitary. With the assistance of its front claw, it feeds on the nests of ants and termites.

Great long-nosed armadillo (*Dasypus kappleri*) Medium-sized body (55cm/45cm/10kg) with a snout that isn't as long as you'd expect with the name. Its bony shell has seven to nine movable scales on the mid-back, much like an accordion.

Found on the forest floor near swamps and streams, they are nocturnal, terrestrial and solitary. Their three-toed tracks appear bird-like.

BATS More than 120 different species of bats have been documented in Guyana. The Kanuku Mountains alone have at least 89 species, accounting for more than half of the total mammal species diversity. In the forest they are important seed dispersers and pollinators, in addition to consuming tonnes of mosquitoes every night. Some of Guyana's diversity includes fruit-, insect-, frog-, nectar-, blood- and small-mammal-eating species.

REPTILES, AMPHIBIANS AND INVERTEBRATES

The Smithsonian's reptile and amphibian preliminary checklist records more than 300 species. Some highlight species include **poison dart frogs** (*Dendrobatidae*) that come in a range of colours including orange, black, blue and yellow and are used by some Amerindian tribes to poison their arrows and blow-gun darts. Another frog of note is the **golden rocket frog** (*Anomaloglossus beebei*), which is endemic to the giant bromeliads atop Kaieteur Falls.

Besides the four species of **sea turtles** that nest on Guyana's coast (see page 47), there are a couple others of note. The endangered **giant river turtle** (*Podocnemis expansa*) is found in Guyana's interior, but like the marine turtles their population is endangered because their meat and eggs have long been seen as delicacies. The female turtles, which typically weigh around 50lb and measure 2ft in length, are easy prey for hunters because they nest in large colonies. Visitors can witness them nesting near the Iwokrama Field Station, near the village of Rewa and at other locations along the Rupununi River. Currently the village of Rewa and the South Rupununi Conservation Society (based at Dadanawa Ranch) have conservation projects to protect the turtles.

The **matamata turtle** (*Chelus fimbriatus*) is certainly one of the more bizarre turtle species. Its shell is covered with horny plates that make it look like a rough dead leaf, but it's the head that's really strange. The large and flat head and neck are covered with ridges, warts and numerous other bumps. It has a very wide mouth and long snout used to breathe while submerged. It sucks prey into its mouth like a vacuum. Their heads also have flap-like appendages that allow them to sense fish swimming by, which is necessary with their poor eyesight.

Guyana is also home to the world's largest alligator, the **black caiman** (*Melanosuchus niger*). There are healthy populations in the interior, especially along the Essequibo, Rewa and Rupununi rivers. They prefer slow-moving rivers, wetlands and flooded savannas and the nocturnal creatures can reach lengths of more than 15ft. Their diet consists of fish, turtles, large rodents and sometimes deer.

While black caimans are more easily spotted in the dry season, visitors to Guyana can easily see them at Iwokrama, Karanambu Lodge and the Caiman House, where there is ongoing research with the species. Other species of caiman in Guyana include **spectacled caiman** (*Caiman crocodiles*), **Schneider's dwarf caiman** (*Paleosuchus trigonatus*) and the world's smallest caiman, **Cuvier's dwarf caiman** (*Paleosuchus palpebrosus*).

As for snakes there are highly poisonous species including the **labaria** (*Bothrops atrox*), **bushmaster** (*Lachesis muta*), the largest venomous snake in the Americas, the **rattlesnake** (*Crotalus durissus*) and **himeralli coral snake** (*Micrurus surinamensis*), most of which visitors will likely not see. There are also several species of tree boas, such as the emerald tree boa, that can be spotted at night along the riverbanks. The most famous boa constrictor is the **anaconda** (*Eunectes murinus*), which grows throughout its life and can reach lengths of more than 30ft. These nocturnal carnivores spend most of their time in swamps and near rivers and eat just about anything, including peccary, deer, caiman, birds, fish, capybara and agouti.

You're also likely to see green iguanas, geckos and several other species of lizards scampering around.

As much of Guyana is covered in tropical rainforest, the number of ants, millipedes, centipedes, spiders, butterflies, beetles, ticks, flies, gnats, bees, roaches, scorpions, etc are endless. It will be these little critters that you're likely to see (or feel) the most.

Mosquitoes are notorious transmitters of disease, including malaria, dengue, yellow fever and filariasis (see *Health*, page 64). The tiny parasitic ticks that are prevalent during the dry season are also disease carriers.

Scorpions, tarantulas and spiders large enough to eat birds can make one recoil at the thought of setting off on a rainforest walk, but you'll likely find that ants are the worse pests of them all.

The tiny insects account for more than 10% of the entire biomass created by animals in the rainforest. One species, the **bullet ant** (*ParapFonera clavata*) is the second-largest in the world and they have a sting to match their size. Locals say they are so named because if they bite you, you'll be off like a bullet.

But ants also play an important role in cleaning up the forest of dead animals and forest plants in a cycle that creates new matter for plants to feed on.

BIRDS

(*Information provided by the Guyana Amazon Tropical Birds Society and www. guyanabirding.com*)

Because other continental birding hotspots such as Peru, Ecuador and Venezuela were better-known, Guyana used to be an overlooked birdwatching destination in South America, attracting only the most adventurous and hardy twitchers. However, in the years since the first edition of this guide was published, Guyana has become a recognised and respected birdwatching destination in its own right.

The Guyana Sustainable Tourism Initiative, a joint programme between the Guyana Tourism Authority and the United States Agency for International Development, began developing Guyana's birding tourism industry in 2006 by bringing international tour operators and media to Guyana. Comments and suggestions provided by the participants are used to improve birdwatching destinations and the tourism industry as a whole. Improvements are ongoing, but the international feedback has been overwhelming. Guyana may not have the numbers of birds found in some other South American countries, but the birds that are found here are incredibly accessible. It's not uncommon to identify nearly half of Guyana's species on a two-week trip.

As part of the initiative a new website was developed (*www.guyanabirding.com;* e *info@guyanabirding.com*) to highlight birding opportunities in Guyana and provide trip-planning information. In 2007, *A Field Checklist of the Birds of Guyana,* compiled by the Smithsonian Institution, was updated and can be found at: http://botany.si.edu/bdg/pdf/bird_checklist_2ndedition.pdf. However most birdwatchers coming to Guyana, and local guides, use *Birds of Northern South America* or *A Guide to the Birds of Venezuela* (see *Appendix,* page 295) as their bird identification book.

OVERVIEW Within Guyana's diverse habitat from the savannas to the forested highlands to the low-level coastal areas more than 815 species from 72 different families have been documented, and there are likely many more that remain unidentified. In Georgetown alone there are more than 200 species from some 40 different families.

The families found in Guyana include many sought-after bird species of the neotropics including: herons; hawks and eagles; falcons and caracaras; rails; sandpipers; gulls, terns and skimmers; parrots; nighthawks and nightjars; swifts; hummingbirds; woodpeckers; ovenbirds; woodcreepers; typical antbirds; tyrant flycatchers; cotingas; emberizine finches; and new world blackbirds.

While no species have been found to be endemic to Guyana, more than 60 of the 104 species endemic to the Guiana Shield have been identified in Guyana. Highlights of known species include blood-coloured woodpecker, Guianan cock-of-the-rock, toco toucan, crimson fruitcrow, caica parrot, little shearwater, little chachalaca, sun parakeet, red-shouldered macaw, roraima screech-owl, scissor-tailed nightjar, racket-tailed coquette, green aracari, black-spotted barbet, Guianan piculet, ferruginous-backed antbird, Rio Branco antbird, Guianan streaked antwren, olive-green tyrannulet, Guianan red cotinga, crimson-hooded manakin, cayenne jay, Finsch's euphonia, and rose-breasted chat warbler.

NATURAL REGIONS Geographically Guyana is part of the neotropics (an area including Central America, the Caribbean and northern South America), which is home to roughly one-quarter of the world's bird species. Within Guyana, there are three main natural regions: the coastlands, the rainforest and the savannas. Each provides a different habitat for an array of bird species.

The coastlands These extend from Venezuela in the west to Suriname in the east. Within this area there are three general habitats: coastal forest and mangrove; cultivated lands; and populated areas. This area also hosts many migrant species of birds while travelling throughout the neotropics.

The Pomeroon River, in the northwestern area of Guyana, divides the coastlands into two distinct regions. Moving west, mangrove and coastal forest habitats are found that widely remain in their wild state and support a mixture of forest and seashore species, including the scarlet ibis. The eastern coastlands are the most populated area of Guyana, with much of the land consisting of farmlands used for cultivating rice and sugar. This area is where birdwatchers can see the strange hoatzin, in addition to egrets, gulls, herons, ibises, hawks, tanagers, flycatchers, finches, blackbirds and orioles.

Tropical rainforests Blanketing roughly 80% of Guyana's landmass, these are home to more than half of Guyana's bird species. The different levels of the rainforest canopy, understorey and floor each host distinct species of birds.

Within the canopy are such species as the harpy eagle, toucans, parrots and macaws. In the middle section are the hummingbirds, trogans, jacamars, tanagers, woodpeckers, cotingas and antbirds. On the forest floor are tinamous, curassows, guans, chachalacas and trumpeters.

Savannas These are found in two areas of Guyana: intermediate savannas are along the banks of the Berbice River in the northeast and the more extensive grasslands of the Rupununi are in the south. The savannas have a range of species including hawks, falcons, caracaras, quail, finches, tanagers and flycatchers. Because of the extreme seasonal fluctuations in the Rupununi that cause a transformation from dry grasslands to wetlands, the ecosystem here is largely independent. The area is rich in waterbirds such as storks, ibises, ducks as well as species found within the forested mountains of the area, including harpy eagles and Guianan cock-of-the-rock.

HABITATS Guyana's natural regions have been further broken down into six separate birding zones, largely based on the different habitats and geographic characteristics found throughout the country.

Zone one Georgetown, with such a wide diversity of birds, is considered a separate zone. The capital city consists of six square miles of parks, cultivated lands and coastline; all have good access. Key families include woodpeckers, tanagers, plovers, parrots, macaws, flycatchers, hummingbirds, raptors and terns. Out of the 200-plus species, highlights include the blood-coloured woodpecker and festive parrot.

Zone two Mainly the 5,000-square-mile area along Guyana's coast, with swamps, mangrove forest and cultivated lands. More than 400 species are found in this zone, with key families including ibises, tanagers, sandpipers, plovers, herons, tyrant flycatchers and parrots.

Zone three In the southwestern area of Guyana, this includes 10,000 square miles of lowland grass and scrub savannas with mixed forests. There are more than 500 species here; key families include storks, herons, hawks, falcons, finches, ducks, toucans, vireos and herons.

Zone four The 6,200 square miles of this area are mainly along the Berbice and Demerara rivers, and consist of white sand forest and mixed scrub and white sand savannas. There are some 350 species in this zone, including woodpeckers, tanagers, flycatchers, nightjars, raptors, jacamars, jays and hummingbirds.

Zone five In the middle of Guyana is this small band of 1,800 square miles of mixed marsh and white sand forests home to more than 300 species of birds. Key families include finches, new world blackbirds, potoos, tanagers and owls.

Zone six The largest zone has 60,000 square miles of mountainous rainforests in the north and mixed flooded forests and mountains to the south. This zone is home to at least 650 species, including many that are migratory, uncommon and rare.

Families include eagles, falcons, cotingas, parrots, tanagers, flycatchers, toucans and hummingbirds. Highlight birds include the harpy eagle, Guianan cock-of-the-rock, red siskin and Amazonian umbrellabird.

UNIQUE SPECIES Guyana is home to many different birds that will have even non-birdwatchers craning their necks skywards more often than not, but there are a few standouts that for visitors lucky enough to see them will likely end up as highlights among the many flora and fauna spotted on a trip to Guyana.

Guianan cock-of-the-rock (*Rupicola rupicola*) is Guyana's poster bird, literally gracing nearly every tourism brochure, website and magazine advertising the country. And with the male's brilliant orange colourings, complete with an attention-grabbing Mohawk, it makes it one of the most sought after and easily identifiable birds of the tropics (the females have a less exciting brown plumage).

Guyana has a healthy population of the birds, which are common in birding zone six. But perhaps the most notable places for seeing the birds in Guyana are at the identified *leks*, or the patches of ground that males use for display during the breeding season, at Kaieteur Falls, the Amerindian village of Wowetta and the Iwokrama International Centre. At these sites, visitors have a decent chance of seeing the birds nesting, bathing, perching and dancing, while the males compete for female attention.

Harpy eagle (*Harpia harpyja*) With weights reaching 18lb, a wingspan of more than 6ft, and a healthy diet of mammals including sloths and monkeys, the largest eagle in the Americas is often referred to as the 'flying wolf'. Harpy eagles are becoming increasingly rare in the wild, but Guyana still provides a refuge for this endangered species. In fact, Guyana's relatively large population of harpy eagles caught the attention of National Geographic who filmed the documentary *Flight of the Harpy Eagle* in Guyana's Kanuku Mountains.

Sightings are rare but do occur with relative regularity at Iwokrama, in the Kanuku Mountains, in the northwest and sometimes even along the Essequibo not far from the coast. Those dedicated to seeing one should enquire with GATBS or send an email through the Guyana Birding website to see if there are any active nests that will be accessible during your visit. At the time of writing, there were active nests providing excellent views near Surama and Rewa villages and within the Kanuku Mountains.

Hoatzin (*Opisthocomus hoazin*) Guyana's national bird is a strange primitive creature. The hoatzin's plump body and reddish-brown feathers may not appear antediluvian, but the bird's blood-red eyes set in patches of bright blue skin and unruly crest of long feathers are throwbacks to another time. Hoatzins are also born with two claws protruding from their wings, a characteristic that leads many to believe that it's a direct link to the archaeopteryx, the first known bird.

Canje pheasants (as they are often called in Guyana) are most common in birding zone four; Mahaica Creek, an offshoot of the Demerara River not far from Georgetown, has healthy populations of the birds. Listen for the smoker's cough.

Red siskin (*Carduelis cucullata*) The red siskin used to flourish in Venezuela and Colombia, but more than 150 years of trappings, in an attempt to breed a red canary, greatly diminished its population in the wild. It was believed to be nearing extinction until April 2000 when, during a survey of Guyana's birds, researchers from the University of Kansas and the Smithsonian Institution discovered a population of several thousand red siskins in southern Guyana. Not only was it the first time the bird had been discovered in Guyana, but also the number found is much larger than the previously recorded wild population.

The South Rupununi Conservation Society is currently leading a project that is studying the bird's distribution, behaviour, habitat and population. Using Dadanawa Ranch as your outpost, Guyana is one of the few places left offering birders an excellent chance at viewing this endangered bird.

BIRDWATCHING AREAS Almost anywhere in Guyana is great for watching birds; the few listed below are just some of the more developed highlight areas. One of the unique experiences of birding in Guyana comes through the local guides, especially the Amerindian guides in the interior.

Guyana's guides are incredibly in tune with nature and see and hear the jungle in a way that's impossible for most Westerners. They will be your eyes and ears and their stories provide a cultural backdrop to any trip.

Georgetown Botanical Gardens and Coastal Rivers
With more than 200 species, including the endemic blood-coloured woodpecker, the Botanical Gardens are a great start to a birdwatching trip. To guide you, enlist Andy Narine, of Guyana Feathered Friends, and to explore further, have him take you to the nearby Abary and Demerara rivers where you may see the hoatzin, scarlet ibis, rufous crab-hawk, and the Guianan gnatcatcher and piculet.

Arrowpoint Nature Resort
Located just two hours from Georgetown on the banks of the Pokerero Creek, Arrowpoint Nature Resort offers great views of hummingbirds, including crimson topaz and reddish hermit. Other specialities include red-bellied macaw, crimson topaz, paradise jacamar, and point-tailed palmcreeper. Don't miss birdwatching via kayak a visit to the nearby Amerindian village of Santa Mission.

Baganara Island Resort
Close to the junction of the Essequibo and Mazaruni rivers, Baganara is a short trip from Georgetown. Speciality birds include the caica parrot, pygmy antwren, Guianan warbling antbird, and spotted antpitta. Also visit Parrot Island to watch hundreds of parrots returning to roost.

Kaieteur National Park
Most people visit to view Kaieteur Falls, one of the world's longest single-drop waterfalls, but keen birdwatchers will want to see the Guianan cock-of-the-rock and orange-breasted falcon. The white-chinned and white-tipped swifts, or Makonaima birds, nest under the vast shield of rock hidden behind the curtain of falling water. At sunset thousands return to the falls and provide an acrobatic display of feeding before disappearing behind the water.

Iwokrama International Centre
With nearly one million acres of protected forests and 500 species of birds, there is a lot to see here, including many speciality birds like blue-cheeked Amazon, marail guan, Guianan red-cotinga, rufous-throated antbird, and several macaw species.

Atta Rainforest Lodge and Iwokrama Canopy Walkway Also in the Iwokrama Forest, you can stay at the Atta Rainforest Lodge where eight new cabins are in place and explore the Canopy Walkway with guide Huxley Moses. From 30m above the forest floor you can look for waved woodpecker, dusky purpletuft, painted parakeet, and white-winged potoo. Nearby there is also an excellent Guianan cock-of-the-rock *lek*, or display ground.

Surama Village If you're lucky, guide Ron Allicock (see page 59) will be home when you visit Surama Village and Eco-Lodge. His keen eyes and ears will increase your chances of getting good looks at harpy eagle, bronzy jacamar, zigzag heron, and the elusive rufous-winged ground-cuckoo.

Rock View Lodge This oasis provides access to good deciduous forest and savanna birding. Allow guide Hendricks Daniel to lead you in search of brown-throated parakeet, Finsch's euphonia, cayenne jay, and double-striped thick-knee, and don't miss sunrise from the top of the lodge's namesake rock.

Wowetta The community-based tourism project at this small Amerindian village in the northern Rupununi savannas features a beautiful trail through pristine primary forest that leads to the *lekking* (or display) grounds of Guianan cock-of-the-rock. But the area is rich in other species of birds, with other highlights including red and green macaw, golden-handed manakin, toucanette, capuchin bird, green oropendola, rufous-winged ground-cuckoo and black currasow.

Karanambu Lodge Many people visit the magnificent Karanambu Lodge, located on the Rupununi River, to meet owner Diane McTurk and learn about her work rehabilitating giant river otters. When not playing with otters or looking for giant anteaters in the savannas, guide Manuel Mandook can lead you in search of capuchinbird, spotted puffbird, bearded tachuri, agami heron, crestless curassow, and the brilliant rose-breasted chat.

Yupukari Village and Caiman House Just a short distance from Karanambu on the Rupununi River, Yupukari village has great savanna, gallery forest and river-edge birds, including pinnated bittern, green-tailed jacamar, black-chinned antbird, and capuchinbird.

Rewa Village and Eco-Lodge At the junction of the Rewa and Rupununi rivers is this idyllic village that is rapidly becoming prized for excellent sport fishing, birdwatching and wildlife viewing. Guide Rovin Alvin will be happy to take you to several spots in search of ornate hawk-eagle, Guianan puffbird, Todd's antwren, spotted tanager, bay-headed tanager, and a high density of macaws. Take time to hike to the top of Awarmie Mountain to absorb the stunning views.

Nappi Village and Maipaima Eco-Lodge Nestled at the base of the Kanuku Mountains, the Maipaima Eco-Lodge at Nappi Village provides excellent access to pristine rainforests, home to an abundance of macaws and parrots, including red-fan parrot. White-bearded bellbird and southern screamer are also in the area.

Dadanawa Ranch You shouldn't miss birding in Guyana's southern Rupununi, and the best place to stay is at Dadanawa Ranch. Guides Duane and Justin de Freitas or Asaph Wilson are your keys to finding Guianan cock-of-the-rock, harpy eagle, jabiru stork and the highly endangered red siskin. The area also has healthy populations of jaguar and giant anteater.

MARINE LIFE

SEA TURTLES (*Information provided by Michelle Kalamandeen, Guyana Marine Turtle Conservation Project*) From March to August, Shell Beach, a 90-mile stretch of undeveloped beach in northwestern Guyana, becomes the nesting ground for four of the world's eight endangered species of marine turtles: leatherback, green, hawksbill and olive ridley.

The Amerindian communities of Guyana have long relied on turtle meat as a staple of their diet. Nesting season for the turtles was hunting season for many, although 'hunting' turtles seems to stretch the use of the word. Regardless, sea turtles were valued for their large amounts of meat, the numerous eggs and their beautiful shells. The hunting was unsustainable and numbers began dropping quickly.

But turtle hunters aren't the only ones to blame for a decline in sea turtle populations. Climate change certainly plays a role, but one of the biggest culprits is fishermen using nets. Turtles often get caught in trawling nets and die. In Guyana commercial fishermen are required to use turtle exclusion devices, or TEDs, but it is still suspected that dozens of turtles die in fishing nets every year.

In 1988, to protect the declining numbers of sea turtles nesting in Guyana, Dr Peter Pritchard, a leading marine turtle biologist who had been doing research in Guyana for a couple of decades, recruited a converted turtle hunter to help him work with the local communities and act as a 'turtle warden' and protect the once-hunted species.

The concept grew over the years and in 2000, the Guyana Marine Turtle Conservation Society (GMTCS) was established (*www.gmtcs.org*). The GMTCS has many roles including helping to facilitate the work of the turtle wardens, and conducting research on the biodiversity of the area while working towards getting Shell Beach designated as a Protected Area. GMTCS also works with the local indigenous communities to develop projects that provide an alternative income to sea turtle egg and meat harvesting. The projects educate locals on the importance of conservation in their villages and surroundings.

For more detailed information on Shell Beach, GMTCS and planning a visit, see *Shell Beach*, page 196.

Species Known turtle species in the world number around 300, of which only eight are sea turtles. Roughly five times that number are land-living, or tortoises, and the remainder are mainly freshwater species.

Sea turtles range from 80 to 1,000lb at maturity and all have forelimbs modified into paddle-like flippers, which typically have one claw instead of distinct digits. Also unique is the fact that the heads of sea turtles cannot be pulled into their shells for protection. Instead the skulls are topped with a very strong bone that acts much like a shell.

In all sea turtle species, breeding females must crawl ashore on a beach to nest (males typically never leave the sea). Once on shore the females excavate a broad 'body pit' and a deep narrow hole into which the eggs will be deposited. Sea turtles usually lay a clutch of around 100 soft-shelled eggs. The eggs are then covered and the female lumbers back to the sea.

Sea turtles normally mate more than once in a season, and often close to the same spot. Green turtles and leatherbacks have been known to nest eight or nine times in one season. These species also tend to take a year or two off before nesting again.

Besides the four sea turtle species that nest in northwestern Guyana, loggerheads have been found washed up on the shores of Shell Beach but have never been recorded nesting here.

Leatherback (*Dermochelys coriacea*) With a shell that can reach about 6ft in length and an overall body mass that can weigh more than 1,000lb, the leatherback is the largest of the sea turtle species. It is a prehistoric beast that is a marvel to see in its natural environment.

The giant size of the leatherback doesn't impede its mobility in water; they can rapidly descend to 1,000ft and have been known to travel thousands of miles in a matter of a few months. Their diet consists mainly of jellyfish.

For obvious reasons, leatherbacks were prized by Guyanese turtle hunters, but since the protection patrols began in 1988, numbers have been on the rise. The leatherback is listed by IUCN as critically endangered.

Green turtle (*Chelonia mydas*) Green turtles can have a shell length of roughly 4ft and weigh upwards of 600lb. They are easily identified by their small heads tipped with a short, rounded snout and their smooth shell, which has four scutes, or horny plates, on each side.

Colour is one aspect that does not work well in identification. The 'green' in their name actually refers to the colour of their fat; outer colouring varies from black above and white below on hatchlings and brown streaks, spots or a uniform grey colour in adults. The green turtles that nest in Guyana are amongst the biggest in the world, and can be twice the weight of some Caribbean green turtles found nesting in Costa Rica.

Green turtles eat mainly sea grasses and seaweeds that are typically found growing in calm waters, but the ideal nesting grounds occur where there is strong wave action. As a result, the turtles must migrate hundreds of miles from feeding to nesting grounds. Many that nest in Guyana come from Brazil.

After years of slaughter, populations in Guyana dwindled to a very low level, but the turtles have been on the increase in recent years. The nesting season in 2007 was one of the best on record, with as many as ten to 12 turtles nesting on a given night. Green turtles are listed by IUCN as endangered.

Hawksbill (*Eretmochelys imbricata*) The average shell length of an adult hawksbill is about 3ft, with a weight of around 160lb. Its head is narrow with a straight pointed, protruding beak (strangely it does not resemble a hawk's bill, which curves down).

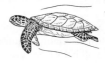

The hawksbill is found throughout the tropics, mainly around coral reefs where they mainly feed on sponges. They have been hunted for many years for their thick, decorative shells, often called 'tortoiseshell', which used to fetch high prices on international jewellery markets (they are currently banned internationally).

Only small numbers of hawksbills nest in Guyana, but the ones that do are amongst the largest recorded species in the world. They are very rarely seen nesting in Suriname and French Guiana. Hawksbill turtles are listed by IUCN as critically endangered.

Olive ridley (*Lepidochelys olivacea*) With an average length of about 26 inches and a weight of 80–100lb, this is the smallest sea turtle species. It has a short, nearly circular shell that is yellowish-olive in colour. When seen from above, the head is triangular and the shell has five to nine plates along each side.

Olive ridleys are a tropical species that nest in mass groups on remote beaches in locations such as Mexico, Costa Rica and India. They were not recorded in the western Atlantic until 1964 when renowned turtle biologist Peter Pritchard discovered them nesting in northwestern Guyana. Today, olive ridleys nesting in Guyana remain a rare occurrence, and some years can pass before one is recorded. It is believed that populations are both shifting and collapsing. The olive ridley is listed by IUCN as endangered.

WEST INDIAN MANATEE (*Trichechus manatus*) This aquatic species, commonly called the sea cow, is grey or brown in colour with an average length of 3m and a weight of 400–800lb. It has a split upper lip for feeding and is typically found in shallow coastal areas and rivers, but you're most likely to see them in the ponds of Georgetown's Botanical Gardens or National Park.

FISH Species of fish in Guyana are incredibly diverse; within the area around Iwokrama and the North Rupununi Wetlands alone, more than 400 species of fish have been identified and it's estimated that roughly 200 more remain unidentified. The fish thrive in a range of habitats, including rivers, creeks, ponds, ox-bow lakes and flooded forests and savannas. During the rainy season, when much of southern Guyana is flooded, fish species are able to move between the Orinoco River delta, the eastern Guiana Shield and the Amazon basin, providing for a rich diversity of fish.

Unique species include the world's largest scaled freshwater fish, the **arapaima** (*Arapaima gigas*), which can reach 3m in length and weigh up to 440lb, **silver arowana** (*Osteglossum bicirrhosum*) and several very large catfish species.

Some of the more unfriendly fish species include the incredibly toothy **red-bellied piranha** (*Pygocentrus natteri*), barb-yielding **freshwater stingrays** (*Potamotrygon sp*), 6ft-long **electric eels** (*Electrophorus electricus*) that pack 500 volts and the tiny parasitic catfish known as **candiru** (*Vandellia cirrhosa*).

Candiru typically get their blood by lodging themselves into the gill chambers of other fish, feasting and then removing themselves. But on very rare occasions, these spined and mostly transparent fish have also been known to lodge themselves in the urethras of unsuspecting swimmers. It's believed that they are attracted to urine streams mistaking them for a fish's gill streams and will swim up the small hole, in which they get stuck; surgery is required for removal. This is rare, but best advice is to not pee in the river and always wear a swimsuit or underwear.

Sport fishing species (*Bruce and Julia Roberts*)
Lukanani It is in the clear, tannin-tinted section of these waters that rod-and-reel anglers can find their quest. Over the last 20 years the *tucunare*, or *lukanani* and peacock bass as it's widely known, has become recognised throughout the angling world as a true heavyweight in the freshwater divisions.

Initially misidentified as the peacock bass of North America, this fish is really a member of the cichlid family. Other than its shape, it bears little resemblance to that of the freshwater, large-mouth bass of North America. This fish is as feisty and as determined as they come. A relentless predator, he has been known to straighten salt water hooks, make multiple runs at the same lure, and put up a battle that gains respect from the most intrepid of anglers.

The species mainly found in northern South America in the Guiana Shield drainage is the *Cichla ocellaris*. Due to its temperature tolerance, this fish was transplanted to the lakes and canals of southern Florida in the 1960s. Unlike its giant cousins further south in Brazil, *Cichla temenisis* (which can grow up to 20lb), these little scrappers average 3–7lb, but can grow up to 12lb in the larger rivers.

Payara Ranked second for purely fly- or spin fishing is the payara. Saber-toothed and prehistoric in appearance, this fish is a denizen of the fast-moving rocky sections of the rivers. A formidable fighter and jumper, the average catch is 4–6lb, but some have been caught up to 20lb.

Arawana In the extensive shallows and along sand bars, dead drifted bait could produce hook-ups with the eel-like arawana. These fish are also known to take flies, poppers and the occasional spoon. Pound for pound, it's one of the strongest fighters in these waters.

Pacu The freshwater 'permit' of South America, is a vegetarian and can be found in the most pristine untouched areas wherever there are rapids and waterfalls. Hooking into one of these on light tackle is an experience of a lifetime.

Basha The jewel in the crown of Guyana's bottom fishing must be the basha, which is a member of the drum family. In the dry season they can be found in pools sometimes deeper than 100ft, and with the right live bait, fishing for these schooling fish can be phenomenal. The average of this species is 3–5lb and trophies up to 10lb have been caught. A beer-filled icebox and a large umbrella are as necessary as bait and tackle for this type of fishing.

Catfish If you're a bottom fisherman, there is probably the biggest concentration of catfish species anywhere on the globe. Starting with the 100lb skeet, the beautiful tiger fish, the prehistoric zip fish and the microscopic twee twee, catfish rule in Guyana. Fishing season, for this underrated species, stretches 365 days of the year.

For more information on fishing see pages 27–8.

3

Practical Information

WHEN TO VISIT

Thanks to its proximity to the Equator, there are only two seasons in Guyana: rainy and dry. On the coast, the rainy season occurs from May to mid-July and mid-November to mid-January. The rainy season in Guyana's interior, however, is different. The heavy rains come from May to August; during these months huge swathes of the savannas flood and rivers can rise some 30ft above their dry season levels. The interior also experiences a shorter period of lighter showers towards the end of December. The 'cashew rains', as they are called because they occur during cashew harvesting, last two or three weeks and are often seen as more refreshing than anything else. Most of Guyana is tropical rainforest and so even during the dry season there can be showers, although they are often brief and welcomed, as they cool the soaring temperatures of the dry season. During the rainy season, there are days when not a drop falls, and even on the rainiest of days there are often extended periods of sunshine.

Choosing when to plan your visit – rainy or dry season – depends on personal preference and desired activities. The dry season offers little relief from the heat, while rainy season days are cooler (relatively speaking) but more humid. Also, Guyana is in the tropics and insects should be expected year-round, but the wet season can tend to offer a denser population of beloved creatures such as mosquitoes and kaboura flies.

Travel to and around Guyana's interior is much easier during the dry season as the rains can render many roads (including the main unpaved road that runs from Linden to Lethem) impassable without the most reliable 4x4 vehicle. On the other hand, the rainy season in the interior means much more travel by boat, which can make for a peaceful, personal way of exploring the interior, especially when you find yourself nearly level with treetops full of birds and monkeys.

Guyana is still a relatively untapped destination for tourists (while there is a tourist trail of sorts that runs through Guyana, it is still a long way from the well-trodden path running through much of South America) but visitor arrivals are increasing. The busiest months for travel to the interior of Guyana are September to November and January to April. However, at any time you may find yourself the only visitor staying at an interior lodge.

Currently, most of the traffic that goes through the international airport is either part of Guyana's expatriate community or returning Guyanese. The former occurs throughout the year while the latter experiences surges over the Christmas holidays and during summer breaks, during July and August. Airline tickets to and from Guyana during these times can sometimes drop in availability and rise in costs.

HIGHLIGHTS

For many visitors to Guyana, the highlights will revolve around interior locations that offer no crowds, plenty of nature and a lifestyle that is at odds with the coastal populations.

ACCOMMODATION In Georgetown there are a host of places to stay, but few will stand out as a highlight of your trip. For colonial-style architecture that harkens back to Guyana's glory days, **Cara Lodge** (see page 105) consists of two renovated houses dating back to the 1840s. The Bottle Bar Restaurant is also one of Georgetown's best. Newcomer **Duke Lodge** (see page 108) is is the place for those looking to combine colonial architecture with a swimming pool.

Along the Essequibo River, **Baganara Island Resort** (see page 160) is the place to go for true relaxation; a taste of the Guyanese Caribbean after a long trip in the interior. For a slightly more intimate feel, visit the **Hurukabra River Resort** (see page 166), which offers many of the same activities.

For those who like to self-cater, house rentals along the Essequibo River are a must. With a swimming pool, sweeping verandas, modern accessories and plenty of space for a large group, **Bidrabu House** (see page 168) provides casual luxury. **Bucksands Lodge** (see page 166) is more rustic, but the isolation and beautiful setting makes the trip.

For an easy transition upon arrival, **Arrowpoint Nature Resort** (see page 130) offers a comfortable lodge, mountain biking, kayaking trips and nature hikes a short distance from the international airport.

If you're spending a night in Linden, the **Watooka Guest House** (see page 212) is the place to see how the other half lived, including visiting royalty. While certainly past its prime, the grand colonial building has riverside grounds and suites that transport visitors back a few decades.

In the interior, **Iwokrama's River Lodge** (see page 229) is stunningly beautiful and provides easy access to protected rainforest. The new rooms at nearby **Atta Rainforest Lodge** (see page 230) offer the unmissable overnight canopy walkway experience. With beautiful gardens, a swimming pool and a central location, the stylish **Rock View Lodge** (see page 248) is an oasis in the northern savannas. Nature lovers shouldn't miss the extraordinary **Karanambu Lodge** (see page 264). You'll be treated like family while exploring the 125 acres of protected lands, home to more than 300 species of birds and a significant population of threatened or endangered species, including giant anteater and an orphaned giant river otter programme.

After **Surama's** much-deserved success (see page 246), eco-lodges in remote Amerindian villages are being built with a relative frequency. Standouts include the **Rewa Eco-lodge** (see page 262) and **Nappi's Maipaima Eco-lodge** (see page 275), both of which offer comfortable lodging and easy access to some of Guyana's more undisturbed forests.

In the southern Rupununi, **Dadanawa Ranch** (see page 290) offers one of Guyana's most unique experiences. Once the world's largest cattle ranch, Dadanawa is still home to more than 6,000 head of cattle. In a given day guests can chase cows with the local cowboys, explore bush islands in ancient Land Rovers and discuss everything from conservation issues to cattle rustlers.

For the experience of camping in the bush, **Carahaa Landing** (see page 246) at Surama, is perfect for walking and boating through the rainforest. **Turtle Mountain Camp** (see page 230) at Iwokrama is good for those wanting to spend a night in a hammock without roughing it too much. Wildlife lovers and birdwatchers won't be disappointed at the isolated **Mapari Wilderness Camp** (see page 273). If you're prepared to battle the mosquitoes, the best remote beach camping is at **Shell Beach** (see page 196); nesting sea turtles are an added bonus.

SIGHTSEEING For many visitors to Guyana, trip highlights (and the reason for coming in the first place) will revolve around the interior and its pristine nature, lack of crowds, welcoming locals, traditional villages and the overall sense of stumbling upon an undiscovered secret. The rainforest and savannas will be a highlight as a whole, but there are some gems that will stand out.

Kaieteur Falls (see page 218) is Guyana's tourism poster child; flights aren't cheap but few will leave feeling like they didn't get their money's worth. Those with the time and sense of adventure may want to do an overland trek (see page 222).

Setting aside one million acres as an experiment on sustainable forest use (everything from ecotourism to scientific research to logging) is a complex endeavour; visitors can see the progress at the **Iwokrama International Centre for Rainforest Conservation and Development** (see page 224). Highlights include night-time boat trips along the Essequibo River to view **nocturnal wildlife**, including giant black caiman, tree boas and capybaras. Another unique look at the jungle is found at the **Canopy Walkway** (see page 235), which at 100ft high gives visitors a peek into the lively upper canopy of the jungle.

You also shouldn't leave Guyana without **paddling a dugout canoe**; it's one of the quietest and most efficient ways to explore the forest. Opportunities abound, but the Burro Burro River trip offered at Surama (see page 247) is particularly good (ask the guides to bring a hand line so you can try fishing for piranha). A trip to **Rewa** (see page 260) is worth it for a sunset paddle on Grass Pond alone.

At Wowetta (see page 254), take an easy (but long) hike through pristine primary forest to watch bright orange male **Guianan cock-of-the-rocks** compete for the females' attention by dancing on the forest floor. For those with less time or endurance, a shorter hike for the same birds is just north along the southern border of **Iwokrama** (see page 224).

Some say that life doesn't get any better than a sunset river trip at Karanambu (page 268) to see **Guyana's national flower**, *Victoria amazonica*, open while sipping on owner and otter-aficionado Diane McTurk's famous rum punch. The return trip involves nocturnal wildlife spotting.

Support **community tourism** (see pages 250–1); many Amerindian villages throughout Guyana are looking to tourism as a way to generate much-needed income. This entails everything from a participatory black caiman research project and nature hikes to eco-lodges and community tours to locally made products. Helping the projects become viable can help discourage villagers from finding work in mining, timber or the wildlife trade.

Relive the days of the Wild West on a **cattle drive** at Dadanawa (see page 287). Join the Amerindian cowboys as they bring the cows home for branding and castration.

Get extremely intimate with the forest in a jungle survival course offered by Bushmasters (see page 59); the isolation period is not for the meek.

Also, while in Guyana, visitors have three main modes of transportation to choose from; each should be experienced. An interior flight is the best way to see the seemingly endless and uninterrupted rainforest stretch out beneath you and, as you head south, the land's sudden transformation into open savannas.

Driving into the interior provides a completely different perspective. A journey down Guyana's main (and unpaved) interior highway gives a true sense of just how much unpopulated land there is in Guyana. And there aren't many international roads that have primary rainforest towering over them.

Whether it's to rent a house, stay at a resort or just for a day trip, take a boat trip on the **Essequibo River** (see page 151). South America's third-largest river has many moods; it's best to stay overnight and experience them all.

From March to August, watch four of the world's eight endangered **marine turtle** species nest at Shell Beach (see page 196). This rustic camping trip isn't for everyone, but those who can hack it will reap great rewards (note that at the time of writing a new lodge was under construction). It's best combined with an overland river trip through Guyana's northwest.

Whether or not you see Georgetown as a highlight depends on your frame of mind. It's a different world from the interior, but it has its charms. Markets are a lively place to experience the culture and see the amazing selection of fruits and vegetables grown in Guyana; two must-sees include the historic **Stabroek Market** (see page 121) and **Bourda Market** (see page 122).

Take a stroll through Georgetown to admire the wooden colonial architecture (in all states of repair); perhaps the most celebrated is **St George's Cathedral** (see page 121).

Serious and novice birdwatchers won't want to miss birdwatching at the **Botanical Gardens** (see page 122). Members of the Guyana Amazon Tropical Birds Society often identify more than 50 of Georgetown's 200-plus species of birds during a guided tour.

History buffs should visit the often-overlooked **Guyanese Heritage Museum** (see page 133). The combination of owner Gary Serrao's private collection and personal passion trumps any other museum in Guyana.

Other museums to visit include the **Roy Geddes Steel Pan Museum** (see page 121), where you'll receive a personal historical tour and mini-concert from steel pan pioneer Roy Geddes, and the **El Dorado Rum Museum** (see page 126), which is the culmination of a Demerara Distillery tour, where you can see how some of the world's finest rum is made.

FOOD With the population of Guyana being a melting pot of East Indian, African, Amerindian, Chinese, Portuguese and Brazilian, there is a variety of interesting dishes to sample. Guyanese like to eat, and often in large portions, so rest assured you will eat well during your stay in Guyana.

Outside of Georgetown there are few splendid restaurants to highlight. Many serve up a similar variety of baked or fried fish and chicken, rice and chow mein. Vegetarian and seafood dishes can often be standouts.

At most interior lodges meals are served family-style and they're often great times to try a variety of dishes with Creole, Brazilian and Amerindian influences. One thing you will not lack for at interior lodges is food.

Restaurants in Georgetown can be hit or miss, but there are a few reliable exemplars. **Shanta's** (see page 114) is the place for a variety of curries enjoyed with roti. The Rastafarian **House of Flavors** (see page 113) serves up good and cheap *ital* (vegetarian) food. **Brasil Churrascaria & Pizzaria** (see page 113) will be favoured by anybody looking to gorge themselves on grilled meats. **Oasis** (see page 113) has some of Georgetown's best coffee drinks and pastries, as well as good, if not a bit pricey, lunches.

The ambience at Cara Lodge's **Bottle Bar Restaurant** (see page 112) often makes up for any shortfalls that occasionally occur during the meal. **El Dorado** at Pegasus (see page 105) is a decent option for fine dining in Georgetown.

SUGGESTED ITINERARIES

Be it birdwatching, jungle trekking, wildlife spotting, Amerindian heritage, relaxation, rustic isolation or something a lot more adventurous, each destination in Guyana offers something a little bit different, and specific itineraries will likely revolve around the desired activities of each visitor.

The itineraries below are laid out so as to maximise the traveller's time, which means they also may leave some feeling exhausted. Travelling in Guyana, especially in the interior, can be arduous at times and many visitors may find it more rewarding to spend more time at fewer places, thus limiting the amount of time spent bouncing over bumpy roads or rolling rivers.

The following are only suggested itineraries, and not necessarily the best options for you. The best way to plan a trip to Guyana is to research the activities offered at each destination and cater a trip to your personal desires, adding and subtracting days to your preference. (Keep in mind that within the itineraries, specific activities aren't listed for each location, as those are best left for travellers to decide.) You will be rewarded by spending more time in one location and really getting to know your hosts and the locals.

Itineraries will also have to be fine-tuned according to chosen modes of travel. For example, interior flights to some destinations run only on certain days of the week, and flexibility is always important when planning a trip to Kaieteur Falls as tourist flights go only when there are enough people to make the trip economically feasible.

Finally – as these itineraries will reflect – every visit to Guyana should include a trip into the interior, preferably including both the rainforest and the Rupununi Savanna. A couple of days on the Essequibo River won't be regretted, and during the right season, those willing to rough it should try to make it to Shell Beach. If Georgetown doesn't excite you, swap it for a night at Arrowpoint Nature Resort (see page 130).

ONE WEEK Georgetown – Iwokrama – Surama – Rock View, with area day trip – Karanambu – Georgetown

TEN DAYS Georgetown – Iwokrama – Rock View – Karanambu – Lethem – Dadanawa – Lethem – Georgetown – Kaieteur Falls – Baganara – Georgetown

TWO WEEKS
Nature Georgetown – Iwokrama – Surama – Rock View, with area day trip – Karanambu – Lethem – Dadanawa – Lethem – Georgetown – Kaieteur Falls – Baganara and Essequibo River – Georgetown

Amerindian Culture Iwokrama – Surama – Rewa – Rock View, with day trip to Wowetta – Karanambu – Yupukari – Nappi – Lethem – Georgetown – Kaieteur and Orinduik Falls

THREE WEEKS Georgetown – Iwokrama – Surama – Rock View, with area day trip – Rewa – Rock View – Karanambu – Yupukari – Lethem – Nappi – Dadanawa – Lethem – Georgetown – Kaieteur Falls – Essequibo – Georgetown

FOUR WEEKS If you're lucky enough to have four weeks to spend exploring Guyana, either extend the time spent at places in the above itineraries or add on the following one-week suggestion: Georgetown – Essequibo River – Georgetown – Mabaruma – Shell Beach – Mabaruma – Georgetown.

Also consider spending two weeks of your holiday on a specialised trip offered by Bushmasters, Ashley Holland or Rupununi Trails (see page 289).

TOUR OPERATORS

One of the purposes of this guidebook is to make it easier for visitors coming to Guyana to plan their own trips. To use a tour operator or not is a personal preference. Some like the ease of having everything planned and sorted for them on their holiday. It is meant to be a holiday, after all, and the less work the better.

Improvisational travel can be rewarding but with travel in Guyana, especially to the more remote lodges and interior locations, a self-arranged trip can be very difficult to plan. While internet is becoming more commonplace at interior lodges, making individual trip planning much easier, many places do not have a phone and a short-wave radio is still a common form of communication. Most venues have email addresses but it can be days before messages are checked and answered. If you show up unannounced at some of the smaller villages, the availability of food and drinking water may be an issue. (Also note that if you visit an Amerindian village without previous arrangements, upon arrival you are required to check in with the Village Council.) In the interior, vehicles are limited; there is a simple system of organising them to shuttle around visitors that can be thrown out of kilter by last-minute requests.

In short, the obstacles of travelling through Guyana can make self-planning some aspects of your trip difficult, or at the very least a frustrating and time-consuming process.

The majority of tour operators in Guyana are reliable and can save you the hassle of arranging the details of your trip. Large or small, they will play a pivotal role in planning any trip to Guyana. The good ones know the industry, understand how the interior functions and they are likely to get answers much quicker than you. They are the middlemen who can save you much frustration.

In any case, most can be helpful in providing you with valuable information whether you book a trip through them or not. And since many work on a commission basis, you often pay the same price as booking direct.

Besides longer trips to locations in the interior – Iwokrama, Surama, Karanambu, etc – the most popular trips booked through tour operators are day tours. These include those to Kaieteur and Orinduik Falls (see page 219), the Georgetown city tour (see page 120), resorts and sites along the Essequibo and Mazaruni rivers (see page 151), and Santa Mission (see page 132).

Most of the local tour operators listed below quote their prices in US dollars, but will accept Guyana dollars and other currencies. Nearly all accept credit cards (with a 4–7% surcharge added on) and a few take travellers' cheques.

Prices for the most common tours don't vary as the tour operators often work together to fill tours to make them more affordable or feasible, as some require a minimum number of people.

Most, if not all, of the international tour operators listed below rely on local ground tour operators to plan the logistics of their trips, but they often use their own professional guides and supplement with local ones.

Keep in mind that as tourism continues to grow in Guyana, the list of international and local tour operators can change often. The list below should by no means be considered as exhaustive.

IN THE UK

Andean Trails 33 Sandport St, Leith, Edinburgh EH6 6EP; 0131 467 7086; e info@andeantrails.co.uk; www.andeantrails.co.uk. Tailor-made & group nature trips.

Audley Travel New Mill, New Mill Lane, Witney, Oxon OX29 9SX; 01993 838 000; e info@ audleytravel.com; www.audleytravel.com. Tailor-made individual itineraries for discerning travellers.

Birdfinders Westbank, Cheselbourne, Dorset DT2 7NW; 01258 839066; e info@birdfinders.co.uk; www.birdfinders.co.uk. Specialised birdwatching tours.

Cox & Kings Flr 6, 30 Millbank, London SW1P 4EE; 020 7873 5000; e cox.kings@coxandkings.co.uk; www.coxandkings.co.uk. Culture, nature & wildlife tours for groups or individuals.

Explore 55 Victoria Rd, Farnborough, Hants GU14 7PA; 0845 013 1537; e res@explore.co.uk; www.explore.co.uk. Wildlife & birdwatching trips.

Geodyssey 116 Tollington Park, London N4 3RB; 020 7281 7788; e enquiries@geodyssey.co.uk; www.geodyssey.co.uk. Tailor-made & group natural history & birdwatching tours.

Journey Latin America 12 & 13 Heathfield Tce, Chiswick, London W4 4JE; 020 8747 8315; e tours@journeylatinamerica.co.uk; www.journeylatinamerica.co.uk. Natural history tours to Guyana's main lodges & destinations.

Jacada Travel 1–3 Dufferin St, London EC1Y 8NA; 020 7562 8288; e enquiries@jacadatravel.com; www.jacadatravel.com. Private, tailor-made expedition tours.

Last Frontiers The Mill, Quainton Rd, Waddesdon, Bucks HP18 0LP; 01296 653000; e info@lastfrontiers.com; www.lastfrontiers.com. Natural history tours to locations throughout Guyana.

Naturetrek Cheriton Mill, Cheriton, Alresford, Hants SO24 0NG; 44 1962 733051; e info@naturetrek.co.uk; www.naturetrek.co.uk. Extended natural history tours to Guyana's rainforests, rivers & savannas.

Ornitholidays 29 Straight Mile, Romsey, Hants SO51 9BB; 01794 519445; e info@ornitholidays.co.uk; www.ornitholidays.co.uk. Specialised group birdwatching tours.

The Adventure Company 1 Cross & Pillory Hse, Cross & Pillory Ln, Alton, Hants GU34 1HL; 0845 287 6132; e customerservice@adventurecompany.co.uk; www.adventurecompany.co.uk. Group wilderness holidays.

The Travelling Naturalist PO Box 3141, Dorchester, Dorset DT1 2XD; 01305 267994; e jamie@naturalist.co.uk; www.naturalist.co.uk. Group wildlife & birdwatching tours.

Undiscovered Destinations PO Box 746, North Tyneside NE29 1EG; 0191 296 2674; e info@undiscovered-destinations.com; www.undiscovered-destinations.com. Group & tailor-made trips spotlighting nature & culture.

WEXAS 45–49 Brompton Rd, Knightsbridge, London SW3 1DE; 020 7589 3315; e mship@wexas.com; www.wexas.com. Membership travel club offering tailor-made trips to Guyana.

Wilderness In Depth 93 Dale Rd, Buxton, Derbys SK17 6PD; 01298 214900; e travel@wilderness-indepth.co.uk; www.wilderness-indepth.co.uk. Tailor-made adventure holidays highlighting Guyana's wilderness.

Wildlife Worldwide Long Barn South, Bishop's Sutton, Alresford, Hants SO24 0AA; 0845 130 6982; e sales@wildlifeworldwide.com; www.wildlifeworldwide.com. Tours of Guyana's interior rainforests & savannas geared towards wildlife & bird enthusiasts.

IN NORTH AMERICA

Adventure Life 1655 S Third St, W, Suite 1, Missoula, MT 59801; 406 541 2677; e trip.center@adventure-life.com; www.adventure-life.com. Custom natural history & cultural tours.

Bird Treks 216 Spring Ln, Peach Bottom, PA 17563; 717 548 3303; e info@birdtreks.com; www.birdtreks.com. Tours highlighting the birds & mammals of Guyana.

Cheesemans' Ecology Safaris 20800 Kittredge Rd, Saratoga, CA 95070; 408 741 5330; e info@cheesemans.com; www.cheesemans.com. Specialist birding & wildlife tours.

Eagle-eye Tours 4711 Galena St, Windermere, British Columbia, V0B 2L2, Canada; 250 342 8640; e travel@eagle-eye.com; www.eagle-eye.com. Birdwatching & natural history trips with small groups.

Eco-Adventure International W6022 Creamery Rd, Fort Atkinson, WI 53538; 888 710 9453; e info@eaiadventure.com; www.eaiadventure.com. Offering several organised & customised nature, wildlife & birdwatching tours throughout Guyana, including to remote interior locations.

EcoVentures PO Box 3881, Charlottesville, VA 22903, USA; 434 831 2575; e info@ecoventurestravel.com; www.ecoventurestravel.com. Wildlife & birdwatching trips to Guyana's interior.

Exotic Birding Colorado; 303 325 5188 e info@exoticbirding.com; www.exoticbirding.com. Small-group birdwatching trips.

Field Guides Incorporated 9433 Bee Cave Rd, #150, Austin, TX 78733; 512 263 7295; e fieldguides@fieldguides.com; www.fieldguides.com. Specialist birdwatching trips.

Foster Parrots PO Box 650, Rockland, MA 02370; 781 878 3733; e marc@fosterparrots.com; www.fosterparrots.com. Birdwatching & nature-based trips to interior locations including Nappi eco-lodge (which they funded), Rewa & Yupukari.

Gap Adventures 19 Charlotte St, Toronto, Ontario, Canada M5V 2H5; 888 800 4100 e sales@gap.ca; www.gapadventures.com. Group wildlife trips through Guyana's interior.

IN EUROPE

Travelwide Reisen Wilhelmstrasse 20, D 59581, Warstein, Germany; 40 02902 3758; e info@travelwide.de; www.travelwide.de.

IN SOUTH AMERICA

Neblina Forest Tours Isla Floreana Av, E8–129, El Sol Apartment Bldg, 3rd Flr, Quito, Ecuador; 593 2 226 7436; e info@neblinaforest.com; www.neblinaforest.com. Birdwatching tours along the Essequibo River & in the interior rainforests & savannas.

IN GUYANA

Air Guyana Ogle Aerodrome, Ogle; 222 6513; e info@airguyana.net; www.airguyana.net. Day trips around Georgetown & tours to Kaieteur, Orinduik, Baganara, Rock View, Iwokrama or just about anywhere else you want to charter a flight to, including Suriname, French Guyana & Brazil.

Geographic Expeditions 1008 General Kennedy Av, San Francisco, CA 94129; 800 777 8183; e info@geoex.com; www.geoex.com. Specialised natural history & cultural tours to Guyana & the Guianas.

International Bicycle Fund (Ibike) 4887 Columbia Dr S, Seattle, WA 98108; 206 767 0848; e ibike@ibike.org; www.ibike.org. Non-profit organisation promotes sustainable transport & international understanding; runs cultural bike tours to Guyana.

Latin American Escapes 3209 Esplanade, Suite 130, Chico, CA 95973; 530 879 9292; e travel@latinamericanescapes.com; www.latinamericanescapes.com. Custom natural history trips.

Tours of Exploration 1114 Cartwright Rd, Gibsons, British Columbia, V0N 1V1, Canada; 604 886 7300; e info@toursexplore.com; www.toursexplore.com. Birdwatching, wildlife & other natural history tours.

Wildside Nature Tours 539 Prince Frederick St, King of Prussia, PA 19406; 610 564 0941; e info@wildsidenaturetours.com; www.wildsidenaturetours.com. Group birdwatching tours.

Wings 1643 N Alvernon, Suite 109, Tuscon, Arizona 85712; 520 320 9868; e wings@wingsbirds.com; www.wingsbirds.com. Small group birding tours.

Specialised birdwatching & wildlife tours to Guyana's interior lodges & the Demerara & Essequibo rivers.

Tropical Birding Quito, Ecuador; 409 515 0514; e info@tropicalbirding.com; www.tropicalbirding.com. Custom birdwatching tours.

Ashley Holland Yupukari Village, North Rupununi; e ashley_p_Holland@yahoo.com; www.rupununilearners.org/r_r_drifters. River & fishing guide extraordinaire based in Yupukari (near Karanambu) & owner of Rupununi River Drifters. Specialises in extended river trips on the Rewa,

Rupununi & Essequibo rivers & into the Kanuku Mountains. Often works with naturalists, scientists, birdwatchers, fishers & general explorers.

Bushmasters 40 Beverly Hills Dr, Lethem; 660 8107; e amazon@bushmasters.co.uk; www.bushmasters.co.uk. Offering specialised trips through Guyana's interior, including jungle survival, 4x4, cattle drives & extended adventure treks, both for small groups or individuals. Trips always involve indigenous communities.

Dagron Tours International 91 Middle St, Georgetown; 223 7921; e dagron@dagron-tours.com; www.dagron-tours.com. Covering most of Guyana & region with tours to Sloth Island Reserve, Kaieteur Falls, Santa Mission, Shell Beach & Essequibo, Mazaruni & all Rupununi, interior resorts & lodges.

Evergreen Adventures Offices at Guyana Pegasus Hotel, Princess Hotel & Ogle Airport; 225 4484/222 8046–55; e reservations@evergreenadventuresgy.com; www.evergreenadventuresgy.com. Specialising in nature & adventure tourism in Guyana with bookings for lodges in the Rupununi, & along the Demerara & Essequibo rivers. Also organises trips to Shell Beach & day outings to Kaieteur & Orinduik Falls, Essequibo River, Marshall Falls, Georgetown city tour. Books trips to Suriname, French Guiana & Brazil. Friendly service (parent company owns TGA & Intraserv).

Guyana Feather Friends 77 C-1 Light St, Alberttown; 231 5684; e gff_birdingtours@yahoo.com; www.birdingguyana.gy. Tours run by Andy Narine, founder of the Guyana Amazon Tropical Birds Society, who specialises in birdwatching trips to Georgetown's Botanical Gardens & coastal & mangrove sites to see the hoatzin & scarlet ibis. Other trips include Rockstone for tour of Gluck Island & Kaieteur Falls.

Hurakabra Tours 168 Century Palm Gdns, D'Urban Backlands Lodge, Georgetown; 225 3557/624 8694; e booking@hurakabragy.com/gemmadhoo@gmail.com; www.hurakabragy.com. Day & overnight trips to locations on Essequibo & Mazaruni rivers, interior lodges, Kaieteur & Orinduik falls & Georgetown city tours.

Rainforest Tours 5 Av of the Republic & Robb St, Georgetown; 231 5661; e rainforesttours@networksgy.com; www.rftours.com. Very friendly, professional & noted for their overland treks to

Kaieteur & Orinduik Falls, but also day trips to Kaieteur & Orinduik Falls, Essequibo River, Santa Mission, & Georgetown, Linden & Berbice. Books Guyana's major resorts, offers weekend trips to Suriname & Brazil & does annual Pakaraima 4x4 safari. Can organise expeditions to Mount Roraima.

Ron Allicock Surama Village; e ronallicock@gmail.com; www.rupicola.net. One of Guyana's best guides, expert birder and naturalist now organising and leading trips throughout Guyana; can also be booked through other tour operators.

Roraima Tours R8 Eping Av, Bel Air Pk; 225 9650; e ral@roraimaairways.com; www.roraimaairways.com. Trips to Kaieteur & Orinduik Falls, Arrowpoint Nature Resort & Santa Mission. Also Georgetown city tours, Iwokrama, Rupununi Savanna destinations & Essequibo River trips. Certified agent for booking international flights & destinations throughout South America & overseas.

Rupununi Trails c/o Dadanawa Ranch, South Rupununi; +44 796 152 1951; e defreitasduane@yahoo.com; www.rupununitrails.com. Tour operator run by Dadanawa manager Duane de Freitas & wife Sandy. Building on 40 years of area experience, offers specialised adventure tours (treks, horseriding, canoeing, boating) to remote locations (especially in southern Guyana) including Kanuku Mountains, Rewa & Rupununi rivers, Rodeo trail drive & Wai Wai country. Organises trips for birdwatchers, fishers, film crews & researchers & books throughout Guyana & to parts of Venezuela & Brazil.

Savannah Inn Tours Savannah Inn, Lethem; 772 2035; e linda@savannahguyana.com; www.savannahguyana.com. Arranges tours & vehicles throughout the Rupununi & nearby locations in Brazil.

Torong Guyana 56 Coralita Av, Bel Air Pk; 226 5298; e toronggy@networksgy.com. The speciality of Malcolm & Margaret Chan-a-Sue is the Kaieteur & Orinduik day trip, but they offer some of the best personal service in organising air, land & water transport in Guyana.

Waldyke (Wally) Prince Yakarinta Village, North Rupununi; e frogprince2010@gmail.com. Excellent naturalist and a top birding guide leads tours throughout Guyana. Can be booked directly or through operators.

Wilderness Explorers Cara Suites, 176 Middle & Waterloo Sts, Cummingsburg; 227 7698; e tours@wilderness-explorers.com;

www.wilderness-explorers.com. This well-established & knowledgeable company is one of Guyana's best. It has the most extensive selection of itineraries & organises trips to most interior locations throughout Guyana, from birdwatching & wildlife spotting tours to remote jungle treks & fishing excursions. Also books Georgetown city tours, Essequibo resorts, Kaieteur & other South American & Caribbean countries.
Worldwide Travel Services 64D Middle St,

South Cummingsburg; ☎ 226 4099; e world@ networksgy.com. Friendly & helpful staff, specialises in overseas, Caribbean & South American flights. Also books Bidrabu House (see page 168) & other resorts in Guyana.
Wonderland Tours 158 Waterloo St, ☎ 225 3122; e gtalisha@yahoo.com; www. wonderlandtoursgy.com. Trips to Kaieteur & Orinduik falls, Essequibo & Mazaruni rivers, Santa Mission, Georgetown city tour & interior nature tours.

TOURIST INFORMATION

Guyana Tourism Authority (GTA) National Exhibition Centre, Sophia; ☎ 219 0094; e info@ guyana-tourism.com; www.guyana-tourism.com; ⊕ 08.00–16.00 Mon–Thu, 08.00–15.30 Fri. Visit the informative website before the office.
Tourism & Hospitality Association of Guyana (THAG) 157 Waterloo St, North Cummingsburg; ☎ 225 0807; e thag.secretariat@gmail.com;

www.exploreguyana.org; ⊕ 08.30–16.30 Mon–Fri. Updated website & office offer helpful advice; publishes free annual Explore Guyana guide.
Ministry of Tourism, Industry & Commerce 229 South Rd, Lacytown; ☎ 226 2505; www.mintic.gov.gy; ⊕ 08.00–16.30 Mon–Thu, 08.30–15.30 Fri.

RED TAPE

Visas are required for all visitors except for nationals of the following countries: Commonwealth countries, Belgium, Denmark, Finland, France, Germany, Greece, Ireland, Italy, Japan, Korea, Luxembourg, the Netherlands, Norway, Portugal, Spain, Sweden and the USA. Visitors from these countries will receive a stamped visa upon entry that is good for up to three months (depending on your length of stay). If you will be staying for more than three months and need to extend or renew your stamp, take your passport to the **Ministry of Home Affairs** (*60 Brickdam, Stabroek;* ☎ *226 2445;* ⊕ *08.00–16.00 Mon–Thu, 08.00–15.30 Fri*) and be prepared to wait.

Visitors arriving by air are required to have an onward ticket. If you plan on hiring a car, bring an International Driving Permit, available from your national motoring association (in Britain contact the AA or RAC; in the USA contact AAA). All visitors are advised to contact their nearest Guyana Embassy, consulate or tourist office before departing.

Ⓔ EMBASSIES AND CONSULATES

ABROAD

UK 3 Palace Ct, Bayswater Rd, London W2 4LP; ☎ 020 7229 7684; f 020 7727 9809; e guyanahc1@ btconnect.com; www.guyanahclondon.co.uk
USA Washington: 2490 Tracy Pl, NW, Washington, DC 20008; ☎ 202 265 3834; f 202 232 1297; e guyanaembassydc@verizon.net; New York: 370 Seventh Av, Room 402, New York, NY 10017; ☎ 212 947 5110; 801 2nd Av, Suite 501, New York, NY 10017; ☎ 212 573 5828; f 212 573 6225; e guyana@un.int

Brazil SHIS Q1 05 Conjunto 19 Casa 24, Lago Sul, Brasilia; ☎ 61 3 248 0874; f 61 3 248 0886; e embguyana@embguyana.org.br; www.embguyana.org.br
Brussels 12 Av du Brésil, 1050 Brussels; ☎ 322 675 6216; f 322 672 5598; e embassy9.guyana@ skynet.be
Canada Ottawa: Suite 309, 151 Slater St, Ottawa K1P 5H3; ☎ 613 235 7249; f 613 235 1447; e guyanahcott@rogers.com;

www.guyanamissionottawa.org. Toronto: Suite 206, 505 Consumer's Rd, Toronto, Ontario M2J 4V8; ↘416 494 6040; f 416 494 1530; e info@guyanaconsulate.com; www.guyanaconsulate.com

China No 1 Xiu Shui Dong Jie, Jain Guo Men Wai, Beijing; ↘10 6532 1601; f 10 6532 5741; e guyemb@public3.bta.net.cn

Cuba No 506, Calle 18, Miramar, Havana; ↘7 204 2094; f 7 204 2867; e embguyana@enet.cu

Greece 206 Syngrou Av, 2nd Fl, Athens 176 72; ↘210 958 5064; e trader@hol.gr

India F-8/22 Vasant Vihar, New Delhi 110 057; ↘11 51669717; f 11 51669714; e hcommguy.del@gmail.com

Suriname Henckarron No 82, Paramaribo; ↘477 895; f 472 679; e guyembassy@sr.net; 10 Gouverneur Straat & West Kanaal Straat, Nickerie; ↘211 019; f 212 080; e guyconsulnick@sr.net

Venezuela Quinta Roraima, Avenida El Paseo, Prados del Este, Caracas; ↘212 977 1158; f 212 976 3765; e embguy@cantv.net

IN GUYANA

UK 44 Main St, North Cummingsburg; ↘226 5881; f 225 3555; e bhcgeo@networksgy.com; http://ukinguyana.fco.gov.uk/en/

USA 100 Young & Duke Sts, Kingston; ↘225 4900; f 225 8497; e usembassy@hotmail.com; http://georgetown.usembassy.gov

Delegation of European Commission 11 Sendall Pl, Stabroek; ↘226 4004; f 226 2615; www.delguy.ec.europa.eu

Brazil 308 Church St, Queenstown; ↘225 7970; f 226 9063; e bragetown@solutions2000.net

Canada Young & High Sts, Kingston; ↘227 2081; f 225 8380; e grgtn@international.gc.ca; www.international.gc.ca/guyana

China Lot 2 Mandela Av, Georgetown; ↘227 1651; f 225 9228; e chinaemb_gy@mfa.gov.cn; http://gy.china-embassy.org/eng/

Cuba 46 High St, Kingston; ↘225 1881; f 226 1824; e emguyana@networksgy.com; www.cubanembassy.org.gy

India 307 Church & Peter Rose Sts, Queenstown; ↘226 3996; f 225 7012; e hoc.georgetown@mea.gov.in

Mexico 44 Brickdam, South Cummingsburg; ↘226 3987; f 226 3722; e mexicoembassy@gmail.com

Russia 3 Public Rd, Kitty; ↘227 1738; f 227 2975; e embrus.guyana@mail.ru

Suriname 171 Peter Rose St, Queenstown; ↘226 7844; f 225 0759; e surnmemb@gol.net.gy

Venezuela 296 Thomas St, Cummingsburg; ↘226 6749; f 225 3241; e embveguy@gol.net.gy

GETTING THERE

BY AIR

From Europe There are no direct flights to Guyana; all flights from Europe are routed through the Caribbean, Suriname or the USA. It's possible to fly from Europe to a number of the Caribbean islands but all flights to Guyana are eventually routed through Trinidad or Barbados. Options are numerous and many choose to combine a Caribbean stay with their trip to Guyana.

From the USA There are daily direct (via Trinidad) and non-stop flights from Miami and New York City to Georgetown. It's also possible to plan your route through the Caribbean from the USA.

From Canada There are direct flights from Toronto to Georgetown, with a stop to pick up and drop off passengers in Trinidad.

From South America Simply put, outside of Suriname and northern Brazil, travel is difficult to or from other South American countries. As strange as it sounds, barring a long journey of short interior flights and overland buses, the easiest flight plan to/from most South American countries often entails transferring through Trinidad, Barbados or the USA.

From the Caribbean As mentioned above, most flights to and from Georgetown are routed through Trinidad or Barbados, making the island nations to the north very accessible. Depending on the plane (propeller or jet) flying time is one to two hours.

Airports At the time of writing, most international flights were still leaving from and arriving at **Cheddi Jagan International Airport**, which is located at Timehri, 41km (1 hour) south of Georgetown. Runway improvements led to an international designation for **Ogle Airport**, which is now handling flights from Suriname and smaller planes to/from the Caribbean are expected soon. Talk of flights to Venezuela seems to always be present, but the actual flights never materialise. When going to or from the airport with luggage, visitors are advised to forgo the cheap minibuses and hire a taxi (US$25).

Airlines Over the years Guyana has played host to several small charter airlines that fill a demand for flights to/from the US and Canada; some last longer than others and new ones start up regularly. The following airlines service Guyana; prices, dates and times for some international flights change often:

Blue Wing Airlines c/o Roraima Airways, R8 Eping Ave, Georgetown; 225 9648; e ral@ roraimaairways.com; www.bluewingairlines. com. 5 flights per week (Mon–Fri) to/from Paramaribo, Suriname & Ogle International Airport. Note that the EU blacklisted the Surinamese airline after a questionable safety record led to a series of crashes. Improvements may or may not have led to the reversal of this; check before booking.

Caribbean Airlines 92 Av of the Republic, Stabroek; 261 2202; e mail@caribbean-airlines. com; www.caribbean-airlines.com. Picking up where BWIA left off, daily flights to the US (Miami, New York City & Fort Lauderdale); London (via British Airways from Trinidad & Barbados);

Toronto; Paramaribo, Suriname (via Trinidad); & the Caribbean (Trinidad, Barbados, St Maarten, Antigua). **Delta Airlines** 126 Carmichael St, Cummingsburg; ☏ 225 7800; e DELTAGY@ laparkan.com; www.delta.com. 4 non-stop flights per week to/from JFK, New York City. **LIAT** ☏ 268 480 5601; e reservations@ liatairline.com; www.liatairline.com. Daily flights to/from Trinidad & Barbados with connections to more than 20 Caribbean islands.

META Airlines 303 Church St, Queenstown; ☏ 225 5315; e georgetown@voemeta.com; www.voemeta.com. Flights to Paramaribo, Suriname & Belem & Boa Vista, Brazil. **REDjet** www.flyredjet.com. New Caribbean discount airline currently expanding service in region; flies to/from Barbados; contact for additional routes being added at time of writing.

Departure tax There is a departure tax on all international flights leaving from Guyana. It is payable after you have checked in and received a boarding pass for your flight. The fee is G$4,000/£14/US$22/CAN$32. No other currencies are accepted for payment of the departure tax, and no airlines include the tax in the price of their tickets. No departure tax is required for domestic flights.

BY LAND

From Suriname The (contested) border between Suriname and Guyana is the Corentyne River. The legal crossing point is in Moleson Creek, where the Canawaima Ferry makes the return trip from Suriname twice per day (leaving Guyana around 10.00 and 12.00). Customs and immigration is handled at the ferry stelling (landing stage); most countries outside of CARICOM countries need a visa to enter Suriname.

In Village 78, near Moleson Creek, there are many speedboats that shuttle passengers across the river, but note that *backtracking* is illegal, as it entails leaving or entering Guyana without going through the proper immigration requirements. The often overloaded boats are also not the safest passage to or from Suriname.

The ferry stellings on both the Guyana and Suriname sides are well serviced by minibuses and taxis that can provide transportation to the capital cities, Georgetown and Paramaribo. The total travel time between the two cities, including two ferry crossings, is roughly 10 hours. For more detailed information, including prices for passengers and vehicles, see page 83.

Guyana and Suriname are also exploring options for building a bridge connecting the two countries while drastically cutting the travel time from one capital to another (especially with the new Berbice bridge). Both sides are in agreement to building the bridge, but funding must be identified before the project can move forward.

From Brazil The only official border crossing connecting Guyana and Brazil is along the Takatu River, between Bonfim, Brazil and Lethem, Guyana. In the past, the border crossing involved taking a pontoon (vehicles and passengers), small boat or simply walking, swimming or driving during the dry season, but in 2009 the long-delayed Takatu Bridge was officially open.

The bridge, which was funded by Brazil (their first step in what is largely expected to culminate with the paving of the Linden–Lethem road and digging of a deep-sea port in Georgetown) incorporates a unique design that actually transfers drivers to the opposite side of the road while crossing over the Takatu River, which forms the border as in Guyana you drive on the left; in Brazil you drive on the right.

In Guyana, the immigration office is very near the entrance/exit of the bridge and in Bonfim, immigration is located just outside of town. Visits to both are required upon leaving and entering either country, even if it is just for the day.

To travel between Georgetown and Lethem takes roughly 10–15 hours depending on your mode of transport (4x4 vehicle or bus) and the time of year (rainy or dry). From Bonfim there are regular buses to Boa Vista, which provides further access to Manaus and Venezuela.

For more detailed information on travel to or from Lethem and the Brazilian border, see page 278.

From Venezuela Because of the long-standing border dispute between Venezuela and Guyana (see page 12), there is no legal border crossing between the two countries.

The only way to access Venezuela by road, and the route to take when going to or coming from Mount Roraima, is through Boa Vista, Brazil (see previous).

BY SEA Outside of those arriving on commercial boats, very few enter Guyana by way of sea.

From Venezuela Just because there are no legal border crossings between Venezuela and Guyana doesn't mean that you can't move from one country to the other. From Kumaka (see page 191), in the northwestern region of Guyana, there are boats that travel to the Venezuelan city of Curiago, which is an official port of entry.

While you can legally enter Venezuela at this point, there are no immigration offices in this area of Guyana, meaning that it's not possible to enter or leave legally. Unless you are able to hire your own boat in Guyana, this trip isn't recommended. If you must, choose your boat and captain wisely and be aware that many are also involved in the even riskier illegal ventures of transporting drugs and fuel from Venezuela into Guyana.

From Suriname There are currently no passenger ships running between Suriname and Guyana, although private cruise ships sometimes travel between the countries.

Yachting In recent years, certain bodies of the local tourism sector have been marketing Guyana as an upcoming yachting destination in the Caribbean. Guyana is being billed as a safe haven for yachters looking to escape the hurricane belt during the hurricane season.

Guyana lacks the infrastructure many boaters are used to in the Caribbean, but a semblance of it is offered at the resorts along the Essequibo River, which has been pinpointed as *the* destination within the destination.

To facilitate the expected increase of yachting traffic, new immigration services have been established in Bartica. See page 161 for more information on yachting in Guyana. The yachting boom is yet to arrive.

Cruise ships Cruise ships are not big business in Guyana. On average, there are maybe three per year that dock at Georgetown. The boats, which are much smaller than the oversized beasts that ply the Caribbean waters to the north, are often part of specialised nature tours or exploratory trips that travel along the coast of South America or the Guianas.

✚ HEALTH   *Kathryn Boryc with Dr Felicity Nicholson*

People new to exotic travel often worry about tropical diseases, but it is accidents that are most likely to carry you off. Road accidents are common in many parts of Guyana so be aware and do what you can to reduce risks: try to travel during daylight hours, always wear a seatbelt and refuse to be driven by anyone who has been drinking. Listen to local advice about areas where violent crime is common too.

IMMUNISATIONS Preparations to ensure a healthy trip to Guyana require checks on your immunisation status: it is wise to be up to date on tetanus, polio and diphtheria (now given as an all-in-one vaccine, Revaxis, that lasts for ten years), and hepatitis A. Immunisations against hepatitis B and rabies may also be needed. Proof of vaccination against yellow fever is needed for entry into Guyana if you are coming from another yellow fever endemic area with the exceptions of Argentina, Paraguay and Trinidad and Tobago. Strangely they also ask for a certificate when coming from Belize which is not an endemic yellow fever area. The World Health Organisation (WHO) recommends that this vaccine should be taken for Guyana by those over nine months of age, although proof of entry is only officially required for those over one year of age. If the vaccine is not suitable for you then obtain an exemption certificate from your GP or a travel clinic.

A single dose of **hepatitis A** vaccine (eg: Havirx Monodose, Avaxim) provides cover for a year and can be given even close to the time of departure. A second dose given at least 6 months after the first dose will extend protection to around 25 years. The two doses cost in the region of £100 but may be available free of charge on the NHS.

Hepatitis B vaccination should be considered for longer trips (two months or more) or for those working with children or in situations where contact with blood is likely. Three injections are needed for the best protection and can be given over a three-week period if time is short for those aged 16 or over. Longer schedules give more sustained protection and are therefore preferred if time allows. Hepatitis A vaccine can also be given as a combination with hepatitis B as 'Twinrix', though two doses are needed at least seven days apart to be effective for the hepatitis A component, and three doses are needed for the hepatitis B. Again this schedule is only suitable for those aged 16 or over. The newer injectable typhoid vaccines (eg: Typhim Vi) last for three years and are about 85% effective. Oral capsules (Vivotif) may also be available for those aged six and over. Three capsules over five days lasts for approximately three years but may be less effective than injectable forms. They should be encouraged unless the traveller is leaving within a few days for a trip of a week or less, when the vaccine would not be effective in time.

Vaccinations for **rabies** are ideally advised for everyone, but are especially important for travellers visiting more remote areas, especially if you are more than 24 hours from medical help and definitely if you will be working with animals (see *Rabies* page 76).

Experts differ over whether a BCG vaccination against **tuberculosis** (TB) is useful in adults: discuss this with your travel clinic.

In addition to the various vaccinations recommended above, it is important that travellers should be properly protected against malaria. For detailed advice, see page 66.

Ideally you should visit your own doctor or a specialist travel clinic (see page 67) to discuss your requirements if possible at least eight weeks before you plan to travel.

MALARIA The *Anopheles* mosquito that transmits the parasite is most found in all areas of the interior of Guyana. There are sporadic cases reported from the coastal region. This serious and potentially fatal illness is transmitted through the bite of the female *Anopheles* mosquito, which usually bites between dusk and dawn. It is very important to take precautions against being bitten by mosquitoes and take antimalarial drugs while travelling in malaria-risk areas (see above). Symptoms can include fever and flu-like illness, including chills, headache, fatigue, abdominal pains, diarrhoea and muscle aches. Symptoms will occur at least seven days after being bitten by an infected mosquito. Medical attention should be sought immediately if you have a fever or suspect malaria while travelling or up to a year after exposure. If left untreated, malaria can quickly become serious and could lead to kidney failure, coma and death.

Malaria prevention There is not yet a vaccine against malaria that gives enough protection to be useful for travellers, but there are other ways to avoid it. Seek current advice on the best antimalarials to take: usually mefloquine, Malarone or doxycycline. If mefloquine (Lariam) is suggested, start this 2½ weeks (three doses) before departure to check that it suits you; stop it immediately if it seems to cause depression or anxiety, visual or hearing disturbances, severe headaches, fits or changes in heart rhythm. Side effects such as nightmares or dizziness are not medical reasons for stopping unless they are sufficiently debilitating or annoying. Anyone who has been treated for depression or psychiatric problems, has diabetes controlled by oral therapy or who is epileptic (or who has suffered fits in the past) or has a close blood relative who is epileptic, should probably avoid mefloquine.

In the past doctors were nervous about prescribing mefloquine to pregnant women, but experience has shown that it is relatively safe and certainly safer than the risk of malaria. That said, there are other issues, so if you are travelling to Guyana whilst pregnant, seek expert advice before departure.

Malarone (proguanil and atovaquone) is as effective as mefloquine. It has the advantage of having few side effects and need only be continued for one week after returning. However, it is expensive and because of this tends to be reserved for shorter trips. Malarone may not be suitable for everybody, so advice should be taken from a doctor. The licence in the UK has been extended for up to three months' use and a paediatric form of tablet is also available, prescribed on a weight basis.

Another alternative is the antibiotic doxycycline (100mg daily). Like Malarone it can be started one day before arrival. Unlike mefloquine, it may also be used in travellers with epilepsy, although certain anti-epileptic medication may make it less effective. In perhaps 1–3% of people there is the possibility of allergic skin reactions developing in sunlight; the drug should be stopped if this happens. Women using the oral contraceptive should use an additional method of protection for the first four weeks when using doxycycline. It is also unsuitable in pregnancy or for children under 12 years.

Chloroquine and proguanil are no longer considered to be effective enough for Guyana, but may be considered as a last resort if nothing else is deemed suitable.

All tablets should be taken with or after the evening meal, washed down with plenty of fluid and, with the exception of Malarone (see above), continued for four weeks after leaving.

Despite all these precautions, it is important to be aware that no anti-malarial drug is 100% protective, although those on prophylactics who are unlucky enough to catch malaria are less likely to get rapidly into serious trouble. In addition to taking anti-malarials, it is therefore important to avoid mosquito bites between dusk and dawn (see *Insect-borne diseases*, page 72).

There is unfortunately the occasional traveller who prefers to 'acquire resistance' to malaria rather than take preventive tablets, or who takes homeopathic prophylactics thinking these are effective against killer disease. Homeopathy theory dictates treating like with like so there is no place for prophylaxis or immunisation in a well person; bone fide homoeopathists do not advocate it. It takes at least 18 months residing in a holoendemic area for travellers to get some resistance to malaria. Travellers to Guyana will not acquire effective resistance to malaria. The best way is to prevent mosquito bites in the first place and to take a suitable prophylactic agent.

Malaria: diagnosis and treatment Even those who take their malaria tablets meticulously and do everything possible to avoid mosquito bites may contract a strain of malaria that is resistant to prophylactic drugs. Untreated malaria is likely to be fatal, but even strains resistant to prophylaxis respond well to prompt treatment. Because of this, your immediate priority upon displaying possible malaria symptoms – including a rapid rise in temperature (over 38°C), and any combination of a headache, flu-like aches and pains, a general sense of disorientation, and possibly even nausea and diarrhoea – is to establish whether you have malaria, ideally by visiting a clinic.

Diagnosing malaria is not easy, which is why consulting a doctor is sensible: there are other causes of fevers in South America which may require different treatments. Even if you test negative, it would be wise to stay within reach of a laboratory until the symptoms clear up, and to test again after a day or two if they don't. It's worth noting that if you have a fever and the malaria test is negative, you may have typhoid or paratyphoid, which should also receive immediate treatment.

Travellers to remote parts of Guyana would be wise to carry a course of treatment to cure malaria, and a rapid test kit. With malaria, it is normal enough to go from feeling healthy to having a high fever in the space of a few hours (and it is possible to die from falciparum malaria within 24 hours of the first symptoms). In such circumstances, assume that you have malaria and act accordingly – whatever risks are attached to taking an unnecessary cure are outweighed by the dangers of untreated malaria. Experts differ on the costs and benefits of self-treatment, but agree that it leads to over-treatment and to many people taking drugs they do not need; yet treatment may save your life. There is also some division about the best treatment for malaria, but either Malarone or Coarthemeter are the current treatments of choice. Discuss your trip with a specialist either at home or in Guyana.

TRAVEL CLINICS AND HEALTH INFORMATION A full list of current travel clinic websites worldwide is available on www.istm.org/. For other journey preparation information, consult www.nathnac.org/ds/map_world.aspx. Information about various medications may be found on www.netdoctor.co.uk/travel.

UK

Berkeley Travel Clinic 32 Berkeley St, London W1J 8EL (near Green Park tube station); ☎ 020 7629 6233; ⊕ 10.00–18.00 Mon–Fri; 10.00–15.00 Sat
The Travel Clinic Ltd, Cambridge 41 Hills Rd, Cambridge CB2 1NT; ☎ 01223 367362; e enquiries@travelclinic.ltd.uk; www. travelcliniccambridge.co.uk; ⊕ 10.00–16.00 Mon, Tue & Sat, 12.00–19.00 Wed & Thu, 11.00–18.00 Fri
The Travel Clinic Ltd, Ipswich Gilmour Piper, 10 Fonnereau Rd, Ipswich IP1 3JP; ☎ 01223 367362; ⊕ 09.00–19.00 Wed, 09.00–13.00 Sat

Edinburgh Travel Health Clinic 14 East Preston St, Newington, Edinburgh EH8 9QA; ☎ 0131 667 1030; www.edinburghtravelhealthclinic.co.uk; ⊕ 09.00–19.00 Mon–Wed, 09.00–18.00 Thu & Fri. Travel vaccinations & advice on all aspects of malaria prevention. All current UK prescribed anti-malaria tablets in stock.
Fleet Street Travel Clinic 29 Fleet St, London EC4Y 1AA; ☎ 020 7353 5678; e info@ fleetstreetclinic.com; www.fleetstreetclinic.com; ⊕ 08.45–17.30 Mon–Fri. Injections, travel products & latest advice.

Hospital for Tropical Diseases Travel Clinic
Mortimer Market Building, Capper St (off Tottenham
Ct Rd), London WC1E 6AU; ☏ 020 7387 4411; www.
thehtd.org. ⏰ 13.00–17.00 Wed & 09.00–13.00
Fri. Consultations are by appointment only & are
offered only to those with more complex problems.
Check the website for inclusions. Runs a Travellers'
Healthline Advisory Service (☏ *020 7950 7799*) for
country-specific information & health hazards. Also
stocks nets, water purification equipment & personal
protection measures. Travellers who have returned
from the tropics & are unwell, with fever or bloody
diarrhoea, can attend the walk-in emergency clinic
at the hospital without an appointment.

InterHealth Travel Clinic 111 Westminster
Bridge Rd, London SE1 7HR; ☏ 020 7902 9000;
e info@interhealth.org.uk;
www.interhealth.org.uk; ⏰ 08.30–17.30 Mon–
Fri. Competitively priced, one-stop travel health
service by appointment only.

MASTA (Medical Advisory Service for Travellers
Abroad) At the London School of Hygiene &
Tropical Medicine, Keppel St, London WC1E 7HT;
☏ 09068 224100 (this is a premium-line number,
charged at 60p per min); e enquiries@
masta.org; www.masta-travel-health.com. For
a fee, they will provide an individually tailored
health brief, with up-to-date information on how
to stay healthy, inoculations & what to take.
MASTA pre-travel clinics ☏ 01276 685040;
www.masta-travel-health.com/

Irish Republic

Tropical Medical Bureau 54 Grafton St, Dublin
2; ☏ +353 1 2715200; e graftonstreet@tmb.
ie; www.tmb.ie; ⏰ until 20.00 Mon–Fri & Sat

USA

Centers for Disease Control 1600 Clifton Rd,
Atlanta, GA 30333; ☏ (800) 232 4636 or (888) 232
6348; e cdcinfo@cdc.gov; www.cdc.gov/travel.
The central source of travel information in the
USA. Each summer they publish the invaluable
Health Information for International Travel.

Canada

IAMAT (International Association for Medical
Assistance to Travellers) Suite 10, 1287 St Clair
Street West, Toronto, Ontario M6E 1B8; ☏ 416 652
0137; www.iamat.org

travel-clinic.aspx. Call or check the website for
the nearest; there are currently 50 in Britain.
They also sell malaria prophylaxis, memory cards,
treatment kits, bednets, net treatment kits, etc.
NHS travel websites www.fitfortravel.nhs.uk
or www.fitfortravel.scot.nhs.uk . Provide country-
by-country advice on immunisation & malaria
prevention, plus details of recent developments,
& a list of relevant health organisations.

Nomad Travel Clinics Flagship store: 3–4
Wellington Terrace, Turnpike Lane, London N8 0PX;
☏ 020 8889 7014; e turnpike@
nomadtravel.co.uk; www.nomadtravel.co.uk; walk
in or appointments ⏰ 09.15–17.00 everyday with
late night Thu. Also has clinics in west & central
London, Bristol, Southampton & Manchester –
see website for further information. As well as
dispensing health advice, Nomad stocks mosquito
nets & other anti-bug devices, & an excellent range
of adventure travel gear. Runs a Travel Health
Advice line on ☏ 0906 863 3414.

Trailfinders Immunisation Centre 194
Kensington High St, London W8 7RG; ☏ 020 7938
3999; www.trailfinders.com/travelessentials/
travelclinic.htm; ⏰ 09.00–17.00 Mon, Tue, Wed
& Fri, 09.00–18.00 Thu, 10.00–17.15 Sat. No
appointment necessary.

Travelpharm www.travelpharm.com. The
Travelpharm website offers up-to-date guidance on
travel-related health & has a range of medications
available through their online mini-pharmacy.

mornings. For other clinic locations, & useful
information specific to tropical destinations,
check their website.

IAMAT (International Association for Medical
Assistance to Travelers) 1623 Military Rd, #279
Niagara Falls, NY 14304-1745; ☏ 716 754 4883;
e info@iamat.org; www.iamat.org. A non-profit
organisation with free membership that provides
lists of English-speaking doctors abroad.

TMVC Suite 314, 1030 W Georgia St, Vancouver,
BC V6E 2Y3; ☏ (604) 681 5656; e vancouver@
tmvc.com; www.tmvc.com. One-stop medical
clinic for all your international travel health &
vaccination needs.

Australia and New Zealand

TMVC (Travel Doctors Group) ☎ 1300 65 88 44; www.tmvc.com.au. 30 clinics in Australia & New Zealand, including: *Auckland* Canterbury Arcade, 174 Queen St, Auckland 1010, New Zealand; ☎ (64) 9 373 3531; e auckland@traveldoctor. co.nz; *Brisbane* 75a Astor Terrace, Spring Hill, Brisbane, QLD 4000, Australia; ☎ (07) 3815 6900; e brisbane@traveldoctor.com.au; *Melbourne* 393 Little Bourke St, Melbourne, Vic 3000, Australia; ☎ (03) 9935 8100; e melbourne@traveldoctor. com.au; *Sydney* 428 George St, Sydney, NSW 2000, Australia; ☎ (2) 9221 7133; e sydney@ traveldoctor.com.au

IAMAT (International Association for Medical Assistance to Travellers) 206 Papanui Rd, Christchurch 5, New Zealand; www.iamat.org

South Africa

SAA-Netcare Travel Clinics ☎ 011 802 0059; e travelinfo@netcare.co.za; www.travelclinic. co.za. 11 clinics throughout South Africa.

TMVC NHC Health Centre, Cnr Beyers Naude & Waugh Northcliff; ☎ 0861 300 911; e info@ traveldoctor.co.za; www.traveldoctor.co.za. Consult the website for clinic locations.

PERSONAL FIRST-AID KIT A minimal kit contains:

- A good drying antiseptic, eg: iodine or potassium permanganate (don't take antiseptic cream)
- A few small dressings (Band-Aids)
- Suncream
- Insect repellent; anti-malarial tablets; impregnated bed-net or permethrin spray
- Aspirin or paracetamol
- Antifungal cream (eg: Canesten)
- Ciprofloxacin or norfloxacin, for severe diarrhoea
- Tinidazole for giardia or amoebic dysentery (see page 72 for regime)
- Antibiotic eye drops, for sore, 'gritty', stuck-together eyes (conjunctivitis)
- A pair of fine-pointed tweezers (to remove hairy caterpillar hairs, thorns, splinters, coral, etc)
- Alcohol-based hand rub or bar of soap in plastic box
- Condoms or femidoms
- A digital thermometer (for those going to remote areas)

MEDICAL FACILITIES IN GUYANA The medical facilities in Guyana will almost certainly be limited which is another reason for having appropriate and robust medical insurance. Always contact them sooner rather than later if you are unwell. Also ensure that you take all your prescription medications with you as it is extremely unlikely that they will be available in Guyana.

Water sterilisation You can fall ill from drinking contaminated water so try to drink from safe sources eg: bottled water where available. Alternatively water should be boiled or passed through a good bacteriological filter or purified with chlorine dioxide tablets.

COMMON MEDICAL PROBLEMS

Travellers' diarrhoea Travelling in Guyana carries a fairly high risk of getting a dose of travellers' diarrhoea; perhaps half of all visitors will suffer and the newer you are to exotic travel, the more likely you will be to suffer. By taking precautions against travellers' diarrhoea you will also avoid typhoid, paratyphoid, cholera, hepatitis, dysentery, worms, etc. Travellers' diarrhoea and the other faecal-oral

Any prolonged immobility including travel by land or air can result in deep vein thrombosis (DVT) with the risk of embolus to the lungs. Certain factors can increase the risk and these include:

- Previous clot or a close relative with a history
- Being over 40, with increased risk over 80 years old
- Recent major operation or varicose-veins surgery
- Cancer
- Stroke
- Heart disease
- Obesity
- Pregnancy
- Hormone therapy
- Heavy smoking
- Severe varicose veins
- Being very tall (over 6ft/1.8m) or short (under 5ft/1.5m)

DVT causes painful swelling and redness of the calf or sometimes the thigh. It is only dangerous if a clot travels to the lungs (pulmonary embolus). Symptoms of a pulmonary embolus (PE) include chest pain, shortness of breath, and sometimes coughing up small amounts of blood and commonly start three to ten days after a long flight. Anyone who thinks that they might have a DVT needs to see a doctor immediately.

PREVENTION OF DVT
- Keep mobile before and during the flight; move around every couple of hours
- Drink plenty of fluids during the flight
- Avoid taking sleeping pills and excessive tea, coffee and alcohol
- Consider wearing flight socks or support stockings (see *www.legshealth.com*)

If you think you are at increased risk of a clot, ask your doctor if it is safe to travel.

diseases come from getting other peoples' faeces in your mouth. This most often happens from cooks not washing their hands after a trip to the toilet, but even if the restaurant cook does not understand basic hygiene you will be safe if your food has been properly cooked and arrives piping hot. The most important prevention strategy is to wash your hands before eating anything. You can pick up salmonella and shigella from toilet door handles and possibly bank notes. The maxim to remind you what you can safely eat is:

PEEL IT, BOIL IT, COOK IT OR FORGET IT.

This means that fruit you have washed and peeled yourself, and hot foods, should be safe but raw foods, cold cooked foods, salads, fruit salads which have been prepared by others, ice cream and ice are all risky, and foods kept lukewarm in hotel buffets are often dangerous. That said, plenty of travellers and expatriates enjoy fruit and vegetables, so do keep a sense of perspective: food served in a fairly decent hotel in a large town or a place regularly frequented by expatriates is likely to be safe. If you are struck, see box on page 72 for treatment.

Heat exhaustion Heat exhaustion can occur from dehydration and loss of salts as a result of excessive sweating. It is important to drink plenty of fluids and not do anything too physically challenging until you acclimatise to the hot climate. Warning signs include lethargy, weakness, muscle cramps, headaches, nausea or vomiting, and fainting. If you experience heat exhaustion, you should take measures to cool off – drink cool beverages (non-alcoholic), rest, take a cold shower or bath, or sit in an air-conditioned room. You must also replace salts – add extra salt to your food and drink fruit juice or a sports drink.

Heatstroke Heatstroke is a serious and potentially fatal condition when the body's cooling system breaks down and the body temperature rises without being able to cool down. Take preventive measures by drinking plenty of fluids and avoiding prolonged exposure to high temperatures. If emergency care is not given, death or permanent disability can occur. Symptoms include a high body temperature (above 39°C or 103°F), red dry skin (no sweating), rapid pulse, throbbing headache, dizziness, nausea and confusion. If you see someone with any of these signs, call for emergency medical attention while trying to cool the victim – move the victim out of the sun, remove their clothing, spray with cool water or cover with a cool wet sheet and fan vigorously.

Motion sickness Motion sickness usually causes mild discomfort but in severe cases can be debilitating. If you are prone to motion sickness you can minimise your symptoms by choosing seats in the front of a car, in the middle of a bus, near the centre of a boat or over the wings of an airplane. Motion sickness medications, which may cause drowsiness, should be taken before departure. A natural preventive is high levels of ginger (available in tablets).

Protection from the sun Give some thought to packing suncream. The incidence of skin cancer is rocketing as Caucasians are travelling more and spending more time exposing themselves to the sun. Keep out of the sun during the middle of the day and, if you must expose yourself to the sun, build up gradually from 20 minutes per day. Be especially careful of exposure in the middle of the day and of sun reflected off water, and wear a T-shirt and lots of waterproof suncream (at least factor 25) when swimming. Sun exposure ages the skin, makes people prematurely wrinkly and increases the risk of skin cancer. Cover up with long, loose clothes and wear a hat when you can. The glare and the dust can be hard on the eyes, too, so bring UV-protecting sunglasses and, perhaps, a soothing eyebath.

Skin infections Any mosquito bite or small nick in the skin gives an opportunity for bacteria to foil the body's usually excellent defences; it will surprise many travellers how quickly skin infections start in warm humid climates and it is essential to clean and cover even the slightest wound. Creams are not as effective as a good drying antiseptic such as dilute iodine, potassium permanganate (a few crystals in half a cup of water), or crystal (or gentian) violet. One of these should be available in most towns. If the wound starts to throb, or becomes red and the redness starts to spread, or the wound oozes, and especially if you develop a fever, antibiotics will probably be needed: flucloxacillin (250mg four times a day) or

TREATING TRAVELLERS' DIARRHOEA

The most important part of treatment for travellers' diarrhoea is replacing all the water lost by drinking lots of clear fluids. Sachets of oral rehydration salts give the perfect biochemical mix to replace all that is pouring out of your bottom but other recipes taste nicer. Any dilute mixture of sugar and salt in water will do you good: try Coke or orange squash with a three-finger pinch of salt added to each glass (if you are salt-depleted you won't taste the salt). Otherwise make a solution of a four-finger scoop of sugar with a three-finger pinch of salt in a 500ml glass. Or add eight level teaspoons of sugar (18g) and one level teaspoon of salt (3g) to one litre (five cups) of safe water. A squeeze of lemon or orange juice improves the taste and adds potassium, which is also lost in diarrhoea. Drink two large glasses after every bowel action, and more if you are thirsty. These solutions are still absorbed well if you are vomiting, but you will need to take sips at a time. If you are not eating you need to drink three litres a day plus whatever is pouring into the toilet. If you feel like eating, take a bland, high carbohydrate diet. Heavy greasy or spicy foods will probably give you cramps.

There is good evidence now that early intervention with an antibiotic such as ciprofloxacin (500mg) and a stopping agent (eg: two capsules of Imodium) taken at the first sign of diarrhoea is effective in over 70% of cases. A second dose of ciprofloxacin can be taken 10–12 hours later if needed together with one further Imodium.

If the diarrhoea is bad, or you are passing blood or slime, or you have a fever, you will probably need a course of antibiotics in addition to fluid replacement. A dose of norfloxacin or ciprofloxacin repeated twice a day until better may be appropriate (if you are planning to take an antibiotic with you, note that both norfloxacin and ciprofloxacin are available only on prescription in the UK). If the diarrhoea is greasy and bulky and is accompanied by sulphurous (eggy) burps, one likely cause is giardia. This is best treated with tinidazole (four times 500mg in one dose, repeated seven days later if symptoms persist).

cloxacillin (500mg four times a day). For those allergic to penicillin, erythromycin (500mg twice a day) for five days should help. See a doctor if the symptoms do not start to improve within 48 hours.

Fungal infections also get a hold easily in hot, moist climates so wear 100%-cotton socks and underwear and shower frequently. An itchy rash in the groin or flaking between the toes is likely to be a fungal infection. This needs treatment with an antifungal cream such as Canesten (clotrimazole); if this is not available try Whitfield's ointment (compound benzoic acid ointment) or crystal violet (although this will turn you purple!).

INSECT-BORNE DISEASES Travellers should take precautions to avoid being bitten by mosquitoes at all times by using insect repellents (at least 30% DEET on exposed skin).

As the sun is going down, don long clothes and apply repellent on any exposed flesh. Pack a DEET-based insect repellent (roll-ons or stick are the least messy preparations for travelling). You also need either a permethrin-impregnated bednet or a permethrin spray so that you can 'treat' bednets in hotels. Permethrin treatment makes even very tatty nets protective and prevents mosquitoes from biting through the impregnated net when you roll against it; it also deters other biters. Otherwise retire to an air-conditioned room or burn mosquito coils or sleep under a fan. Coils and fans reduce rather than eliminate bites. Travel clinics usually sell a good range of nets, treatment kits and repellents.

Mosquitoes and many other insects are attracted to light. If you are camping, never put a lamp near the opening of your tent, or you will have a swarm of biters waiting to join you when you retire. In hotel rooms, be aware that the longer your light is on, the greater the number of insects will be sharing your accommodation.

Aside from avoiding mosquito bites between dusk and dawn, which will protect you from elephantiasis and a range of nasty insect-borne viruses, as well as malaria (see page 65), it is important to take precautions against other insect bites. During the day it is wise to wear long, loose (preferably 100% cotton) clothes if you are pushing through scrubby country; this will keep off ticks and also tsetse and day-biting *Aedes* mosquitoes which may spread dengue fever and yellow fever.

Bites and stings Travellers who have a history of allergic reactions to insect bites or stings should consider carrying an epinephrine autoinjector (EpiPen) with them. Most insect bites and stings are painful or uncomfortable rather than dangerous; however, if a bite or sting causes bruising, persistent pain or swelling, medical attention should be sought. Shake out clothing and shoes before putting them on to avoid scorpion bites.

Ticks Like an endless host of other insects, ticks are common in Guyana, especially in the interior regions during the dry season. Most visitors won't have any major problems with the parasites unless they are venturing deeper into the forest on some of the lesser-used trails, but caution should always be exercised, especially when you're climbing over or around dead trees. Wear cover-up clothing including long trousers tucked into boots and hats. Insect repellents may be of benefit to so apply to exposed skin.

Ticks should ideally be removed as soon as possible as leaving them on the body increases the chance of infection. They should be removed with special tick tweezers that can be bought in good travel shops. Failing that you can use your finger nails: grasp the tick as close to your body as possible and pull steadily and firmly away at right angles to your skin. The tick will then come away complete, as long as you do not jerk or twist. If possible douse the wound with alcohol (any spirit will do) or iodine. Irritants (eg: Olbas oil) or lit cigarettes are to be discouraged since they can cause the ticks to regurgitate and therefore increase the risk of disease. It is best to get a travelling companion to check you for ticks; if you are travelling with small children, remember to check their heads, and particularly behind the ears.

Spreading redness around the bite and/or fever and/or aching joints after a tick bite imply that you have an infection that requires antibiotic treatment, so seek advice.

Malaria See page 65.

Yellow fever Yellow fever, a viral illness found in tropical countries, is transmitted through the bite of an infected mosquito. Symptoms of yellow fever range from a flu-like illness to hepatitis and haemorrhagic fever. If infection is suspected, seek immediate medical attention and drink plenty of fluids.

An international certificate of vaccination is required for entry into Guyana if travelling from an endemic zone and visitors travelling onwards from Guyana may be required to present proof of yellow fever vaccination for crossing other

3

international borders. Guyana also considers Belize, Guatemala, Honduras and Costa Rica to be infected so will ask for proof of vaccination if you are coming from these countries. The vaccine must be administered at an approved yellow fever vaccination centre. It takes ten days to be fully effective and lasts for ten years. Vaccination poses some risk but is usually advised since Guyana lies in the yellow fever endemic zone. The risk to travellers is highest in rural or jungle areas. Your doctor will discuss risks and contraindications. If the vaccine is not considered suitable for you then you will need to carry an Exemption Certificate instead. These can be obtained from most GPs and all travel clinics and are generally accepted by Guyana though it is wise to check with the relevant embassies before you go.

Dengue fever Often referred to as 'breakbone fever' because of the symptoms of joint and muscle pain, dengue fever and dengue haemorrhagic fever are viral diseases transmitted by mosquitoes. The mosquitoes that transmit the illness are most frequently found in or around human habitations and bite during the day, particularly in the morning for a couple of hours after sunrise and in the late afternoon for a couple of hours until sunset. Symptoms tend to occur 3–14 days after being bitten by an infected mosquito and include high fevers, headaches, joint and muscle pain, nausea, vomiting, and rash. Severe manifestations of dengue can present with haemorrhagic fevers and can be fatal. No vaccine is available, so travellers should take precautions against mosquito bites. Acetaminophen should be used for treating fever, while aspirin and ibuprofen should be avoided. If infected, you should rest and drink plenty of fluids and closely monitor vital signs.

Lymphatic filariasis Lymphatic filariasis is an infection caused by threadlike worms spread by mosquito bites. The worms can live in the bloodstream and the body for many years without a person showing any signs of the infection. In some cases symptoms include fever, swelling of the lymph nodes in the groin, armpit, arms, legs, scrotum or breast. There is no cure for filariasis but it can be prevented by avoiding mosquito bites by using salt with Diethylcarbamazine (DEC) regularly in the preparation of food. DEC, which kills the filaria worm and stops the disease before signs and symptoms develop, is also available in tablet form from licensed physicians in the US for treatment of travellers with the infection.

Leishmaniasis Leishmaniasis is a parasitic disease caused by the bite of a sand fly and presents in two forms: cutaneous (skin) or visceral (internal organ). The cutaneous form is distinguished by a skin sore(s) that develops weeks to months after being bitten by an infected sand fly. The sores can last from weeks to years and will eventually develop a raised edge with a crater-like centre. Signs and symptoms of visceral leishmaniasis include fever, weight loss, enlargement of the spleen or liver, and anaemia, and develop months to years after infection. If untreated, visceral leishmaniasis is typically fatal. Travellers should avoid sand fly bites by using insect sprays and wearing protective clothing, and should sleep with a bed net.

Chagas disease Chagas disease or American trypanosomiasis is a potentially serious disease caused by the protozoan Trypanosoma cruzi and is spread by the biting or Reduviid 'kissing' bug (*Panstrongylus megistus*) which is endemic in Central and South America. The disease is most prevalent in rural areas where the bugs live in mud walls and only come out at night. Avoidance is the best method so when travelling through an endemic region try not to sleep in adobe huts where the locals sleep, keep away from walls when sleeping and use mosquito nets. Spraying the insides of rooms with an insecticide spray is also a good idea.

Symptoms include swelling around the site of the bite followed by enlargement of the lymph glands and fever. Long term symptoms include damage to the heart causing sudden death and paralysis of the gut causing difficulty in swallowing and severe constipation.

There is no preventative vaccine or medication for Chagas disease and treatment is difficult as agents toxic to the trypanosomes are also toxic to humans.

Bilharzia or schistosomiasis Bilharzia or schistosomiasis is a disease that commonly afflicts the rural poor of the tropics. There is one form in South America – schistosoma mansoni. It is an unpleasant disease which is worth avoiding but can be treated if you get it. It is easier to understand how to diagnose it, treat it and prevent it if you know a little about the life cycle. Contaminated faeces are washed into the lake, the eggs hatch and the larva infects certain species of snail. The snails then produce about 10,000 cercariae a day for the rest of their lives. The parasites can digest their way through your skin when you wade, or bathe in infested fresh water.

Winds disperse the snails and cercariae. The snails in particular can drift a long way, especially on windblown weed, so nowhere is really safe. However, deep water and running water are safer, while shallow water presents the greatest risk. The cercariae penetrate intact skin, and find their way to the liver. There male and female meet and spend the rest of their lives in permanent copulation. No wonder you feel tired! Most finish up in the wall of the lower bowel, but others can get lost and can cause damage to many different organs. Although the adults do not cause any harm in themselves, after about 4–6 weeks they start to lay eggs, which cause an intense but usually ineffective immune reaction, including fever, cough, abdominal pain, and a fleeting, itching rash called 'safari itch'. The absence of early symptoms does not necessarily mean there is no infection. Later symptoms can be more localised and more severe, but the general symptoms settle down fairly quickly and eventually you are just tired. Although bilharzia is difficult to diagnose, it can be tested at specialist travel clinics or hospitals. Ideally tests need to be done at least six weeks after likely exposure and will determine whether you need treatment. Fortunately it is easy to treat at present.

Avoiding bilharzia If you are bathing, swimming, paddling or wading in fresh water which you think may carry a bilharzia risk, try to get out of the water within ten minutes.

- Avoid bathing or paddling on shores within 200m of villages or places where people use the water a great deal, especially reedy shores or where there is lots of water weed.
- Dry off thoroughly with a towel; rub vigorously.
- If your bathing water comes from a risky source try to ensure that the water is taken from the lake in the early morning and stored snail-free, otherwise it should be filtered or Dettol or Cresol added.
- Bathing early in the morning is safer than bathing in the last half of the day.
- Cover yourself with DEET insect repellent before swimming: it may offer some protection.

SEXUALLY TRANSMITTED INFECTIONS Sexually transmitted infections include bacterial infections such as gonorrhoea, chlamydia, and syphilis and viral infections such as herpes, human papilloma virus, genital warts and HIV. Symptoms of sexually transmitted infections may include burning, itching, abnormal discharge, bumps, blisters, abdominal pain, fever, painful urination and painful intercourse. However, symptoms may not be obvious or present at all, especially in women. Antibiotics are used to treat bacterial infections, whereas there is no cure for the viral infections (although treatment exists to alleviate the symptoms). Condoms are a very effective method against most sexually transmitted infections.

HIV Special attention should be paid to protect oneself against HIV (human immunodeficiency virus) in Guyana. Exposure to blood, blood products or body fluids may put a person at risk. Infection rates have been found to be as high as 16% in some most-at-risk populations such as sex workers. It is estimated that 2.5% of the general population in Guyana is infected with HIV; this is one of the highest prevalence rates in Latin America and the Caribbean. Travellers should avoid unprotected sex and sharing of drug injection equipment. If you need an injection, request that the syringe be unwrapped in front of you. Condoms are widely available in pharmacies and supermarkets in Guyana; take care to store them in a cool, dry place.

RABIES Rabies is carried by all mammals (beware the village dogs and small monkeys that are used to being fed in the parks) and is passed on to man through a bite, scratch or a lick of an open wound. You must always assume any animal is rabid, and seek medical help as soon as possible. Meanwhile scrub the wound with soap under a running tap or while pouring water from a jug. Find a reasonably clear-looking source of water (but at this stage the quality of the water is not important), then pour on a strong iodine or alcohol solution of gin, whisky or rum. This helps stop the rabies virus entering the body and will guard against wound infections, including tetanus.

Pre-exposure vaccinations for rabies is ideally advised for everyone, but is particularly important if you intend to have contact with animals and/or are likely to be more than 24 hours away from medical help. Ideally three doses should be taken over a minimum of 21 days. Having one or two doses will not change what treatment is needed and can indeed cause confusion among the treating doctors. If three doses of pre-exposure vaccine are taken then only two further doses of vaccine are needed three days apart following a potential exposure. If you have not had the pre-exposure vaccine then you will need a blood product (rabies immunoglobulin, ideally human but horse will do) and five doses of vaccine. RIG is hard to come by, very expensive and is painful to have administered. This is a good reason to have the pre-exposure vaccines.

SNAKEBITE Snakes rarely attack unless provoked, and bites in travellers are unusual. You are less likely to get bitten if you wear stout shoes and long trousers when in the bush. Most snakes are harmless and even venomous species will dispense venom in only about half of their bites. If bitten, then, you are unlikely to have received venom; keeping this fact in mind may help you to stay calm. Many so-called first-aid techniques do more harm than good: cutting into the wound is harmful; tourniquets are dangerous; suction and electrical inactivation devices do not work. The only treatment is antivenom. In case of a bite that you fear may have been from a venomous snake:

- Try to keep calm – it is likely that no venom has been dispensed.
- Prevent movement of the bitten limb by applying a splint.
- Keep the bitten limb BELOW heart height to slow the spread of any venom.

- If you have a crêpe bandage, wrap it around the whole limb (eg: all the way from the toes to the thigh), as tight as you would for a sprained ankle or a muscle pull.
- Evacuate to a hospital that has antivenom.

And remember:

- NEVER give aspirin; you may take paracetamol, which is safe.
- NEVER cut or suck the wound.
- DO NOT apply ice packs.
- DO NOT apply potassium permanganate.

If the offending snake can be captured without risk of someone else being bitten, take this to show the doctor – but beware since even a decapitated head is able to bite.

SAFETY

When doing initial pre-trip research on Guyana, it would be easy to be turned off by the crime in the country. The media love to sensationalise stories of bandits, pirates and machete-wielding husbands. Crime rates are indeed high in Guyana, but they are mainly concentrated along the coastal areas and foreign tourists are rarely targeted. Keep in mind that most visits to Guyana are trouble-free, and occurrences of crime in the interior are fairly uncommon.

Guyana is a developing country with a noticeable disparity of wealth. Guyana is also a major drug transhipment country, with a large amount of cocaine funnelling into the country from Venezuela and being shipped out to other Caribbean countries, the US and Europe. Both are behind many of the crimes that take place in Georgetown and other coastal towns and rarely affect those not involved.

Petty crimes such as pickpocketing, purse snatching and theft of other goods occur throughout Georgetown and travellers should always remain on the defensive. The best way to avoid crime is by not showcasing any signs of wealth. Don't travel with valuable jewellery. In Georgetown and other areas along the coast, don't prominently display cameras, music players or other high-priced electronics. (In fact, in Georgetown, unless you are on an organised tour or with locals, you may want to consider keeping any expensive cameras at the hotel and purchasing postcards.)

When going to banks or *cambios* (businesses that exchange foreign currencies) to change money it's advisable to always use a reputable taxi company (hailing an unmarked car from the street in front of the bank may not be the best option). Don't carry large sums of money around town and it may be a good idea to disperse your notes throughout a few different pockets so that you don't pull out a large wad of money when paying for something.

If you ever find yourself the victim of a robbery, it's best to hand over whatever is being demanded without resisting. Most injuries that are the result of a robbery occur because of resistance. All crimes should be reported to the local police, but don't have expectations of your case being solved.

Walking in Georgetown is generally okay during daylight hours, but taxis should be used at night. Most hotels and restaurants have security. Exercise extra caution while walking on Sundays, when the city's streets are much less populated.

When visiting the sea wall it's recommended to avoid deserted stretches (east of Celina's Atlantic Resort is best) and to go only when it is most populated with walkers and joggers (roughly 17.00–18.00). The sea wall has been the scene of various crimes in the past so it's advised to go with at least one other person and avoid the area at dark (except on Sunday night when it becomes a gathering place for the entire town).

In the waters there are also attacks by pirates on fishing vessels. It is very rare for such an occurrence to take place on public speedboats or ferries.

Again, if you exercise caution, don't flaunt any valuables and remain alert and vigilant your time in Guyana will most likely be trouble-free.

WOMEN TRAVELLERS

In general, the most common problems women travelling in Guyana will encounter are inappropriate comments and verbal harassment. Maintain your composure and do not react to verbal comments or hissing/sucking. Be sensitive to the local dress standards; you may want to dress more conservatively to help avoid unwelcome attention. You may also want to wear a ring to fend off unwanted suitors. Use common sense – don't walk alone at night and be aware of your surroundings at all times. Stay in well-populated areas, as most acts of robbery or assault take place on lonely streets. Sundays and holidays tend to be particularly quiet, so be careful if walking around Georgetown alone on these days. Look and act confident; walk like you know where you are going – if you display self-assurance, you may ward off some potential danger.

GAY TRAVELLERS

Guyana is, unfortunately, the only country in South America where homosexuality remains illegal. According to the country's draconian penal code, any male persons committing or attempting to commit an act of 'gross indecency…shall be guilty of misdemeanour and liable to imprisonment for two years.' 'Buggery' is listed as a felony and can carry penalties from ten years to life in prison. There is no reference to lesbianism in the books, making it technically legal, but not necessarily tolerated.

In 2001, Guyana's parliament voted to outlaw discrimination based on sexual orientation, but under extreme pressure from religious groups, President Jagdeo refused to assent to the amendment bill. In 2003, parliament was scheduled to again discuss the bill. To garner public support and advocate against homophobia, the Society Against Sexual Orientation Discrimination (SASOD; *www.sasod.org.gy*) was formed at this time. Parliament proposed another bill, but the ruling party once again said it would not vote on it.

Since 2003, SASOD has continued its advocacy work in Guyana and regularly organises LGBT film festivals, poetry nights and other special events at locations in Georgetown including the Sidewalk Café (see page 115) and Oasis Café (see page 113).

Actual enforcement of, and punishment associated with, the law outlawing homosexuality is extremely rare in Guyana. Gay travellers are unlikely to encounter any problems during a visit to Guyana, but it isn't recommended to make a point of drawing attention to their sexual orientation. Other than the sporadic events organised by SASOD (who have offices in Georgetown), there is nothing that can be called a gay scene anywhere in the country.

DISABLED TRAVELLERS

Guyana, as a whole, is relatively inaccessible for people with disabilities. In Georgetown and other coastal towns, pavements are a rarity and potholed road surfaces would prove challenging for those in a wheelchair. Accessibility to public areas is limited. But with patience, people with disabilities can still travel throughout Guyana.

In Georgetown, few hotels have lifts (namely Pegasus Guyana and Princess Hotel), but others will have some rooms on the main level; enquire when making your booking or seek assistance from a local tour operator. At interior lodges, few are built to accommodate people with disabilities. Many are elevated off the ground and use steps for access. Some, like Rock View Lodge and Karanambu Lodge, have cabins and rooms that are on ground level. If travelling to the interior, it is recommended to use a local tour operator that is familiar with the infrastructure of each individual lodge so proper arrangements can be made.

For transportation, taxis or private vehicles are recommended. Minibuses are often overcrowded and the drivers are likely to be less patient with riders needing extra time to get in and out of the vehicle.

While it won't always be easy, most people with disabilities will likely be pleasantly surprised by the amount of assistance and help they receive. Getting in and out of small aircraft, aluminium boats, and 4x4 vehicles can be a challenge, but helping hands will always be available to make experiencing Guyana's interior a possibility.

TRAVELLING WITH CHILDREN

Depending on their age, travelling in Guyana with children, particularly in the interior, could be considered challenging. Simply put, child-specific facilities do not exist. This could make travelling with young children difficult. If the child is a bit older, however, and enjoys hiking, boat trips, fishing, 4x4 trips on rough roads and generally being outdoors, Guyana could prove a wonderful experience.

At interior lodges, while there is much to do that revolves around nature, the travel can be arduous and parents may worry about safety precautions not being up to Western standards. Child-size life jackets, for example, would likely be hard to come by and child seats for vehicles are not common (better to bring one).

If considering travelling with children in Guyana, parents should review the health section (see page 64) in detail and make sure all necessary precautions and vaccinations are considered.

WHAT TO TAKE

CLOTHING Guyana is equatorial and the temperatures reflect this. Daytime is hot; night-time cools slightly, but it is still warm. These stable temperatures make packing easy, with the only concern being what you will need for the interior.

Dress codes throughout the country are very casual and relaxed, but locals do enjoy dressing smartly in the city.

Lightweight and loose-fitting casual clothing is best. A rain jacket is a must for the rainy season and recommended for the dry season when showers still occur. A sturdy pair of walking shoes and a good pair of sandals or flip-flops make a good match. A good hat to provide shade and protect you from the sun is also a good idea.

Along the coast it will be rare that you will ever want long-sleeved clothing due to being cold, but in the higher-altitude interior locations it can get a bit chillier at night. One lightweight long-sleeved shirt is a good idea to provide protection from bugs. Remember that very dark clothes tend to attract mosquitoes and other insects.

For trips to the rainforests you'll need to add a bit of kit. A pair of quick-drying trousers and long-sleeved shirt offer good protection against bugs and thorny flora. (Two sets are advised for those who will be spending many days in the jungle as they will become sweaty and dirty quickly.) Good hiking boots that perform well when saturated with water are best for longer jungle treks, but for the nature trails around most resorts and lodges, a good pair of walking shoes will suffice.

It's important not to over-pack, especially if you will be taking domestic flights in Guyana, as they have strict weight limits. Most hotels and interior lodges have laundry services to help travellers deal with restricted bag sizes.

EQUIPMENT The kit that you will need to pack depends largely on where you will be going on your trip. Journeys into the interior require more equipment, but for trips along the coast, where most everything is available, you can pack lighter.

If you are coming on an organised tour where all transfers are arranged then a suitcase will suit just fine for packing. But keep in mind that driving in the interior often covers everything in a fine red dust, so travelling with your best luggage is not recommended.

If you will be moving around a lot and relying on many different forms of transportation, a rucksack works best. Having something that is small enough to stay on your person, or between your legs, on minibuses, speedboats, ferries, etc is preferable.

All personal items (toiletries, sun cream, medicines) can be bought locally along the coast, but unless you want to pay slightly higher prices you should pack what you need. Before heading into the interior, it's best to make sure you have all the items you will require.

Bug repellent is a must for your trip, but there is no need to pack a product containing 100% DEET. The locally made extra-strength Mozipel (30% DEET) will give you just as good protection and it's widely available.

A torch is a necessity. Power cuts are still common throughout Guyana and many interior locations that rely on generators provide power for only a few hours each night. Batteries are readily available in Guyana, but poor quality knock-offs are common; consider packing extras. All necessary camera equipment should be packed. Film can be purchased here but the expiry dates can be questionable. For digital cameras, extra memory cards are available in Georgetown, but expensive.

An umbrella can come in handy for both protection against the rain and to provide shade from the sun. Also, don't leave home without a good pair of sunglasses. The sun is blindingly bright on most days.

Most hotels and lodges provide towels, but if you'll be staying at some of the remote eco-lodges or plan on camping, pack a quick-drying travel towel.

Bottled water is sold everywhere in Guyana (never drink tap water), but if you will be travelling to more remote areas or just want to save money, pack a water bottle and purification tablets.

Mosquito nets are provided at all lodges; there is no need to pack one unless you are going camping.

If you plan on camping while in Guyana, the preferred mode of shelter is a hammock and mosquito net. In the jungle, the ground is where the creatures lurk so it's best to be elevated above it. Tents can be used in the savannas and along some riverside beaches, but a hammock can be hung anywhere. Cheap travel hammocks and mosquito nets are available at many locations in Georgetown, but you can also check with your local sports shop. The nylon hammocks are not only lighter than cotton ones but they also dry much faster. If you are looking to invest in a hammock that you will use for years to come, the Hennessy hammock (*www. hennessyhammock.com*) is a great contraption that combines the hammock with a net. It's like a hammock tent and many locals going on longer treks prefer it.

For any trip, but especially one involving travel through the interior and along rivers, it's wise to pack waterproof bags for your valuables. Guyana is a land of humidity and water and things often get wet. Zip-lock plastic bags work fine, but outdoor shops often carry a host of quality waterproof vessels for reasonable prices. These also help to keep out the persistent dust of the savanna dry season.

A first-aid medical kit is also recommended; see page 69 for a list of items to include.

MAPS For pre-trip planning the only commercially produced map of Guyana that is widely available is from **International Travel Maps & Books** (*12300 Bridgeport Road, Richmond, BC, V6V 1J5, Canada;* 604 273 1400; e *itmb@itmb.com; www. itmb.com*). The map of Guyana is at a scale of 1:850,000; the map of the Guianas, which is on the other side, is at a scale of 1:1,200,000. Small maps of capital cities are also included.

The Guyana Tourism Authority publishes a good two-sided tourism map, with a Georgetown city map on one side and a Guyana country map on the other. The free map is available at the GTA office, Timehri International Airport and at many hotels, restaurants and gift shops in Georgetown. Both maps have basic information on Guyana and most major landmarks are marked. Cutting away the excess advertisements can reduce the bulk.

For larger and more detailed maps of Guyana, visit the **Guyana Lands and Surveys Commission** (*22 Upper Hadfield St, Durban Pk;* 226 0524; *www.lands. gov.gy.* ⊕ *08.00–12.00 & 13.00–16.30 Mon—Thu, 08.00–12.00 & 13.00–15.30 Fri*). They have a collection of city maps, Guyana regional maps and Guyana country maps for sale. A few are outdated but work is always being carried out to update them. They are also working towards designing maps for visitors.

ELECTRICITY Electricity in Guyana is 110/220V in 50–60 cycles: in Georgetown it is 110V, with 220V in most other places, including parts of suburban Georgetown. Interior lodges with electricity provided by generators are often 110V, but be sure to always double check if you don't have an adaptor. Plugs are three-pin American style. Power surges are common in most areas of Guyana so when charging electronic equipment ask for a surge protector or carry a small one.

$ MONEY

CURRENCY Guyana's unit of currency is the Guyana dollar (G$). Normal transactions are undertaken in local currency, but most hotels, lodges and travel agents quote prices in US dollars and will accept either. When packing for your trip, the best currency to bring is US dollars, as they are widely accepted by most tourism bodies and are easily exchanged. Banks and cambios will exchange most major foreign currencies.

In July 2011, the rate of exchange was: £1 = G$330, US$1 = G$205, €1 = G$298.

Note that some hotels will accept foreign currency but will charge you to convert it into local Guyana dollars and this is often done at a horrible rate. Always query before paying with foreign currency. The interior is largely a cash economy, and outside of the lodges, Guyana dollars are preferred.

CHANGING MONEY The best place to exchange money is Georgetown, but there are branches of the main banks at most major towns throughout the country. In Georgetown the best rates (and shortest queues) are usually found at cambios, but they will only exchange cash. Banks offer slightly lower rates of exchange, and they often involve waiting in a long queue, but they are the only places that will exchange travellers' cheques and give cash advances on credit cards.

Many major hotels offer foreign exchange for cash and travellers' cheques, but the rates are often poor. There are also moneychangers who frequent the international airport arrivals area and the Stabroek Market vicinity. While they typically offer good exchange rates, it's not wise to flash your cash in such public areas, as muggings have occurred right after changing money. There have also been instances where the moneychangers were dealing with counterfeit bills.

CREDIT CARDS The number of businesses that now accept credit cards in Guyana has increased greatly in the past few years, but they are still few and are all mainly in Georgetown. Most of the bigger hotels and tour operators will accept payment by credit card, as will a few restaurants (mainly in hotels) and grocery stores; the drawback is that you are charged a commission. The fee charged by the credit card companies is passed on to the consumer in Guyana. It is usually 3–7%, but can be as much as 10%. Credit cards can be convenient but cash is definitely cheaper.

Banks are the only places in Guyana that will offer credit card cash advances. Expect the same commission to be charged and only mediocre rates to be given.

ATM It wasn't until 2007, in preparation for hosting games for the cricket World Cup, that a few ATMs in Guyana were configured to accept international cards. All Scotiabank ATMs accept most international bankcards, and other banks are beginning to follow suit.

BUDGETING

Travelling in Guyana, especially when compared with other South American countries, is relatively expensive. But the cost of a trip largely depends on personal standards. If you travel with a hammock, are OK with roughing it a bit and get creative with transportation, trips can actually be quite affordable. If you'll be staying at all of the lodges, eating big meals and like to travel with a bit of comfort, a trip to Guyana can quickly become expensive.

LODGING In Georgetown, the cheapest (without being rundown and dingy) hotels cost about US$20 a night, per person (based on double occupancy). For mid-range hotels, expect to pay about US$50–90 for a double. Upmarket hotels begin around US$100 and go up to US$300 for suites.

For meals, the cheapest way to eat is by dining at small restaurants and roti shops frequented by the majority of locals; if you're willing to eat a staple of rice, chicken and vegetables then you can save money (snacks US$1, rice US$1–2, curry US$2–4, fried/baked fish or chicken US$2–4) and easily spend less than US$10 per day on meals. Fresh fruits and vegetables from market vendors also make for cheap eats.

If you have a simple breakfast (US$2–3), lunch at a local restaurant (US$3–4), and splurge a bit on dinner (US$10–15; US$15–20 with drinks) then your food budget will range from US$15–30 per day (this will easily increase if you are eating at hotels).

Drinking local Banks beer (US$1–2) and the excellent El Dorado rum (US$1–5, depending on age) will save you on any alcoholic drinks.

For smaller towns prices are typically cheaper, but there are fewer options. An average lunch or dinner costs between US$2 and US$4, more with drinks. Cheap hotels are under US$30 for a double; mid-range (it's tough to find anything above this) average about US$45 for a double.

The rates for most interior lodges and resorts include all meals and some activities and they range from US$85 to US$200 per person per night. A few will let visitors opt out of certain meals or self-cater their trips, which can make things more affordable. Keep in mind though that the reason the prices include all meals is because the lodges are typically isolated and there are no other options.

Many lodges will let people hang a hammock for US$2.50–10. Meals can often be paid for separately and cost between US$4 and US$15.

TRANSPORTATION The cost of transportation must also be figured heavily into any trip to Guyana. Minibuses are always the cheapest (US$0.40 around town; up to US$5 for longer trips) but taxis can be relatively affordable (and safer) as well (US$1.50–2 in town; US$20–40 for trips of more distance). Car hire is approximately US$40 per day.

Public speedboats charge US$5–10, while ferries cost US$0.50–2.50. Hiring boats can be prohibitively expensive without a group and cost roughly US$50 for short trips; US$150 for trips of about one hour; and up to US$600 for journeys of 5–6 hours. Prices vary with the price of petrol throughout the country.

To get into the interior and Rupununi, the cheapest way is to use minibuses (US$40) or the Intraserv bus (US$50). When using 4x4 transportation for transfers in the interior, prices vary wildly according to destination and road conditions. Costs range from US$20 for five miles to US$300 for 50 miles. Domestic flights range from US$70 to 120 each way.

Organised day trips vary depending on the activity and the number of people. Kaieteur and Orinduik Falls by plane is US$270. Georgetown city tours cost roughly US$30. Trips to the Essequibo and Mazaruni rivers are US$100 and most day trips to resorts are US$75–100.

As of 2011 Guyana has a VAT that adds 16% to most purchases, including hotel rooms, restaurant bills and tour prices. A few items have been zero-rated, including most local foodstuffs and domestic flights. At the time of writing, Guyana's tourism industry was still heavily lobbying the government to zero-rate certain aspects of the industry to allow for growth. Be sure to clarify VAT charges when paying for any trips, hotel rooms, bus tickets, etc.

GETTING AROUND

Travel in Guyana involves utilising a variety of transportation modes, including walking, taxi, minibuses, buses, 4x4 vehicles, speedboats, ferries, dugout canoes and small aircraft. With paved roads along most of the coastal belt and into Linden, travel is fairly straightforward, but transportation can get progressively more interesting as you move further into the interior. Roads there are unpaved dirt trails and their condition varies wildly throughout the year. In the rainy season many become impassable and rivers and creeks become the preferred 'roadways'.

In many areas of Guyana, rivers are the only way of getting around. Where there are established public boat services, be it on speedboats or ferries, the prices are often affordable. But if you need to hire a boat, prepare to pay.

The fastest and most convenient way of getting to interior locations is by flying. There are regularly scheduled passenger flights that go to many main tourism destinations, but once you arrive you will have to rely on other forms of transportation to get around.

In this book, many of the small towns/villages and interior resorts and lodges do not have their own *Getting Around* section. This is because the information is largely covered in each destination's *Getting There* section. Most resorts and lodges are destinations in themselves and any getting around is inherent in your travels to arrive or depart. For the small villages, walking is the main means of getting around, and any necessary transportation will be covered under the taxis, minibuses, boats, etc used to arrive and depart.

BY AIR In Georgetown, scheduled and chartered domestic flights leave from and arrive at Ogle International Airport (7km east of town). There are several local airlines that offer charter flights within Guyana; at the time of writing, Trans Guyana Airways (TGA) still had the most extensive offering of scheduled passenger flights, but Roraima Airways and Air Services Ltd were beginning to respond to increasing demand with more scheduled services, particularly to Lethem.

Internal flights within Guyana aren't cheap (about US$75–140 one-way) but when considering the time saved and the ease of travel, the value for money increases. Many prove their money's worth in the scenery alone. For a truly panoramic view, ask if the co-pilot seat is available for your flight.

Flying in Guyana may not be for everyone. Aircraft used are small prop planes that hold up to 12 passengers; and airstrips are often precarious-looking dirt runways. Checking in involves stepping onto scales, sometimes small bathroom scales or an ancient contraption of heavy metal weights, so that the plane can be properly balanced. It's bush flying, but the airlines also operate with stringent safety standards, so all in all, the flying isn't as risky as it may sometimes seem.

It isn't uncommon for interior flights to be booked weeks in advance – especially the Georgetown–Lethem flight – so if you're planning on flying during your trip, it can be difficult to spontaneously choose dates. To plan ahead, TGA takes reservations over the phone and tickets can be purchased once you arrive in Guyana.

Most domestic flights have a baggage weight limit of 20lb per passenger. Charge for excess baggage is US$0.50–1 per pound, but there is no guarantee that space is available. TGA sometimes allows passengers to book excess weight in advance, but its best to travel light into the interior (many lodges have laundry services).

Note that as tourism slowly begins to increase in Guyana, and as demand rises for Georgetown and Lethem flights, several of Guyana's local companies are planning on adding regularly scheduled flights. If TGA flights are booked or the times don't work, enquire with others.

The following companies operate flights within Guyana:

Air Services Ltd Ogle International Airport, Ogle; 222 4357; e res@aslgy.com; www.aslgy.com. Domestic & overseas charter flights, medical evacuation & scheduled flights 3 times per week to Lethem (US$105 one-way, US$210 return) & Kaieteur (US$105 one-way, US$210 return) & twice to remote mining villages in Region 7.

Roraima Airways Ltd R8 Eping Av, Bel Air Pk; 225 9648; e ral@roraimaairways.com; www.roraimaairways.com. Charter flights, tours & medical evacuation.

Trans Guyana Airways (TGA) Ogle Aerodrome, Ogle; 222 2525; e commercial@transguyana.com; www.transguyana.com. Scheduled & chartered flights to more than 35 destinations in Guyana, including regular flights to interior locations.

Wings Aviation Limited/Air Guyana Ogle Aerodrome, Ogle; 222 6513; e info@airguyana.net; www.airguyana.net. Charter flights around Guyana & to Suriname, French Guiana Trinidad & Tobago & Brazil; also organises day & multi-day tours in Guyana; exploring scheduled domestic flights, including to Lethem and Bartica; contact for updates.

BY LAND Along the coast, most people rely on public transportation (buses, minibuses, ferries, speedboats and taxis), which keeps prices affordable. But start branching out from the populated areas and transportation becomes more complicated and rather expensive.

Driving conditions are rough on vehicles and those using interior transportation often feel the high cost of upkeep, maintenance and fuel. Most interior lodges provide transportation but it can be prohibitively expensive for solo and smaller groups of passengers.

Car hire It's possible to hire a vehicle in Guyana, but it's recommended to leave the driving up to somebody else. Along the coast, and especially in Georgetown, driving conditions are largely anarchic. Many of the roads are in a bad state of repair and when combined with speeding minibuses accidents are frequent. If you do hire a car, remember that traffic drives on the left in Guyana.

In the interior, the off-road conditions are best handled by an experienced driver. Many of the areas are remote and if you find yourself stuck or have an accident or car troubles, the nearest help could be miles, and hours, away.

Warning given, if you feel the need to throw yourself into the mix, see page 104 for a list of companies that hire cars.

Driving licences To drive legally any vehicle or motorbike in Guyana, you need to have an International Driving Permit (IDP) or a local licence. Visitors can apply for and receive a licence at the international airport upon arrival, but it is still a good idea to travel with an IDP. They are available from your national motoring association (in Britain contact the AA or RAC; in the USA contact AAA). To obtain one you must have a standard driver's licence in your country of residence; the IDP must also always be accompanied by your driver's licence from home.

Police roadblocks are common and if you are found driving without a licence it will likely entail paying an on-the-spot fee (read: bribe) or dealing with a fine and court date.

Petrol and diesel Both petrol and diesel are regularly available throughout Guyana's coastal belt. When driving your own vehicle into the interior, it's necessary to carry extra fuel as distances between places to purchase it can be lengthy. The situation seems to be improving slowly with more locations and some lodges selling fuel, albeit for inflated costs.

On average in Guyana, petrol costs US$1.25 per litre and diesel is cheaper at US$1.15. Fuel is always more expensive in more remote locations where it has to be shipped in. As in any country, fuel prices change rapidly, affecting the costs of transportation throughout the country.

Motorbike and scooter hire Motorbikes and scooters are a popular form of transportation in Guyana, but at the time of writing there were no companies that hired them.

Bicycle hire Besides the chaotic transportation, bicycles are a great way to get around Georgetown. Unfortunately, like motorbikes and scooters, at the time of writing no companies hired them.

In the interior, Rock View Lodge (see page 248) and Bina Hill (see page 253) rent bicycles, as does New Kanuku Bar in Lethem (see page 282). Arrowpoint Resort (page 130) also has mountain bikes available for use on their trails. Personal hire is also an option; just ask around.

By taxi Where there are paved roads in Guyana, there are taxis in plenitude and they are reasonably priced. Recommended taxi companies for cities and towns are covered in the relevant sections of this book, but it's always easy to hail one on the road, especially now that a new law states they must be painted bright yellow (also look for a licence plate beginning with 'H').

Most rides within Georgetown cost roughly US$2 (the same applies for other towns in Guyana). An airport transfer to/from Georgetown is US$25. Around town, taxis can also be hired by the hour for US$5–10; discounts are sometimes given for long trips or day-rentals.

For longer distances minibuses are always much cheaper, but when a taxi driver is driving too fast, they usually listen when you ask them to slow down. Hiring a taxi can also be a wonderful time to chat about life in Guyana. Most drivers are more than happy to launch into conversations on everything from local politics to overseas relatives.

By bus Public buses are not common in Guyana and are normally only used to cover longer distances. A public bus runs between Georgetown and Linden (see page 211), and while this is slower than taking a minibus, it is often a safer and more comfortable option.

Guyana's private bus company, **Intraserv** (*177 Waterloo St, South Cummingsburg; ╲ 226 0605; e commercial61@live.com*), was travelling between Georgetown and Lethem. However, they have just ceased all services until interior road conditions improve. Contact the Correia group for more information (╲ *222 2525*).

By minibus The most common form of public transportation in Guyana is minibus. Locals rely on them because they are cheap, not because they are preferred. In many cases the drivers of the highly personalised vehicles use their vans as a way to express their machismo. They overload their vehicles, have the music entirely too loud, honk with abandon, suck at women and drive recklessly fast. Accidents are all too common on the highways.

For trips of any distance (around Georgetown is usually OK), unless you are on a very tight budget or really want the experience, you should hail a taxi before a minibus. If for any reason you don't feel safe while travelling in a minibus don't be afraid to ask the conductor to stop the bus so you can exit. It has saved lives in the past.

Minibuses are privately owned but they operate along specific routes and their fares are regulated. Minibus routes will get you almost anywhere in Guyana accessed by roads. In Georgetown, the main bus park, where most buses officially begin and end their route, is scattered around Stabroek Market, mainly in the area of the Croal St Demico House. Routes can be confusing, especially within Georgetown, but almost any local will be able to provide assistance with information on which bus goes where.

Minibuses follow no set schedule. For longer trips (Georgetown to Linden, for example) they often won't leave until the bus is full, hence the reason for the battle over customers at bus parks. At night the number of buses on the road decreases greatly, but visitors should be using a taxi at this time of day for safety.

Minibuses are the cheapest (although not the safest) form of transportation. Fares around Georgetown are between US$0.40 and US$1; for destinations throughout the country, fares run up to US$5 (Lethem is US$40). For the most useful bus route numbers and destinations see *Getting around*, page 103.

By 4x4 When getting from place to place in the interior, if you're not using a boat then you'll likely be in a 4x4 vehicle. There are a few places in Georgetown that rent 4x4 vehicles but this isn't always recommended unless you are used to the driving conditions and are able to inspect the vehicle to make sure it will withstand interior roads.

Many resorts have their own 4x4 vehicles to provide transportation within the interior. It's not cheap, but the drivers are experienced and know the roads well. Some of the vehicles have seen better days, and seatbelts or even properly closing doors aren't always in order, but it's often still the safest option and part of the experience.

Hitchhiking Hitching in Guyana is not a normal practice. Along the coast where there are paved roads, if you stand at the side of the road with your thumb up, the only vehicles likely to stop are taxis and minibuses. And unless you find yourself completely out of money, you should be able to afford at least the latter.

Away from main roads and along the Linden–Lethem road, where traffic is less frequent, it would likely be possible to get a lift from passing vehicles. But relying on hitchhiking, as a way to get from one destination to another, is unreliable and not your safest option.

BY RIVER Outside of the coastal belt, Guyana is a land of many waterways and few well-maintained roadways. As a result, it is nearly impossible to travel around Guyana without using a boat of some sort, be it a large transport ferry or a traditional dugout canoe, a wooden speedboat or a jet boat. During the rainy season when many interior roads disappear under metres of water, boats become even more prevalent.

Sometimes using a boat is your only option of getting from point A to point B. Relevant details regarding travel by boat throughout Guyana are given in the individual chapters of *Part Two* of this guide.

The boat rides are essential in more than just practical ways; they also offer some of the best glimpses into daily life in Guyana and are excellent vessels for nature watching.

ACCOMMODATION

In Georgetown the accommodation options are quite varied. Lodging options outside of Georgetown become more limited and this section will give you an idea of what to expect.

HOTELS AND GUESTHOUSES
Georgetown From dingy and unsafe to over the top and overpriced, the capital city has the widest range of accommodation options. On the high end is Princess Hotel Guyana (formerly Buddy's International Hotel), which was built to four-star standards. It's a hotel for people who like to be self-contained as it has shops, restaurants, pool, gym, cinema, casino, bank and almost everything else you may need, but it's location isn't ideal and you also get charged for the services (US$150–300) which aren't always up to standard. With a better location, Pegasus Hotel Guyana (it is no longer a Le Meridien property) remains the most popular full-service hotel, but thanks to ageing rooms and lack of upkeep, their basic rooms now seem terribly overpriced (US$150). If it actually materialises, Marriott has plans to shake things up when they open their first branded hotel in Guyana in 2013. The 160-room Georgetown Marriott Hotel will be on the corner of the Atlantic Ocean and Demerara River (just around the corner from the Pegasus), and plans call for a casino, nightclub, restaurant and boardwalk.

Most hotels fall into the mid-range category. For between US$50 and 100 for a double, the rooms are self-contained, clean, air-conditioned and perfectly comfortable. Room furnishings, from garish to quality, locally-made furniture, vary wildly.

At the lower end, roughly US$10 and 20 per person, there are some comfortable guesthouses where the service is friendly and personalised and the rooms are basic but clean. It's also possible to find good hotel rooms in this range that have most amenities, including air conditioning.

Other towns Most established towns outside of Georgetown have a few lodging options and some are surprisingly nice. None could be considered upmarket, but it's possible to get a perfectly comfortable room with all amenities – television, air conditioning, en-suite bathroom – for around US$30–50 for a double. More basic rooms with fans and mosquito nets are US$10–20, and are clean and comfortable enough. Don't overlook the government guesthouses recommended in this book, as they are often good value.

Take note that many of the rock-bottom hotels and guesthouses in small towns have a chance of being frequented by short-term customers and may not be the cleanest places to stay.

INTERIOR LODGES AND RESORTS Guyana's lodges are where travellers will be spending most of their time and the accommodation ranges from rustic to very comfortable, but don't expect any upmarket all-inclusive resorts similar to those of the Caribbean islands.

Most lodges are equipped only for small groups of, on average, eight to 20 guests at a time. This is done on purpose as the proprietors like to keep operations small and intimate so that they can welcome their guests as friends. Expect to be called by your first name during your stay and it also isn't uncommon for your party to be the only guests at a lodge. Meals, usually served family-style, are often very good and plentiful. Rates for full board range from US$80 to 200 per person per night.

SELF-CATERING Throughout Guyana there is a range of hotels and lodges that have facilities that allow guests to self-cater. As buying food from local markets is quite cheap, this can be a way to save money on any trip. Places that do allow, or have the facilities for, self-catering are covered under hotel and lodge listings.

CAMPING There are no official campsites in Guyana, but camping is still common. Most camping is done with hammocks as tents place you on wet ground full of insects and other creatures.

ACCOMMODATION PRICE CODES

Accommodation listings are laid out in decreasing price order, under the following categories: Exclusive, Upmarket, Mid-range, Budget and Shoestring. The following key (also on the inside front cover) gives an indication of prices. Prices are based on a double room per night, including any taxes.

Exclusive	$$$$$	US$150+	G$30,000+
Upmarket	$$$$	US$90–150	G$18,000–30,000
Mid-range	$$$	US$50–90	G$10,000–18,000
Budget	$$	US$25–50	G$5,000–10,000
Shoestring	$	< US$25	<G$5,000

In the interior some locations have very basic shelters and hammock *benabs* (a traditional Amerindian shelter, usually open sided and with a roof made from palm thatch) to provide a cheaper form of accommodation to travellers (US$2–10). Bathroom facilities range from pit to flush toilets and bathing can be in a river, from a bucket or under a pipe.

At any interior location it never hurts to enquire about the possibility of hanging a hammock for the night; for those who don't mind roughing it, this is the cheapest way to travel.

PAYMENTS AND RESERVATIONS Most major hotels in Georgetown will accept credit card payments and some will also accept travellers' cheques although there is a surcharge. Smaller hotels and interior lodges (when paying direct) accept only hard currency, either Guyana or US dollars. If you prefer to pay for interior lodges with a credit card (or in advance with cash, to limit the amount you must carry), this can be done with most tour operators.

As tourism in Guyana begins to grow, lodges are seeing peak bookings in the dry season and much lower occupancy rates over the holidays and during the interior rainy season (May–August). To lure travellers during their slow months, many are now offering special rates and it never hurts to enquire when making a booking during these times.

Most places offer lower rates to Guyanese residents and people in the country working for volunteer organisations. Enquire at individual lodges or hotels.

Rates are also often negotiable for groups of people (usually more than four) and long-term stays (usually more than four nights).

Overall occupancy rates in Guyana are still relatively low, but growing; reservations are never a bad idea. Reservations are especially recommended for any interior locations, not always because they are likely to fill up, but because advance notice allows them to make sure they have everything required by visitors, including enough food.

✖ EATING AND DRINKING

A range of cultures, including East Indian, African, Amerindian, Brazilian and Chinese, influence Guyanese cuisine.

Perhaps the best thing about Guyanese cuisine is that it's almost always made with fresh ingredients from the farm, tree, river or sea.

As should be expected, Guyanese cuisine is more Caribbean than Latin. Staple dishes include various curries, often eaten with *roti*, a fried flatbread, and dhal; cookup rice (rice cooked with coconut milk and whatever is on hand: peas, okra, beans, plantains) that is often served with fried chicken or fish; fried rice; Caribbean-style chow mein (stir-fried soft noodles often topped with fried chicken); and all meals are accompanied with excellent fiery pepper sauces. Mango achar also makes a wonderful complement for most meals.

Speciality dishes include *pepperpot*, an Amerindian stew made with meat, peppers and cassareep, an extract of cassava that has long been valued for its preservative qualities, allowing pepperpot to last indefinitely (it's widely available to buy in Guyana); and *metemgie*, a thick coconut-based soup filled with dumplings, fish or chicken and a host of provisions including eddoes, yams, cassava and plantains. Garlic pork, which is a form of pickled pork, is a Portuguese dish traditionally served for Christmas.

Breakfasts often mirror lunch, with many eating hearty curries and rotis. Bakes, which are most often fried pieces of dough, are often served with salt fish; pepperpot is also popular for breakfast.

Homemade breads are popular in the interior where Amerindian populations have perfected the craft over the years. Favourite pastries with a British influence include cheese flaps, pine (pineapple) tart and *solara*, a cake rolled around a red coconut filling. The densely-moist and savoury-sweet cassava pone is also a popular dessert featuring coconut.

Adventurous eaters can also sample a range of wild meats while in Guyana; they are commonly found on menus in many smaller villages. Labba, agouti, peccary and paca are just a few.

SAMPLING Any eating tour should start with street snacks. Fried plantain chips topped with mango sour (boiled green mangos and peppers) provide a good salty backdrop to a superb selection of fresh fruit; the pineapples are not to be missed.

A good lunch option (besides chicken and rice) is a bowl of curry eaten with roti. Curried ingredients range from mutton to shrimp, pumpkin to eggplant, and all are worth sampling.

Come dinner, sample the seafood, which is plentiful and cheap. Usually the freshest options are snapper, trout, and prawns. Have the prawns marinated in garlic and butter, the trout served with a tropical salsa or the snapper lightly fried. And don't be afraid to accompany any meal with the always present homemade and quite hot pepper sauces.

RESTAURANTS

In Georgetown There are a handful of good restaurants that cater to the well-established expat scene, well-off Guyanese and the occasional tourists. Most have varied menus of different meats (chicken, beef, pork) and seafood (prawns, fish) cooked in a variety of ways. Meals in Georgetown's nicer restaurants cost between US$6 and 20, for food only.

By eating at small establishments favoured by locals you can get very large portions for around US$2–4. The only thing lacking is a wide variety and ambience (which can be relative).

Outside of Georgetown Options grow slimmer here. Most restaurants and smaller places that serve food are geared towards local tastes. Variety is limited, but the portions are often huge, the food good and the prices low (US$2–4).

Expect variable service wherever you eat. Even the nicest restaurants can sometimes take more than an hour to bring the wrong plate to your table. The mystery of the service you'll receive is part of the experience.

RESTAURANT PRICE CODES

Restaurant listings are laid out in decreasing price order, under the following categories: Expensive, Above average, Mid-range, Cheap & cheerful and Rock bottom. The following key (also on the inside front cover) gives an indication of prices. Prices are based on the cost of a main course per person.

Expensive	$$$$$	US$15+	G$3,200+
Above average	$$$$	US$9–15	G$1,800–3,200
Mid-range	$$$	US$5–9	G$1,000–1,800
Cheap & cheerful	$$	US$3–5	G$600–1,000
Rock bottom	$	<US$0.50–3	<G$100–600

CAFÉS AND BARS In Guyana most restaurants also double as a place to have a drink. For a quieter atmosphere it's best to seek out a hotel bar or higher-class restaurant. For a bit more of a local experience, often accompanied by blaring music, visit a rum shop. Rum shops are the cheapest options and it's where most head to do some serious drinking.

Prices for drinks vary according to the establishment you are at. The cheapest option is to drink local beer (Banks) and rum (El Dorado); the beer is good and the rum is world-renowned. Local bars will charge around US$1.50 for a local bottle of beer, but this can be doubled at restaurants. Nicer restaurants will have a stocked bar full of local and imported spirits, a few red and white wines and a limited selection of local and imported beer. Most international brands of sodas, soft drinks and other such sugar or fizz-laden beverages are widely available.

SELF-CATERING Preparing your own meals is not a problem in much of the coastal areas, provided you have cooking facilities. Georgetown and most other towns have grocery stores stocked with local and imported products. There are also very good markets throughout the country where you can buy fresh fruits, vegetables, meats and fish. Buying local food is much cheaper than purchasing imported goods.

In smaller interior locations it can be harder to come by fresh vegetables but most shops stock basic tinned foods.

PUBLIC HOLIDAYS

On public holidays most businesses and all government offices close, but some grocery shops, petrol stations and markets will be open for limited hours. Many restaurants in hotels also remain open. With Guyana's vibrant blend of cultures, there are many holidays to celebrate; they include:

1 January	New Year's Day
23 February	Republic Day/Mashramani
1 May	Labour Day
5 May	Indian Arrival Day
26 May	Independence Day
16 June	Enmore Martyrs' Day
First Monday in July	CARICOM Day
1 August	Emancipation Day
25 December	Christmas Day
26 December	Boxing Day

Public holidays with changing dates include: Good Friday, Easter Monday, Phagwah (Festival of Spring; usually March), Deepavali (Festival of Lights; usually November), Eid-ul-Fitr (end of Ramadan), Youman Nabi (Birth of the Prophet Mohammed), Eid-ul-Adhah (Feast of the Sacrifice). See page 24 for festivals.

SHOPPING

Guyana has never been internationally renowned for any particular handicraft or distinct style of art, but that could just be because Guyana is under the radar with most things. Travellers to Guyana will probably find plenty of locally made items to buy. Most of Guyana's main gift shops are in Georgetown (see *Shopping*, page 115), but many interior lodges and some Amerindian villages have small craft shops.

The best items to buy in Guyana include pottery, anything made with or carved from the plethora of beautiful Guyanese hardwoods, items woven from forest vines and reeds, figurines made of balata (see box on page 275), paintings, jewellery, hammocks and antique Dutch bottles.

Items made by Amerindians are often of high quality and encompass most items listed above (baskets and jewellery made from natural forest products are most popular). If you plan to travel to in the interior or visit any Amerindian villages, you will likely have the opportunity to buy items directly from the artist, but most items are also available in Georgetown.

The beautiful hammocks for sale throughout Guyana also make good souvenirs. The brightly coloured cotton hammocks sold everywhere are imported from Brazil. They're beautiful and a good bargain, but for a local souvenir look for one woven by the Makushi or Wapishana Amerindians of the Rupununi. The hand-woven cotton hammocks differ in that the Makushi is a single weave and the Wapishana is a double weave. The Makushi style is better for hot climates, but the thicker Wapishana provides more warmth. Both are more expensive than the imported Brazilian hammocks but they are of outstanding quality (a sample of a double-weave Wapishana hammock hangs in the Smithsonian).

Guyana has long been rumoured to be the site of the long-lost (or never found) El Dorado, the city of gold. Truth or not, plenty of gold and diamonds are mined in Guyana, and Georgetown has endless jewellery shops to prove it. Unless you are confident in your ability to appraise the quality of gold and diamonds, it's best to buy from more reputable dealers. Remember that while you're closer to the source, you're still buying precious minerals; if the price seems too good to be true, double-check the quality.

Visitors to Guyana should not leave without a bottle of El Dorado rum. The 15-year-old has been voted world's best, but even the five-year-old possibly tastes better than most rums you've ever had. It can be purchased throughout Georgetown and Guyana, or duty free at the airport.

ARTS AND ENTERTAINMENT

Georgetown, the only city of size in Guyana, has the largest offering of arts and entertainment, but it could still be considered limited for a country's capital city.

For visual arts, the best museum is Castellani House (see page 121), which is home of the National Art Gallery and rotating exhibits ranging from photographs to paintings. Castellani House also hosts special events such as classic movie nights. In Georgetown it's also becoming more common for restaurants and cafés to display and sell local artworks.

Entertainment options are fairly limited in Georgetown. The local form of entertainment involves heading to a rum shop and imbibing, perhaps while playing a game or two of pool. Later in the night, there are a handful of nightclubs that play loud music for dancing.

Film festivals occur throughout the year. Some are sponsored by the various embassies in Georgetown, and the Sidewalk Café (see page 115) also regularly hosts weekly film nights (in addition to live jazz).

International live music concerts also pass through Georgetown from time to time; acts are mostly from the Caribbean, but also come from as far away as India. There are also a handful of local music acts that perform at different venues in Guyana and the National Cultural Centre hosts many cultural celebrations that involve theatre, music and dance.

NEWSPAPERS Guyana has four daily newspapers: *Stabroek News, Guyana Times* and *Kaieteur News* are private papers while the *Guyana Chronicle* is state owned. *Stabroek News* is often regarded as the best for reporting non-biased and honest news (and often feels pressure from the government for doing so); *Kaieteur News* likes to sell papers with sensationalised stories and all too graphic front-page photos; and the *Guyana Chronicle* is more geared towards positive reports on the ruling party. All mainly cover local news (there is much overlap between the papers) and also run stories from international wires. All post much of their daily content on the web (*www.stabroeknews.com; www.guyanatimesgy.com; www.kaieteurnews. com; www.guyanachronicle.com*).

Two other papers, the *Catholic Standard* and *The Mirror* (*www.mirrornewsonline. com*) are published weekly. *Guyana Entertainment Magazine* (GEM; *www. gemmagonline.com*) is Guyana's glossy bi-monthly magazine covering local culture and entertainment figures.

TELEVISION There are roughly a dozen television stations (they come and go) in Guyana, with the majority in Georgetown. Many do little more than rebroadcast US (and sometimes Indian) imports. Television programming is wildly unpredictable, but CNN, BBC and nightly world news from the US are staples, as is Oprah. Local news programmes are also shown in the early morning and evening. America's most popular shows of the time are also shown on television in Guyana. Bootlegged movies are also regulars, and it's not uncommon to see a movie on television in Guyana the same week it was released to theatres in the States.

RADIO Voice of Guyana 98.1 FM is the main radio station. In the Rupununi, be sure to tune in to Radio Paiwomak (97.1 FM), a community-managed radio station based at Bina Hill.

POST Most towns in Guyana have post offices, but it's best to send any mail from Georgetown. Mail is reliable, but delivery times to Europe and North America can vary. A good average is two weeks, but it can be surprisingly quicker or slower. Letters inside Guyana cost US$0.15; to North America and Europe they range from US$0.50 to US$1. See *Communications*, page 118 for more detailed information on Georgetown's post offices.

TELEPHONE AND FAX The cheapest way to make international phone calls from Guyana is at one of the many internet service providers. They are common along the coast and outlined in relevant areas of this book. Calls to North America and Europe cost between US$0.10 and 0.50 per minute. To forgo the slight delay found on internet calls, purchase a phonecard that works with public phones. They are widely sold at markets, grocery stores, pharmacies and petrol stations and calls to the US or UK cost about US$0.50 per minute. Many hotels offer international direct dialling, but rates can be very high; the cards should work from their phones.

The phonecards also work for local cards from public phones that are found at locations throughout Guyana. For all of Guyana the country code is 592, followed by a seven-digit number.

Guyana now has two mobile phone service providers: GT&T Cellink and Digicel. Service reaches most areas along the coast, into Linden and around Lethem, with plans to expand coverage along the main interior highway to Brazil. Digicel, the

Some of the best souvenirs to take home from Guyana are the crafts that are made by Guyana's indigenous population. Many Amerindian communities in Guyana are involved in producing traditional and non-traditional handicrafts for sale; by supporting these projects, visitors help provide a much-needed source of income that is a viable alternative to some of the less sustainable options, including mining, logging, wildlife trade and over-hunting and fishing. One of the best places to shop for a range of Amerindian crafts from throughout Guyana is at the Ministry of Amerindian Affairs gift shop in Georgetown (see page 116). The co-op of crafters and related gift shop at Santa Mission (see page 132) is also an excellent place to purchase gifts and souvenirs.

There are a handful of craft projects in Guyana that are working hard to promote the importance of crafts for local families. The projects seek to prove that the traditional skills can have an economic value, and by providing an alternative means of income, promote conservation.

Some items to look out for while at lodges in the Rupununi, include: salad servers, bowls, cutlery, jewellery boxes and animal figurines carved out of leopard wood by the Parashara Carving Group. Surama Village also sells bows and arrows made from the same beautiful wood. The Massara Ladies Sewing Group uses needlepoint to capture everyday life of the Rupununi. If you have space, the hammocks, baby slings and bags made from home-grown cotton are worth the cost.

YUPUKARI CRAFTERS Near Karanambu, in the village of Yupukari, the Yupukari Crafters is a project that is working to develop a line of home furnishings made with a combination of wood, rawhide and cotton. The group makes tables, chairs, sofas, hammocks, baskets and the like. They are also using balata (see box on page 275) in creative ways, including in the making of tiles. The craft projects are available at the Caiman House (see page 270), at locations in the Rupununi and soon by order. See www.rupununilearners.org for more info.

MORUCA EMBROIDERY Composed of women from the Santa Rosa and Waramuri communities of northwestern Guyana, Moruca Embroidery was started by the Guyana Marine Turtle Conservation Society (GMTCS) as part of their efforts to protect the endangered species of sea turtles that nest on Shell Beach (see page 196). The items, which include hats, pillowcases, bags and towels, feature Images of local flora and fauna, with the focus on sea turtles. As Santa Rosa and Waramuri are the two main sea turtle harvesting communities near Shell Beach, creating alternative income is of utmost importance. The crafts are available at the main office for Iwokrama in Georgetown [110 C1].

ECO JEWELRY Like Moruca Embroidery, this new initiative was also founded by Michelle Kalamandeen of the GMTCS. The project involves women from the North Rupununi and Moruca communities who make a range of jewellery from natural and recycled materials found in Guyana. The project focuses on providing the members with an income through skills and products that utilises their traditional knowledge and culture.

newest provider to Guyana, brought some much-needed competition and service is rapidly expanding. Mobile phones with GSM capability should work in Guyana, but local SIM cards are available at cellular shops throughout the country.

Fax services are available at several hotels and some office supply stores in Georgetown (see *Telephone and fax*, page 118).

INTERNET While the service isn't as fast as in more developed countries of the world, high-speed internet is common throughout Guyana. Many hotels in Georgetown, and some other locations along the coast, now offer free Wi-Fi service to their guests; computers are also often available for those not travelling with one.

Internet cafés are common throughout the country, and in some more remote towns and lodges internet services is provided via satellite. Cost for browsing ranges from free to US$1–2 per hour.

BUSINESS HOURS

Most shops and tour operators are open for business from 08.00 to 17.00, although some fluctuate by an hour or so on either side. The majority of banks keep the following hours: Monday–Thursday 08.00–14.00, Friday 08.00–14.30.

TRAVELLING POSITIVELY

The fact that Guyana is an English-speaking country makes interactions with the locals (for other English speakers) an added benefit to any trip. Guyanese people are friendly, educated and always have an opinion so don't be afraid to strike up a conversation. Talking with locals is the best way to get a true understanding for the country. Taxi drivers are particularly keen to offer up their input on any subject from politics to food.

In Amerindian communities, the people are often initially much more shy and quiet, but once you've spent some time with them they usually open up and you'll find it easy to coax stories from them that offer insights into their culture.

Whenever possible support small-scale shops and businesses, and avoid imported food and other products. This is the best way to ensure that your money is going to the local grassroots community, where it is needed most.

Buy crafts made locally and try to get the history on a product whenever possible to make sure you are supporting a sustainable project.

It is always polite to ask permission before taking photographs of locals.

For travellers who are looking for ways to give something back to Guyana, there are a variety of options. Basic necessities such as clothes, children's toys, school supplies and basic over-the-counter medical supplies are always needed, either for the remote interior communities or for locations along the coast. When booking a trip through any tour operator, they will be able to assist you in the best way of dispersing any donation items you bring to Guyana.

For those with more specialised skills who like to combine their holiday with a stint of volunteering, there are a few projects in Guyana that are always looking for assistance.

REMOTE AREA MEDICAL (RAM) (*www.ramusa.org*) During the 15 years Stan Brock spent in southern Guyana he saw how limited medical facilities for the villages of the area were. With this in mind, Remote Area Medical Volunteer Corps was started as a volunteer airborne relief corps that provides free health care, dental care, eye care, veterinary services and technical and educational assistance to remote areas throughout the world. In Guyana, RAM works though an air ambulance service based in Lethem that serves some 25 of Guyana's most remote and inaccessible villages and a cervical cancer team that provides women's health services in Guyana. As RAM relies entirely on volunteers, help is always needed.

IWOKRAMA INTERNATIONAL CENTRE FOR RAIN FOREST CONSERVATION AND DEVELOPMENT For those with a scientific background, Iwokrama always has research projects with space for volunteers. For more information, see page 45.

KARANAMBU TRUST The Karanambu Trust has a rotating list of volunteer opportunities that range from otter keeper to researcher. The charity works to ensure the sustainable use of the Karanambu Wetlands through wildlife and habitat conservation, research and education in partnership with local communities. For more information, see page 265.

RUPUNUNI LEARNERS FOUNDATION (e *info@rupununilearners.org; www. rupununilearners.com*) Based at the Caiman House in Yupukari (see page 270), the Rupununi Learners Foundation seeks to improve the quality of life for the indigenous population of the Rupununi, by enhancing literacy, access to information and preserving local customs. More detailed information on their projects, including the libraries that have been built and stocked with thousands of books, is covered on page 270, but the foundation is always in need of donations and volunteers.

Volunteers are needed with skills in arts and crafts, videography, home furnishings design, librarianship, public health, teaching, tourism, wildlife research and a host of other areas. If you are interested in volunteering or donating, please contact Alice Layton for current information.

Practical Information   TRAVELLING POSITIVELY

3

Part Two

THE GUIDE

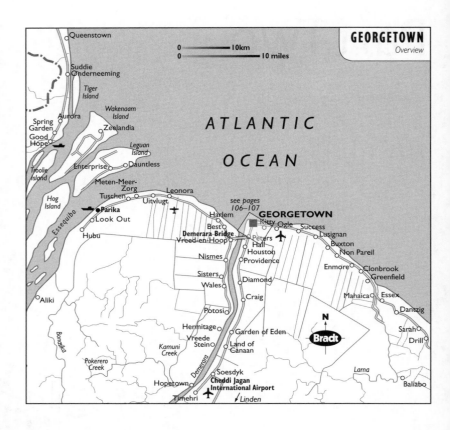

ATLANTIC

OCEAN

0 _____ 10km
0 _____ 10 miles

Queenstown

Suddie
Onderneeming

Tiger
Island

Wakenaam
Island

Aurora

Spring
Garden
Good
Hope

Zeelandia

Leguan
Island

Enterprise

Dauntless

Troolie
Island

Meten-Meer-
Zorg

Tuschen

Leonora

Hog
Island

Uitvlugt

Parika

Look Out

Hubu

Harlem

Best

Demerara Bridge
Vreed-en-Hoop

Nismes

Sisters

Wales

Potosi

Hermitage

Vreede
Steino

Kamuni
Creek

Pokerero
Creek

Hopetown

Timehri

Soesdyk

Cheddi Jagan
International Airport

Linden

Land of
Canaan

Garden of Eden

Diamond

Craig

Providence

Houston

Hall

Peters

see pages
106–107

GEORGETOWN

Kitty Ogle

Success

Lusignan

Buxton

Non Pareil

Enmore

Clonbrook
Greenfield

Mahaica

Essex

Dantzig

Sarah

Drill

Larna

Baliabo

N

Bradt

Essequibo

Bonasika

Demerara

Aliki

4

Georgetown

In the world of tourism, Georgetown could be considered a tough sell. Guyana's slightly rundown capital city of 170,000 people (250,000 with surrounding towns/villages) was once touted as the 'Garden City of the Caribbean', but that name has been fading since the British pulled up their imperialistic stakes (and maintenance money) in the 1960s. Even though there are more than 200 species of bird found within the capital and still enough green patches, flowering plants and fruit-bearing trees to make the most sceptical see the origins of the city's nickname, when Georgetown appears in Guyana's tourism guides and brochures amongst conglomerations of nature shots and worn-out adjectives flaunting this 'Paradise for Nature Lovers', the city does not come off as quite so appealing.

But why make travel plans based on old epithets? Or visit cities for nature? Guyana's interior is the draw for most visitors and Georgetown is the gateway, a final dose of hurried civilisation before the vast emptiness of the jungle and savanna.

British and Dutch heritage and a melting pot of lively English-speaking locals make the city decidedly more Caribbean than Latin. Colonial buildings, both lovingly restored and barely standing, dominate the town's architecture. Minibuses share the streets with cows, horse-drawn carts and the speeding cars that are at odds with the laidback pace of life. And with its thriving markets, a few decent museums, some good restaurants and a handful of manatees, Garden City or not, Georgetown certainly merits a day or two of the visitor's time.

HISTORY

Originally, the area comprising Georgetown was an uninhabitable tangled mess of coastal floodplains unfit for development. Thus the reason why, when the European settlers finally got around to exploring the area in the 1740s, they chose an island 27km up the Demerara River as the site for Borselen, the capital of the new colony, Demerara.

The colonists quickly realised the soil along the Demerara River was ideal for sugarcane production and it wasn't long before the area dominated the region's sugar industry: by 1769 there were 206 plantations.

The profitable plantations soon attracted the attention of the British, who in 1781 became the bullying majority. This was the beginning of an era when many land rights were disputed, wars were fought and control of the colonies frequently changed hands. The British set about protecting their new claim and built Fort St George at the mouth of the Demerara River. In 1782, the French, who were allies with the Dutch, took control of the colonies and renamed the area around Fort St George, Longchamps.

In 1783, the French handed control back to the Dutch, who, seeing the developments around Longchamps, deemed their interior capital insufficient and moved to the coast. The city was renamed Stabroek. The Dutch settlers, using their forefathers' knowledge and the efforts of African slaves, expanded the area by building canals, dykes and '*kokers*', or sluices, to conquer the unruly waters. Floodlands were reclaimed, plantations were built, the foundation of a new capital city was laid, and the Dutch undoubtedly congratulated themselves.

In 1796 the British returned with force and controlled the area until 1802 when the Dutch made a final stand that lasted until the British re-seized the colonies about one year later. Finally in 1814, the determined British re-christened Stabroek, Georgetown, after King George III or IV (depending on which historical story you believe), and decreed it to be the new capital of the colony of British Guiana.

In 1966 the British relinquished control, leaving an occasionally divisive population of descendants of African slaves and indentured labourers from India, Portugal and China, who worked on British plantations after slavery was abolished.

GETTING THERE

Georgetown will be the main entry and exit point for many visitors, as all international flights arrive and depart just outside of the capital city. Other visitors who arrive in Guyana from Brazil or Suriname and are making their way to Georgetown have a variety of public transportation options to choose from.

BY AIR All international flights leave from and arrive at **Cheddi Jagan International Airport** (✆ *261 2244; www.cjairport-gy.com*). The airport is located at Timehri, 41km or one hour south of Georgetown (the airport is often called Timehri International Airport).

For transportation, at US$2, minibus route 42 is a cheap daytime option; for early morning or night-time flights, official airport taxis (US$25) are a wiser choice.

Most domestic flights leave from and arrive at Ogle International Airport (7km from town). Local airlines offering scheduled and chartered flights from destinations within Guyana are listed on page 84.

There is a queue of taxis waiting to take passengers to Georgetown from Ogle (US$6).

BY LAND Travelling by land to and from Georgetown is by way of taxi, minibus or larger buses. Minibuses are often cheapest, but not always the safest. Larger buses are cheap and relatively safe, but are also slower. Taxis provide more flexibility and a bit more control of the driving, but for longer trips they can be more expensive.

Travel between Georgetown and most major towns in Guyana is covered under each relevant section of this book. For information on travel between Georgetown and Lethem, or most destinations in southern Guyana, see pages 205 and 278. For information on travelling between Georgetown and Moleson Creek (location of the ferry crossing to Suriname), see page 138.

More information on travelling by land is covered in the *Practical information* chapter, *Getting around* section, page 85.

BY RIVER Most travel to and from Georgetown doesn't involve using the river. With a paved road in place, travel to Linden by way of ferries on the Demerara River is no longer available. The main form of boat travel from Georgetown is by crossing the Demerara River to Vreed-en-Hoop with speedboats. The boats leave from the docks behind Stabroek Market [110 B7] (US$0.50) and allow travellers to bypass the Demerara Bridge.

By ferry A passenger and cargo ferry travels between Georgetown's Kingston wharf and Kumaka's wharf on a fortnightly basis (adult/child US$10/5). The long, arduous and seasick-inducing journey takes 24 hours by way of the Atlantic, but it's the cheapest way of getting from Georgetown to the Mabaruma area.

At the time of writing, the ferry left Georgetown on Wednesday afternoons, arriving in Kumaka on Thursday afternoon. The boat is typically docked in Kumaka for five to seven days before returning to Georgetown. Schedules and departure times can vary greatly depending on weather and other unforeseen circumstances. For updated departure times call the Transport and Harbours Department/Georgetown Ferry (✆ 225 6471).

ORIENTATION

Georgetown's streets were laid out in a neat grid pattern and lined with canals during the Dutch efforts to protect the city from flooding, a constant threat due to its precarious position seven feet below sea level. The Demerara River forms the western boundary, and to the north is the Atlantic Ocean, the source of cooling coastal winds.

Georgetown is divided into small boroughs; knowing the neighbourhoods is helpful as street names change often and numbering can be nonsensical. West of Vlissingen Road: Kingston and Thomas Lands (north); Cummingsburg, Alberttown and Queenstown (centre); Robbstown, New Town, Lacytown and Bourda (south-central); Stabroek, Werk-en-Rust, New Burg and Wortmanville (south); East of Vlissingen Road: Subryanville, Bel Air Gardens, Bel Air Springs and Bel Air (north); Kitty, Campbellville and Newtown (central); Bel Air Park (south); Prashad Nagar, Lamaha Gardens and Sophia (east).

GETTING AROUND

Transportation for Georgetown locals ranges from minibuses, motorbikes and cars to taxis and bicycles; visitors are best off getting around by minibus, walking and by taxis during the day and using taxis at night.

BY TAXI The safest way to manoeuvre the streets of Georgetown (read: cow dodging, horn honking, and dealing with an overall disregard for traffic laws) is to let a taxi driver do it for you. Thankfully, taxis are both plentiful and cheap. Around town rides cost US$1.50–2 per stop or US$10 per hour. A longer ride, to the outskirts of town, costs US$2–4, while a ride to or from the airport is around US$25. There is no main taxi rank but you can find plenty of companies listed in the phonebook or flag down a taxi on the street – always look for the yellow car and plates beginning with an H. Most hotels have good taxi service that sometimes charge slightly more. A few reliable companies include:

🚐 **Cyril's Taxi Service** ✆ 227 1700
🚐 **Gem's Taxi Service** ✆ 225 5075
🚐 **Sherry Taxi Service** ✆ 231 7777

BY MINIBUS Georgetown's answer to public transportation comes through a series of minibuses, which, although privately owned, operate along specific routes with regulated fares (US$0.40–1 around town). There is no set schedule but there is a constant flow of buses plying each route; note that bus frequency thins greatly during late night hours, at which time it is strongly recommended that visitors use taxis anyway. Unfortunately the same entrepreneurial spirit that provides a plethora of buses also results in aggressive bus drivers and overcrowded vans travelling at breakneck speeds. Accidents are not uncommon and unless you are seeking the experience, visitors are advised to hail a taxi before a bus.

While there are car parks where each bus officially begins and ends its route (for destinations within Georgetown, the chaotic car park is located near Stabroek Market at the Croal Street Demico House), it's possible for passengers to board and exit anywhere along the route. Routes can be confusing for those unfamiliar with Georgetown, so don't be afraid to ask someone on the street as most locals rely on minibuses for transportation. Those most useful for visitors are:

Bus 31, to Wales
Bus 32, to Parika
Bus 40, to Kitty/Campbellville areas
Bus 41, to Lodge/South, East & West Ruimveldt
Bus 42, to Timehri (Cheddi Jagan International Airport)
Bus 43, to Linden
Bus 44, to Mahaica
Bus 45, to Main, Lamaha & Albert streets

Bus 50, to Rosignol (location of Bus 56, which crosses Berbice Bridge to New Amsterdam)
Bus 56, Rosignol to New Amsterdam (route which crosses Berbice Bridge, replacing old ferry)
Bus 63, New Amsterdam to Corriverton
Bus 72, to Mahdia
Bus 94, to Lethem (Brazilian border) leaving from P&A Ice Cream and Transport Service (*75 Church St, Georgetown;* 225 5058) & Rockies International Hotel (*43 Light St, Bourda;* 225 5058)

BY CAR Renting a car is not necessary for most visitors to Georgetown as taxis and minibuses are cheap and plentiful, but for the adventure of navigating Georgetown's crowded streets on your own, there are several options for renting vehicles. Many require a deposit of around US$250 and a valid local or international driver's licence. Discounts are often given for long-term rental.

Auto Tech Car Rentals 59 Bel Air Springs; 225 8761; e info@guyanacarrental.com; US$30–60/day
Regency Suites Auto Rentals 98 Hadfield St, Werk-en-Rust; 225 4785; e hotelregency3@hotmail.com; US$30/day
Ease Auto Rental 118 Aubrey Barker St, South Rumveldt; 218 2014; e easeauto@ networksgy.com; US$30/day with 2-day min

Dolly's Auto Rental 272 Bissessar Av, Prashad Nagar; 225 7126; e dollysautorental@ yahoo.com; sedans US$30–40/day; 4x4 US$75–125/day
Knight Rider Bus Service 35 Delhi St, Prashad Nagar; 225 1429; minibus US$80–110/ day. Specialises in bus rentals of all sizes; call for detailed rates, which include driver & fuel.

BY BICYCLE While a bike can be a quick and convenient way for getting around Georgetown, at the time of writing, there is unfortunately no place in town that rents them.

SAFETY Georgetown's streets pose risks, but mainly at night when their emptiness and poor lighting offer criminals opportunity. Daytime muggings and petty thefts do occur however, so don't carry valuables (if not with a group, consider leaving your expensive camera and buying postcards) and take taxis from banks and cambios. Firearms are abundant in Georgetown, but violence is rarely directed at foreigners. Walking is fine during daylight but taking taxis at night is recommended. As in any unfamiliar city, remain alert and vigilant, and your chances of experiencing any problems are slim.

WHERE TO STAY

Georgetown offers visitors a wide range of lodging options including cheap and dodgy, cheap and comfortable, expensive and overpriced, expensive and worth it and nicely middle of the road. When comparing rates with other South American cities, you'll likely find hotels in Georgetown to be pricier, perhaps because of the alignment with the Caribbean. There are room options in the US$10 price range, but they don't offer the cleanest or most secure lodging. The accommodation below is recommended and worth any extra money. Unless otherwise noted, all rooms are en suite and have air conditioning and televisions.

It's also worth noting that in 2010 Marriott announced plans to open their first branded hotel in Georgetown in 2013. The planned (no promises; many say it is unlikely) 160-room Georgetown Marriot Hotel will be on the corner of the Atlantic Ocean and Demerara River (just around the corner from the Pegasus), and there are also plans for a casino, night club, restaurant and boardwalk.

EXCLUSIVE $$$$$
Princess Hotel Guyana [106 A7] (200 rooms) Providence, East Bank Demerara; 265 7001; e info@princesshotelguyana.com; www.princesshotelguyana.com. Formerly Buddy's International Hotel, this behemoth was built next to Guyana's new cricket stadium to host the top brass for 2007 World Cup matches, meaning it's self-contained. The massive marble lobby complete with leather sofas, garish chandeliers & gaudy picture frames sets the tone of this hotel. The rooms are spacious with shared balconies, all the necessary furnishings, free Wi-Fi & high ceilings. By spending more you get more outlandish furniture, extra sitting rooms & jacuzzi tubs. Extras include a sprawling pool, a Creole & Chinese restaurant, a bank, on-site travel agent, enough shops to constitute a mini shopping

centre & a casino only open to hotel guests & foreigners. All that said, low occupancy rates have led to a lack of maintenance, poor upkeep & staff that are sometimes ill-equipped to deal with guests. Bigger doesn't mean better.
Pegasus Hotel Guyana [106 B3] (130 rooms) Seawall Rd, Kingston; 225 2856; e reservations@pegasushotelguyana.com; www.pegasushotelguyana.com. Hotel guests enjoy shops, business centre, beauty salon, bars, restaurants, pool, gym, tennis courts, yoga, tour operator & 24hr room service, but the rooms are basic, sorely in need of renovation & overpriced. Unless you need a self-contained hotel, stay elsewhere & enjoy the well-kept grounds by coming for dinner or drinks at El Dorado or Le Poolside (see page 114).

UPMARKET $$$$
Blue Wave Apartments [111 G5] (21 rooms) 89 North Rd, Bourda; 226 1418; www.bluewave-gy.com. This hotel isn't cheap & little makes up for the prices charged. It has a good location near Bourda Market, but it's on a busy street & crowded by residential houses. The drab & sometimes musty rooms are at least clean & have free Wi-Fi; some have kitchenettes. The mock waterfall in the stairway is the best touch. This is also the place to buy overpriced Eddie Grant merchandise. *Suites* $$$$$

Cara Lodge [111 F4] (34 rooms) 294 Quamina St, Alberttown; 225 5301; e caralodge@carahotels.com; www.carahotels.com. Comfortably renovated houses with a rich local history dating back to the 1840s make up Georgetown's most popular colonial-style hotel. Clean & spacious rooms have all amenities including minibar, free coffee & tea, internet access, local artwork & creaky hardwood floors. Complimentary business centre on site, & beautiful courtyard doubles as Mango Tree bar; the

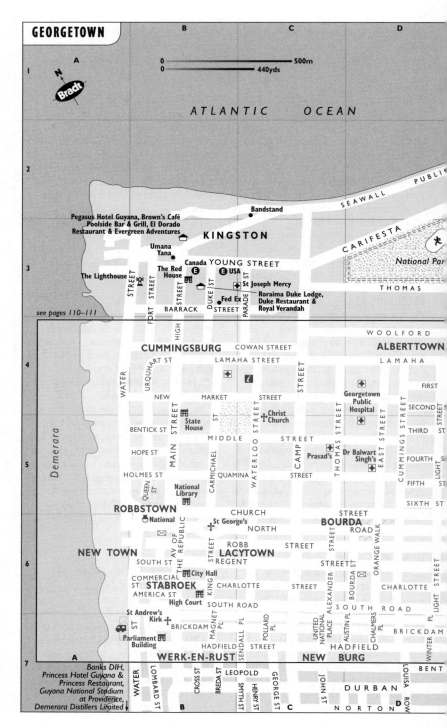

GEORGETOWN

ATLANTIC OCEAN

Pegasus Hotel Guyana, Brown's Café
Poolside Bar & Grill, El Dorado
Restaurant & Evergreen Adventures

Umana Yana

KINGSTON

Bandstand

SEAWALL

PUBLI

CARIFESTA

National Par

The Lighthouse

The Red House

Canada

USA

YOUNG STREET

THOMAS

St Joseph Mercy

Fed Ex

Roraima Duke Lodge,
Duke Restaurant &
Royal Verandah

BARRACK STREET

DUKE ST

PARADE

see pages 110–111

HIGH

WOOLFORD

CUMMINGSBURG

COWAN STREET

ALBERTTOWN

LAMAHA STREET

LAMAHA

URQUHART ST

WATER

NEW

MARKET

STREET

Georgetown
Public
Hospital

FIRST

SECOND

State House

Christ Church

BENTICK ST

MAIN STREET

MIDDLE

STREET

THIRD

ST

HOPE ST

CARMICHAEL

WATERLOO STREET

CAMP

STREET

Prasad's

Dr Balwart
Singh's

EAST STREET

CUMMINGS STREET

FOURTH

HOLMES ST

QUAMINA

STREET

FIFTH

ST

QUEEN ST

National Library

SIXTH ST

ROBBSTOWN

National

CHURCH

STREET

BOURDA

St George's

NORTH

ROAD

ORANGE WALK

NEW TOWN

AV OF THE REPUBLIC

ROBB

STREET

LACYTOWN

REGENT

SOUTH ST

STREET

LIGHT STREET

COMMERCIAL ST

City Hall

STABROEK

KING STREET

CHARLOTTE

STREET

CHARLOTTE

AMERICA ST

High Court

SOUTH ROAD

ALEXANDER

BOURDA ST

PL

St Andrew's
Kirk

BRICKDAM

MAGNET PL

SENDALL PL

POLLARD PL

SOUTH ROAD

UNITED NATIONAL PLACE

AUSTIN PL

CHALMERS PL

BRICKDAM

WINTER PL

Parliament Building

HADFIELD STREET

HADFIELD

WERK-EN-RUST

NEW BURG

Banks DIH,
Princess Hotel Guyana &
Princess Restaurant,
Guyana National Stadium
at Providence,
Demerara Distillers Limited

WATER

LOMBARD ST

CROSS ST

BREDA ST

LEOPOLD

SMITHS ST

HENRY ST

GEORGE ST

JOHN ST

LOUISA ROW

BENT

DURBAN

NORTON

0 ——— 500m
0 ——— 440yds

Demerara

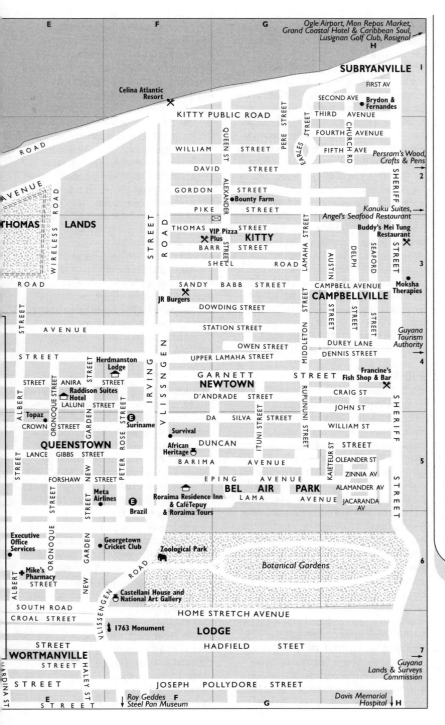

Ogle Airport, Mon Repos Market,
Grand Coastal Hotel & Caribbean Soul,
Lusignan Golf Club, Rosignol

SUBRYANVILLE

FIRST AV

Celina Atlantic
Resort

SECOND AVE   **Brydon &
Fernandes**

KITTY PUBLIC ROAD   THIRD   AVENUE

FOURTH   AVENUE

WILLIAM   STREET   FIFTH   AVE

Persram's Wood,
Crafts & Pens

DAVID   STREET

GORDON   STREET

Bounty Farm

PIKE   STREET

Kanuku Suites,
Angel's Seafood Restaurant

THOMAS   STREET   **Buddy's Mei Tung
Restaurant**

VIP Pizza
Plus   **KITTY**

BARR   STREET

SHELL   ROAD

THOMAS   LANDS

ROAD

SANDY   BABB   STREET   CAMPBELL AVENUE   Moksha
Therapies

JR Burgers   **CAMPBELLVILLE**

DOWDING STREET

STATION STREET

Guyana
Tourism
Authority

AVENUE

OWEN STREET   DUREY LANE

STREET   UPPER LAMAHA STREET   DENNIS STREET

Herdmanston
Lodge

STREET   ANIRA   STREET   **GARNETT**   STREET   **Francine's
Fish Shop & Bar**

Raddison Suites
Hotel   **NEWTOWN**

LALUNI   STREET   D'ANDRADE   STREET   CRAIG ST

JOHN ST

Topaz

Suriname   DA   SILVA   STREET   WILLIAM ST

CROWN   STREET

Survival

QUEENSTOWN   African
Heritage   DUNCAN   STREET   OLEANDER ST

LANCE GIBBS   STREET   BARIMA   AVENUE   ZINNIA AV

FORSHAW   STREET   EPING   AVENUE   ALAMANDER AV

Meta
Airlines   **BEL   AIR   PARK**   JACARANDA
AV

Roraima Residence Inn   LAMA   AVENUE
& CaféTepuy
& Roraima Tours

Brazil

Executive
Office
Services   Georgetown
Cricket Club   Zoological Park

Mike's
Pharmacy
STREET   *Botanical Gardens*

Castellani House and
National Art Gallery

SOUTH ROAD

CROAL   STREET   HOME STRETCH AVENUE

1763 Monument   **LODGE**

STREET   HADFIELD   STEET

WORTMANVILLE   Guyana
Lands & Surveys
Commission

STREET

STREET   JOSEPH   POLLYDORE   STREET

Roy Geddes   **F**   Davis Memorial
Steel Pan Museum   **G**   Hospital   **H**

Bottle Bar restaurant (see page 112) is also one of Georgetown's best. Central location & craft shop on site. *Suites* $$$$$

🏠 **Cara Suites**   [111 E3] (15 rooms) 176 Middle St, Cummingsburg; 📞 226 1612; e carasuites@carahotels.com. Sister hotel of Cara Lodge focuses on long-term visitors with studio & suites with all amenities, including furnished kitchens. Good bar, restaurant, tour operator & jewellery store on site. *Executive suites* $$$$$

🏠 **Roraima Duke Lodge**   [106 B3] (9 rooms) 94-95 Duke St, Kingston; 📞 231 7220; e roraimadukelodge@hotmail.com; www.roraimaairways.com. Located opposite the American Embassy, this beautiful colonial hotel is housed in what used to be one of Guyana's most prestigious reception halls. Professional staff oversee clean rooms fully furnished with the regulars & stocked mini-fridge, iron, hair dryer & coffee/tea maker. The restaurant, pool & poolside bar attract a crowd of guests & locals, which can get noisy in some rooms on the w/ends. *B&B.* *Suites* $$$$$

🏠 **Hotel Tower**   [110 C4] (76 rooms) 74 & 75 Main St; Cummingsburg; 📞 227 2011;

MID-RANGE $$$

🏠 **El Dorado Inn** (9 rooms) 295 [111 F4] Thomas & Quamina Sts, Cummingsburg; 📞 225 3966; e reservations@eldorado-inn.com; www.eldorado-inn.com. This friendly, immaculately clean & well-decorated inn should serve as a model to other area hotels. Each room has its own style & is furnished with feather-top mattresses & fluffy pillows (rarities in Guyana), flat screen TVs, DVDs, fans & desks. The building is cement but with dark hardwoods throughout & vaulted roof it has colonial air. Main floor has interior & exterior lounge with locally crafted cane furniture & bar; upstairs balcony provides good breeze. To splurge, request the reasonably priced executive suite complete with jumbo big screen TV, full kitchen, dining table for 6, personal balcony, & 2 bathrooms. Proprietor has extensive experience with local tourism & is very helpful in booking trips. *Suite* $$$$ *all B&B.*

🏠 **Grand Coastal Hotel**   [107 H1] (43 rooms) 2 Area M, Le Ressouvenir, East Coast Demerara; 📞 220 1091; e reservations@grandcoastal.com; www.grandcoastal.com. This hotel is about 8km from downtown but many find it's a distance

e Hotel.Tower@solutions2000.net; www. hoteltowerguyana.com. At the time of writing, the Tower, one of Guyana's oldest hotels, was undergoing an extensive renovation. The booming Edge Lounge nightclub was complete but the new rooms & planned gym & restaurants (including a hibachi grill) were slated for a 2011 completion. Hopefully the renovation will turn around a hotel that has seen better days. The pool is a plus (also available to non-guests), but the location in the middle of busy downtown can be seen as either a perk or drawback. Nightclub noise while trying to sleep is definitely not a bonus. *Suites* $$$$$

🏠 **Roraima Residence Inn**   [107 F5] (11 rooms) R8 Eping Av, Bel Air Pk; 📞 225 9648; e ral@roraimaairways.com; www. roraimaairways.com. This central boutique hotel is a place of high standards, which shows throughout. Staff are friendly & professional, rooms are tidy, spotless & fully furnished with the regulars & stocked mini-fridge, iron, hair dryer & coffee/tea maker. The pool (& poolside bar) is clean & inviting, the top-level patio is breezy & the restaurant, while it lacks ambience, serves good food. *B&B.*

worth travelling (taxis cost US$4–5). The hotel was all either recently built or refurbished. The rooms are spacious & have all the amenities, including desks & free Wi-Fi. There is a pool & small gym & other services such as massages & haircuts can be arranged, & the restaurant serves some of Georgetown's best food. *Some rooms* $$$$.

🏠 **Herdmanston Lodge**   [107 F4] (8 rooms) 65 Peter Rose & Anira Sts, Queenstown; 📞 225 0808; e stay@herdmanstonlodge.com; www.herdmanstonlodge.com. Beautiful colonial home in quiet, central neighbourhood gives visitors a taste of Georgetown's past glory days. Rooms are sparsely decorated, but clean & spacious & all have wooden floors, free internet & fans. Upstairs lounge & balcony provide breezy, relaxed atmosphere perfect for b/fast & evening cocktails while admiring the architectural splendour of the Brazilian ambassador's residence located across the street. *Suites* $$$$, *all B&B.*

🏠 **Hotel Ariantze**   [111 E3] (8 rooms) 176 Middle St, Cummingsburg; 📞 226 5363; e ariantze@networksgy.com; www.ariantzesidewalk.com. Full of character, this beautiful wooden colonial building also houses Sidewalk Café (see page 115); well-appointed rooms include free Wi-Fi. *All B&B*.

🏠 **Kanuku Suites** [107 H2] (19 rooms) 123 Kanuku St, Section M, Campbellville; 📞 226 4001; e reservations@kanukusuites.com; www.kanukusuites.com. This nondescript hotel tucked in a quiet neighbourhood is cosy, friendly & has a sense of style often overlooked in Georgetown. The clean rooms are well appointed with local furniture & extras like mini-fridges & microwaves; suites have even more space, beautiful wood floors & kitchenettes. The upper level of the tower-like hotel has a comfortable, breezy lounge with computer (Wi-Fi is free throughout) & TV & outdoor patio. Seafood restaurant & bar on site also good. *Suite* **$$$$**.

🏠 **Prairie International Hotel** (18 rooms) 11 S Half Coverden, East Bank Demerara; 📞 261 2260; e prairie.hotel@networksgy.com. Located just 8 miles from CJI Airport & 18 from Georgetown, this is well out of town, but it's a clean & comfortable place to stay for early departures or trips to the interior. Some rooms

have river views from private balconies. The restaurant built over the Demerara is great for sundowners. *Some rooms* **$$$$**.

🏠 **Raddison Suites Hotel** [107 E4] (24 rooms) 83 Laluni St, Queenstown; 📞 226 2145; e info@guyanahotel.com; www.guyanahotel.com. Friendly, centrally located hotel provides good mid-range option for visitors looking to self-cater. Most of the well-appointed rooms have kitchenettes with microwave, fridge, stovetop & table, all well used but clean. Nice rooftop garden & bar provide good views of city. Meals can be provided for non-cookers. *Businessman suite* **$$$$**.

🏠 **Regency Suites/Hotel** [111 E7] (40 rooms) 98 Hadfield St, Werk-en-Rust; 📞 225 4785; www.regencyhotelguyana.com. Massive concrete hotel has spacious & clean rooms lacking in style. All have free Wi-Fi & suites have kitchenettes. The sprawling shared balconies are good places to watch the busy street life filter to & from nearby Stabroek Market. Guests get free access to gym & club at Buddy's (see page 114). *Suites* **$$$$**.

BUDGET $$

🏠 **Rima Guest House** [110 C3] (12 rooms) 92 Middle St, N Cummingsburg; 📞 225 7401; e rima@networksgy.com. This wooden colonial home has the vibe of a welcoming grandmother's house. The simple rooms & shared bathrooms are spotless, food is cooked to order & the relaxing lobby has a TV, piano & old magazines. Rooms are fan cooled only, but AC is unnecessary with Demerara-shuttered windows, cool Atlantic breezes & mosquito nets.

🏠 **Sleepin Guest House** [111 H4] (23 rooms) 151 Church St, Queenstown & 24 Brickdam, Stabroek; 📞 231 7667; e reservations@ sleepinguesthouse.com; www. sleepinguesthouse.com. The central locations, comfortable rooms with bathrooms, TV, phone & friendly staff make for a good bargain. *Studio* **$$$**.

SHOESTRING $

🏠 **Florentene's Hotel** [111 E5] (15 rooms) 3 North Rd, Lacytown; 📞 226 2283. The hotel's basic, semi-clean rooms (some en suite), furnished with beds, mosquito nets & fans (no

AC), are merely places to lay your head for those in need of a centrally located cheap hotel. If you're travelling with valuables, consider paying a bit more for a more secure hotel.

✖ WHERE TO EAT AND DRINK

EXPENSIVE $$$$$

✖ **El Dorado** [106 B3] Pegasus Guyana Hotel, Seawall Rd, Kingston; 📞 225 2856; e reservations@pegasushotelguyana.com; www.pegasushotelguyana.com; ⏰ 19.00–22.30 Tue–Sat. Georgetown's only fine-dining

establishment usually delivers. Service is unmatched & the food comes just as you ordered. The steaks & seafood dishes are good options, as are vegetarian plates & soups.

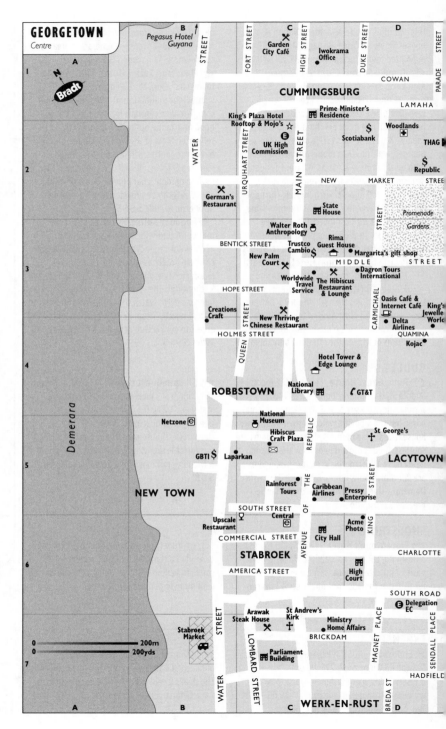

GEORGETOWN
Centre

N
Brandt

A | B | C | D

Pegasus Hotel
Guyana

FORT STREET
HIGH STREET
DUKE STREET
PARADE STREET

Garden
City Café
Iwokrama
Office

COWAN

1

CUMMINGSBURG

LAMAHA

WATER STREET

URQUHART STREET

MAIN STREET

King's Plaza Hotel
Rooftop & Mojo's ☆
UK High
Commission

Prime Minister's
Residence

Scotiabank $

Woodlands

THAG

Republic $

2

German's
Restaurant

NEW   MARKET   STREE

State
House

STREET

Promenade
Gardens

Walter Roth
Anthropology

Rima
Guest House

Trustco
Cambio $

Margarita's gift shop

BENTICK STREET

New Palm
Court

MIDDLE   STREET

Dagron Tours
International

3

Worldwide
Travel
Service

The Hibiscus
Restaurant
& Lounge

HOPE STREET

CARMICHAEL STREET

Oasis Café &
Internet Café
King's
Jewelle
Worl

Creations
Craft

QUEEN STREET

New Thriving
Chinese Restaurant

Delta
Airlines

HOLMES STREET

QUAMINA

Kojac

Hotel Tower &
Edge Lounge

4

ROBBSTOWN

National
Library

GT&T

National
Museum

Netzone

Hibiscus
Craft Plaza

REPUBLIC STREET

St George's

LACYTOWN

GBTI $ Laparkan

5

NEW TOWN

Rainforest
Tours

AVENUE OF THE

Caribbean
Airlines
Pressy
Enterprise

KING STREET

SOUTH STREET

Upscale
Restaurant

Central

Acme
Photo

COMMERCIAL STREET

City Hall

CHARLOTTE

STABROEK

6

AMERICA STREET

High
Court

SOUTH ROAD

Delegation
EC

Arawak
Steak House

St Andrew's
Kirk

Ministry
Home Affairs

MAGNET PLACE

SENDALL PLACE

BRICKDAM

0   200m
0   200yds

Stabroek
Market

WATER STREET

LOMBARD STREET

Parliament
Building

BREDA ST

HADFIELD

7

A | B | C   WERK-EN-RUST   D

Demerara

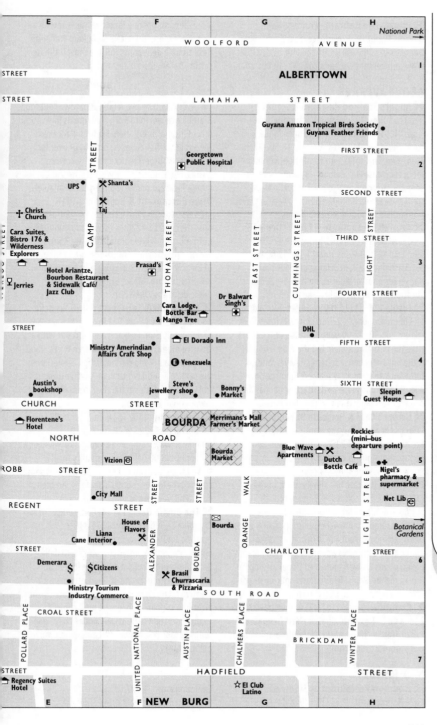

E   F   G   H

National Park

WOOLFORD   AVENUE

STREET

STREET   ALBERTTOWN   1

STREET   LAMAHA   STREET

Guyana Amazon Tropical Birds Society
Guyana Feather Friends

FIRST STREET

Georgetown
Public Hospital   2

UPS   Shanta's   SECOND STREET

Taj

Christ
Church

Cara Suites,
Bistro 176 &
Wilderness
Explorers   THIRD STREET   3

Prasad's

Jerries   Hotel Ariantze,
Bourbon Restaurant
& Sidewalk Café/
Jazz Club   FOURTH STREET

Dr Balwart
Singh's

Cara Lodge,
Bottle Bar
& Mango Tree   DHL

El Dorado Inn   FIFTH STREET   4

Ministry Amerindian
Affairs Craft Shop

Venezuela

Austin's
bookshop   Steve's
jewellery shop   Bonny's
Market   SIXTH STREET

Sleepin
Guest House

CHURCH   STREET

Florentene's
Hotel   Merrimans's Mall
Farmer's Market   Rockies
(mini-bus
departure point)

BOURDA

NORTH   ROAD

Bourda
Market   Blue Wave
Apartments   Dutch
Bottle Café   5

ROBB   STREET   Vizion   Nigel's
pharmacy &
supermarket

Net Lib

City Mall

REGENT   STREET

House of
Flavors   Bourda   Botanical
Gardens

Liana
Cane Interior

STREET   CHARLOTTE   STREET

Demerara   Citizens   6

Ministry Tourism
Industry Commerce   Brasil
Churrascaria
& Pizzaria   SOUTH ROAD

CROAL STREET   BRICKDAM

7

STREET

Regency Suites
Hotel   HADFIELD   STREET

El Club
Latino

E   F NEW BURG   G   H

✖ Princess Restaurant Princess Hotel Guyana, Public Rd, Providence, East Bank Demerara; ☏ 265 7001; www.princesshotelguyana.com; ⏲ 10.00–24.00

Mon–Sun. An upscale Creole restaurant with an ambitious menu & waiters & cooking staff who have trouble delivering. Not the most intimate setting for an upscale restaurant.

ABOVE AVERAGE $$$$

✖ Angel's Seafood Restaurant [107 H2] Kanuku Suites, 123 Section M, Campbellville; ☏ 226 4001; e reservations@kanukusuites. com; www.kanukusuites.com; ⏲ 18.30–22.30 Mon–Sun. This small, but comfortable dining room specialises in seafood – prawns, salmon, snapper, trout – but also has lamb, chicken & steaks. All are well prepared in a variety of ways, from grilled to added to pasta dishes.

✖ Arawak Steak House [110 C7] Demico Hse, Brickdam & Stabroek Mrkt; ☏ 225 3297; ⏲ 11.30–21.00 Mon–Thu, 11.30–22.00 Fri/ Sat. Casual restaurant & large outdoor patio bar serves good griddle-cooked steaks & fish. Location a bit iffy at night; take a taxi.

✖ Bistro 176 [111 E3] Cara Suites, 176 Middle St, Cummingsburg; ☏ 226 1612; www.carahotels. com; ⏲ 06.30–22.00 daily. AC restaurant doesn't have the best atmosphere but the food is good & the full menu has something for everyone, including great steaks & seafood. Small patio allows for dining al fresco & attached bar has menu of appetisers & good sandwiches & burgers.

✖ Brown's Café & Poolside Bar & Grill [106 B3] Pegasus Guyana Hotel, Seawall Rd, Kingston; ☏ 225 2856; e reservations@ pegasushotelguyana.com; www.pegasushotelguyana.com; ⏲ 07.00– 23.00 daily. The café has a daily lunch buffet (12.00–15.00) & extensive Sunday brunch (11.00–15.00); or order from the à-la-carte menu of salads, sandwiches, burgers, fish & chips or grilled meats. Poolside is casual, al fresco dining with a range of appetisers, grilled meats, pasta, pizzas & a very non-traditional attempt at Indian dishes. Poolside also hosts special all-you-can-eat nights: pizza, BBQ & pasta.

✖ Caribbean Soul [107 H1] Grand Coastal Inn, 2 Area M, Le Ressouvenir, East Coast Demerara; ☏ 220 1091; e reservations@grandcoastal.com; www.grandcoastal.com;

⏲ 07.00–23.00 daily. A bit out of town, but food & ambience worth the drive. All meals have good mix of local & international dishes. Pancakes & eggs or saltfish & bakes; prawns or liver for appetisers; burgers, chicken wraps, curries, pastas, chilli, garlic prawns & more round out the menu. Pleasant poolside dining (AC available).

Duke Restaurant & Royal Verandah [106 B3] Roraima Duke Lodge, 94-95 Duke St, Kingston; ☏ 231 7220; e roraimadukelodge@ hotmail.com; www.roraimaairways.com. Popular new restaurant serves good range of local & international cuisine in beautiful colonial setting. Meals can also be taken poolside at the Duke Bar.

✖ Dutch Bottle Café [111 H5] 10 North Rd, Bourda; ☏ 231 6561; ⏲ 11.00–23.00 Mon–Sat, 17.00–23.00 Sun. Cosy restaurant & bar with a creative menu, large portions & free Wi-Fi. Good lunch specials & vegetarian dishes. Sometimes the service & food is excellent & other times it's frustratingly off the mark. Best in small groups; always good for a drink.

✖ Café Tepuy [107 F5] Roraima Inn, R8 Eping Av, Bel Air Pk; ☏ 225 9648; e ral@ roraimaairways.com; www.roraimaairways.com; ⏲ 06.00–23.00 daily. Good-quality meals served with fresh ingredients. Menu shows some creativity; excellent soups & seafood. Ambience lacks a bit; request to sit poolside.

✖ The Bottle Bar [111 F4] Cara Lodge, Quamina St, Alberttown; ☏ 225 5301; e caralodge@carahotels.com; www.carahotels.com; ⏲ 07.00–21.30 daily. Beautiful restaurant set at the bottom of an old colonial hotel is one of Georgetown's best. Creative menu changes often but features dishes including rack of lamb, pesto, pork chops & snapper served Creole style. Lunches have good soups, salads & sandwiches. Come when you're not in a hurry.

MID-RANGE $$$

✖ Bourbon Restaurant at Sidewalk Café & Jazz Club [111 E3] 176 Middle St,

Cummingsburg; ☏ 227 0152; www.ariantzesidewalk.com; ⏲ 11.30–21.30

Mon–Fri, 18.00–21.30 Sat–Sun. From the food to the furniture & the entertainment to the artwork, local culture is on display. Popular lunchtime buffet (⏰ *11.30–14.30 Mon–Fri*) has 12+ Creole dishes. Regular menu is typical array of sandwiches, salads, soups, seafood, meat & vegetarian dishes cooked with a local ingredients & flair. All best enjoyed al fresco.

✖ Brasil Churrascaria & Pizzaria [111 F6] 208 Alexander St, Lacytown; ✆ 231 1268; ⏰ 11.00–23.00 Mon–Sun. Unsophisticated outdoor Brazilian restaurant worth visiting for the impressive list of pizzas, but most come for the barbecued meats. For one reasonable price you can stuff yourself silly on the salad bar & grilled meats carved tableside. Potent *caipirinhas* are extra, but worth it.

✖ Buddy's Mei Tung Restaurant [107 H3] 137 Sheriff St, Kitty; ✆ 231 7260; ⏰ 11.00–midnight Mon–Thu, 11.00–03.00 Fri/Sat, 11.00–02.00 Sun. Expansive Chinese restaurant serving all the favourites; good dinner can be combined with dancing, game of pool or workout.

✖ New Palm Court [110 C3] 35 Main St; ✆ 227 0008; ⏰ 11.00–02.00 daily. Popular lunch & dinner spot is also a bar by night. Menu is wide mix of Guyanese & Creole favourites cooked with a Western influence. Look for the garish neon palm trees.

✖ New Thriving Chinese Restaurant [110 C3] 37 Main St, Georgetown; 227 5140;

CHEAP AND CHEERFUL $$

✖ Francine's Fish Shop & Bar [107 H4] 47 Sheriff & Garnett Sts, Campbellville; ✆ 227 2753; ⏰ 11.00–01.00 Mon–Thu, 11.00–03.00 Fri–Sun. Popular hangout for fried food & local beer.

✖ Garden City Café [110 C1] 45 High St, Kingston; ✆ 223 7312; ⏰ 07.30–16.00. Simple, but popular lunch spot serving a variety of pre-made Creole dishes, including fish, chicken, curries & rice dishes.

✖ German's Restaurant [110 B2] 8 New Market St, Cummingsburg; ✆ 227 0079; ⏰ 09.30–16.00 Mon–Sat, 09.30–15.00 Sun. Popular restaurant with locals who pile in during lunch for good & cheap soups & curries.

ROCK BOTTOM $

✖ House of Flavors [111 F6] 177 Charlotte St, Lacytown; ⏰ 06.00–21.00 Mon–Sat, 06.00–

⏰ 8.00–24.00 daily. After opening restaurants all over the city, New Thriving topped everyone with their new over-the-top restaurant that is part Vegas & part Chinese overindulgence. Good Chinese, Thai & Japanese food (the latter two are relative) served in numerous indoor and outdoor dining rooms and extravagant VIP rooms. Also popular on Sun when they serve dim sum. Come hungry.

✖ Oasis Café [110 D3] 125 Carmichael St, Cummingsburg; ✆ 226 9916; www.oasiscafegy.com; ⏰ 07.30–18.30 Mon–Wed, 07.30–19.30 Thu–Fri, 09.00–19.30 Sat, 10.00–18.00 Sun. Unofficial meeting place for Georgetown's expats, from embassy workers to volunteers, but also draws a good crowd of locals. Known for inventive entrées and delicious lunch buffet, sandwiches, bagels, croissants & range of desserts. Some of the best coffee drinks in town & free Wi-Fi.

✖ VIP Pizza Plus [107 F3] 164 Barr St, Kitty; ✆ 227 0781; ⏰ 08.00–22.00 daily. Decent pizza restaurant that delivers; also has variety of OK Guyanese dishes.

✖ The Hibiscus Restaurant & Lounge [110 C3] 91 Middle St, Cummingsburg; ✆ 231 5857; ⏰ 11.00–23.00 Sun–Thu, 11.00–midnight Fri/Sat. Popular bar has extensive menu of Guyanese favourites with gourmet touches. Nice outdoor seating & happy hour specials.

✖ JR Burgers [107 F3] 3 Sandy Babb St, Kitty; ✆ 226 6614; ⏰ 09.30–23.00 Mon–Sat, 16.00–23.00 Sun. Georgetown's place for local fast food burgers, fries & shakes.

✖ Taj [111 E2] 228 Camp St; ✆ 223 1630; ⏰ 11.00–21.00 Mon–Sat. While it's not authentic Indian food, it's the closest you'll get in Georgetown. The menu changes daily but features all the staples, including biryani rice, tandoori chicken, rogan josh, chapattis, naan, samosas & lassis. The basic dining room, with outdoor patio seating, is best for lunch or a simple dinner.

16.00 Sun. This Rastafarian *ital* (vegetarian) restaurant serves only one meal – a calabash

4

filled with rice & a secret mixture of vegetables, beans & the pickled condiment mango achar– in a space bedecked with fruit-covered tablecloths, red & white curtains, bright green walls, purple tiles, murals of boats & a TV muted by loud reggae music. It is simplicity amongst confused interior decorating, & as the lines of customers attest, it works wonderfully.

✗ **Shanta's** [111 F2] 225 Camp & New Market Sts, Cummingsburg; ✆ 226 4365; ⊘ 08.00–18.00 Mon–Sat. If the dining room sink doesn't clue you in to the fact that lunch can get messy, customers slopping up curries with roti (a fried flatbread) certainly will. For more than 50 years, Shanta's has been serving up the city's best curries; try *boulanger choka* (eggplant), pumpkin curry or boneless chicken curry paired with a homemade peanut punch.

ENTERTAINMENT AND NIGHTLIFE

Georgetown does not have the thriving entertainment and nightclub scene usually associated with most capital cities. For drinks and conversation, it's best to head to restaurants or bars in hotels; for a taste of the local scene, and perhaps a game of pool, visit a rum shop; and if you are looking to dance into the early hours there are several nightclubs playing a mix of thumping Caribbean soca music, East Indian chutney songs and popular music from the 1980s.

Sheriff Street [107 H1–7], the irrationally self-proclaimed Las Vegas of Guyana, is filled with restaurants and discos open throughout the night, although many are not considered safe for non-locals.

Many of Georgetown's hotels have bars that are great places to have a drink in a slightly quieter and more relaxing atmosphere. The **Mango Tree** at Cara Lodge [111 F4] (see page 105) has a beautiful patio area, shaded by, strangely enough, an old mango tree. Drinks and cutters are available. **Poolside** at Pegasus Hotel Guyana [106 B3] (see page 112) is a popular place for a drink with the international and local scene; there is also live music on Friday nights. Relative newcomer **Duke Lodge** [106 B3] (see page 108) and sister hotel **Roraima Residence Inn** [107 F5] (see page 108) also have poolside bars that are much smaller and more personal; there's also a rooftop area at the latter. The nondescript **King's Plaza Hotel** [110 C2] (*45 Main St, Cummingsburg;* ✆ *225 7775*) has a basic rooftop bar that is one of the best places in town for sunset. Of course **Princess Hotel Guyana** [106 A7] (see page 105), the we-have-it-all hotel, has nice poolside tables perfect for enjoying a drink plus live entertainment on weekends; drinks in the casino are free for gamblers.

☆ **Buddy's Nite Club** [107 H3] 137 Sheriff St, Kitty; ✆ 223 7658. A popular & safe pick, this ever-growing complex features a disco, pool hall, Chinese restaurant & exercise gym (not necessarily best enjoyed in that order).

☆ **Celina Atlantic Resort** [107 F1] Kitty Foreshore, Seawall Rd; Kitty; ✆ 231 6648. Resort it's not, but Celina's is the city's only waterfront restaurant & bar. Have a drink in an open-air benab as a reminder that Georgetown actually is on the ocean, & let the sunset & capuchin monkeys distract you from the sometimes slow & aloof service.

☆ **El Club Latino** [111 G7] 57 Hadfield & Lime Sts, Werk-en-Rust; ✆ 227 4600. Popular w/end hangout with large bar & separate dancefloor.

☆ **Jerries** [111 E3] 177 Waterloo St; ✆ 227 5701. Popular hangout for drinking beer, dancing & buying late-night snacks after other bars have closed. Jerrie's is open all night.

☆ **Mojo's** [110 C2] King's Plaza, 45 Main St, Cummingsburg; ✆ 225 6065. Recently refurbished & newly popular nightclub with indoor & outdoor bar.

☆ **New Palm Court** [110 C3] 35 Main St; ✆ 227 0008. Long-time Georgetown staple for nightlife recently received new building complete with giant, garish neon palm trees; outdoor patio has a range of entertainment options including karaoke, live music, DJs & happy hours. Normally has small cover charge.

☆ **Sidewalk Café & Jazz Club** [111 E3] 176 Middle St, Cummingsburg; ✆ 226 5363. Georgetown is short on entertainment options that branch out beyond pool tables & bumping soca music, so Sidewalk Café's live jazz, dinner theatres, karaoke & films draw an appreciative crowd. The fact that the local goods on display are artwork & furniture, rather than scantily clad bodies, doesn't hurt either.

☆ **The Edge** [110 C4] Hotel Tower, 74 & 75 Main St; Cummingsburg; ✆ 227 2011. Popular new nightclub in ageing hotel features regular DJs & less-regular live music.

☆ **Upscale Restaurant** [110 C6] 32–33 Regent & Hinck Sts, Lacytown; ✆ 225 4721. Intimate setting is home to Guyana's only spoken word & poetry nights; poetry is first Tue of every month & stand-up comedy is first & last Fri of every month. Drinks are served every night.

SHOPPING

The best souvenirs from Guyana are hand-crafted and range from woven baskets and wooden bowls to hammocks and jewellery (for more information on what to buy in Guyana, see *Shopping*, page 91), most of which can be found in stores and gift shops in Georgetown. If you have a day in Georgetown after your travels in Guyana, you may want to wait to shop, because if you're travelling to the interior, you will likely have opportunities to purchase items directly from the craftsmen, artisans or communities that produce them.

Georgetown's main shopping avenue is **Regent Street** [110–111, C5–H5]. Its shops all sell remarkably similar items, mainly in the line of electronics, household goods and clothes. On a busy Saturday morning, a walk down Regent Street can be an experience in itself, especially if you add in time at **Stabroek Market** [110 B7] (see page 121).

FOOD Whether or not you are staying at a place with kitchen facilities, food shopping at the local markets is an activity not to be missed in Georgetown. There is no need to buy, but if you see a piece of exotic fruit (of which there are many) that piques your interest, prices are cheap, and sampling is encouraged. In front of Stabroek Market on Water Street (see page 121), there is a daily gathering of vendors selling a wide variety of fruits and vegetables (among everything else from watches to underwear), with the busiest day being Saturday. Inside the market, there are more food vendors in addition to butchers displaying slabs of raw meat.

The best market for admiring and buying the wide array of fresh fruits and vegetables grown in Guyana is **Bourda Market** [111 G5]. See page 122 for details.

For seafood connoisseurs, and early risers, the place to visit is the daily fish market near Stabroek Market. Here fishmongers sell a wide range of Guyana's finest seafood, fresh from the boats on which they were caught. On the outskirts of the market, there are also people who will skin or peel your purchases for a nominal fee.

Roughly five miles from Georgetown along the east coast public road, is **Mon Repos Market**, the place for carnivores. The vendors crowding the main road display and sell fresh (sometimes killed and cleaned to order) meat including goat, cow, chicken and rabbit, among others. The market isn't for those with a queasy stomach but makes for an interesting morning outing. The market takes place every Saturday; go early for the freshest meats. Fruits, vegetables and other odds and ends are also sold here. The petrol stations south of Survival [107 F5] (see page 116) on Vlissengen Road double as mini grocery stores with longer opening hours, and are especially handy when the other markets are closed.

For those looking to stock up on more normal staples, there are several small grocery stores with good selections of cheaper local goods and more expensive items imported from the US. A few of the better options include:

Bonny's Market [111 G4] 310 Church St, Cummingsburg; ☎226 2076; ☼ 08.00–20.00 Mon–Sat, 08.00–14.00 Sun

Bounty Farm [107 G2] Pike & Alexander Sts, Kitty; ☎226 7154; ☼ 08.00–20.00 daily.

Bryden & Fernandes [107 H1] 58B Second Av, Subryanville; ☎225 5105; ☼ 08.30–16.30 Mon–Fri, 09.00–13.00 Sat. Expensive imported speciality items popular with the expat crowd.

Nigel's Supermarket & Pharmacy [111 H5] 45 Robb St, Bourda; ☎226 6200; ☼ 08.00–20.00 Mon–Sat, 08.00–13.30 Sun.

Survival [107 F5] 10 Vlissengen Rd, Newtown; ☎227 7574; ☼ 08.00–21.00 Mon–Sat, 08.00–14.00 Sun. This store lives up to its name by offering basic necessities &some of the cheapest beer, wine & spirits in town. This is a good place to stock up on El Dorado rum to carry home.

CRAFTS In addition to below, the median on **Main Street**, in front of Hotel Tower [110 C4], is also a popular spot for local artists to sell their crafts, mainly woodcarvings. **Pegasus Hotel** [116 B3], **Princess Hotel** and **Cara Lodge** [111 F4] also have small craft shops selling a variety of items but expect to pay higher prices.

Creations Craft [110 B4] 7A Water St, Cummingsburg; ☎226 0073; ☼ 08.30–16.30 Mon–Fri, 09.00–13.00 Sat. Large variety of locally made crafts.

Hibiscus Craft Plaza [110 C5] Cnr North Rd & Av of the Republic, Robbstown; ☼ 09.00–17.00 Mon–Fri, 09.00–15.00 Sat. Collection of small shops selling everything from woodcarvings to T-shirts & woven baskets to purple heart bowls. Also good place for collectors of Dutch bottles.

Liana Cane Interior [111 F6] 173 Charlotte St, Lacytown; ☎226 2009; ☼ 08.00–16.30 Mon–Fri, 08.00–12.00 Sat. Owner Jocelyn Dow is internationally acclaimed for her beautifully crafted cane furniture, which warrants a visit to the shop in itself. Jocelyn is also very involved in the arts in Guyana, from Georgetown to southern Wai Wai communities, & has a large selection of items on sale in the back room. Beware though, as you may find yourself coming for a balata animal & leaving with a new set of furniture. On special request, tours can also be arranged to the nearby factory where the furniture is handmade.

Margarita's Gift Shop [110 D3] 92 Middle St, Cummingsburg; ☎226 3966; ☼ 08.00–16.00 Mon–Fri, 09.00–13.00 Sat. Wooden crafts, Amerindian jewellery, arrows/bows & woven goods. Also have gold & silver jewellery & imported selection.

Ministry of Amerindian Affairs Craft Shop [111 F4] 236 Thomas St, Cummingsburg; ☎223 7392; ☼ 08.00–16.30 Mon–Thu, 08.00–15.30 Fri. Located on the main level of the Ministry building is this small shop that has the cheapest selection of Amerindian crafts in Georgetown. Almost everything you could want is available – woodcarvings, baskets, balata, jewellery, hammocks, paintings – but sometimes the selection is limited.

Persram's Wood, Crafts & Pens 24 Belvoir Ct, Bel Air; ☎226 1757; e kpersram@networksgy.com; ☼ 08.00–16.00 Mon–Fri, 08.00–13.00 Sat. Samples of 400+ species of wood in labelled boxes & boards, pens, wooden eggs, bowls, chess boards & plenty more. Persram's work is highest quality & sold in many area gift shops, but his showroom has the best selection. Accepts special orders.

The City Mall [111 E5] Cnr Regent & Camp Sts, Lacytown; ☎225 6644; ☼ 08.30–20.00 Mon–Sat, 10.00–16.00 Sun. Guyana's first shopping centre opened with a splash as it also houses the country's first & only escalator. The automatic stairs initially drew more shoppers than did the slightly overpriced shops selling typical wares: clothes, shoes, electronics, jewellery & the like.

HANDCRAFTED JEWELLERY

King's Jewellery World [110 D4] 141 Quamina St, Cummingsburg; ☎226 0704; www.kingsjewelleryworld.com; ☼ 09.00–17.00 Mon–Fri, 09.00–14.45 Sat

Steve's Jewellery [111 F4] 301 Church St, Cummingsburg; ☎223 9641; e SLN22k@

yahoo.com; www.stevesjewellery.com; ☼ Mon–Sat 09.00–17.30

Topaz [111 E5] 143 Crown & Oronoque Sts, Queenstown; ☎227 3968; e topaz@networksgy.com; www.theonlyjewellers.com; ☼ 09.00–16.30 Mon–Fri, 09.00–13.00 Sat

NEWSPAPERS AND BOOKSHOPS The local newspapers, *Stabroek News*, *Guyana Chronicle*, *Guyana Times* and *Kaieteur News*, can be purchased at grocery shops, filling stations and from street vendors. *GEM*, a magazine offering a good insight into local culture, can also be bought at grocery shops and bookshops. Georgetown is short on bookshops but there is one good choice if you are in need of a new novel or field guide. **Austin's Book Services** [111 E4] (*190 Church St, Cummingsburg;* 227 7395; ⏰ *08.30–16.30 Mon–Fri, 08.30–12.30 Sat*) has a good selection of novels, nature guides, history books, local authors and stationery supplies. International magazines can also be purchased at Nigel's supermarket and the filling stations on Vlissingen Road.

FILM AND CAMERA SUPPLIES When buying film in Guyana, check the expiry dates. The best places to purchase all camera supplies are:

Acme Photo [110 D6] 123–124 Regent & King Sts; 226 2344; ⏰ 08.00–17.00 Mon–Fri, 08.00–13.00 Sat

Pressy Enterprise [110 C5] 94 Regent St, Lacytown; 226 0814; ⏰ 07.45–19.30 Mon, 07.45–17.00 Tue–Fri, 07.45–15.00 Sat, 09.45–17.00 Sun

OTHER PRACTICALITIES

AIRLINES For a list of airlines with offices or representation in Georgetown see *Getting there*, page 102. If you are looking to book flights to the Caribbean, Suriname, Brazil or even further afield, contact the airline office or a travel agency from the list under *Tour operators*, page 56.

BANKS AND MONEYCHANGING General information on banks, cambios and the use of ATM and credit cards is given on page 81.

Keep in mind that when changing cash, cambios often have shorter lines and better rates than banks. Many of the better hotels will also change money for rates similar to, or slightly less than, banks. And while there are often moneychangers at the airport and in front of Stabroek Market [110 B7] who have good exchange rates, keep in mind that it may not be the safest place to flash your cash and many often involve scams. Use a taxi when changing large amounts of money.

Banks Banks don't always offer the best rates, and they often involve waiting in long queues, but they are the only places that will exchange travellers' cheques and give credit card cash advances. Try to go early and avoid Fridays if possible.

$ **Citizens Bank** [111 E6] 201 Camp St, Lacytown; 226 1705; ⏰ 08.00–14.00 Mon–Thu, 08.00–14.30 Fri. Accepts foreign currency & travellers' cheques.

$ **Demerara Bank Limited** [111 E6] 230 Camp St, Lacytown; 225 0610; ⏰ 08.00–14.00 Mon–Thu, 08.00–14.30 Fri. Exchanges foreign currency & travellers' cheques.

$ **Guyana Bank for Trade & Industry (GBTI)** [110 B5] 47–48 Water St, Robbstown; 226 8439; ⏰ 08.00–14.00 Mon–Thu, 08.00–14.30 Fri. Exchanges foreign currency & travellers' cheques & gives credit card cash advances.

$ **Republic Bank** [110 D2] 155–6 New Market St, Cummingsburg; 223 7938; ⏰ 08.00–14.00 Mon–Thu, 08.00–14.30 Fri. Foreign currency & travellers' cheques exchanged.

$ **Scotiabank** [110 D2] 104 Carmichael St, Cummingsburg; 225 9222; ⏰ 08.00–14.00 Mon–Thu, 08.00–14.30 Fri. Exchanges foreign currency, travellers' cheques, gives credit card cash advances & has an ATM accepting international cards.

Cambios While cambios will only buy and sell currency, the process is often faster and rates better than at banks.

Laparkan Financial Services [110 B5] Fogarty's Department Store, 347 Water St, Robbstown; ☎225 6870; ⏰ 08.30–18.00 Mon–Sat, 10.00–14.00 Sun

Trustco Cambio [110 C3] 623 Middle St, Cummingsburg; ☎226 9781; ⏰ 08.00–15.30 Mon–Thu, 08.00–14.30 Fri

COMMUNICATIONS

Post For general information on postal services and costs see page 93. Postal services in Guyana are generally reliable, although the process of sending anything more than a letter can be trying. Visit the main post office [110 C5] to send or receive packages and be sure to bring identification; don't be afraid to ask for guidance as the process involves visiting several different windows. In any case, expect queues, which many Guyanese blatantly ignore; stand firm.

✉**Main Post Office** [106 B6] Robb St, Robbstown; ☎226 3123; ⏰ 07.00–16.00 Mon–Fri, 07.00–11.00 Sat. Enter on North Rd, west of Av of the Republic.
✉**Bourda Post Office** [111 G6] Regent St, Bourda; ☎226 5122; ⏰ 07.00–16.00 Mon–Fri, 07.00–11.00 Sat.
✉**Kitty Post Office** [107 F3] 36 Pike & Alexander Sts; Kitty; ☎225 6790; ⏰ 07.00–16.00 Mon–Fri, 07.00–11.00 Sat

✉**DHL** [111 G4] 50 E Fifth St, Alberttown; ☎277 4742; ⏰ 08.00–17.00 Mon–Fri, 09.00–12.00 Sat
✉**Federal Express** [106 B3] 125 Barrack St, Kingston; ☎227 6976; ⏰ 08.00–16.30 Mon–Fri, 08.30–12.00 Sat
✉**United Parcel Service (UPS)** [111 E2] 210 Camp St, Cummingsburg; ☎227 8524; ⏰ 08.00–16.00 Mon–Fri, 08.00–12.00 Sat

Email and internet Surprisingly, many of Georgetown's hotels are now offering free Wi-Fi internet connections to their guests, and if you're not travelling with a laptop, most of the same hotels have a desktop computer for use. Hotels, however, do not offer public internet or email services.

There is also a handful of good internet cafés around Georgetown, but note that 'café' is used lightly as most have poor ambience and little more to offer than web access. Rates average US$1–2 per hour.

🖥**Central Netsurf** [110 C6] 7 Av of the Republic; ☎226 2401; ⏰ 08.00–20.00 Mon–Sat
🖥**Oasis Café** [110 D3] 125 Carmichael St, Cummingsburg; ☎226 9916; ⏰ 07.30–06.30 Mon–Wed, 07.30–19.30 Thu–Fri, 09.00–19.30 Sat, 10.00–18.00 Sun. Georgetown's cosiest café features free Wi-Fi, 2 desktop computers, baked goods, sandwiches, cooked lunch, salad bar, smoothies, ice cream & great coffee; computers available.
🖥**Netzone Internet Café & Business Centre** [110 B5] 42 Water St, Robbstown; ☎231 7101; ⏰ 08.00–17.00 Mon–Sat
🖥**Vizion Internet Café** [111 F5] 56 Robb St; ☎227 7716; ⏰ 08.00–22.00 Mon–Sat, 10.00–22.00 Sun

Telephone and fax The cheapest way to make international phone calls from Georgetown is at one of the many internet cafés (see page 119) where they cost US$0.10–0.50 per minute. If you don't want to deal with the slight delay, another option is to buy one of the phonecards sold throughout town at electronic shops, small markets, grocery stores, pharmacies and filling stations; expect to pay around US$0.50 per minute. Many hotels also offer international direct dialling but rates are high.

The phonecards also work for local calls and can be used at the phone booths scattered throughout the city, including several in front of the **Guyana Telephone & Telegraph Company**'s offices (*78 Church St, Cummingsburg & 79 Brickdam, Stabroek*). Local calls from hotels are often free or have a minor charge. The area code for all of Guyana is 592.

Fax services are available at several hotels and some office supply stores including **Executive Office Services** [107 E6] (*82 Albert St, Bourda;* ☎ *223 8176,* ⊕ *08.00–17.00 Mon–Fri, 08.00–12.00 Sat*) and **Kojac** [110 D4] (*140B Quamina St, Cummingsburg;* ☎ *225-2387,* ⊕ *08.00–16.30 Mon–Fri, 09.00–13.00 Sat*); international faxes cost US$2–4 per page.

Mobile phones Guyana now has two cellular phone service providers: GT&T Cellink and Digicel. Service reaches most areas along the coast, to Linden and around Lethem. Digicel, the newest provider to Guyana, brought some much-needed competition and service is rapidly expanding. Mobile phones with GSM capability should work in Guyana, but local SIM cards are available at cellular shops throughout the country.

HOSPITALS, DOCTORS AND PHARMACIES Medical attention at the **Georgetown Public Hospital** [111 F2] (*Thomas St, between Middle and Lamaha Sts, Cummingsburg;* ☎ *227 8232*) is free and there are 24-hour emergency services, but the meagre facilities within this antiquated structure (the oldest ward was built in 1838) lack sufficient supplies and staff.

For anything from an emergency to a general medical consultation, visitors are advised to go to one of the private clinics and hospitals favoured by expatriates and locals who can afford the nominal fees. Be prepared to wait at all locations.

No clinic or hospital in Guyana is up to Western standards, and if a serious medical emergency arises, visitors may want to consider being evacuated to a hospital in Port of Spain, Trinidad (flying time is 1–2 hours). Roraima Airways (see page 84) offers medical evacuation flights.

For a medical emergency requiring an ambulance, dial 913.

Hospitals and clinics

✚ **Davis Memorial Hospital** [107 H7] 121 Durban St, Durban Backlands; ☎ 227 2041. Full services offered including pharmacy.

✚ **Dr Balwant Singh's Hospital** [111 G4] 314 East St, Cummingsburg; ☎ 226 4279. Small private clinic is Guyana's most modern.

✚ **Georgetown Medical Centre/Prasad's Hospital** [111 F3] 258–259 Middle & Thomas Sts, Cummingsburg; ☎ 226 7210. Private clinic

with full range of services, including dentistry & pharmacy.

✚ **St Joseph's Mercy Hospital** [106 C3] 130–32 Parade St, Kingston; ☎ 227 2072. Private hospital with 24hr emergency services & pharmacy.

✚ **Woodland's Hospital** [110 D2] 110 Carmichael St, Cummingsburg; ☎ 226 2024. Popular & busy (read: long wait) private hospital.

Pharmacies Georgetown has plenty of pharmacies that are well stocked with quality medicines, drugs and essential items such as cosmetics and toiletries that have been imported. While most of the hospitals listed above have onsite pharmacies, they are often understocked.

✚ **Mike's Pharmacy** [107 E6] 147 Regent & Albert Sts, Bourda; ☎ 223 9700; ⊕ 08.30–17.00 Mon–Sat. Large stock of prescription & over the

counter drugs, cosmetics & toiletries; call for other branches.

Massage If you find yourself in need of a massage after a particularly exhausting trip into the interior, some of Georgetown's top hotels can arrange for a massage therapist. Also recommended:

Moksha Therapies [107 H3] 102 Campbell Av, Campbellville; ☎ 231 0691; e moksha_therapies@ hotmail.com; ⏰ 10.30–20.30 Mon–Fri, 10.30–17.00 Sat, Sun by appointment only. Offering aromatherapy, Swedish, sports recovery, Thai & other massages. Also reflexology & reiki. Appointments recommended. *US$10–30*.

POLICE In an emergency, dial ☎ 911. If you need to report a theft or crime for insurance reasons, call or visit Police Headquarters (*39 Brickdam, Stabroek;* ☎ *226 2487*) with low expectations, as chances of recovering stolen items are quite slim.

Police are also often seen patrolling the city while holding large weapons and they will provide assistance if flagged down for help, but keep in mind that, as is the case in most developing countries, corruption is common and police don't always act in your best interests.

SWIMMING A few of Georgetown's hotels allow non-guests to use their swimming pools for a daily rate. These include Pegasus Hotel Guyana [106 B3], Hotel Tower [110 C4] and Princess Hotel Guyana.

TOURIST INFORMATION For detailed information on the **Ministry of Tourism**, the **Tourism & Hospitality Association of Guyana** and the **Guyana Tourism Authority**, see page 60. For general tourist enquiries about Georgetown you may be better off asking at your hotel or any of the tour operators listed on page 56.

VISA EXTENSIONS Depending on the mood of the airport customs officer, passports of visitors not requiring a visa are stamped upon entry for 30 to 90 days; to stay longer visit the **Ministry of Home Affairs** [110 C7] (*60 Brickdam, Stabroek;* ☎ *226 2445;* ⏰ *08.00–16.00 Mon–Thu, 08.00–15.30 Fri*).

WHAT TO SEE AND DO

Georgetown's highlights can be seen in two days of walking and exploring. Many of the local tour operators (see *Tour operators*, pages 56) offer Georgetown city tours that are a good way of seeing the major sites while getting good background information. Georgetown's streets pose some normal risks, but mainly at night; greatly minimise threats by walking during daylight hours, taking taxis at night and not carrying valuables or flashing expensive cameras.

MUSEUMS AND GALLERIES
National Museum [110 C5] (*North Rd & Hincks St;* ☎ *225 7191;* ⏰ *09.00–17.00 Mon–Fri, 09.00–12.00 Sat; free*) This eclectic museum is a bit dated but worth visiting. Collection contains oddities such as a Rolls-Royce gifted to the government, an opium pipe from Singapore and a frightening life-sized model of a pork-knocker (miner). The large assortment of native fauna on display appear to have been stuffed when King George IV was alive, which would explain their mangy state. The exception is a new model of a giant sloth based on fossils found in Guyana.

Walter Roth Museum of Anthropology [110 C3] (*61 Main St;* ☎ *225 8486;* ⏰ *08.00–16.30 Mon–Thu, 08.00–15.30 Fri; free*) The museum, named after an

Englishman who pioneered research of Amerindian life and folklore in British Guiana, has an impressive collection of artefacts documenting Guyana's nine Amerindian tribes. It's housed in a beautiful example of a colonial Georgetown house; built in the 1890s, the wooden building elegantly showcases timber columns and moulding, and the signature Demerara shutters (louvred wooden shutters that rest on fretted window boxes when closed).

Castellani House [107 F6] (*Cnr Vlissengen Rd & Homestretch Av;* ✎ *225 0579;* ⊕ *10.00–17.00 Mon–Fri, 14.00–18.00 Sat; free*) Designed by Cesar Castellani and completed in 1877, it was originally the home of Guyana's director of agriculture. It was later the home of former Guyana president Forbes Burnham. In 1993 it officially became the **National Art Gallery**. It also hosts the National Art Collection, rotating exhibits of local artists and cultural activities.

Roy Geddes Steel Pan Museum [107 F7] (*190 Roxanne Burnham Gdns, South Ruimveldt;* ✎ *226 9844;* ⊕ *10.00–17.00 daily; free*) Having been playing for more than 50 years, Roy Geddes could be called a pioneer of steel pan music. Roy is a player, teacher and creator of steel pans and he's opened a museum to share his passion. In the gardens around his house visitors learn about the history of steel pan (dating back only to the 1940s) through photographs, recorded and written music, implements used to craft steel drums into the instruments and demonstrations of how to play steel pan, all from a living legend in the field.

Museum of African Heritage [107 F5] (*13 Barima Av, Bel Air Pk;* ✎ *226 5519;* ⊕ *08.00–16.30 Mon–Thu, 08.30–15.30 Fri; free*) Small but good museum includes African art, musical instruments, games and clothing, all with instructive background information on meaning and importance.

CHURCHES
St George's Cathedral [110 D5] (*North Rd at Carmichael St;* ✎ *226 5067; www. stgeorges.org.gy;* ⊕ *08.30–17.00 daily; free*) Often regarded as Georgetown's gem is this towering church completed in 1894. As Georgetown expanded so did St George's. Three previous cathedrals were outgrown, so when designing the fourth St George's, size mattered – at 143ft, it's one of the world's tallest free-standing wooden buildings. The Gothic church is constructed almost entirely with local materials; the cool and breezy interior displays Guyana's many hardwoods and is a welcome reprive from the nearby market's pandemonium. Take some time to read the historical tablets and memorials adorning the walls as they provide interesting insights into Guyana's early settlers and the hardships they endured.

Two more examples of Gothic wooden architecture are found at **St Andrew's Kirk** (*cnr Ave of the Republic & Brickdam*) which, having been open for worship since 1818, is the oldest church in Georgetown; and **Christ Church** (*Waterloo St, between New Market & Middle*), which opened its doors in 1843 to appease those Anglicans who felt services at St George's Cathedral were too ritualistic.

MARKETS
Stabroek Market [110 B7] (*Water St, between Croal St & Brickdam*) With a bustling shopping Mecca drawing life in, and a chaotic bus park pumping it out, this is the heartbeat of Georgetown. In 1881, the corrugated-iron building and signature four-faced clock covered an open-air market dating to 1792. Inside the market, the scene is fairly typical: merchants peddle everything from leather goods

and gold to pirated DVDs, butchered meat and songbirds to knock-off designer clothes; outside a mass of people moves without direction through even more vendors while minibuses part the sea with their proclamations ('I'm On My Way Up', 'I've Been Touched'). While the scene at Stabroek can be a bit chaotic (especially on Saturday, which is the main market day) it should certainly be experienced, for people-watching if nothing else. It is advised however, that you don't carry any valuables and stay alert.

Bourda Market [111 G5] (*North Rd & Robb St, between Orange Walk & Alexander St*) The best market for admiring and buying the wide array of fresh fruits and vegetables grown in Guyana is Bourda Market, a daily, permanent market dating back to 1880. While the market is generally safe, it's best to enter from North Rd and peruse only the first few aisles instead of diving too far into the depths.

On Wednesday afternoon, and all day Thursday and Saturday, a recommended farmers' market is set up in the wide median (just east of the permanent shops in the median which sell everything from tailor-made clothes to cane furniture). Not only is this a good time to admire the tropical fruits, it also provides for good people-watching as many locals crowd the stalls to do their weekly shopping.

PARKS AND GARDENS
Promenade Gardens [110 D3] (*Entrance on Middle St, between Carmichael St & Waterloo St*) Promenade Gardens are what remain of the original Parade Grounds, which were used in the 19th century for militia drills and parades. A section of the old Parade Grounds has been renamed **Independence Park**; this was the site of the public execution of slaves involved in the 1823 slave uprising on the east coast of Demerara (see page 134). In 1851 it was decided to dedicate a portion of the land to be used as a public garden. While the gardens once claimed the widest collection of wild orchids in the Caribbean, in recent years they could only be described as dilapidated and seemed to display merely their potential. But thanks to rehabilitation in 2006, the area is once more reminiscent of the days when Georgetown was known as the 'Garden City'. The gardens have several fountains, a bandstand erected in 1897 and a bronze statue of Mahatma Gandhi.

National Park [106–7 D3–E3] (*Bordered by Carifesta Av to the north and Thomas Rd to the south; enter on Thomas Rd*) This 57-acre city park was originally the site of a sugar estate and later a golf course. In 1965 it became Queen Elizabeth Park, to honour Her Majesty during her visit to Guyana that year. It was renamed on 25 May 1966 after the British flag was lowered for the last time and the Guyana flag was raised for the first time in the park. The fields are often filled with weekend picnickers, football, cricket and rugby matches, and the mile-long track circling the park's edge is a good place for running or walking (there are manatees in the ponds on the northern side of the park). There is also a stadium inside the park which hosts special events and celebrations such as Emancipation Day and the judging of Mash floats.

Botanical Gardens & Zoological Park [107 F6–H6] (*Regent St & Vlissengen Rd;* ✎ *225 9142; www.guyanazoo.org.gy;* ⊕ *gardens: dawn–dusk; zoo: 07.30–17.30 daily; gardens free, zoo costs adult/child US$0.50/0.25*) The rundown zoo needs more funding, and if you've just been to see many of the zoo's species in the interior of Guyana, it can be downright depressing. But if you missed the jaguar, harpy or sloth they are here in substandard conditions.

The Botanical Gardens are pleasant, with the biggest draw being the manatees in the pond near the zoo entrance and the birds that are everywhere. The Seven Ponds Monument, Mausoleum and the much-photographed Kissing Bridge are also notable sites.

Perhaps the best way to see the gardens, and safest way to explore the furthest reaches, is on a birdwatching tour offered by the knowledgeable guides at Guyana Feather Friends (see page 59). The best time to go is at dawn or dusk, and in two or three hours you're likely to see roughly 50 of Georgetown's 200-plus species of birds.

Also located near the entrance to the zoo is the **Guyana Marine Turtle Conservation Society Eco-Museum**, which opens on request (ask at zoo ticket office). It houses a collection of artefacts related to marine turtle conservation and protections and also provides background information on establishing Shell Beach as a protected area. There is also a collection of souvenirs on sale.

Sea wall Thanks to constant sea breezes, the sea wall, the long dyke protecting Georgetown from the Atlantic's high tide, is a popular spot for exercising, kite flying or people-watching – especially on festive Sunday evenings. At 280 miles, the seawall runs along the coast of much of Guyana and all of Georgetown, but there are some lonely stretches in the city that are unsafe. It's best to stay east of Celina Atlantic Resort and west of where the wide platform of the sea wall ends (a distance of roughly three miles) or near Pegasus Hotel. Going on the sea wall at night is not recommended except along the crowded stretches on Sundays when it becomes the place to be in Georgetown.

On the western end is the **Bandstand** [106 C2], which was built in 1903 as a memorial to Queen Victoria and the remnants of the **Round House**, used to guard the entry to Port Georgetown in the 19th century.

HISTORICAL BUILDINGS AND MONUMENTS
Parliament Building [110 C7] (*Cnr High St & Brickdam*) This building designed by Joseph Hadfield was completed in 1834 and officially handed over to the court of policy on 5 August, just days after the abolition of slavery. Guyana's current parliament still meets under the carved dome.

The High Court [110 D6] (*Cnr Charlotte & King Sts*) This building, which dates to 1887, beautifully mixes Gothic and Tudor architecture. It was originally called Victoria Law Court and is still stood guard by a marble statue of Queen Victoria that was unveiled on the site in 1894. During a time of anti-imperial attitudes in Guyana the statue was vandalised with a charge of dynamite. It was repaired in England and returned to Guyana but then spent years tucked into a corner of the Botanical Gardens until a past mayor restored the queen to her original post.

City Hall [110 C6] (*Cnr Regent St & Av of the Republic*) This neo-Gothic wooden building completed in 1889 still houses the city's administrative offices. One of Georgetown's most distinguished architects of the time, Father Ignatius Scoles, designed this impressive structure, which is still one of the city's most striking displays of colonial wooden architecture.

The Red House [106 B3] (*High St, between Barrack & Young Sts*) This recently refurbished colonial-style building gains its name from the red wallaba shingles that cover the house. It has held various government officials since it was built in the 19th century and now houses the Cheddi Jagan Research Centre.

National Library [110 C4] (*76–7 Church & Main Sts, Cummingsburg;* 226 2690; ☺ *08.30–17.15 Mon–Fri, 09.00–14.45 Sat*) The ageing books of Georgetown's public library can be found in this building that was paid for by Andrew Carnegie and opened in 1909. It's worth a look around inside for the wooden architecture and medley of old books.

State House and Prime Minister's Residence While you can see them only from their gates, the houses of Guyana's president and prime minister are worth admiring. **State House** [110 C2] (*Main St, between Middle & New Market Sts*) was built in 1858 and used to be the residence of the governor general of British Guiana. In 1970 Guyana's first president, Arthur Chung, moved in and it is still used as the residence of the president of Guyana. The **Prime Minister's Residence** [110 C1] (*Main St, between Lamaha & New Market Sts*) however is often considered to be the superior home. This Italian-influenced wooden home was built in the late 19th century for Mr Sandbach, the director of Booker Bros, a shipping firm. Legend has it that he used to sit in the top of the square cupola to watch the ships come into Georgetown's port and the captains, aware of who was watching from the sidelines, always made sure the port side of their boats were freshly painted.

Umana Yana [106 B3] (*High St at Battery Rd*) Wai Wai for 'Meeting place of the people', this 55ft-tall thatched roof hut, or *benab*, was built by the Wai Wai Amerindians in 1972 to host a meeting of the Non-Aligned Movement of Third World Nations. Some 60 Wai Wai citizens came to Georgetown to construct the *benab* (see page 89 for explanation of this term) using mostly traditional materials and methods. Today, the venue is used for various functions ranging from art shows to Amerindian heritage festivals.

Also in the grounds of Umana Yana is the **African Liberation Monument**, a sculpture consisting of five greenheart poles commemorating African freedom fighters. It was constructed for the 1974 meeting of the United Nations Commission.

The 1763 Monument [107 F7] (*Brickdam & Vlissingen Rd*) Located in the Square of the Revolution, this 15ft-high statue of an African slave, Cuffy, commemorates the efforts he made in leading the unsuccessful 1763 slave rebellion in Berbice (see page 137). It was unveiled in 1976 by then president Burnham to celebrate Guyana's tenth anniversary of independence.

The Lighthouse [106 B3] (*Water St*) Built very near the mouth of the Demerara River, this stone lighthouse was erected in 1830, replacing the original wooden structure that was constructed in 1817 by the Dutch. It is no longer in use.

SPORT
Georgetown Cricket Club (GCC) [107 E6] (*221 New Garden St, Bourda;* ✆ 226 3404) These historic grounds were opened on the site in 1865, and are commonly referred to as Bourda Cricket Ground. Guyana's most popular sports arena, GCC is the only international cricket club beneath sea level and the oldest cricket ground in the Caribbean. While all future matches will be played at the newly built cricket ground in Providence, Bourda is still likely to host some Test matches and serves as a holy shrine for serious cricket fans who want to see the old home of cricket heroes such as Clive Lloyd and Lance Gibbs.

Guyana National Stadium at Providence [106 A7] (*Providence, East Bank Demerara;* ✆ 265 7083) Guyana's newest cricket stadium was completed in 2007, just in time for the Super Eight matches that were hosted here during the ICC World Cup. This very modern facility came with a US$25 million price tag and doesn't have the history of Bourda (yet) but within its massive structure there is space for some 15,000 spectators, six pitches and four practice nets and warm-up pitches. This is where all international cricket games will be played and die-hard fans can arrange tours by calling the stadium.

Lusignan Golf Club [107 H1] (*Lusignan, East Coast Demerara;* ✆ 220 5660; ☉ *08.00–20.00 Mon–Fri, 08.00–23.00 Sat–Sun; golfing ends at dusk; US$10*) This private nine-hole golf course is located about 15 minutes outside of Georgetown. Visitors are welcome and clubs are available for rent. Clubhouse is on site.

DISTILLERIES AND BREWERIES
Demerara Distillers Limited (DDL) [106 A7] (*Plantation Diamond, East Bank Demerara;* ✆ 265 5019; e *export@demrum.com/info@theeldoradorum.com; www.*

theeldoradorum.com; ⊕ *tours 09.00 & 13.00 Mon, Wed & Fri, or by appointment; US$15)* Learn of Guyana's 300-year-old rum tradition that has produced rums voted to be best in the world. Hour-long tours begin at the Diamond Distillery, which has the capacity to produce 26 million litres of pure alcohol annually. Here visitors are shown the stills, including the continuous still, wooden pot still and wooden coffey still, the last operating still of its kind in the world. Tours also include the warehouse, where some 65,000 barrels of rum are stored every year, and some sit for 25 years. At the Heritage Centre there is a photographic exhibition, documentaries, display of old machinery and parts, and models of distilleries past and present. There's also a gift shop and each tour includes a free bottle of five-year-old rum; connoisseurs will want to leave with a bottle of the 12- or 15-year-old rum.

Banks DIH [106 A7] (*Thirst Pk;* ✆ *226 2491;* e *banks@banksdih.com; www. banksdih.com;* ⊕ *tours 13.00 Mon–Thu, or by appointment; free admission*) Hour-long tours show visitors the bottling plant, and an inside look at the making of a range of products, including baked goods, bottled water, beer and rum. The latter two are the reason to visit, but the DDL tour provides much more historical context.

5

Around Georgetown

What follows below are details of locations that can be reached from Georgetown within an hour or two of travel. They range from full-fledged nature resorts and creekside *benabs* to a history museum; all are good day-trip options, and some make for pleasant overnight stays as well. As is the case throughout Guyana, access varies, meaning that some trips can be easily organised on your own while others are best done with the use of a local tour operator.

SOUTH OF GEORGETOWN

SOESDYKE–LINDEN HIGHWAY The easy access granted by this 45-mile (72km) stretch of road has led to a series of resorts being developed along the banks of creeks in the area. The resorts all vary in their offerings and level of development. Some are well maintained while others have apparently been sinking into a state of disrepair for years. Heading to the creek is a popular weekend and holiday activity for locals; if you want to avoid crowds visit on a weekday. The roadside resorts seem to come and go with regularity and most offer the same thing: *benabs* for shade and a black water creek for swimming. The resorts listed below are more established.

Getting there and away All locations on the Soesdyke–Linden Highway are within an hour of Georgetown and less than 30 minutes from Linden. The paved highway makes access easy by vehicle. Without your own, hire a taxi (around US$20 from Georgetown) or take any Linden-bound bus or minibus 43 from Stabroek Market and have the driver drop you off. The resorts that are not built along the highway have signs posted along the access road and drivers should be familiar with them as well. They are listed below heading from north to south (towards Linden) along the highway.

Marudi Creek Resort (*Soesdyke–Linden Highway;* ✆ *624 6011;* e *marudicreek@ yahoo.com;* ⏰ *08.00–17.00 Mon–Fri, 08.00–18.00 Sat–Sun; adult/child US$2.50/1.25*) This small resort is one of the few in the area created with environmental concerns in mind and the 'no music allowed' policy means that you can actually hear the sounds of nature that surround you. This rustic resort has some 20 small *benabs* scattered throughout the site, each with a table, benches and chairs perfect for picnicking (food and beverages are also available at the basic bar). The black water creek is surrounded by white sand that leads into the dense forest on the edge of the resort. Marudi Creek Resort is located one mile off the main highway so walking in is possible if you take a bus.

Splashmin's Fun Park & Resort (*Madewini Creek, Soesdyke–Linden Highway;* ✆ *223 7301;* e *info@splashmins.com; www.splashmins.com;* ⏰ *09.00–17.00 daily;*

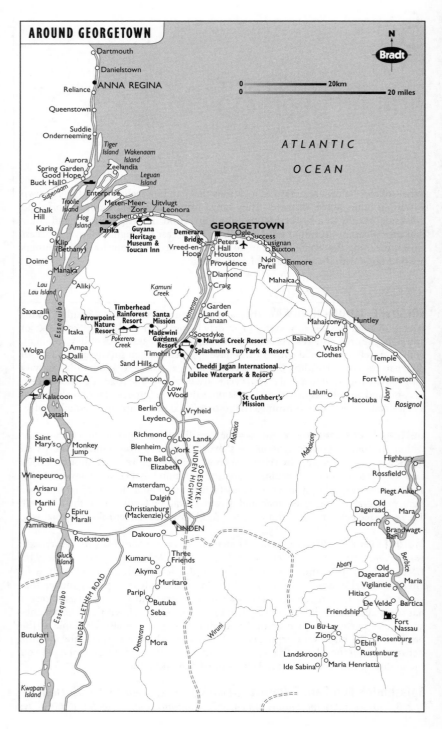

AROUND GEORGETOWN

N

Bradt

Dartmouth

Danielstown

Reliance ANNA REGINA

Queenstown

Suddie
Onderneeming

Tiger
Island   Wakenaam
Island

Aurora   Zeelandia
Spring Garden
Good Hope   Leguan
Buck Hall   Island

Supenaam

Enterprise

Troolie   Meten-Meer-   Uitvlugt
Chalk   Island   Zorg   Leonora
Hill   Tuschen

Karia   Hog
Island

Klip   Parika   Guyana   Demerara   GEORGETOWN
(Bethany)   Heritage   Bridge   Ogle   Success
                             Museum &   Vreed-en-   Peters   Lusignan
Doime   Toucan Inn   Hoop   Hall   Buxton
                                                          Houston   Non
Manaka   Providence   Pareil   Enmore

Aliki   Diamond
Lau   Craig   Mahaica
Lau Island
                            Kamuni
Saxacalli   Creek

Itaka   Arrowpoint   Timberhead   Santa   Garden   Mahaicony   Huntley
                Nature   Rainforest   Mission   Land of
Wolga   Resort   Resort   Canaan   Perth
                Ampa   Soesdyke   Baliabo
                Dalli   Pokerero   Madewini   Marudi Creek Resort   Wash
                             Creek   Gardens   Clothes
                                          Resort   Splashmin's Fun Park & Resort
                Sand Hills   Timehri   Temple
                                                         Cheddi Jagan International
BARTICA   Dunoon   Jubilee Waterpark & Resort   Fort Wellington

Kalacoon   Low   Abary
                Wood   St Cuthbert's   Laluni
Agatash   Berlin   Mission   Macouba   Rosignol
                Leyden   Vryheid
Saint   Richmond   Loo Lands
Mary's   Blenheim   York
Monkey   The Bell
Hipaia   Jump   Elizabeth   Highbury

Winepeuro   Amsterdam   Rossfield

Arisaru   Dalgin   Piegt Anker

Marihi   Epiru   Christianburg   Old
                Marali   (Mackenzie)   Dageraad   Mara
Taminada   Hoorn   Brandwagt-
                Rockstone   Dakouro   LINDEN   Bari
Gluck
Island   Kumaru   Three
                                          Friends   Abary   Old
Butukari   Akyma   Dageraad
                                          Muritaro   Vigilantie Maria
                             Paripi   Hitia
                                          Butuba   De Velde   Bartica
                             Seba   Friendship
                                                         Du Bu Lay   Fort
Kwapani   Mora   Zion   Nassau
Island   Rosenburg
                                                         Ebini   Rustenburg
                                          Landskroon
                                          Ide Sabina   Maria Henriatta

ATLANTIC

OCEAN

0   20km
0   20 miles

Essequibo

Demerara

Mahaica

Mahaicony

Berbice

Wiruni

Demerara

Essequibo

LINDEN–LETHEM ROAD

SOESDYKE–LINDEN HIGHWAY

adult/child US$3/2) Located 45 minutes from Georgetown, Splashmin's is a popular weekend destination for locals seeking to capture a piece of the Caribbean that eludes Guyana's shores: white sand beaches and water fit for swimming. The resort has developed more than 60 acres of land that offers different slices of Guyana in a clean, contained and well-manicured environment. With a lot of dredging and clearing, Splashmin's took control of nature and was able to form a lake out of the normally narrow Madewini Creek. The white sand beach stretches for nearly a mile and the lake is divided into sections for swimming, lounging in a floating chair (US$1/hour), kayaking (US$6–10/hour), pedal boating (US$12–20/hour) or jet skiing (US$65/hour).

Other options at Splashmin's include a tour of their farm where tropical fruits and vegetables are grown (US$6/6 persons); some people choose to skip the sometimes chaotic beach scene and spend an afternoon picnicking in the shade of the farm's palm trees. There is also a 45-minute creek and savanna tour (US$5/person) that offers a glimpse of the untamed side of the resort.

For the more active there is basketball, volleyball and cricket. A bar, snack shop and full restaurant are on site, but there are also plenty of small thatched *benabs* with tables and benches for picnicking.

For those seeking more than a day trip, on-site lodging is available in two forms. The new hotel (24 rooms; **$$$**) has clean rooms with new furnishings. All are en suite and have air conditioning; televisions and telephones were purposely left out. Camping is also an option on the farm (**$**) and you can rent hammocks, grills, tents and fishing rods (US$1–5).

Splashmin's know their market, which is loud, boisterous and fond of alcohol, and hosts almost monthly special events ranging from water-ski shows to cricket matches to body-building competitions. If you're seeking relaxation and a bit of quiet, visit on a weekday; during weekends (Sundays are busier than Saturdays) and special events, the rumbling speedboats and whining jet skis compete with the blaring music and screaming kids.

St Cuthbert's Mission Activities at this small Amerindian village are limited to swimming and shopping, which make for a lovely way to pass an afternoon. While swimming in the Mahaica River you're likely to be sharing it with families bathing and doing their laundry and daredevil kids jumping from overhanging branches. The area also has a healthy population of hoatzin, Guyana's strange national bird.

The shopping is undertaken at the village craft shop that sells a good selection of the exceptional crafts produced here. On sale are items finely woven from local liana and grasses – baskets, place settings, jewellery and the like – and beautiful wooden carvings, especially those of resident woodcarver Oswald Hussein. When buying from the village, there's also a good chance that you'll get to speak to the person who made your purchased goods.

St Cuthbert's is located roughly ten miles from the highway and as the access road can be in poor condition, especially in the rainy season, a 4x4 is often necessary. If you are coming on your own be sure to see the Captain or village council member upon arrival to pay the village fee (US$5/person). Many local travel agencies can also arrange special day trips to St Cuthbert's on request.

DEMERARA: WEST BANK

Because of their proximity to Georgetown, the two resorts and Amerindian community in this section are popular for both day trips and short overnight stays.

5

Being close to the airport, a stop at one of the resorts makes for a good introduction to the rivers, jungles and savannas of Guyana, or a comfortable way to bid farewell.

Arrowpoint and Timberhead resorts are both located within the Amerindian reserve of Santa; the main village is called Santa Mission. While they are located close to Georgetown, they are in an isolated area where all transportation is via the waterways. Although it's always possible in Guyana to hire a boat along the docks, the best way to get to the resorts or the village is on an organised tour or overnight stay.

River trips begin on the Demerara River, not far from the airport. From here you cross over the river and begin heading up Kamuni Creek, which is a beautiful black water creek covered over in low-hanging jungle foliage. After a short ride through the jungle, the surroundings open up into wide savanna lands and you come first to the Amerindian community of Santa Mission, then to Timberhead Rainforest Resort and finally to Arrowpoint Nature Resort. From the docks on the Demerara River the trip takes roughly 45 minutes; from Georgetown, the entire trip takes about 90 minutes.

The area is rich in wildlife and birds, including several monkey species, macaws, parrots, toucans and hummingbirds.

ARROWPOINT NATURE RESORT (*Roraima Airways, Lot R8 Eping Av, Bel Air Pk;* \ *225 9650;* e *ral@roraimaairways.com; www.roraimaairways.com*) Located within the Santa Mission and on the banks of the Kamuni Creek, this eco-friendly nature resort has plenty of activity options and a tightly structured schedule to make sure guests can sample them all. The resort itself, with four self-contained cabins and one large central building, is designed and operated as an expression of Amerindian culture. While the mountain biking, surf biking and pedal boating may not be reflections of Amerindian culture, the cassava bread making, *wabani* expedition, canoeing, spear fishing and jungle hikes are more reflective of their traditional lifestyle.

Arrowpoint, which is named after the many arrow trees in the area that are used by Amerindians in the construction of arrows, is a good mixture of the traditional and the modern, of the relaxing and the scheduled. Close to Georgetown, it's a good location for a day or one-night trip to enjoy a bit of nature without leaving many of the creature comforts behind.

All day trips to Arrowpoint are inclusive of all road and river transportation from Georgetown, lunch, activities and guides; overnight rates include all meals and limited local bar; alcoholic drinks and some soft drinks are extra. The all-inclusive packages, and plethora of activities offered by the resort, unfortunately make Arrowpoint one of Guyana's more expensive resorts. Discounts are often offered for larger groups.

Getting there While the resort isn't too far from Georgetown, it's in an area that isn't easily accessed. If you are going for either a day trip (US$95p/person, minimum 8) or to spend the night, all transportation is included in the package trips, which can be organised through Roraima Airways.

Arrowpoint is also often combined with day trips to Kaieteur Falls. Contact local tour operators for more information.

Where to stay (*FB* $$$$$) Accommodation is in one of ten self-contained rooms set inside cabins that were constructed by local Amerindian craftsmen, with wood from the manicole palms for walls and troolie leaves for the roof. The rooms are fully furnished with comfortable beds and mosquito nets, locally crafted furniture and tasteful decorations and fixtures and each cabin has a balcony.

With a generator producing electricity and perks such as Wi-Fi, it's a nature resort that doesn't require too much roughing it. The main building is where meals are served, drinks are poured, television is watched (more modern perks) and football is played. On an overnight stay, dinners are often served outside next to a bonfire.

What to see and do From birdwatching and mountain biking to fishing and touring Santa Mission, Arrowpoint has a long list of activities available to visitors and a very structured schedule on day and overnight trips in an attempt to fit it all in. Arrowpoint is definitely not a resort where visitors are normally left to their own devices (at least for periods of more than an hour or so), but if you really insist on just sitting in a hammock and reading, during the scheduled jungle outing, it is allowed.

Most visits begin with a *wabani* jungle expedition. Wabani is an Amerindian word for a platform set up in a tree and used for hunting. Bait is placed below, and when an animal arrives it is shot with an arrow from above. The expedition is said to retrace the path of an Amerindian hunter through the forest, up a tree and out to the creek, where you then get in a canoe and paddle back to the resort. Essentially, it's a glorified jungle walk and creek paddle.

There's always some scheduled time for swimming from the white sand beach along the creek and participating in water activities, including kayaking, canoeing, pedal boating, surf biking. Volleyball, cricket and dominoes are also offered.

One of Arrowpoint's greatest highlights is the extensive series of well-marked and well-groomed trails that can be used for hiking or mountain biking. This is the only resort in Guyana that has mountain bikes available and a series of sandy trails, from novice to experienced, to use them on. The trails can also be used for extended hikes that can take as long as four hours.

With more than 200 species of birds in the area, Arrowpoint is also a good spot for birdwatching. It has long been a destination resort for tickers looking to mark off the crimson topaz hummingbird, of which a healthy population is found here.

Spear fishing, cassava bread making demonstrations, night-time walks and boat trips in search of nocturnal animals and tours of Santa Mission round out the exhausting list of activities.

TIMBERHEAD RAINFOREST RESORT (*Office: 810 Providence, East Bank Demerara;* \ *233 5108;* e *timberhead@solutions2000.net;* *www.timberheadguyana.com*) Timberhead is another small resort located on the banks of Kamuni Creek in the Amerindian reserve of Santa Mission. While Timberhead still has plenty to do, it is more intimate than Arrowpoint, a bit more attuned with nature. With a beautiful jungle backdrop on the edge of the savanna, the lodges mesh well with the trees, life is less structured, and there are no televisions or internet to worry about.

The down side of Timberhead is that they aren't very proactive about promoting the resort and the low number of visitors means that operation costs push prices up. However for those willing to pay, it's a relaxing and beautiful getaway for a day trip.

Day trips (US$90; minimum 4 persons) to Timberhead include road and river transportation, lunch, activities and guides. The resort used to offer overnight stays (**$$$$$**, minimum 3 persons) including the above plus accommodation, all meals and limited bar, but at the time of writing they discontinued this part of their business. Management was planning on refurbishing the resort (including the construction of new cabins) and reopening for regular business by 2012. Contact the resort for updates.

Local, hearty meals are served in the main house, which also has a bar.

Getting there Transportation from Georgetown is included in all day trips and overnight stays. The trip to the resort is outlined at the beginning of this section.

What to see and do Timberhead also has a range of activities to choose from, and when they are done it's at a bit more of the visitor's leisure. Miles of trails run through the jungle for walking, canoes are available to explore the numerous creeks in the area, birdwatching here is also excellent, the beach is good for swimming and fishing and at night nocturnal animal spotting is done with the canoes. Visits to Santa Mission are also part of every visit.

SANTA MISSION Santa Mission is a small Amerindian village with mainly Arawak and Carib inhabitants set in the sandy savannas on the Kamuni Creek. The village is a popular day trip destination from Georgetown, and with the nearby resorts of Arrowpoint and Timberhead, villagers have grown used to visitors coming for a glimpse of their traditional lifestyles.

Visitors get a tour of the village, often with stops to see a stage of cassava processing and a visit to the community church. Besides using a crashed aircraft frame as a bell-tower, this otherwise nondescript church's claim to fame is that Queen Elizabeth II and Prince Phillip once attended a service here.

Tours always end at the community's large craft shop, one of the finest in Guyana. Santa Mission is famed for its woven handicrafts, and in the shop, if there is something that can be created by weaving local forest products, you're likely to find it. Other indigenous crafts are also available.

Day trips to the area usually include time for a jungle hike or swim in the black water creek.

Getting there and away Visiting Santa Mission is available through a day trip from Georgetown (contact any local tour operator, see page 58) or as part of a trip to Arrowpoint or Timberhead resorts. All trips include road and river transportation from Georgetown. For details on the roughly 90-minute trip (from Georgetown) see page 127.

 Where to stay The village of Santa Mission does not have accommodation set up for visitors, but Arrowpoint is within the boundaries of the reservation.

DEMERARA: EAST BANK

MADEWINI GARDENS RESORT & HOTEL (*Timehri Public Rd, Madewini;* ✆ *615 6512; www.madewinigardensgy.com;* ⊕ *non-guests 08.00–18.00 Sat/Sun & hols; call on other days; resort admission: adult/child US$2/1.50;* **$$–$$$**) The resort consists of two swimming pools, a bar and small *benabs* that line a narrow creek. The hotel (12 rooms) is new and the rooms are clean, self-contained and have air conditioning, television and balconies that overlook the pools and manmade swamp/pond. Two rooms have a kitchenette, small dining room and separate bedroom. If you have a hammock or tent, camping (**$**) is an option. The friendly proprietors prepare meals on order for guests. And while the location close to the busy public road doesn't quite offer visitors a nature sanctuary, the hotel's proximity to the airport is a definite bonus for early morning flights.

JUBILEE WATERPARK AND RESORT (*Jubilee Rd, Timerhi;* 2258915; reservations@ *jubileeresort.com; www.jubileeresort.com;* 10.00–18.00 *Sat/Sun; US$6*) This resort, aimed at the local market, is situated on the Dakara Creek, about five minutes from the Cheddi Jagan International Airport. While there are nature trails and pedal boats, the real draw for locals is the Olympic-sized swimming pool and 400ft waterslide ('Only one of its kind in Guyana'). There is nothing extraordinary for overseas visitors, but if you have spare time in the vicinity of the airport and need to cool off, it's an option.

Getting there and away Located behind the international airport, the resort can be reached by taxi (US$20 from Georgetown). To keep your price down, it would be possible to take minibus 42 to the airport and hire a taxi for the short trip from there.

What to see and do Besides the waterslide and swimming pool, there is a nearby creek with canoes and pedal boats available and short nature walks cut through the grasslands. On site there is a bar and restaurant, volleyball, cricket, pool, table tennis and loud music (dancing is optional).

The grounds are kept neat and tidy and there are several *benabs* around the pool to provide shade. Lifeguards are always on duty, strict dress codes are enforced and the one price gives visitors access to everything.

DEMERARA: WEST COAST

West coast Demerara means the villages along the Atlantic coast on the western side of the Demerara River. It is the road that runs from Vreed-en-Hoop to Parika.

GUYANESE HERITAGE MUSEUM AND TOUCAN INN (*17 Meten-Meer-Zorg, West Coast Demerara;* 275 0028; e *toucan-s@networksgy.com;* 08.00–17.30 *daily; US$1.50*) Even though this private museum has been around since 2001, it seems to be a little-known spot in Guyana, perhaps due to its unlikely location in a quiet village roughly halfway between Georgetown and Parika. The museum grew as a result of owner Gary Serrao's passion for his country's heritage; while living in the UK for 20 years he quelled his homesickness by collecting historical artefacts from Guyana. After returning to Guyana, Gary continued collecting until, without realising it, he had enough to turn his home into a museum.

Besides the few rooms set aside for the museum, the relics fill all areas of this multi-tiered home and inn. The pieces span hundreds of years and cover all periods of Guyana's history. The collection includes (but is hardly limited to) Dutch bottles by the hundreds, stamps dating from the 1860s, Amerindian trading beads, stone mortars, shelves and shelves of books on Guyana, cannonballs, records by Guyanese singers, and historic photos. There is a special light-sensitive room dedicated to maps, the oldest dating back to 1633.

The Guyana Heritage Museum is a must for any level of history buff; even those normally not interested in history will likely find Gary's enthusiasm for his collection, and country, hard to resist.

To help supplement his pastime of buying expensive historical pieces, Gary opened the **Toucan Inn** (14 rooms; **$$–$$$**). All the rooms are self-contained and decorated with historical artefacts and bright paintings. Each has its own charm so be sure to ask for a tour before choosing a room. Air conditioning is available in some rooms but they aren't the cheeriest of the lot; the upstairs doubles get plenty of light and the breeze makes air conditioning unnecessary. There is also a small pool and a tower patio with views of the Essequibo River feeding into the Atlantic Ocean.

Museum guests can also have access to the tower patio and other lounges (US$0.50/hour) as well as the pool (US$1.50/hour). Meals are prepared on order for guests of both the museum and lodge (US$3–7). Gary also runs a small museum shop with a large number of Dutch bottles for sale.

DEMERARA: EAST COAST

This area is along the Atlantic Ocean on the eastern side of the Demerara River, mainly the road between Georgetown and Rosignol. The Mahaica and Abary rivers are popular with birdwatchers for the range of species they harbour. This area is also the best to see the hoatzin, Guyana's strange national bird.

The best trips (including transport and birding guides) to this area can be arranged through Guyana Feather Friends and Wilderness Explorers (see *Tour operators*, pages 59).

MAHAICA RIVER This little-visited area of Guyana is a good destination for a half-day birdwatching trip. A short 45-minute drive from Georgetown takes you to the Mahaica River where, with further travel by boat, you can explore a variety of wetlands and savannas. The area is home to more than 150 species of birds, including large populations of the hoatzin, and seeing as how they live in groups along the river, chances of seeing them are quite good. Even for non-birdwatchers, it's a beautiful area to explore.

ABARY RIVER Just a short drive from the Mahaica River site is some excellent birding along an easy walking trail within the protected Abary River mangrove forest. The trail provides great chances of seeing many endemic and coastal species, including the blood-coloured woodpecker, Guianan gnatcatcher, and white-bellied and white-barred piculet. As the trail gets closer to the Atlantic, you may also see the endangered rufous crab-hawks scour the marshes for their namesake food.

6

Berbice

When listening to some Guyanese talk about Berbice (maybe they'll ask if you've been to Berbice, telling you that they come from there, adding that everybody knows Berbice is home to the friendliest folks and finest food) it would be easy for any visitor to assume Berbice is a city. In actuality, Berbice is an entire area of Guyana home to a few towns and dozens of small villages. There is a West Berbice and an East Berbice but hardly anybody differentiates between the two.

Berbice is a rather large chunk of land south of the Atlantic; West Berbice is found just west of the Berbice River, while East Berbice stretches east to the Corentyne River, which is also the border with Suriname. But just Berbice will do, and when most people speak of Berbice they are referring to the stretch of coastal road that runs between New Amsterdam and Moleson Creek. Much of the land south of this area is sugarcane fields, aquaculture ponds, fruit and vegetable farms, timber concessions or largely unpopulated tracts of forest and savanna.

The mostly pristine state of the interior of Berbice, with its countless rivers and endless flora and fauna, holds much tourism potential that still remains mostly unrealised. There are a few options covered in this chapter for intrepid travellers looking to explore sections of Guyana that see very few visitors, but most of the chapter covers the lived-upon lands to the north and the places that travellers will pass through on their way to or from Suriname, which is likely to be the only reason many people on holiday in Guyana would find themselves in Berbice anyway.

HISTORY

Berbice was the name given to Guyana's second colony settled by the Dutch. In 1627, Abraham Van Pere, a merchant who had his sights set beyond the Essequibo colony, asked the Dutch West India Company for permission to explore, and hopefully colonise, the land around the Berbice River. They consented, and Van Pere rounded up a group of other willing merchants and their families, and before long they were calling Fort Nassau, a small settlement roughly 70 miles up the Berbice River, home.

Many plantations blossomed (thanks to the poorly treated slaves), bringing wealth to many of the settlers. Frequent trading was also done with local Amerindians. Van Pere must have certainly been pleased with the results of his grand plan of striking out to start his own colony. However, nobody said the business of colonisers was an easy one, and the inhabitants of Berbice certainly had their share of setbacks.

In 1665 the English attacked. In 1689 and 1708 the French took their turn. In 1712, the French raided again, this time holding Fort Nassau until a ransom was paid. The large payout resulted in a period of economic decline for the Berbice colony.

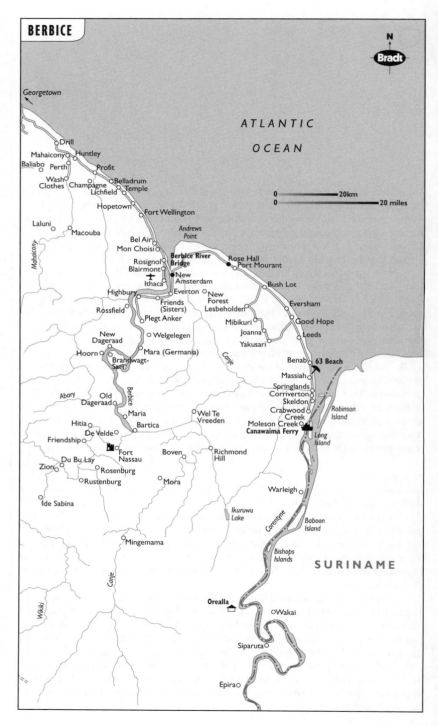

Perhaps the biggest blow to the colony came with the Berbice revolt, a slave uprising that began on 23 February 1763 and lasted for more than a year. What started on a couple of plantations along the Berbice River quickly gained momentum as groups of fed-up slaves made their way towards Fort Nassau. The plantation owners and their families were aware of the discrepancy in population sizes – roughly 350 of them and nearly 4,000 slaves – and fled for their lives. The Dutch had originally sought refuge at Fort Nassau, but they quickly realised they would be cornered there and decided to make their way towards the coast; the Fort was burned before they left.

The entire incident is covered in more detail on page 6, but by March the slaves controlled most of the plantations in Berbice. The Dutch retreated to a plantation closer to the coast and the two sides had a stand-off with many large and small-scale battles. The Africans wanted to be granted freedom; the colonists, knowing that would mean the decline of their plantations, refused.

Military reinforcements eventually arrived from Europe and by January 1764 the Dutch had reclaimed Berbice. The last of the rebel slaves were caught in April. Those who weren't re-enslaved were publicly executed. While the slaves lost their fight for freedom, their efforts left huge financial and mental scars on the plantation owners of Berbice.

Berbice fell upon tough times and, in 1784, the government of Berbice decided to move their capital closer to the Atlantic coast in an attempt to revitalise the economy. Building began near a small settlement on the confluence of the Berbice and Canje rivers and by 1791 New Amsterdam was declared the new capital of Berbice.

Agriculture is still the economic focus of Berbice, and a visit to this region is a visit to Guyana's countryside. Neat rows of sugarcane disappear in the distance; rice is laid out to dry in the road along with coconut shells; cows wander everywhere; and palm groves stand proudly, knowing the sight of them matches the vision of any tropical paradise (minus the clear blue waters of course).

However, it is hard to call Berbice a tourist destination in itself. New Amsterdam is home to a handful of historical buildings showcasing colonial architecture (the old New Amsterdam Hospital is arguably one of Guyana's grandest wooden buildings) but unfortunately many are in a terrible state of disrepair, and if rehabilitation efforts aren't started soon will be lost altogether. Tours of the sugar estates are an interesting way to spend an hour or two and a river trip into the interior is an even better option if you have the extra time and money.

In the end, Berbice is probably a place that you'll find yourself only passing through if you are travelling overland to or from Suriname. If this is the case, don't pass through in a hurry; the locals are friendly and you may catch a glimpse of paradise in the distance.

GETTING THERE AND AWAY

A fleet of taxis, an army of ever-present minibuses, a new floating bridge and a flock of the strange-looking Tapirs (the only vehicle ever made in Guyana) comprise travel to, from and around Berbice. Whatever your chosen mode of transportation, the journey is sure to be far from dull, as the narrow coastal road is also the hub of life. Villages are built along its edge, meaning the road also serves as a pavement, bike path, playground for children, gathering place for elders and illogical grazing ground for a veritable farmyard of animals – cows, goats, roosters, donkeys, horses, dogs – that roam freely.

Needless to say, the hazards are many and your transportation will decide the level of excitement. (Tip: most minibuses drive incredibly fast and accidents are all too common; taxi drivers also like to drive fast, but you have the option of telling them to slow down; Tapirs, far from being a marvel of engineering, don't have the word 'fast' in their vocabulary.)

Travel to Berbice used to be hampered by the fact that the only way to cross the Berbice River was via a ferry that often involved waiting in a frustratingly long queue. Thankfully a new floating toll bridge is now open and the journey is much faster. While the ferry was certainly an experience, the ease of the bridge crossing means it is one that will not be missed by many.

From Georgetown it is roughly 65 miles (105km) to the Berbice River bridge at Rosignol; from New Amsterdam to Moleson Creek is a distance of roughly 50 miles (82km). Note that there is a small fee for vehicles to cross (from US$10, depending on your vehicle). It is charged only when coming from the west. The bridge also closes for 1½ hours every day to allow ships to pass; for closing times, which vary with the tide, check the local papers or call the Transport and Harbour Department (✆ 226 8018).

BY TAXI Most of Georgetown's taxi companies will make the trip to New Amsterdam (US$40 plus toll), and at the bus park in New Amsterdam there are cars willing to drive to Georgetown. Taxis will also go directly to the Rosignol stelling where you can board a minibus for New Amsterdam. Shared taxis are the cheapest option. In Georgetown, they can be found near the number 50 buses at the Stabroek bus park and in Rosignol, at the stelling (be sure to specify that you want a shared taxi). Taxis to Georgetown can also be hired in Rosignol.

In New Amsterdam, taxis can be found gathered at the Berbice Petroleum Establishment. Some sample rates are US$10 to Rose Hall; US$30 to Skeldon; and US$40 to Moleson Creek. Many taxis in Berbice are privately owned; the two main companies in New Amsterdam are **Triple S** (✆ 333 4367) and **Joey's** (✆ 333 4300). Rides around town cost roughly US$1.50.

BY MINIBUS Bus number 50 runs between Stabroek Market in Georgetown (US$4) and the stelling in Rosignol. Bus 56 travels between the Rosignol stelling and the New Amsterdam stelling, crossing the Berbice bridge.

Bus number 63 runs between New Amsterdam and the Corentyne River; the turn-around point is Sukhpaul's car park at the collection of roadside stalls on the public road, directly in front of the Springlands Market (US$3; less for shorter distances).

Travel by minibus is the cheapest option, but, as always, be prepared for overcrowded buses, screaming speeds and loud music (if you find yourself fearing for your life – or hearing – don't be afraid to ask the driver to stop so you can switch and get on another bus, which may or may not be better).

BY TAPIR These boxy and often highly personalised vehicles provide cheap transportation (US$0.50–2) for passengers along the eastern end of Berbice, from Village No. 75 to Crabwood Creek, an area collectively referred to as Corriverton.

BY CAR Hiring a car would have to be done in Georgetown, as there are no car hire agencies in Berbice (see page 104).

BY FERRY Coming to Berbice from Suriname involves taking the Canawaima ferry (see page 139).

Rosignol–New Amsterdam Ferry After the completion of the new Berbice River bridge, the regular ferry stopped service.

Blairmont–New Amsterdam (Note that at the time of writing, this crossing was closed due to a decline in business. There was talk of the boat starting up again, but ask around before travelling to the site.) If you take the public road south for about two miles past the turn for the stelling, the road winds through the Blairmont sugar estate until it ends at the smaller Blairmont stelling. From here a small passenger boat makes the ten-minute journey across the river, starting at 07.00 and ending at 18.00.

Canawaima Ferry: Moleson Creek, Guyana to South Drain, Suriname This passenger and vehicle ferry makes the return trip between Guyana and Suriname twice per day. Times are a bit ambiguous depending on weather and other mysterious factors officials were not able to clarify, but according to the schedule, it is to leave Guyana around 10.00 and 12.00. Passengers should plan on arriving at least one hour before the scheduled departure time to have time to go through customs and immigration, which is at the stelling.

Most countries outside of CARICOM countries will need a valid Suriname visa in order to be allowed to board the boat. If you didn't secure one before leaving for your travels, visas are issued at the Suriname Embassy in Georgetown (see page 61).

Note that the ferry is the only legal way to cross from Guyana to Suriname. In Village 78 on the Corentyne, there are many speedboat captains who will offer to take you to Suriname, but while backtracking, as it is called locally, is tolerated, it's also illegal as it entails leaving Guyana without going through the proper immigration requirements. The often overloaded boats are also not the safest passage to or from Suriname.

Note that Guyana and Suriname are also exploring options for building a bridge connecting the two countries while drastically cutting the travel time from one capital to another (especially with the new Berbice bridge). Both sides are in agreement to building the bridge, but funding must be identified before the project can move forward.

Rates One-way adult/child US$10/5; return adult/child US$15/10; 21+ day return adult/child US$25/15. One-way car/4x4 US$15/20; return car/4x4 US$30/40; 21+ day return car/4x4 US$40/50. Bicycles are free.

NEW AMSTERDAM

Outside of some historical buildings showcasing beautiful colonial architecture (some better preserved than others), New Amsterdam holds little of interest for the average visitor. However, if you find yourself passing through and have some extra time, a walking tour of town can be completed easily in an hour or two; just don't expect clean streets or proper pavements to be part of your tour.

During the day, general safety is not a major issue in New Amsterdam, but caution should be exercised at night, especially on side streets. Also, mosquitoes in New Amsterdam can be particularly fierce so it's always a good idea to keep repellent close at hand.

WHERE TO STAY All rooms below are self-contained and furnished with televisions, fans, mosquito nets, desks and chairs; extra amenities are detailed in the listings.

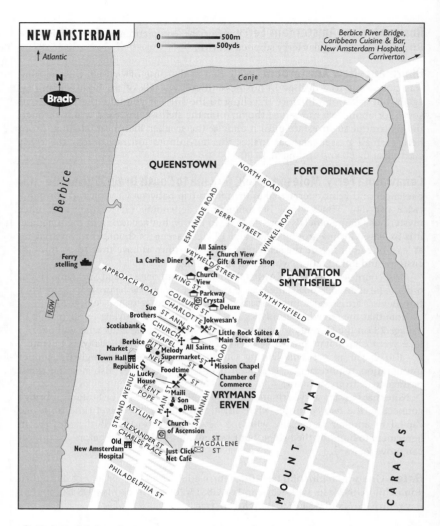

NEW AMSTERDAM

0 ▬▬▬▬ 500m
0 ▬▬▬▬ 500yds

↑ Atlantic

N

Berbice River Bridge,
Caribbean Cuisine & Bar,
New Amsterdam Hospital,
Corriverton

Canje

QUEENSTOWN   FORT ORDNANCE

Berbice

Ferry
stelling

NORTH ROAD

ESPLANADE ROAD

PERRY STREET

WINKEL ROAD

APPROACH ROAD

FLOW

All Saints
✚ Church View
La Caribe Diner ✕ Gift & Flower Shop
VRYHELD STREET
🏠 Church
View
KING ST
COLBURG ST 🍴 Parkway
CHARLOTTE ST ⊙ Crystal
Sue ⊙ Deluxe
Brothers ST ANN ST Jokwesan's
Scotiabank $ ✕ ✕ ST
CHURCH Little Rock Suites &
Berbice CHAPEL Main Street Restaurant
Market PITT ST ✚ All Saints
Town Hall 🏢 🏠 Melody
Republic $ Supermarket
NEW ST
Lucky Foodtime ✕ ✚ Mission Chapel
House KENT ST Chamber of
STRAND AVENUE POPE Commerce
ASYLUM ST 🍴 Maili VRYMANS
MAIN ST & Son ERVEN
ALEXANDER ST ● DHL
CHARLES PLACE ⊙ Church
Old of Ascension
New Amsterdam ST
Hospital 🏢 Just Click MAGDALENE
PHILADELPHIA ST Net Café ST

PLANTATION
SMYTHSFIELD

SMYTHFIELD ROAD

MOUNT SINAI

CARACAS

Bradt

140

🏠 **Little Rock Suites** (25 rooms) 10 Main &
Church Sts; 📞 333 2727; e lrtvs@guyana.net.gy.
If you like your room to be outfitted with new
furnishings & all the amenities, including AC (no
mosquito nets needed), mini-fridges, balconies,
& free Wi-Fi, then you'll get your money's worth
at New Amsterdam's newest, nicest & most
expensive hotel. However, don't expect an
outstanding difference in the service or food, as
the same or better can be found elsewhere for
less money. **$$$–$$$$**

🏠 **Church View Hotel** (19 rooms) 3 Main
& King Sts; 📞 333 2880; e churchviewhotel@
networksgy.com. In this old colonial building are

a variety of rooms adorned with a hotchpotch
of second-hand furnishings that complement
the homey feel created by the friendly staff. AC
& mini-fridges are in some rooms & Wi-Fi is free
throughout. If you have a group or are looking to
spread out, the Private A & B rooms offer plenty
of space & a lounge area. **$**; AC **$$**.

🏠 **Parkway Hotel** (35 rooms) 4 Main St;
📞 333 3929. The basic rooms in this old wooden
structure show their age but are clean enough &
suitable if you're only after a cheap bed & shower,
which, bear in mind, seems to be the case with some
short-term clients. On-site restaurant has as much
ambience as the rooms, which is little. **$**; AC **$$**.

🏠 **Deluxe Guest House** (13 rooms) 5–19 Coburg St; ☎ 333 3004. While not deluxe per se, this converted colonial house has friendly proprietors & clean rooms. The corner rooms are particularly spacious, airy & full of light; ask to see a selection before choosing. No AC; full b/fast can be added for minimal cost. **$**

🍴 **WHERE TO EAT AND DRINK** Nearly all restaurants in New Amsterdam, and all of Berbice for that matter, serve a selection of typical Guyanese cuisine (mainly curried, baked or fried meat or seafood with a selection of side dishes), Chinese food or a combination of both. The restaurants listed below come recommended by locals as making some of the best food, but non-discerning diners may find it all remarkably similar.

New Amsterdam is full of rum shops, but most visitors will find the atmosphere of the restaurants listed below to be preferable when looking for a place to have a drink.

Guyanese

🍴 **Caribbean Cuisine & Bar** 7879 Number 2 Village, E Canje; ☎ 332 0096; ⏰ 11.00–22.30 Mon–Fri, 11.00–midnight Sat, 16.30–22.30 Sun. Just across the Canje Bridge from New Amsterdam is this local attempt at classy dining; & while the food is of good quality & the atmosphere – especially the well-landscaped outdoor patio – is pleasant, it's reflected in the high prices. The extensive menu features such items as salmon salad & prawns in ginger sauce, but daily selections are limited to a few items written on a chalkboard. The list of drinks is also 4 pages long, but the inadequate bar only allows for a fraction of them to be made. **$$$**

🍴 **Main Street Restaurant** Little Rock Suites, 10 Main & Church Sts; ☎ 333 2727; ⏰ 06.00–23.00 daily. More typical Guyanese cuisine served up in an elegant (for New Amsterdam) AC atmosphere. Prices are slightly higher & service can be slow, but the food is good. **$$$**

🍴 **Church View Hotel Restaurant** 3 Main & King Sts; ☎ 333 2880; churchviewhotel@ networksgy.com; ⏰ 06.00–midnight daily. This open & breezy upper-level dining room has a good selection of the usual suspects, with some nice soups thrown in. Patrons are forewarned though that some of the fauna they may be hoping to see in the wild are on the menu, including iguana, turtle, peccary & labba. Also a nice place to enjoy a few cold beverages. **$$**

🍴 **La Caribe Diner** Lot 1 Main St; ☎ 333 5540; ⏰ 08.00–23.00 Mon–Fri, 08.00–12.00 Sat. La Caribe serves up high-quality dishes with an array of vegetables, seafood & meat (including wild labba & deer). There's indoor & outdoor seating & the portions are large (many will find the half-order to be plenty). **$$**

🍴 **Foodtime** 16 Main & New Sts; ☎ 333 6658; ⏰ 07.30–22.00 Mon–Sat, 15.00–22.00 Sun. Another popular place for locals, the friendly owner & staff here cook & display enough Creole food every day to please anybody's palette. Also have good homemade doughnuts, juice & milkshakes. **$**

🍴 **Jokwesan's Creole Junction** 7 Charlotte St; ☎ 333 2464; ⏰ 10.00–22.00 Mon–Sat. A favourite lunch spot with the locals, Jokwesan's prepares several dishes daily, including good curries, pasta salad & fried chicken & fish; also good selection of fresh juice & snacks, including homemade bread, cakes & pastries. Come early as the selection diminishes greatly after lunch rush. **$**

Chinese
Berbice is also home to an endless selection of Chinese restaurants, all serving similar dishes out of establishments with varying degrees of cleanliness. A couple of your best bets in New Amsterdam are:

Lucky House Chinese Restaurant 17 Main St; ☎ 333 4287; ⏰ 09.00–midnight Mon–Sun. **$$**

Sue Brothers Restaurant Main & St Ann's Sts; ☎ 333 2408; ⏰ 09.00–midnight daily. **$$**

Vegetarian Excellent *ital* (vegetarian) food can also be found at the Rastafarian stands on the corner of Main and Pitt Streets. They have no names but you can't miss their bright colours (⊕ *12.00–midnight daily;* $).

Self-catering Fresh vegetables and fruits can also be found at the daily market (see page156). Basic food and toiletry items can be bought at:

Mali & Son 19 Main St; ☎333 4589; ⊕ 08.00–20.00 Mon–Sat, 08.00–13.00 Sun

Melody Supermarket 14 Pitt St; ☎333 5068; ⊕ 07.30–18.00 Mon–Sat

SHOPPING New Amsterdam is no shopper's paradise but the town's many market stalls and shops selling a little bit of everything can make for some mildly entertaining window shopping.

The Church View Gift & Flower Shop Lot 1 Vryhed St; ☎333 3927; ⊕ 08.00–16.00 Mon–Sat. The place to go for local crafts & souvenirs ranging from wooden rolling pins & Guyana flags to hand-crafted leather sandals to stuffed caiman. Collectors of Dutch bottles will also be pleased with the selection.
The Market Strand Av; ⊕ 06.00–17.15 Mon–Tue & Thu–Sat, 06.00–12.00 Wed, 06.00–09.00 Sun. Located in the old town hall building dating back to 1833. If there's something

specific you're after there's a good chance you'll find it here.
Pitt Street Between Strand & Main Sts. At this outdoor mall of sorts, you can get your hair done, buy a new outfit, purchase the hottest soca CD, get any office supply needs, purchase that metre of fabric you've been wanting & get the makings for a salad. Better yet, just buy a cold drink & watch other people do the shopping.

OTHER PRACTICALITIES This section covers local services that visitors may require during their time in New Amsterdam.

Banks
$ **Republic Bank** Strand Av; ☎223 7938; ⊕ 08.00–14.00 Mon–Thu, 08.00–14.30 Fri. Both foreign currency & travellers' cheques can be exchanged.

$ **Scotiabank** 12 Strand Av; ☎333 4154; ⊕ 08.00–14.00 Mon–Thu, 08.00–14.30 Fri. International ATM machine, exchanges foreign currency, travellers' cheques & gives credit card cash advances.

Communications
Post
DHL 18 Kent St; ☎333 2996; ⊕ 08.00–17.00 Mon–Fri, 09.00–12.00 Sat. A good option for more secure mailings.

New Amsterdam Post Office Cnr St Magdalen St & Savannah Rd; ☎333 2531; ⊕ 07.00–16.00 Mon–Fri, 07.00–11.00 Sat. For general mailing needs.

Email and internet Due to a strong demand for cheap overseas calls, internet cafés seem to be popping up all over. All seem to lack any ambience so any will likely do for basic internet needs. Rates average US$1–1.50 per hour for internet and US$0.10 per minute for calls to the US, Canada and UK.

🖲 **Crystal Net Café** 513 Main St; ☎333 2629; ⊕ 08.00–23.00 daily

🖲 **Just Click Net Café** Main & St Magdalene Sts; ☎333 4043; ⊕ 08.00–22.00 Mon–Sat, 13.00–22.00 Sun

Hospital The New Amsterdam Public Hospital (*Main St & Garden Rd;* \ *333 2494*) is a relatively new facility, but the services are not up to Western standards and waiting time is often long.

Tourist information As tourism is fairly non-existent in New Amsterdam there is no office set up to deal specifically with visitors. Outside of helpful hotel staff, the local Chamber of Commerce (*12 Chapel St;* \ *333 3324*) can provide some useful information.

WHAT TO SEE AND DO As was said earlier, New Amsterdam doesn't have any grand destinations that draw in visitors, but there are a few historical sites worth admiring.

At first glance, the old **New Amsterdam Public Hospital** building (*along Charles Place, between Main St & Strand Av*) looks like the perfect setting for a horror film, but once you get past its decaying state, a beautiful and grand piece of colonial architecture shines through. The hospital, designed by Ceasar Castellani, was built in 1878 and will hopefully see a much-deserved rehabilitation.

There are also a couple of churches from New Amsterdam's earliest days. The beautiful wooden interior of the **All Saints' Anglican Church** (*cnr Main & Church Sts*) is worth a visit. The building dates from 1811 and was recently restored.

The **All Saints' Scots Church** (*Main & Vryheid Sts*) was erected c1838 to serve the growing population of New Amsterdam. It is a basic but charming wooden church with a striking steeple.

The **Mission Chapel Congregational Church** (*eastern end of Chapel St*) that stands now was constructed in the 1840s after the original church, built by slaves in 1819, was destroyed. Plantation owners ordered its destruction after placing blame on the missionaries for the 1823 slave uprising. The church is not in the best shape, but the imposing structure is still a sight to behold. Slaves used to receive their education under the tamarind tree in front.

The **Roman Catholic Church of Ascension** (*19 Main St;* \ *333 2732*) is a well-maintained, but modest wooden building. The dark wooden interior, with high vaulted ceilings and nice stained glass, is worth a quick peek.

The old **Town Hall** building (*Strand Av*) was originally constructed in 1868 and is now the site of the daily market. Again, windows are broken and paint is peeling, but one can still imagine the status its large tower held in the 19th century.

CORRIVERTON

Similar to Berbice, Corriverton is not a village or town in itself, but refers to a collection of villages along the Corentyne River. The main villages of Corriverton are No 78, which is also called Springlands, No 79 and Skeldon. It can all seem very confusing but each village is small and there is no separation between them, hence calling them all Corriverton.

The area serves as the launching pad to Suriname as well as to more isolated villages and logging concessions further up the Corentyne River. Crabwood Creek, a village just south of Skeldon, is home to several logging companies and sawmills that receive boatloads of timber from deep in the interior.

Corriverton is also a large cane-producing area of Guyana, with the new Guyana Sugar Company processing plant being located in Skeldon.

WHERE TO STAY If you find yourself spending the night waiting for the ferry to Suriname or a trip on the Corentyne, there are actually a few good hotels to

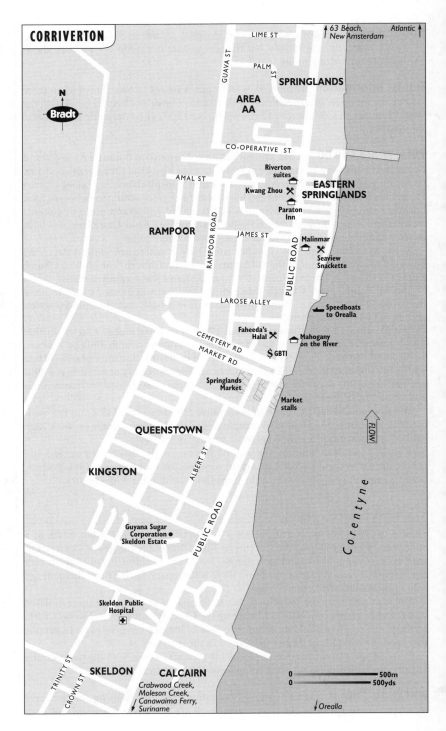

CORRIVERTON

↑ *63 Beach,*   *Atlantic* ↑
New Amsterdam

LIME ST

SPRINGLANDS

GUAVA ST

PALM ST

AREA
AA

CO-OPERATIVE ST

AMAL ST

Riverton
suites

Kwang Zhou

EASTERN
SPRINGLANDS

Paraton
Inn

RAMPOOR

JAMES ST

RAMPOOR ROAD

Malinmar

PUBLIC ROAD

Seaview
Snackette

LAROSE ALLEY

Speedboats
to Orealla

Faheeda's
Halal

CEMETERY RD

Mahogany
on the River

$ GBTI

MARKET RD

Springlands
Market

Market
stalls

QUEENSTOWN

FLOW

ALBERT ST

KINGSTON

Corentyne

Guyana Sugar
Corporation ●
Skeldon Estate

PUBLIC ROAD

Skeldon Public
Hospital

TRINITY ST

SKELDON

CALCAIRN

CROWN ST

Crabwood Creek,
Moleson Creek,
Canawaima Ferry,
Suriname

0 ▬▬▬▬ 500m
0 ▬▬▬▬ 500yds

↓ *Orealla*

choose from. All have self-contained rooms with television and fan; rooms with air conditioning and mini-fridges are available for an extra charge.

🏠 **Mahogany on the River** (9 rooms) 50 Public Rd, Springlands; ☎ 335 2535. Rates for rooms here vary according to size but all are new, well decorated with cane furniture, have fridges & smell of cleaning products. Be warned though that the nightclub downstairs is popular, partly because of the music blaring forth at all hours. **$$**

🏠 **Paraton Inn** (22 rooms) K & L 78, Springlands; ☎ 335 3025. This cavernous hotel can be a bit gloomy, but request a recently renovated room to get sparkling tiles on the floors & new furnishings best described as East Indian Art Deco. **$$**

🏠 **Riverton Suites** (13 rooms) 78 Public Rd, Springlands; ☎ 335 3039. The monochrome colours & maze-like construction of this hotel

make for one of the area's funkiest hotels, & certainly without trying to do so. There must have been a blowout sale on light green paint because everything, including the floors, tables, chairs, desk & beds, in the very spacious & spotless rooms is painted green. Surprisingly, it creates a unique ambience. You won't want for extra space in any of the rooms, but perhaps the best is the tower room. Isolated on top of the building, the room is breezy, full of light & has a little patio with a fantastic view. **$$**

🏠 **Hotel Malinmar** (21 rooms) 13 Public Rd, Springlands; ☎ 335 3328; e hotelmalinmar@ yahoo.com. The rooms are kept very clean, the staff are personable & helpful & the views of the river & into Suriname are a bonus, especially from the small rooftop patio. **$**, AC **$$**

✗ WHERE TO EAT AND DRINK

✗ **Faheeda's Halal Restaurant** 147 Public Rd, No. 78 Village; ☎ 335 3830; ⏱ 09.00–21.00 daily. Locals say Faheeda's makes some of the best Creole dishes in Guyana & they may be right. The dining room is clean, the servers friendly & the portions are substantial. **$$**

✗ **Kwang Zhou Restaurant** Lot X Public Rd, Springlands; ☎ 625 8819; ⏱ 09.30–20.30. The building may not look too appealing but Mr

Zhou cooks up some of the best Chinese food in Berbice, & his cheerful demeanour makes up for any lacking ambience. **$$**

✗ **Seaview Snackette** Corentyne riverfront, Springlands (directly in behind Hotel Malinmar); ☎ 642 3537; ⏱ 06.00–20.00 daily. A small snack bar serving up home-cooked Creolese dishes with a smile. **$**

OTHER PRACTICALITIES
Bank
$ **Guyana Bank for Trade & Industry (GBTI)** Lot 211, No. 78 Village; ☎ 335 3399; ⏱ 08.00–14.00 Mon–Thu. Exchanges foreign

currency & travellers' cheques & gives credit card cash advances.

Email and internet How Corriverton can support so many places offering internet access and overseas phone calls probably has something to do with the fact that many are located in front of private homes. Options along the road are endless; rates are roughly US$1–1.50 per hour.

Hospital The **Skeldon Public Hospital** (☎ 339 2211) is fine for minor illnesses or injuries, but if the ailment is more serious, transportation should be arranged for New Amsterdam at the least and possibly even Georgetown.

WHAT TO SEE AND DO With limited tourism options, chances are slim that you'll be heading to Corriverton as a destination in itself, but there area few ways to pass time while waiting for the ferry to Suriname, or better yet, a boat expedition on the Corentyne River.

Touring a sugar estate and processing plant may not sound like the most captivating activity, but a visit to the Guyana Sugar Corporation's **Skeldon Estate** (✆ *339 2214; www.guysuco.com; advance notice is required*) is an enlightening insight into an industry with a long history in Guyana. Skeldon recently completed a new state-of-the-art processing plant, valued at US$169 million, to complete the ancient factory previously on site. Tours also include trips to the sugarcane fields where the chopped cane is loaded onto punts, or boats, and brought to the factory via canals.

The **Springlands Market** is a good place for sampling an array of strange tropical fruit and browsing through stalls selling cheap goods smuggled in from Suriname.

While technically located just north of Corriverton, **63 Beach**, located in No. 63 Village has long been touted as a tourism site in Guyana with great potential for future development. The beach itself is a long stretch of sand bordered by the brown waters of the Atlantic on one side and spotty patches of coconut palms on the other. It's a pleasant place to go for a walk, but with the appalling amounts of rubbish (especially after a busy Sunday afternoon) that line the edges, it's not going to attract legions of tourists any time soon. If locals stop littering and take care of the beauty at their doorstep, the potential would be a whole lot brighter.

CORENTYNE RIVER

The interior region of Berbice is still largely untouched by mainstream tourism. Most of the traffic heading up the Berbice and Corentyne rivers is related to timber concessions, mining claims, agriculture farms and the small accompanying interior villages. While it can be quite difficult to locate a boat to carry you up the Berbice River, organising a boat trip on the Corentyne, where more activity takes place, is relatively simple, but not inexpensive.

While plenty of logging companies work concessions near the Corentyne River, the scenery along the banks hasn't been completely marred by timber activities, which take place further in. There's a good chance that unless you request to see a concession, the only sign of logging will be boats filled with felled trees heading for the sawmills in Crabwood Creek.

The rewards for the adventurous travellers who decide to venture into this normally unvisited area of Guyana can be many, extensive species of flora and fauna, numerous waterfalls, beautiful creeks, pristine forests and a true sense of isolation among them.

OREALLA This friendly Amerindian village approximately 50 miles up the Corentyne River is perhaps the best option for visitors to Berbice who want to push inland without too much hardship or time invested.

Before finalising and leaving for your trip, it is a polite necessity to notify the village council of any upcoming visit, be it for a couple of hours or a couple of days. The council can be reached on the village phone (✆ *338 9281*).

Getting there and away Travel to Orealla is via boat. The cheapest and safest option is to use the Orealla village boat that makes the trip between Orealla and Corriverton twice weekly (US$4; 3–4hrs). The boat leaves Corriverton on Tuesday and Saturday afternoons and leaves Orealla on Monday and Friday. The boat is a larger vessel that takes longer than a speedboat but has room for moving around and hanging hammocks.

There are also some in the village who have speedboats that sometimes take on passengers. If you prefer speedboats, call the village phone (✆ *338 9281*) to find out

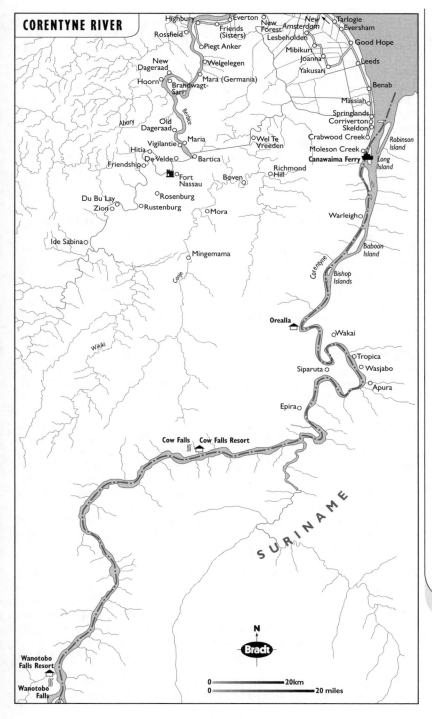

CORENTYNE RIVER

Highbury
Everton
New Amsterdam
New
Tarlogie
Eversham
Rossfield
Friends (Sisters)
New Forest
Lesbeholden
Good Hope
Piegt Anker
Mibikuri
Joanna
Leeds
New Dageraad
Welgelegen
Yakusari
Hoorn
Mara (Germania)
Benab
Brandwagt-Sarr
Massiah
Abary
Old Dageraad
Springlands
Corriverton
Skeldon
Maria
Wel Te Vreeden
Crabwood Creek
Robinson Island
Vigilantie
Moleson Creek
Hitia
De Velde
Bartica
Canawaima Ferry
Long Island
Friendship
Richmond Hill
Fort Nassau
Boven
Du Bu Lay
Rosenburg
Zion
Rustenburg
Mora
Warleigh
Ide Sabina
Mingemama
Baboon Island
Corentyne
Bishop Islands
Canje
Orealla
Wakai
Wikiki
Tropica
Siparuta
Wasjabo
Apura
Epira

Cow Falls   Cow Falls Resort

SURINAME

Wanotobo Falls Resort
Wanotobo Falls

N
Bradt

0 ──────── 20km
0 ──────── 20 miles

if any will be travelling during the time of your visit. Always call to double-check the days the regular boat will be travelling, as they have been known to change.

Two companies located on the riverfront in Springlands that have boats available for charter (up to 7 persons) are **Roy Ramdass & Sons** (✆ *335 3279*; US$275 return; overnight add US$100) and **Eno Bharrat** (✆ *335 3625*; US$250 return; overnight add US$75). Roy's quoted price is slightly more but the difference is made up for in friendlier and more reliable service. Keep in mind that all quotes seem to be a bit ad hoc and it never hurts to try bargaining using the competitor's rates as a starting platform.

The one-way trip takes 1½–2 hours in a speedboat. Bharrat's also charters a larger boat with two engines that can accommodate up to 15 persons (US$375; overnight add US$50) and makes the trip in about an hour.

For an extra charge, both companies will push further up the river to locations such as Siparuta Village, Zambi Island and Cow Falls, but travellers must carry all necessary camping equipment and food and water. When chartering a boat for any trip always make sure that the proper life jackets are on board before leaving.

Where to stay The village of Orealla has one **guesthouse** for rent (**$**), a stand-alone house with one bedroom, kitchen and bathroom. There is space for additional beds and there is also always space to hang hammocks in the village.

Cortours (see below) also recently built a **15-room guesthouse** (**$$**) in Orealla. Located right on the river, the large outdoor balcony is a bonus, but the self-contained rooms are spacious and modestly furnished. Meals are included with the stay.

Where to eat Being a remote Amerindian village means that Orealla doesn't have any restaurants. It's best to bring all necessary food and water, but with advance notice it's possible to arrange a cook to cater meals for a reasonable charge. If you're staying at the Cortours guesthouse, meals will be provided.

What to see The main thing to do in Orealla is go for nature walks through the rainforest, and there are always friendly and knowledgeable residents willing to guide visitors. As the locals know the surrounding forests intimately, the distance of the trek is entirely up to you, and could range from a short walk in the vicinity to a day-long march to more isolated villages. Whatever distance is decided upon, while walking, take the opportunity to pick the guide's brains for a fascinating insight into the jungle and the many local uses for the surrounding flora.

Guides also give village tours and can introduce you to the most skilled craft makers and show you the best swimming and fishing spots in the river. Also be sure to see the ancient Amerindian artefacts in the area.

ZAMBI ISLAND, COW FALLS AND WANOTOBO Cortours (*Lot 34, Grant 1651, Crabwood Creek, Corentyne, Berbice;* ✆ *339 2741;* e *cortoursinc@yahoo.com*) Claims to run the first, and at this point only, ecotourism resorts on the Corentyne River at Cow Falls and Wanotobo. The fact that Cortours, which is owned and operated by a logging company based in Crabwood Creek, built the eco-lodges on logging concessions may raise questions about what ecotourism really consists of, but at least the cabins are located on protected lands: 700 acres at Cow Falls and 500 acres at Wanotobo.

Whether or not they are technically eco, the fact is that Cortours has built two well-appointed lodges in a very remote and pristine area of Guyana. As a measure of reference, Wanotobo is located roughly 210 miles in by river – the Iwokrama Mountains are due west of the camp. The trips offered by Cortours provide the perfect opportunity for the adventurous to explore a section of Guyana that is difficult to access and is largely unknown to Guyanese, let alone outsiders.

In 2010 Cortours also opened a guesthouse in Orealla (see page 146) that is used on their tours.

Getting there and away The main access to the camps is by boat, but Cortours is currently working on building airstrips at both locations that would allow for guests to arrive on chartered planes. Cortours arranges all necessary boat transportation and provides trained captains and tour guides who accompany each trip.

The trips begin and end at their sawmill in Crabwood Creek, a decidedly strange way to begin any ecotourism trip, but it does provide an interesting insight into the industry.

While beautiful, the boat journey is long. The distance to Cow Falls is 120 miles, a six-hour journey. Wanotobo is 90 miles past Cow Falls, or an additional five-hour trip. The trips are broken up with stops at Amerindian villages such as Orealla, sandbanks, beaches, waterfalls and lakes, all according to the wishes of the group.

The trip to Cow Falls is normally done on a large boat complete with benches on top, space to hang hammocks and makeshift beds. From Cow Falls the river gets narrower and shallower necessitating the use of smaller speedboats.

Where to stay and eat At **Cow Falls** there is one building with eight self-contained rooms, a second building with six rooms that share a bathroom and a large dining hall and bar. All are built on rocks raised above the river. Each room is appointed with beds and mosquito nets, and a generator provides limited electricity at night (unless guests desire the peace and quiet).

Wanotobo has three log cabins, two with four rooms and the other with six rooms, situated on top of a hill with a view of Wanotobo Falls. Each cabin has a shared bathroom. There is also a dining hall and bar.

Cooks are provided and all meals are included in the trips.

What to see and do

Cow Falls Resort trip It is recommended to plan at least three days for a trip to Cow Falls. The six-hour boat trip can be split up with short stops at the Amerindian villages of Orealla and Siparuta, as well as many beaches along the way.

Zambi Island, located ten miles before Cow Falls, is used for guests who want to spend one night camping out. The clear water is perfect for swimming and a nearby lake is a breeding ground for the prized catch, lukanani, as well as other species including yakato and kaduri.

Activities at Cow Falls include hiking the forest trails, birdwatching, fishing, swimming in the clear waters and exploring the many rock formations. There is also a volleyball net and small cricket field.

Wanotobo Resort trip Due to the lengthy travel, at least five days should be planned for a trip to Wanotobo Resort. The trip includes the same stops as Cow Falls, but pushes further upriver an additional 90 miles. The river narrows and grows shallower. The sense of isolation increases, as does the wildlife. During the dry season, it's often necessary to push the boat over shallow stretches and barely flowing rapids. It can be an arduous journey.

Along the way there are stops at many rapids, small waterfalls, beaches and islands, including Iguana Island where iguanas can be seen breeding in August and September. There is another optional overnight camp set up near Big Timehri Rapids, which is also the site of an ancient Amerindian petroglyph.

Wanotobo Resort is located where three falls – Wanotobo, Frenchman and Blue Crane – are arranged in a semicircle. Again, from the resort, there are hiking trails, paths to the tops of the waterfalls, and many pristine bathing spots in and around the falls.

Costs Trip prices vary according to the number of people and distance being covered. Cortours prefers a minimum of five persons to make the trip, but it can be done with fewer people if they're willing to pay more. The large boat can accommodate 12 persons and the smaller boats can accommodate eight to ten.

The average price for a three-day trip to Cow Falls is US$240 per person; a five-day trip to Wanotobo averages US$350 per person. Prices include all meals, accommodation and transportation. Special packages can be designed.

7

Lower Essequibo, Cuyuni and Mazaruni Rivers

The combined landmass of the area where the Essequibo, Cuyuni and Mazaruni rivers flow through is an overwhelming amount of Guyana's terrain. The length of the Essequibo River covered in this section of the book is roughly 50 miles, about one-tenth of its full size. In this lower section of the Essequibo is the most development, and it's also very easily accessed from Georgetown and other coastal regions.

Outside of their extreme lower reaches, near their confluence with each other and the Essequibo River, the Cuyuni and Mazaruni rivers run through fairly inaccessible terrain. Both are sites of much of Guyana's gold and diamond mining, and outside of the most adventurous tourists, many will not likely venture too far past Bartica. For those seeking a different type of tourism experience in Guyana, there is fairly regular transportation along the Mazaruni River. It's a beautiful area if you can see past the scarring effects that mining and timber concessions can have on the land.

ESSEQUIBO RIVER

From its humble source in the Acarai Mountains along Guyana's southern border with Brazil, the Essequibo River flows north for more than 600 miles – winding, twisting and roaring through savannas and tropical forests along the way – until its mouth opens up some 20 miles (32km) in width and it spills into the Atlantic Ocean. During its journey, the Essequibo, which is Guyana's largest river, and South America's third-largest (behind the Amazon and Orinoco), flows around some 365 different islands. The three largest – Wakenaam, Leguan and Hog – create a large tongue in the Essequibo's mouth. Together their girth measures nearly 60 square miles; alone the islands are larger than some of the famed Caribbean countries to the north.

Many of Guyana's other great rivers flow into the Essequibo, including the Cuyuni, Mazaruni, Potaro, Rupununi and the Siparuni. The Essequibo is a grand, beautifully moody river that transports the brown muddy waters from wide reaches of Guyana. It was the area that attracted Guyana's first European settlers and its lower section (for the purpose of this book, from its mouth to just past Bartica, some 50 miles to the south) continues to bustle with activity and is easily accessible for visitors.

PARIKA

Parika is the main port town located very near where the Essequibo River pours into the Atlantic Ocean. The main stelling is where boats and ferries can be found heading further up and across the Essequibo. Getting a boat going elsewhere is precisely the reason many visitors find themselves passing through Parika.

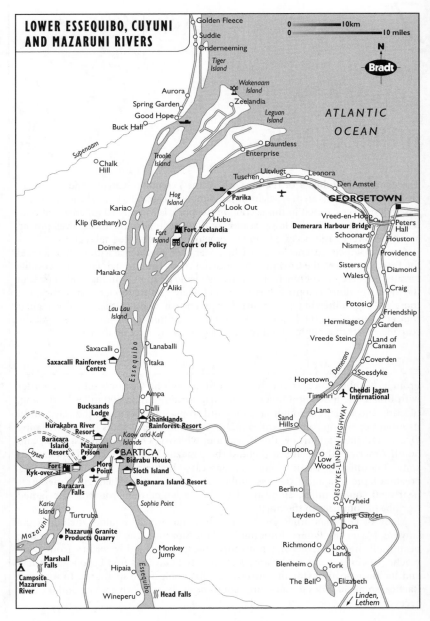

LOWER ESSEQUIBO, CUYUNI AND MAZARUNI RIVERS

0   10km
0   10 miles

N

Bradt

ATLANTIC OCEAN

Golden Fleece
Suddie
Onderneeming
Tiger Island
Aurora
Wakenaam Island
Zeelandia
Spring Garden
Good Hope
Buck Hall
Leguan Island
Supenaam
Chalk Hill
Troolie Island
Dauntless
Enterprise
Uitvlugt
Tuschen
Leonora
Den Amstel
Hog Island
Kariao
Parika
Look Out
GEORGETOWN
Klip (Bethany)
Hubu
Vreed-en-Hoop
Peters Hall
Fort Island
Fort Zeelandia
Demerara Harbour Bridge
Schoonard
Houston
Doime
Court of Policy
Nismes
Providence
Manaka
Sisters
Diamond
Aliki
Wales
Craig
Potosi
Friendship
Lau Lau Island
Hermitage
Garden
Vreede Stein
Land of Canaan
Saxacalli
Lanaballi
Coverden
Saxacalli Rainforest Centre
Itaka
Soesdyke
Essequibo
Hopetown
Ampa
Cheddi Jagan International
Bucksands Lodge
Dalli
Timehri
Lana
Hurakabra River Resort
Shanklands Rainforest Resort
Sand Hills
Baracara Island Resort
Kaow and Kalf Islands
Mazaruni Prison
Dunoon
Fort Kyk-over-al
BARTICA
Moro Point
Bidrabu House
Low Wood
Baracara Falls
Sloth Island
Berlin
Karia Island
Baganara Island Resort
Turtruba
Sophia Point
Leyden
Vryheid
Spring Garden
Mazaruni
Mazaruni Granite Products Quarry
Dora
Richmond
Loo Lands
Marshall Falls
Monkey Jump
Blenheim
York
Campsite Mazaruni River
Hipaia
The Bell
Elizabeth
Wineperu
Head Falls
Linden, Lethem
SOESDYKE-LINDEN HIGHWAY
Demerara
Cuyuni

With too much litter in the streets and an apparent fondness for rum-shop offerings, Parika can come off as being a bit rough around the edges. While tourists can expect special attention in the way of harmless comments, and safety is not a large concern in Parika, visitors should always keep their wits about them and keep a watchful eye on their belongings.

With boats loading and unloading on one end, and minibuses doing the same

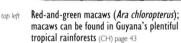

top left   Red-and-green macaws (*Ara chloropterus*); macaws can be found in Guyana's plentiful tropical rainforests (CH) page 43

top right   The area near Dadanawa is an excellent spot for birdwatching, and offers the possibility of sighting jabiru storks (*Jabiru mycteria*) (KS) page 292

above   The stunning Mobai Pond is covered with *Victoria amazonica* lilies, on which you can watch wattled jacanas nest (KSt) page 268

right   The hoatzin (*Opisthocomus hoazin*) is Guyana's national bird (FDN/FN/M/FLPA) page 44

below   Red-billed toucan (*Ramphastos tucanus*); the southwestern area of Guyana boasts more than 500 bird species, including toucans (SAT/FN/M/FLPA) page 43

above left Ocelots (*Leopardus pardalis*) are mainly nocturnal and usually terrestrial, climbing and swimming only occasionally (SAT/FN/M/FLPA) page 31

above Because of their large size and dark reddish and orangish fur, red howler monkeys (*Alouatta seniculus*) are locally called baboons (PO/MP/FLPA) page 36

left Paca (*Agouti paca*) are often called *labba* (CH) page 38

below Giant anteaters (*Myrmecophaga tridactyla*) are found in forest and savanna, especially in open areas with large termite mounds (DF) page 38

above left Giant river otters (*Pteronura brasiliensis*) are often seen in groups of five or more, mostly in remote large rivers, lakes and flooded areas (KS) page 35

above right The capybara (*Hydrochaeris hydrochaeris*) is the world's largest (90cm/30kg), and certainly strangest-looking, rodent (CH) page 38

right The golden-handed tamarin (*Saguinus midas*) is Guyana's smallest primate (PO/MP/FLPA) page 36

below South America's largest native mammal, the tapir (*Tapirus terrestris*) is commonly called the bush cow in Guyana (SAT/FN/M/FLPA) page 37

above left The anaconda (*Eunectes murinus*) grows throughout its life and can reach lengths of more than 30ft (PO/MP/FLPA) page 41

above The thought of a Goliath bird-eating spider (*Theraphosa blondi*) may make you recoil at the idea of setting off on a rainforest walk, but you'll likely find that ants are the worst pests of them all (PO/MP/FLPA) page 41

left With a shell that can reach about 6ft in length and an overall body mass that can weigh more than 1,000lb, the leatherback (*Dermochelys coriacea*) is the largest of the sea turtle species (SAT/FN/M/FLPA) page 48

below There are over 300 reptile and amphibian species in Guyana, including the cane toad (*Bufo marinus*) (SS) page 40

above   Guyana is home to the world's
           largest alligator, the black caiman
           (*Melanosuchus niger*)
           (KS) page 40

right   Yellow-banded poison dart frog
           (*Dendrobates leucomelas*); poison
           dart frogs come in a range of
           colours and are used by some
           Amerindian tribes to poison their
           arrows and blowgun darts
           (CH) page 40

below   Pierid butterflies (*Phoebis*) basking
           on the road; insects are the form of
           wildlife that you're likely to see the
           most in Guyana (CH) page 41

above During its peak, some 30,000 gallons of water cascade over a 741ft-sheer drop, making Kaieteur Falls one of the world's largest and most powerful single-drop waterfalls (KSt) page 218

left The petroglyphs at Iwokrama Gorge date back more than 6,000 years (KS) page 233

below From March to August, Shell Beach, a 90-mile stretch of undeveloped beach in northwestern Guyana, becomes the nesting ground for four of the world's eight endangered species of marine turtles (KS) page 196

above   Guyana's national flower is the giant water lily *Victoria amazonica* (KSt) page 29

right   The Essequibo River is South America's third-largest river and runs the entire length of Guyana (SS) page 3

below   The Iwokrama Canopy Walkway offers a unique opportunity for visitors to immerse themselves in the mid-level canopy of the forest (SS) page 235

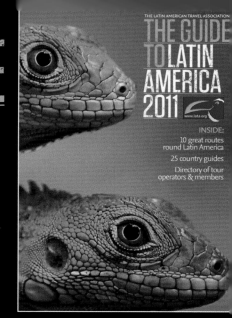

on the other, the stelling is the main pulse of the town, and the dock can provide some good photo opportunities of brightly coloured wooden boats and a seemingly endless supply of fruits and vegetables being unloaded and taken to market.

GETTING THERE AND AWAY Parika is well serviced by minibuses and taxis from Georgetown and all along the west bank and west coast roads. The driving route from Georgetown includes a trip over the locally touted tourist attraction that is the floating **Demerara Harbour Bridge**, reportedly the world's longest floating bridge (it's not). Note that there is a small fee for vehicles to cross (US$0.40), which is included in the taxi or minibus fare. It is charged only when coming from the east bank. The bridge also closes for 1½ hours every day to allow ships to pass; for closing times, which vary, check the local papers or call the **Transport & Harbour Department** (226 8018).

Another option for crossing the Demerara River is by taking a speedboat (US$0.50) from the dock behind Stabroek Market to the Vreed-en-Hoop stelling.

Public river transportation from Parika is either on smaller passenger speedboats or on larger ferries that transport cargo, vehicles and passengers. The main destinations are to the Supenaam stelling, directly across the river in Good Hope, and Bartica, the small frontier town located up the Essequibo, near the convergence of the Cuyuni and Mazaruni rivers.

If you are travelling with a vehicle and need to stop, either for an afternoon or overnight, parking is available at **Lot 162** (*Junction Rd;* 260 4297; US$5 overnight), on a first-come, first-served basis.

By taxi From Georgetown, any taxi company will drive the 30-mile, one-hour trip to Parika (US$15–20). From the Vreed-en-Hoop stelling, there are plenty of taxis that drive to and from Parika (US$10). In Parika, taxis to Georgetown and Vreed-en-Hoop are found in front of the stelling.

By minibus Bus number 32 travels between Stabroek Market and Parika (US$2). There is also always a pack of buses waiting at the Vreed-en-Hoop stelling that travel to Parika (US$1). In Parika, the minibuses converge around the Junction (the crossing of the two main roads) in front of the Two Brothers Restaurant.

By boat As there are many options for travel by boat to and from Parika, this section has been split up by destination and type of transport, speedboat or ferry. The charge for speedboat transportation is paid to the captain at the destination, while tickets for the ferry are purchased in advance at the stelling.

Stelling phone numbers: Georgetown (225 6471), Parika (260 4498), Adventure (774 4272), Bartica (455 2273).

Speedboat This is by far the fastest mode of travel, although it can entail waiting, as public boats don't normally leave until filled with passengers. The Essequibo is a large moody river and the trip can be serenely calm or jarringly rough. Nylon tarpaulins are kept in all boats and do a good job of keeping you dry during rain and rough waters. The river is usually calmest early in the morning or late in the afternoon.

Speedboats from Parika are either going to Bartica or Supenaam; be sure to clarify the boat's destination before boarding. Boats to Bartica often leave from the beach just south of the stelling, while boats to Supenaam are typically boarded from the dock of the stelling, but it never hurts to ask.

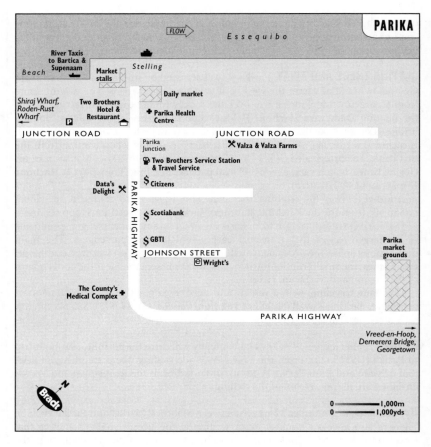

Essequibo

FLOW

Beach

River Taxis
to Bartica &
Supenaam

Market
stalls

Stelling

Shiraj Wharf,
Roden-Rust
Wharf

Two Brothers
Hotel &
Restaurant

Daily market

Parika Health
Centre

JUNCTION ROAD

JUNCTION ROAD

Parika
Junction

Valza & Valza Farms

Two Brothers Service Station
& Travel Service

Data's
Delight

Citizens

PARIKA HIGHWAY

Scotiabank

GBTI

JOHNSON STREET

Wright's

Parika
market
grounds

The County's
Medical Complex

PARIKA HIGHWAY

Vreed-en-Hoop,
Demerera Bridge,
Georgetown

N

0 ————— 1,000m
0 ————— 1,000yds

With speedboats there are no set departure or arrival times; roughly from dawn until dusk they leave whenever full.

It is also possible to hire a private boat. While there are always plenty of people at the stelling offering the services of their boat, one recommended company is Belle's (↖ 455 2253 or 624 1066). Most captains at Belle's know both sides of the Essequibo River and are reliable.

Georgetown–Vreed-en-Hoop Speedboats make frequent trips between Stabroek Market and the Vreed-en-Hoop stelling (US$0.50; 10 minutes), providing a fast alternative to the Demerara bridge route.

Parika–Supenaam This route crosses the Essequibo River to Good Hope, landing at the mouth of the Supenaam River. The 45-minute trip (US$5; more for excess baggage) involves crossing the Essequibo's 20-mile-wide mouth; the river's battle to flow out and the Atlantic's battle to push in can make for a rough, wet journey.

Parika–Bartica Barring the sometimes rough water and (usually) cramped boats, this one-hour boat ride (US$12.50; more for excess baggage) is often a pleasure in itself. The scenery while moving up the Essequibo is stunning, and those who are able to spot wildlife while travelling at fast speeds may be rewarded with a host of birds and monkeys along the bank.

Ferry While travel on the ferry is cheaper, it also is much slower and less frequent. If you have an aversion to speedboats and decide to travel on the ferry, bring patience, binoculars and a good book to pass the time.

Parika–Adventure Due to menacing sandbars, this ferry (passenger US$2; vehicle US$6; 3 hours) leaves with the tide, resulting in an erratic schedule of departure and arrival times. A new ferry stelling in Good Hope was recently completed, but at the time of writing was still marred with problems, so the Adventure stelling was still in use. It is hoped that the Good Hope stelling, along with two new ferries, will eventually alleviate the current travel woes. For updated times, call the Parika stelling.

Parika–Bartica This route has a schedule (to Bartica: 09.00 Thursday and Saturday; to Parika: 06.00 Friday and Sunday; passenger US$3.00, vehicle US$7.00; 5 hours), which is usually followed closely, but the loading of vehicles can take some time.

Parika–Leguan Island The island of Leguan is directly across from Parika in the Essequibo, but it has little of interest for the average visitor (to Leguan Island: 10.00 and 16.00 daily; to Parika: 06.00 and 15.00 daily; passenger US$0.50, vehicle US$4; 45 minutes).

WHERE TO STAY Considering the close proximity of Parika to Georgetown, and the little of interest that the town has for visitors (other than boats going elsewhere) there is little reason for visitors to overnight here. If you need to get a very early boat, the best lodging option nearby is the Toucan Inn, located ten miles (16km) away in Meten-Meer-Zorg (see page 133).

For those who want to stay within walking distance of the stelling, Parika has one newly refurbished hotel that will likely meet the standards expected by travellers.

Two Brothers Hotel (12 rooms) 215 Parika Junction; 260 4014. These new self-contained rooms are clean & furnished with AC, TV & private balconies, but their cramped quarters provide little respite from the noisy street below. **$$**

WHERE TO EAT Parika has plenty of Chinese restaurants, snackettes and rum shops that serve food, but many are a bit rough and a keen eye should be used in checking for cleanliness. The places below come recommended by locals.

Data's Delight 315 Parika Highway; 260 4228; ⏱ 07.00–21.00 daily. This roadside restaurant is only delightful for those looking to sample wild meat, including labba, peccary & deer. Chicken, fish & mutton are also on the menu. **$$**

Two Brothers Restaurant 215 Parika Highway; 260 4016; ⏱ 07.00–19.00 daily. Downstairs is a casual café with range of good pre-made items to choose from, including pizza, fried rice, chicken, fried fish, pastries & the like. The upstairs restaurant has a more spacious dining area & menu of similar fare. **$–$$**

Valza Lot 212; 260 4052; ⏱ 09.00–19.00 Mon–Fri, 09.00–21.00 Sat, 09.00–17.30 Sun. This small restaurant serving a menu of typical Guyanese fare is regularly packed with locals, & not just because of the hearty portions & friendly service, but because they say the food is as good as their mothers'. **$**

SHOPPING Parika is known for its **Sunday market**, said to be one of the largest in Guyana. Once a week, farmers and villagers from all around the agricultural region, including up and down the Essequibo River, converge on the Parika Market Ground and transform it into a throbbing mass of people buying, selling, drinking, eating and sharing the latest gossip. The tropical fruits and fresh vegetables are endless, as are the other goods ranging from underwear to plastic buckets. Come early for the best selection.

The **Daily Market**, located just in front of the stelling, consists of a few snackettes, and vendors selling fruit, vegetables and the typical cheap watches, sunglasses and other imported plastic items.

For grocery items and toiletries, the small **Valza Farms** (*Lot 212;* \ *260 4052;* ⊕ *07.00–19.00 Mon–Fri, 07.00–21.00 Sat, 07.00–17.00 Sun*) has a decent selection.

OTHER PRACTICALITIES This section covers local services that visitors may require while passing through Parika.

Banks Thanks to the thriving Sunday market, Parika has three banks, all of which are open on Sunday.

$ **Citizens Bank** 298 Parika Highway; \ 262 4005; ⊕ 08.00–14.00 Mon/Tue/Thu/Fri, 08.00–12.00 Sun, closed Wed/Sat. Accepts foreign currency & travellers' cheques.

$ **Guyana Bank for Trade & Industry (GBTI)** 300 Parika Highway; \ 260 4400; ⊕ 08.00–14.00. Mon/Tue/Thu/Fri, 08.00–12.30 Sun, closed Wed/Sat. Exchanges foreign currency & travellers' cheques & gives credit card cash advances.

$ **Scotiabank** 299 Parika Highway; \ 260 4205; ⊕ 08.00–14.00 Mon/Tue/Thu, 08.00–14.30 Fri, 08.00–12.30 Sun, closed Wed/Sat. Exchanges foreign currency, travellers' cheques, gives credit card cash advances & has an ATM accepting international cards.

Email and internet

🖥 **Wright's Internet Café** 279 Johnson St; \ 260 4721; ⊕ 07.00–20.00 daily

Hospitals, doctors and pharmacies For serious medical attention it is advised to go to Georgetown, where the nearest hospital is located. For minor concerns, Parika has a **health centre** (\ *260 4040*) directly in front of the stelling, but expect overburdened staff and a long wait. Another option is the **County's Medical Complex** (*2000 Parika Highway;* \ *260 4394;* ⊕ *07.00–19.00 daily*), which houses a doctor's office offering lab and X-ray services, and a pharmacy and Western Union branch.

Tourist information

ℹ **Two Brothers Travel Service** 175 Parika Highway; \ 260 4012; e two2brothersgy@ yahoo.com. Tour operator in Parika strangely does nothing in the way of organising boats for Essequibo trips; essentially books trips through other local operators.

BARTICA

Bartica, an Amerindian word meaning 'red earth', is a frontier town located at the point where the Cuyuni and Mazaruni rivers join the Essequibo River. It has developed from an Anglican missionary settlement in the mid 19th century to a bustling town built on the lucrative businesses of forestry and mining and serves as a passing-through point for many migrant workers, mainly miners who come from around Guyana, Brazil and Venezuela in search of riches. Bartica is also often the first place they reach when coming out to cash in their find so there are plenty of places to spend money: shops, bars, restaurants and hotels.

With boats coming and going from Parika and other destinations along the three rivers, Bartica also has a lively stelling and dock area, which is often all that most visitors will see of the town. There are few places of interest in Bartica, but if you find yourself with some extra time, strolling through the main streets exposes a unique town with an interesting vibe created by a constant coming and going of miners happy to partake in the libations found in the city and a growing Brazilian influence.

GETTING THERE AND AWAY The most common way to get to Bartica is by boat, but at the time of writing, local airlines were exploring regularly scheduled flights from Georgetown's Ogle airport to Bartica. This would make travel to the region much faster and easier, but the sustainability of the service remains to be seen. There is also a rough overland trail that can be used to access Bartica.

Navigation around Bartica, which is approximately one square mile in size, is fairly easy as all seven avenues run north–south and all nine streets run east–west. Walking will suffice in most cases, but taxis are available if you're travelling to the outskirts of town.

By plane Charter flights are always possible to Bartica's airstrip, but at the time of writing, Air Guyana (see page 58) and a new company, Bartica Air Services (`226 4898`), had plans of launching regularly scheduled flights. Bartica Air Services planned on two flights daily (US$25/one-way, including transport from the airstrip to central Bartica). Contact the companies or a local tour operator for current information.

By boat Public river transportation to and from Bartica is serviced by the speedboats, or river taxis, and the cargo, vehicle and passenger ferries running on the Essequibo River between here and Parika (see page 153 for detailed information).

Speedboats land at the docks further south of the stelling. The walkway leading to these docks is just south of the WK Shopping Mall (*33 First Av*); the cluster of small bars at the docks are a good place to enquire about hiring a private boat if you need to access destinations further a field.

By 4x4 Next to the WK Shopping Mall, at the point where boat passengers exit the docks, there is often a pack of 4x4 trucks competing for the business of miners looking to head to the interior. These trucks offer access to hinterland locations, but visitors should not just hop on a truck and land unannounced at some interior mining camp. Visits to the interior from Bartica should be well planned and, ideally, taken with a trustworthy and knowledgeable guide.

With a sturdy 4x4 vehicle, Bartica can also be reached by land. The route entails driving to Linden and then following the trail towards Rockstone village on the Essequibo River (see page 215) and on to Sharima village. From there a ferry crosses the Essequibo River (US$40) and another trail connects with the Potaro Road, south of Bartica. The Potaro Road leads directly to Bartica. During the dry season, the entire trip takes roughly four hours; during the wet season the condition of the road can be horrible. There is no public transportation that services this route, and it is not entirely straightforward (there are many wrong turns to take); it should always be driven with somebody familiar with the road.

By taxi In Bartica there are taxis widely available to provide transportation around town and to nearby locations where the road permits. Rates range from US$1.50 per stop or US$10 per hour; one company to call is Krissy's Taxi Service (📞 455 2553). Some locations further out on the Potaro road also have a set fare.

WHERE TO STAY Be they miners, aid workers, residents of nearby villages or travellers, Bartica sees its fair share of visitors passing through town and has a host of hotels to service individual needs. The following are Bartica's more reputable lodgings. To stay a bit more out of town, see also Bidrabu House (page 168).

🏠 **'D' Factor Interior Guest House**
(10 rooms) Lot 2 Triangle St; 📞 455 2544. Set on the edge of Bartica along the river, this guesthouse is quiet & breezy. These self-contained rooms with fans, nets & desks are basic but very clean. There's a large wraparound balcony upstairs with views of Parrot Island & an area on the main floor for the cheaper option of hanging hammocks. Meals can be catered & the owner, Balkarran, offers river trips. *Rooms* **$$**, *hammocks* **$**
🏠 **Zen's Plaza Hotel** (14 rooms) Lot 43 Second Av; 📞 455 2441. This friendly hotel is much quieter than anything found on First Av. The old wooden house has self-contained rooms, which are spacious & outfitted with fans, TVs & desks; some have AC for extra charge. Tour the rooms before choosing because while there's a difference in price, there is little difference in the rooms. **$$**
🏠 **Platinum Inn** (24 rooms) Lot 7 First Av; 📞 455 3041; e platinum_inn_intl@yahoo.com; www.platinumparadise.bravehost.com. This hulking cement building has a selection of self-contained & tidy rooms for every budget. The small & cavernous basic rooms are filled with just a bed & fan, while others offer AC, cable TV, hot & cold water, mini-fridges, desk & tall ceilings; for the extra money, the suites offer only an additional bed. A nice lounge has a big-screen TV, the restaurant serves reliable food & the bar overlooking the river specialises in pounding music on w/ends. This, combined with the noise

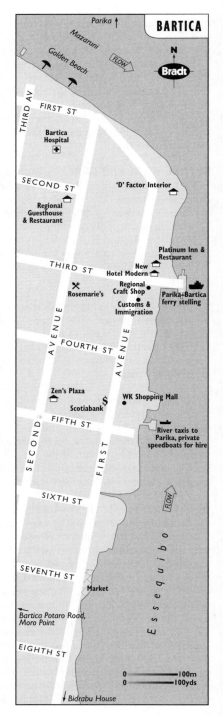

of the nearby stelling, could be a breaking point for some. Helpful & welcoming manager also organises area trips & offers package deals. **$–$$$**

🏠 **New Hotel Modern** (20 rooms) Lot 9 First Av; ☎ 455 2301. The day & night popularity of the downstairs bar & the location right off the stelling make the Hotel Modern a noisy place to seek sleep. The ordinary rooms are very basic & share a dirty bathroom. The standard self-contained rooms are better with fans, tables &

TVs; the suites add AC, small veranda & fridge & dirty carpet over the otherwise nice wooden floors. **$–$$**

🏠 **Regional Guest House** (10 rooms) Lot 8 Second Av; ☎ 455 2244. The best & cheapest basic rooms in town. The tidy rooms all have fans, nets & desks; 4 are self-contained & 6 share clean bathrooms & showers. The location is quiet (minus daytime laughter of kids from nearby school) & the staff treat you like family & serve some of the best food in town. **$**

✖ **WHERE TO EAT** Bartica's First Avenue is full of restaurants and snackettes serving everything from typical Guyanese cuisine to Chinese to increasingly popular Brazilian food. Many serve food that is fine, although meals can be hit or miss. Restaurants below are reliable and recommended, but don't be afraid to ask a local for their favourite.

✖ **Platinum Inn Restaurant** Lot 7 First Av; ☎ 455 3041; e platinum_inn_intl@yahoo.com; www.platinumparadise.bravehost.com; ⊕ 07.00–23.00 daily. The atmosphere is slightly stale but the typical Guyanese cuisine served here is good quality. $$

✖ **Regional Guest House Kitchen** Lot 8 Second Av; ☎ 455 2244; ⊕ 08.00–20.00 daily (flexible hours for guests). The set menu changes daily & features staples like BBQ trout, fried

chicken & buttered plantains, but the cooks also like a challenge & prepare meals to order for special diets, vegetarians or certain cravings. Food is some of the best in town. $$

✖ **Rosemarie's Lot** 21 Second Av; ☎ 455 3088; ⊕ 07.00–23.00 Mon–Sat. Clean & spacious dining room with a large selection of prepared meals. Snacks, pastries & breads all baked fresh in-house. $$

BARTICA REGATTA

The Rupununi has the rodeo (see page 285) and Bartica has the regatta. Every year over Easter weekend Bartica is transformed into a destination location; hotels are booked, the streets are crowded and Golden Beach becomes packed with spectators cheering on small boats travelling at high speeds. The drinking, eating and loud, thumping music goes without saying.

The history of this event goes all the way back to 1947 when the captain of a yacht that had come across the Atlantic Ocean somehow landed in Bartica. Once in Bartica the captain didn't stop and count his blessings after actually making it past all of the Essequibo River's unmarked hazards unscathed. Instead he passed the days by racing his boat, powered by a 22-horsepower outboard engine, up and down the river. His exploits drew appreciative crowds of locals.

The captain soon found himself with a competitor who had an aluminium boat powered by a 22-horsepower engine as well. Word spread of the scheduled race and people came to watch from miles around.

The story of the epic race and the brave captain never lost its lustre and it eventually grew into the current annual Bartica Regatta. Besides the boat races, other activities include the highly anticipated Bartica Regatta pageant, road race, swimming race, kite flying and a host of other sporting events that attract crowds of intoxicated people, including dominoes.

7

SHOPPING As Bartica serves as an outpost for many interior mining communities there are plenty of shops selling an assortment of goods. First Avenue is where most stores are located and it's here you'll find groceries, mining supplies, clothing boutiques, pharmacies, toiletries, jewellery and the like. On the southern end of First Avenue is a collection of market stalls with fresh fruit, vegetables, meat and fish.

The **Regional Craft Shop** (*Third St, across from Platinum Inn;* ⊕ *08.00–16.30 Mon–Fri*) has done a good job of filling a cramped store with a wide selection of local crafts. Here you can find *warashis* (locally crafted backpacks), straw hats, baskets, *matapis* (used in extracting cyanide from cassava), bows and arrows, blowguns, stuffed caiman and animal skins.

Many shops and market stalls close for extended periods over the lunch hour and stay open later in the evening.

OTHER PRACTICALITIES This section covers local services that visitors may require while in Bartica or other nearby areas.

Bank
$ **Scotiabank** 43 Second Av; ✆ 455 2618; ⊕ 08.00–12.00 & 13.30–16.00 Mon/Tue/Thu/Fri, 08.00–13.00 Wed. Only bank in Bartica that exchanges foreign currency, travellers' cheques, gives credit card cash advances & has an ATM accepting international cards.

Email and internet If you are in need of internet, head to First Street where you'll find several good options offering internet access (US$1/hour) and international calls (US$0.20–0.50/minute).

Hospitals In case of an emergency, visit the Bartica Hospital (✆ *455 2339*), but don't come expecting the best conditions.

WHAT TO SEE AND DO The town of Bartica has little to offer visitors in the way of activities outside of frequenting the local rum shop. Most visitors will only find themselves passing through town en route to a destination along one of the rivers.

The **Benedictine Monastery,** located outside of town, closed in 2010, but the nearby **Moro Point** (see page 176) can be easily accessed from town, either by taxi or a long walk.

In town, there is the **Golden Beach** (*between Second Av & Fourth Av*). The sands are as the name says, golden, and the Essequibo River is always good for a swim, but the frequent presence of rubbish is a turn-off.

ESSEQUIBO RIVER: EAST BANK

There are several lodges, resorts and private home rentals on the banks of the Essequibo River. All have their own charm, and while they may appear to be similar at first glance, each offers a unique experience to visitors. A trip, which combines two or three of the locations, is the best way to experience this section of the Essequibo.

The east bank of the Essequibo River is more easily accessible in that the public river taxis that travel between Parika and Bartica follow this side and are willing to drop passengers at locations along the route.

BAGANARA ISLAND RESORT (*c/o Evergreen Adventures, 159 Charlotte St, Lacytown;* ✆ *222 8050;* e *reservations@evergreenadventuresgy.com; www.evergreenadventuresgy. com/resorts/Baganara.html;* **$$$$–$$$$$**) Baganara is a 187-acre island located five miles south of Bartica, near the Essequibo's east bank. The resort, with its football pitch-sized perfectly manicured lawns, white sand beach lined with reclining chairs and watersports, is reminiscent of locations found in the Caribbean Sea to the north. The beautiful setting, relaxed ambience and well-appointed lodge make Baganara the perfect place to decompress after a trip to some of Guyana's more demanding destinations.

Getting there and away Baganara is most often accessed by boat, but with a private runway on the island, chartered flights and day trips that include Kaieteur Falls are also an option.

By boat
From/To Parika Travel time is roughly one hour.

From Parika, take the **river taxi** (see page 154 for details) to Bartica and then arrange for transportation from there to Baganara, either through Baganara or a private boat.

Baganara offers return transportation in the **Baganara jet boat** from Roden-Rust Wharf, just south of Parika (return US$30/person; minimum 12 persons). Private charters are also available (one-way US$415).

Hiring a **private boat** can be a good option for a large enough group to make it economically feasible. Be sure to arrange a pick-up time with the captain, get a back-up phone number and don't pay for any services in advance (ie: the return trip).

From/To Bartica Travel time is roughly 10–15 minutes.

Baganara's boat can arrange transfer to and from Bartica (return US$100; maximum 11 persons).

By querying at the docks in Bartica, **private boats** can be found to take visitors to Baganara (one-way US$40).

YACHTING IN GUYANA

Along with improving the recognition of Guyana as a birdwatching destination, the Ministry of Tourism and the Guyana Tourism Authority (GTA) are trying to push Guyana as a destination for yachters. Since Guyana lies outside of the hurricane belt, those involved in the initiative believe that yachters will come to Guyana instead of other destinations such as Trinidad and Tobago and Venezuela during the hurricane season.

The catch is that Guyana doesn't have the turquoise blue waters or the level of infrastructure yachters will find in many of the other more developed yachting destinations in the Caribbean. However Guyana does have some nice white sand beaches along the Essequibo River and a few places for the boats to anchor, such as Baganara Island Resort and Hurakabra River Resort.

To help ease the logistics for interested yachters, Bartica has been declared an official port of entry and all immigration services can be taken care of there. For those looking to steer their boats off the well-worn nautical paths, more technical information can be found in the *Cruising Guide to Trinidad & Tobago, Barbados and Guyana*, by Chris Doyle. Detailed trip reports from the captains of the few yachts that have come to Guyana can also be downloaded from the GTA website.

By plane There are no scheduled flights to Baganara, but charters are available (20 mins; see page 84). There are also many tours that combine flights to Kaieteur Falls and Baganara Island (see page 58). While many are day trips, it is possible to stay overnight and return to Georgetown with a boat.

⌂ Where to stay

All accommodation at Baganara (17 rooms) is inclusive of all meals and local soft drinks and is in self-contained superior rooms (**$$$$$**) or standard rooms with shared bathrooms (**$$$$**). The meals are hearty and consist of dishes made with local vegetables, fish, meat and fruit.

Sitting on the upper edge of the beach, Baganara House is the centrepiece of the island. Originally built as a family retreat, the beautiful wooden building has five rooms upstairs (1 superior, 4 standard) and an open dining room, bar and lounge area downstairs. The bedrooms are breezy and open onto shared or private balconies with great views of the river.

Downstairs is the dining room where all meals are served, a well-stocked bar and an open lounge area with hammocks, tables and chairs, and elevated sofa beds that deserve as much attention as the beachside chairs. The fact that there are no walls provides great views of the river from nearly anywhere you're sitting.

The remaining ten superior rooms are in a separate building on the opposite end of the beach. The comfortable rooms are tastefully decorated with locally crafted furniture, ceiling fans, hardwood floors and new fixtures. While the building itself isn't as visually stunning as the Baganara House, the rooms are newer, more private and the views are still brilliant.

What to see and do

Between some serious bouts of relaxing, Baganara Island Resort offers a variety of activities to occupy your time. More than 120 species of birds have been identified on or around Baganara Island, but many birdwatchers still don't consider Baganara as an ideal spotting location. The island used to be little more than a floating patch of thick swampy forest; to build the resort a large area was cleared, filled in and planted with grass. The resulting grounds are beautiful, but many of the birds have retreated into the trees on the still untouched half of the island.

There are nature trails winding through the pristine forests located on the northern end of the island, but this land is also highly prone to flooding, often making them inaccessible.

Kayaks are available for rent (US$2.50/hour) and can be paddled around the island or up a small creek located on the mainland. The 1–2-hour creek paddle offers the best chance for spotting wildlife and birds, as well as an interesting mix of flora. It is much like a water-based jungle hike.

Other water-based activities on the island include swimming, pedal boating, water skiing and wake boarding and banana boats. Fishing trips along the Essequibo can also be arranged with advanced notice. There is also a volleyball court and table tennis and pool tables. In the evening, for those not wanting to sit under the stars and absorb the sounds of nature, a television, DVD player and karaoke machine are available.

Off-island trips include excursions to Marshall Falls (US$150/boat; maximum 12 persons); to Parrot Island (US$75/boat; maximum 8 persons) for a not-to-be-missed sunset. Watch droves of parrots return to roost for the night; and to Bartica (US$70/boat; maximum 8 persons) for a tour of the town.

Baganara is also a popular location for day trips, most often in combination with a flight to Kaieteur Falls. These trips usually involve flying to Kaieteur Falls in the morning and making a stop at Baganara Island on the return for lunch and swimming. Evergreen Adventures also offers an overland day trip (US$85; min 15 persons). See page 59 for details.

SLOTH ISLAND (*c/o Dagron Tours International;* \ *223 7921;* e *slothisland@yahoo. com; www.dagron-tours.com;* **$$$$**) The 160-acre Sloth Island is a new resort just opposite Bartica, and while development of nature trails on the island is ongoing, the main buildings of the lodge are complete and ready for visitors.

Getting there Sloth Island is located three miles north of Bartica and is accessible by boat.

From/To Parika The cheapest option is to take a public boat to Bartica and then arrange transportation from there. If you have a large group and are willing to pay slightly more for the convenience of leaving when you want, then hire a private boat to cover the trip from Parika (one-way US$250).

From/To Bartica By querying on the docks, it is easy enough to find somebody willing to take you to the island (one-way US$30). If you arrived in Bartica on a river taxi, ask the captain if he can take you the rest of the way after unloading passengers.

Where to stay All accommodation at Sloth Island (8 rooms) includes all meals and local soft drinks and is in self-contained rooms.

The main concrete house sits on the northern part of the island and has views of the Essequibo River and, in the distance, Bartica. All rooms are fairly spacious and include two beds and fans. Four on the main floor have tiled floors, and the three on the top have wooden floors and better views. If it's available, you should request the more secluded tower room, which has the best views on the island.

The dining room and bar is located in two covered *benabs* behind the main house. Beyond this are more tables and benches shaded by the forest and a covered house for hammocks.

What to see and do Like many of the Essequibo resorts, Sloth island is set up around relaxing and water activities. The island features several natural beaches that come and go with the tides. There are nature trails but much of the island remains unconquered mangroves and rainforests, meaning the wildlife is plentiful.

Fishing, both on and off island, can be arranged and birdwatchers have more than 170 species to identify during their stay. The island is also home to many mammal species, including the namesake sloth.

Off-island trips can be arranged to all area destinations (see page 174), including Marshall Falls, Baracara Falls, Parrot Island (where thousands of parrots roost), and to Bartica for a tour of the town.

SHANKLANDS RAINFOREST RESORT (Note: Shortly after the first edition of this guide was published, Shanklands Resort was closed and put up for sale. At the time of going to print, Shanklands had been purchased with plans to reopen the resort. Details and changes were not available, so it is included here with only general information from the original incarnation. If it does reopen and is anything like it was when the original owners, Joanne and Max Jardim were running it, it's worth contacting a local tour operator to plan a visit.)

Shanklands is located on 145 acres of mostly virgin rainforest on the east bank of the Essequibo River, 20 minutes from Bartica. It's a small affair that began when original owner Joanne Jardim inherited the land from her father in the 1980s. In an effort to build a holiday cottage on the land, Joanne hired local Amerindians to help her clear the area, being careful not to cut down any of the towering hardwood trees which are vital to the natural ecosystem. During the building phase, Joanne spent countless nights camping in the jungle and getting to know the depth of her land intricately. Over time the idea that started as a personal holiday cottage morphed into a full-fledged eco-resort with a laidback atmosphere that gives guests their space while still providing plenty of personal attention.

Getting there The most common way to get to Shanklands is via the Essequibo, but it is also possible to access Shanklands by road from the east. The public **river taxis** (see page 165 for details) going to Bartica follow the east bank of the river, so it's possible to have the captain drop you at Shanklands on request (be sure to notify the captain before departing Parika). For the return trip, ask the Shanklands staff to call Bartica to notify the next departing boat that there are passengers at Shanklands needing transport.

Where to stay Shanklands had four self-contained colonial-style gingerbread cottages and an open dormitory-style building for large groups. From their perches on the hill overlooking the Essequibo, the cottages provide beautiful views from their balconies lined with Berbice chairs and hammocks. The cottages also have furnished kitchens (minus the fridge; ice provided) that allow for groups to rent individual cottages and self-cater.

What to see and do The original Shanklands catered to a wide range of nature lovers including botanists, biologists, backpackers and birdwatchers. A small sample of what has been recorded on the property includes 11 of South America's 12 families of butterflies, seven of Guyana's eight species of primates, 56 species of trees and 210 species of birds, not to mention a wealth of other insects, mammals, reptiles, amphibians and plantlife. This dense concentration of flora and fauna is the main draw for Shanklands.

The great thing about Shanklands is that this melting pot of tropical flora and fauna is incredibly accessible, which makes activities such as birdwatching especially convenient. The best birding is had while walking around the manicured lawns of the main grounds. In just a few hours it's not uncommon to spot upwards of 50 different species of birds, including tropical kingbirds, lineated woodpeckers, swallow-winged puffbirds, common tody-flycatchers, scarlet tanagers, cayenne jays, white-winged potoo, channel-billed toucans, green aracari, ruby-topaz hummingbirds, blue dacnis, red-bellied macaws, green honeycreepers, golden-winged parakeets, black-spotted barbets and silver-beaked tanagers. While the open lawns along the riverbank offer some of the best birdwatching at Shanklands, a nature walk through the rainforest shouldn't be missed.

ESSEQUIBO RIVER: WEST BANK

The Essequibo River, with its many hidden sand banks and other hazards, can be a beast to navigate. For this reason, the captains of the river taxis tend to follow a set route along the Essequibo's east bank and are largely unfamiliar with the west bank. Rarely will river taxis agree to stray from their normal course and drop passengers at locations on the west bank, making special boat arrangements a near necessity to access this side of the river.

The river taxi company, Belle's (☎ 455 2253), has boats for hire and will travel to the west bank (one-way US$125–150) from Parika or Bartica. They are reliable and friendly. Another recommended captain is the river guide Balkarran (☎ 455 2544); he makes trips between west bank locations and Bartica (one-way US$40–50). Once again, be sure to arrange a return pick-up time with the captain, get a back-up phone number and don't pay for any services in advance (ie: the return trip).

More details and transportation options are covered under each location's *Getting there* section.

SAXACALLI RAINFOREST CENTRE (*c/o 60 Area H Ogle, East Coast Demerara;* ☎ *222 4565;* e *emc@networksgy.com; www.emcguyana.com*) While studying environmental studies at the University of Guyana, Shyam Nokta realised a flaw in the programme. Many of the students couldn't afford to travel to some of Guyana's better-known natural sites, and thus their first-hand experience and research was limited. Shyam began searching for an area of untouched forest near Georgetown that could be easily and affordably accessed by students, researchers, locals and tourists alike. The result is Saxacalli Rainforest Centre located on nearly 30 acres adjacent to Saxacalli, an Amerindian village 25 miles south of Parika.

Saxacalli provides a good opportunity for visitors on a day trip or longer stay to explore an area of Guyana's rainforest that is rich in flora and fauna. Saxacalli is an education centre, not a typical resort, but the nature trails are excellent, the lodging is comfortable and the white sand beach at Saxacalli village is said to be one of the best on the Essequibo.

Getting there and away
By boat This is the only way to reach Saxacalli Rainforest Centre.

From/To Parika Travel time is about 40 minutes.
There are the rare times when a captain of a **public boat** will agree to cross to the west bank (it never hurts to ask), but this option should not be relied upon. When chartering a boat to Saxacalli without a large group, it may be cheaper to take the public boat to Bartica and then hire a boat to travel back to the centre.

When organising a day or overnight trip with the **Saxacalli boat**, the rates are inclusive of transportation from Georgetown and vary according to the number of persons. All return boat transportation from Parika can be arranged through Saxacalli. For day trips (US$40–170/person, depending on number of persons; minimum 2, maximum 12) rates include return transport from Georgetown, drinks, snacks, lunch and activities.

With a larger group, hiring a **private boat** can sometimes work out to be the cheapest option. The river taxi company, Belle's (☎ 455 2253) has boats for hire and will travel to the west bank (one-way US$150–175).

From/To Bartica Travel time is 20–25 minutes.
River taxis will not typically take this side of the river when going to Parika, necessitating a private boat.
By querying at the docks in Bartica, a **private boat** can be arranged to make the trip (one-way US$50).

⌂ **Where to stay** The concept behind Saxacalli is that it is a rustic, back-to-nature resort (3 rooms), but most visitors will find that the accommodation, while basic, exceeds the definition of rustic. The main building, the Kabakalli Lodge, is a stilted wooden building with an open lounge, bedroom, bathroom and barbecue pit downstairs, and two additional bedrooms, kitchen, sitting room and large wraparound balcony upstairs. There are two additional beds on the balcony and plenty of space for hammocks. Beds are covered with mosquito nets; the caretakers, who are also available to help prepare the self-catered meals, keep the shared bathrooms clean. A generator provides electricity for a few hours at night. The facilities are comfortable and still maintain a certain harmony with nature.

There are also plans to build two self-contained cabins, with two to three rooms in each. Rates to overnight at Saxacalli are negotiable according to the number of people and number of nights; contact them for quotes.

What to see and do Saxacalli, which means 'kingfisher' in the local Arawak dialect, offers a little bit of everything to the visitor, from the jungle to the beach, the Essequibo to small interior creeks.

There is a virtual maze of nature trails that wind all over the mora/swamp forest and to the nearby village of Saxacalli. These trails offer serious researchers and curious visitors a chance to learn much about the fancy words of science: botany, entomology, herpetology, mammalogy and ornithology.

Massive greenheart, kabukalli, crabwood and mora trees line the trails, as do many species of orchids and ité and kokerite palms. A few of the fauna calling the forests home include agouti, deer, tapir, peccary, armadillo, jaguar, ocelot, sloth, squirrel, capuchin and howler monkeys. Some 100 species of birds have been identified, including hawks, falcons, curassows, hummingbirds, kingfishers, jacamars, woodpeckers, toucans, macaws and parrots. The insects, as is always the case in rainforests, are numerous.

Water-based activities include swimming from the extensive beach, dugout canoe trips up small creeks and night-time boat trips using spotting torches to locate nocturnal creatures. Fishing trips for such species as pacu, haimara and dogfish can also be arranged.

Tours of Saxacalli Village, including a stop at their beautiful beach and trips to other sites along the Essequibo, can also be organised.

HURAKABRA RIVER RESORT AND BUCKSANDS LODGE (\ 226 0240; e *gemmadhoo@gmail.com/gem@hurakabragy.com; www.hurakabagy.com*) Located three miles south of Bartica on the west bank of the Essequibo, and named after an adjacent creek, this resort consists of the extravagant **Mango Tree Villa** and the more modest **Bamboo Cottage**, both set along the river's edge. All the fixings of a resort are here – beautiful manmade beach, long dock stretching over the river, beach bar and grill, noisy wave runners, quiet kayaks, veranda jacuzzi – yet it's not your typical resort. The owners built the whole complex as a retirement/holiday retreat, and they occupy the Mango Villa frequently on weekends and holidays; it has the feel of staying in someone else's fancy house, which in essence, is exactly what you're doing. Hurakabra was also built to give visiting yachts a place to moor.

Bucksands River Cottage, located one mile further south of Hurakabra, was a private holiday home for more than 30 years until recently being opened for public rentals. Bucksands is more rustic – the wood of the doors, floors and homemade beds is unfinished, kitchen furnishings are well used, and there are ants aplenty – yet the sense of isolation and privacy found in its beautiful setting provides a different kind of luxury. Bucksands is ideal for travellers looking for a self-catering and inexpensive retreat.

Getting there and away

By boat Travel by boat is the only way to get to Hurakabra.

From/To Parika Travel time is one hour.

There are the rare times when a captain of a **public boat** (river taxi, see page 165) will agree to cross to the west bank, but this option should not be relied upon. To keep transportation costs to a minimum, the best option is to take a river taxi to Bartica and arrange private transportation from there to the resort.

Hurakabra boat transportation from Parika to Hurakabra or Bucksands can be arranged through the owners, although it's not the cheapest option. If your travel plans happen to coincide with when the owners are making the trip, guests can ride in their boat (return US$50–60/person) otherwise the entire boat can be chartered (one-way US$175; maximum 8 persons).

Chartering a **private boat** from Parika (one-way US$150–175) is a good option for those travelling in a group. Belle's (455 2253) is familiar with Hurakabra and Bucksands.

From/To Bartica Travel time is 10–15 minutes.

River taxis will not typically take this side of the river when going to Parika, necessitating a private boat.

Hurakabra boat When using the river taxi to or from Bartica, arrangements can be made for drop-off or pick-up (one-way US$50; maximum 8 persons).

By querying at the docks in Bartica, a **private boat** can be arranged to make the trip (one-way US$25–40).

Where to stay Three different nouns – villa, cottage, lodge – essentially mean the same thing, yet do a good job of defining the differences between the four accommodation options here.

Hurakabra ($$$$$) are planning to build six additional self-contained rooms to better handle larger groups. The resort has 110V solar electricity, hot and cold water and meals can either be self-catered or provided at an extra charge.

Mango Tree Villa ($$$$$) is the trophy home of the three: a holiday home fit for the entire extended family. This massive yellow, two-level cement structure doesn't necessarily mesh with the jungle backdrop, but it seems to have been built with more of a focus on modern luxuries than natural surroundings.

The downstairs has a spacious dining room and large kitchen fully equipped with solar refrigerator and freezer, stove, oven and grill. The upstairs, which is accessed by a stylish yet best-undertaken-while-sober spiral staircase, has three bedrooms, a living room stuffed with lounging chairs, television and computer with internet access, and a veranda, complete with jacuzzi, that wraps around the entire house. The master bedroom has a private bath, king-sized bed and a walk-in closet. The second bedroom has a queen-sized bed with view of the river while the third room has a twin bunk bed and looks out to the jungle in the back. The entire house is beautifully decorated with furniture locally crafted from natural forest products.

Bucksands Lodge ($$$$) skips all things modern and fancy (except for the small generator supplying limited electricity at night) while still providing a perfectly adequate lodging in a serene jungle setting. Bucksands is the literal cabin in the woods providing a retreat from the hustle and bustle of daily life. It's an ageing wooden building on stilts (necessary during high tide), rustic but not rundown. The two upstairs bedrooms have double bunk beds, and the one downstairs has a double bed; all have mosquito nets and sinks. The kitchen is fully stocked with dishes, pots, pans, stove and oven; it doesn't have a fridge however, meaning the drinks will be warm and the food unpreserved unless you're travelling with an icebox. The two bathrooms and one shower are shared and a caretaker is available for washing up and cleaning.

The real draws of Bucksands are the wide veranda, practically sitting over the river, and the gorgeous natural beach. The view over the Essequibo, especially early in the morning and late in the evening, is fantastic.

Bamboo Cottage (**$$$**) is named after the bamboo furniture with which it is furnished. It's smaller, cosier and a bit more manageable than the villa. There is a bedroom, an open kitchen with stove, oven and ice cooler, a small living room and riverfront veranda with barbecue grill. The living room's sofa turns into a bed, which would be fine for kids, but the cottage would feel a bit cramped with more than two adults.

What to see and do Hurakabra is the place to visit if you're looking for activities other than reading, swimming and lounging to fill your days. For non-peaceful entertainment a wave runner can be rented (US$25/half-hour) and water skiing and knee boarding are also options (US$35/half-hour). More serene options include birdwatching and the rental of pedal boats and kayaks. If it rains, there is a host of indoor board games and books to peruse.

Bucksands is a place to visit for relaxation. There is little to do other than lounge about, swim in the river, read a book and play games. The jungle is just behind the lodge but it's never a good idea to explore its depths without a guide. Bucksands also serves as a good base for river trips around the area.

River trips along the Essequibo, Mazaruni and Cuyuni (see page 173) can also be booked through Hurakabra.

BIDRABU HOUSE (*c/o Worldwide Travel Service, 64D Middle St, South Cummingsburg;* \ *226 4099;* e *world@networksgy.com;* **$$$$$**) Bidrabu is a beautiful three-level wooden house facing the Essequibo River. It is, in the truest sense, a holiday home. There is plenty of space for large groups, yet it's intimate enough for a lone couple to stay and not feel swallowed up by its size.

Getting there and away Bidrabu House is located roughly one mile north of Bartica, from where it's accessible by boat, taxi or walking. If the boat captain, taxi driver or whoever else you ask for directions isn't familiar with the Bidrabu House, refer to it as the Willems' house, as they are the owners.

From/To Parika The cheapest option is to take a public boat to Bartica and then arrange transportation from there. If you have a large group and are willing to pay slightly more for the convenience of leaving when you want, then hire a private boat to cover the trip from Parika (one-way US$150–200).

From/To Bartica Once in Bartica there are several options for reaching Bidrabu.

By boat By querying on the docks, it is easy enough to find somebody willing to make the short drop to Bidrabu (one-way US$15–20). If you arrived in Bartica on a river taxi, ask the captain if he can take you the rest of the way after unloading passengers.

By taxi From town it's possible to take a taxi most of the way (US$5–8). The taxi will drop you just before Bidrabu village, behind the house. Walk towards the river and ask anybody to point you in the right direction (the caretakers also live in Bidrabu village).

On foot Bidrabu House is roughly a 20-minute walk from Bartica.

Where to stay Virtually everything one could want in a holiday retreat is accounted for: a well-stocked, large kitchen with new appliances, including stove, fridge and microwave; dining room table fit for a party; five self-contained bedrooms; lounge area with classic books, TV and DVD player; two verandas with Berbice chairs and tables; a swimming pool; two beaches; electricity; and hot water.

Everything is kept very clean and the open layout of the house provides plenty of space, sunshine and gorgeous river views.

Bidrabu is rented out by the bedroom (from 2 to 5; US$110–240) ; when renting just one or two, request that the top-floor bedrooms be made up, as they have the best views. If renting the entire house, extra mattresses can be made up to accommodate more bodies on the floor. Bidrabu is not usually rented out to more than one party at a time, no matter how many rooms are booked, but it always pays to double-check if you're not interested in sharing a house with strangers. The house is often booked far in advance for weekends and holidays.

Guests must bring food, drinking water and beverages, but the caretaker is an excellent cook if cooking is an undesirable activity for you on holiday. For the price of gasoline used by the caretaker's small boat, they will also make trips into Bartica to pick up any necessary supplies.

What to see and do Bidrabu is a great place for a relaxing weekend. It's not as isolated as Bucksands or Gold Mine, and sometimes the night-time noise of Bartica drifts upriver, but the trade-off is that it's easier to access and offers more amenities. Bartica is close, making a trip in to explore the town a good way to spend a couple of hours. Bidrabu is ideal for non-resort seekers who would still like to experience the Essequibo and this region of Guyana, and with more than two people it becomes affordable.

MAZARUNI RIVER

The source of the nearly 400-mile-long Mazaruni River is located in the Merume Mountains of western Guyana. The Merume Mountains, along with the Pakaraima Mountains, are the highlands of the Roraima Plateau, an incredibly inaccessible area of Guyana formed of sandstone and conglomerate *tepuis*, or tabletop mountains, which are crowned by the roughly nine-mile-long and 9,222ft (2,810m) Mount Roraima.

From its inhospitable source, the Mazaruni River falls south from the mountains before turning its course northwards; its route descends through steep canyons and over numerous falls. Continuing northwards, the river passes through small villages such as Imbaimadai, Kamarang, Kurupung and Issano.

Now heading through the Pakaraima Mountains, the dramatic falls and steep canyons continue. After Peaima Falls the river bends and heads southeast, skirting the edge of the mountains from which it just descended. As it flows over lowland areas of the Precambrian Guiana Shield, other rivers with their sources in the Merume Mountains – the Meamu, Kurupung and Eping – merge with the Mazaruni.

Eventually, just after Tiboku Falls, the Mazaruni begins heading northeast on its final stretch around islands and over sets of small rapids and falls before meeting the Cuyuni River's mouth and pouring into the Essequibo River near Bartica.

Areas all along the Mazaruni River from its source to its mouth have long been a hotbed for mining of gold and diamonds. Alluvial diamonds were first found in Guyana by accident in 1890 when the miner Edward Gilkes was prospecting for gold in the upper Mazaruni River basin. In the decades that have followed, the Mazaruni River and its major tributaries have produced more than half of all alluvial diamonds mined in Guyana.

Dredging the Mazaruni River for gold has also long been a common practice in the area. Large amounts of gold have been pulled out of the river, especially during the 1980s and early 1990s. And with the price of gold once again reaching record highs in 2006, the practice gained a newfound popularity. The search for the fabled city of gold, El Dorado, will probably never cease.

TOURISM Most tourism along the Mazaruni River takes place quite near its mouth. Besides a possible stop at a nearby beach, most visitors won't make it any further than Marshall Falls. Tourism beyond this area of the Mazaruni River is still relatively rare.

The terrain is incredibly rugged and development is limited to isolated Amerindian villages and Wild West mining camps where living conditions are harsh (the area has long been a hotbed for malaria). And while much of the land remains unexplored and untouched, it's the scarred lands of mining camps that welcome people to the area. Needless to say, the effects of mining are a dreadful sight, and a vision most would rather not bring to the forefront of reality on a nature-based holiday.

That said, from Bartica it takes just a short trip up the Mazaruni River – to Marshall Falls for example – for visitors to recognise the beauty along its banks. This can lead to visions of what lies further upriver in the jungle, mountains, rivers and creeks left untouched by human interference. For now, and likely for many more years to come, to the average visitor, it's likely that the upper reaches of the Mazaruni will have to remain imagined.

Nevertheless, for the adventurous travellers, preferably with a rucksack, who are extremely hardy, tolerant of rough mining camps and miners and are never quite content unless they are officially way off the beaten track, it's possible to push far up the Mazaruni, and quite easily.

The Correia Group of Companies owns a dizzying array of businesses in Guyana, including many that have been vital to the growth of tourism, such as Evergreen Adventures, Baganara Island Resort, Trans Guyana Airways and Intraserv Bus Company. The grandfather of all the companies is the Correia Mining Company, which has been involved in gold and diamond mining since 1935. Much of the company's mining claims are in the Mazaruni River area.

When a need for cheaper and more reliable transportation to the mining areas along the Mazaruni arose, the Correia group formed a new company, the Interior Transportation Service (ITS).

ITS operates jet-boat services from Roden-Rust to Tamakay on the upper reaches of the Mazaruni. During the ten-hour trip, many stops are made at mining camps along the way. The boats provide public transportation so it's possible for an

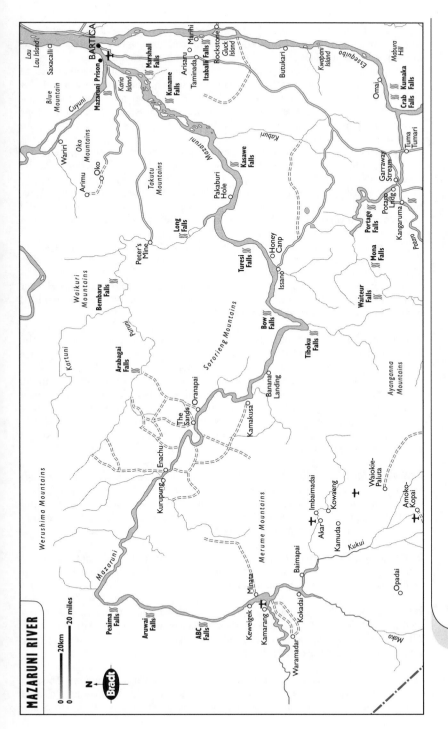

MAZARUNI RIVER

0 ———— 20km
0 ———— 20 miles

N

Bradt

Werushima Mountains

Peaima Falls
Aruwai Falls
ABC Falls
Keweigek
Kamarang
Minata
Waramadan
Kokadai
Kamuda
Baimapai
Merume Mountains
Mako
Opadai
Kukui
Kamuda
Akar
Imbaimadai
Kowaeng
Waiokie-Paluta
Amoko-Kopai
Mazaruni

Kartuni
Waikuri Mountains
Bembaru Falls
Puruni
Arabagai Falls
Oranapai
The Sands
Kamakusa
Kurupung
Enachu

Peter's Mine
Long Falls
Takutu Mountains
Oko Mountains
Arimu
Oko
Wariri
Blue Mountain
Cuyuni
Saxacalli
Lau
Lau Islands

BARTICA
Mazaruni Prison
Karia Island
Kuname Falls
Marshall Falls
Taminada
Arisaru
Marhi
Itaballi Falls
Rockstone
Gluck Island
Butukari
Kwapani Island
Essequibo
Mabura Hill
Kumaka Falls
Crab Falls
Omai
Tuma Tumari
Garraway Stream
Potaro Landing
Kangaruma
Potaro
Portage Falls
Mona Falls
Waiteur Falls
Kabun
Kasawe Falls
Pakaburi Hole
Mazaruni
Honey Camp
Turesi Falls
Issano
Bow Falls
Tiboku Falls
Banana Landing
Sororieng Mountains
Ayanganna Mountains

adventurous tourist to hop on board. They leave on an average of three days each week at around 10.30. Days vary; for more information contact **Correia Interior Transportation Services** (📞 *226 0605;* ✉ *commercial@correiamining.com*).

Many of the more established mining villages have shops selling food and some have government guesthouses or company quarters that have rooms available for the night. Beyond the reaches of the villages are original forests with stunning waterfalls and an abundance of flora and fauna. A guide is an absolute must; after asking for recommendations at the villages, pick one that is trustworthy and can prove their knowledge of the surrounding area.

Places that likely hold the most interest to visitors include Kurupung and Olive Creek. From Kurupung it is possible to hike to the little-known Kumerau Falls. The trek takes two to three hours and a guide can be arranged in Kurpung.

While the villages are generally safe, they are isolated and populated by migrant prostitutes and miners who at times are in possession of very valuable gems and minerals. Skirmishes happen. Valuables should be left behind and women are not advised to travel alone.

Travelling up the Mazaruni is not something that should be done on a whim. Before planning a trip, contact Evergreen Adventures (see page 59) for advice, recommendations, maps and safety tips.

Some of the villages in the area also have airstrips that can be accessed by charter flights; to service mining communities, Air Services also has a couple of scheduled flights to the region every week (see page 84).

⌂ WHERE TO STAY Overnight options for those looking to push further up the Mazaruni (see above) range from your own hammock or tent to a room in a government guesthouse or mining company outpost.

Closer to Bartica, the best option for staying along the river involves camping. Note that the first edition of this guidebook included a listing here for the beautiful Benedictine Monastery that was located on the Mazaruni River. The monastery proved a very popular place with readers, but it unfortunately closed in April 2010. At the time of writing, there was no update on what would happen to the house and grounds; it doesn't hurt to ask around Bartica if you're curious.

Campsite Mazaruni River (c/o 'D' Factor Interior Guest House, Lot 2 Triangle St; 📞 455 2544; $) Local river guide Balkarran (see page 174) has set up a 15-acre riverside hammock camp next to what certainly must be one of the most beautiful beaches along the Mazaruni River. This is a regular swimming stop on his boat tour, but for those who like camping, it's the perfect way to extend your stay.

Getting there and away Access is by boat, and as it's on Balkarran's land, he will likely be your captain. He has set a rate that includes transportation, river tour and use of the site (US$150; maximum 8 persons).

⌂ Where to stay It is a rough camp so accommodation is provided either in a hammock under a basic structure covered by a tarpaulin or in a tent on the beach. All necessary camping equipment, food, beverages and drinking water must be supplied by those going on the trip.

What to see The beautiful white sand beach is the main attraction here. The area is perfect for swimming as the river bottom is also sandy and the water is cleared by the filtration of the small rapids just above the beach. Sliding down the algae-covered rocks under the shallow rapids also provides mild entertainment. There are also some good fishing holes in the area.

CUYUNI RIVER

Located just north of the Mazaruni River, is the 350-mile-long Cuyuni River, another of Guyana's large waterways flowing through inaccessible terrain best known for its rich alluvial gold deposits.

The Cuyuni River has its beginnings in Venezuela's eastern highlands. From here, the river makes a quick descent, widens and follows the international boundary between Venezuela and Guyana for nearly 60 miles (100km). It then flows east, making a fairly direct route through dense rainforest, until its confluence with the Mazaruni River, just before the Essequibo River.

TOURISM Similar to the Mazaruni River, but even more so, much of the Cuyuni River basin is rarely visited by outsiders other than those connected to the migrant mining camps and infrequent Amerindian villages. A combination of nearly impenetrable tropical forests, little development and lack of regular transportation makes visiting the area an option only for truly determined travellers. The best way to source transportation up the Cuyuni is by asking around in Bartica if any boats are scheduled to deliver supplies to any of the interior mining camps, or call Balkarran (455 2544) who runs supplies to interior locations.

WHERE TO STAY At the time of writing, there was only one public place to stay on the Cuyuni River. With the help of locals, the more creative and adventurous may be able to sniff out a beach or two fit for camping.

Baracara Island Resort (*c/o Whitewater Adventure Tours, Lot 3 Sandy Babb St, Kitty; 226 5225*) This small island resort, located five miles from Bartica where the Mazaruni and Cuyuni rivers converge, has a beautiful setting that is at times overrun with loud music and drinking visitors on the weekends. What was once one of Guyana's more popular resorts is now mainly a day trip destination from Georgetown.

In the main building, just above the white sand beach, the beautiful wooden bar filling one wall and the pool tables, many tables and chairs and a fog machine should be your first clue that it's not all about nature at this resort. If the music is bumping and the party happening, there is no escaping it, but if you happen to come on your own at a different time or with a quiet group then the white sand beaches lining the island can be serene, the bar a nice place to relax and the overall experience pleasant.

Getting there and away Access is by boat transportation. Baracara Island Resort is a popular stop for day tours to the area, but it's possible to arrive on your own. If arranging a boat from Bartica or Parika, there is a US$2 landing fee per person.

To/From Parika The cheapest option is to take a public boat to Bartica and then arrange transportation from there. If you're willing to pay for convenience, hire a private boat in Parika (US$250). Whitewater Adventure Tours also arranges all-inclusive day trips that include transportation from Georgetown, activities, lunch and limited local bar (US$100/person; minimum 10 persons).

To/From Bartica From Bartica, private boats can be arranged to provide transport to the island (one-way US$50).

🏠 **Where to stay** The resort's seven rooms are outfitted for overnight stays, but at the moment only day trips are being offered. If a group is interested in staying overnight at the resort, arrangements can be made; contact Whitewater Adventure Tours for rates. When coming outside of an organised trip, you must self-cater, meaning you bring all necessary food, drinks, etc.

The resort consists of one large rustic wooden lodge with an open bar and dining area downstairs and bedrooms upstairs, all surrounded by white sand. The self-contained bedrooms are basic but there's plenty of breeze and the locally crafted furniture adds a welcome sense of style. Each opens onto a shared balcony with views of the beach and river.

What to see and do As mentioned earlier, many people come on day trips to enjoy little more than cold drinks on the airy lounge and sun-drenched deck. Those who are more active can go swimming, play volleyball or take a boat trip to Baracara Falls, just across the river on the mainland, to hike through the jungle and play in the rapids.

ESSEQUIBO, MAZARUNI AND CUYUNI RIVER HIGHLIGHTS

Resorts such as Saxacalli Rainforest Centre and Baganara Island Resort are good destinations in themselves, even if it's only for a day trip. Other sights along the river are usually visited as part of a river trip organised through tour operators in Georgetown, area resorts or through local boat captains.

One of the best area boat captains and river guides is Balkarran (📞 455 2544). Based in Bartica, he has been giving boat tours of the area since 1987. He is highly knowledgeable, reliable and his enthusiasm for the places he has visited countless times remains infectiously childlike. His rates are also some of the cheapest around and he will provide transport to and from any of the resorts and houses along the rivers.

The prices for trips vary depending on the number of people, distance covered, place of pick-up and drop-off and number of places visited. Tours booked through the major resorts are also usually more expensive, but average prices for trips should run between US$150 and 250 per boat.

It can be very easy to find yourself so contended with the surroundings of your chosen resort or lodge that the thought of boarding another boat becomes a tedious thought quickly dismissed. However, a trip past Bartica and up the Mazaruni or Cuyuni rivers is highly recommended. The trip to Marshall Falls for example, takes visitors past a prison, the remains of an old Dutch fort, a large stone quarry and boats dredging for gold. Unlikely attractions indeed but they wonderfully demonstrate the many uses of the river and surrounding lands.

Then, almost without warning, the banks of the Mazaruni River go from scarred to crowded with wonderfully pristine flora and the boat is suddenly engulfed in perfect jungle scenery.

Places described here are listed in a north–south direction, starting at the mouth of the Essequibo River, and do not include resorts covered elsewhere in this chapter.

FORT ZEELANDIA AND THE COURT OF POLICY Located on Fort Island, some 8½ miles (16km) from the mouth of the Essequibo River, these two structures were completed in 1744 after the Dutch began moving their plantations closer to the coast. Fort Island was the seat of the Dutch administration for Essequibo colony and Fort Zeelandia served to protect the Dutch West India Company's holdings and ward off attack from other European enemies.

The relatively small fort was used to store a cache of arms, and was surrounded by ramparts with four bastions. Partial walls remain as do several cannons.

A short walk away is the better-preserved Court of Policy. This clay brick building was much more than just a court. Its three rooms also served as a store, church (three Dutch officials are still entombed here today), seat of government and sales office where the auctioning of slaves took place. The building is said to be the oldest non-military structure in Guyana and it recently received a much-deserved renovation.

The Court of Policy now houses a museum that is full of old Dutch artefacts, pictures and exhibits of the period of Guyana's history that started with the arrival of Dutch settlers.

SAXACALLI This is a small Amerindian village located on the west bank of the Essequibo River, which has been inhabited since before the arrival of the Dutch settlers to the area. Originally an Arawak community (Saxacalli means *Kingfisher* in their native tongue), the population of the village is now mixed with Caribs and people from the coast.

Visitors can have a tour of the community and buy local handicraft when it's available, but the real reason to visit is to swim at one of the Essequibo's finest beaches.

PARROT ISLAND This small island on the Essequibo River is where thousands of parrots come to roost at night. Beginning just before sunset, flocks of the noisy birds fly in from the surrounding jungles where they spent the day eating. The sight, and sound, of so many parrots is impressive and the experience makes for a nice sunset activity.

KAOW AND KALF ISLANDS Once the site of a leprosy colony, Kaow Island bears the name of the English doctor who was in charge. Kalf Island, the smaller of the two, was used as burial grounds and is the source of many current ghost stories.

Today, Kaow Island is the site of a grungy looking sawmill and a beautiful house named the Gazebo. The Gazebo used to be a popular weekend retreat for visitors, but ownership of the island changed hands and it is now for private use only.

MAZARUNI PRISON Located at the confluence of the Essequibo, Mazaruni and Cuyuni rivers is Guyana's largest prison. The Dutch originally settled the area in 1687 and there is a legend of a tunnel that runs from here, under the river to Kyk-over-al. It's a story that's hard to swallow, but it creates interest in a sight that is otherwise mildly depressing.

FORT KYK-OVER-AL Meaning 'see-over-all', this fort is believed to be the earliest Dutch fort in Guyana. Located on a small island at the meeting point of the Mazaruni and Cuyuni rivers, the fort had a strategic vantage point overlooking the Essequibo River. Exact dates of construction are unknown, but it's believed work on the fort began c1613 and was completed c1623.

This small fort had three rooms upstairs that were used as housing; downstairs was used to store food, ammunition and goods received in trade with the Amerindians. Some 400 years later, all that remains standing is an arch.

BARACARA FALLS Located on the mainland across from Baracara Island, near the confluence of the Mazaruni and Cuyuni rivers, Baracara Falls is a small tiered waterfall good for swimming and soaking under the falls. From the shore (accessed by boat) it's a ten-minute hike through the rainforest to the falls. Access to the falls was damaged in 2010 when the local quarry company tore through the area to make a new access road. At the time of writing, the same company was making promises to improve the area for tourism, but nothing had been completed (or even started).

MORO POINT This is a secluded and beautiful white sand beach that stretches for nearly 200m along the Mazaruni River. The beach can either be accessed by private boat hire (be sure to arrange a pick-up time if getting dropped off) or by road from Bartica.

MAZARUNI GRANITE PRODUCTS QUARRY The sight of this large quarry on the bank of the Mazaruni River can be shocking. In full operation, more than 500 tonnes of granite are ripped from the earth. Needless to say, it consists of a large hole exposing the earth's innards, towering piles of rocks and a fleet of large machines.

MARSHALL FALLS A first sight of these falls, which are just over 30ft high and often clogged with a tangle of dead trees, might make you wonder what all the fuss is about. However those who clamber up the rocks and battle through the rushing current will soon realise they've stumbled upon a natural jacuzzi in the jungle.

The falls are reached after a 20–30-minute hike along a good jungle trail that, with a good guide, will reveal many species of trees, plants, birds, insects and many other creatures.

Upon reaching the falls, the first thing you'll notice is the redness of the water, a result of the minerals being leached from the soil and dead plant matter. Once there, follow the guide's lead up the rocks and behind the falls to a natural opening that bubbles with refreshingly cool water. Sturdy shoes or sandals that can be worn in the water are recommended.

MINING OPERATIONS There are no specific mining operations along the Mazaruni and Cuyuni rivers that are frequented by tourists, but on request many tour operators can arrange a trip to a camp where the process of mining can be observed.

8

Essequibo and the Northwest

In Guyana, the area west of the Essequibo River, east of Venezuela, south of the Atlantic and just north of the Cuyuni River, is split into two separate regions commonly referred to as Essequibo and the Northwest. Essequibo was the site of Guyana's first colony and the tightly packed villages along the relatively short coastal road here are where you'll find the highest population density in this large swathe of Guyana.

This region of Guyana is an intriguing mixture of Atlantic coast, mangrove swamps, rice fields, broad savannas, dense forests and a tangle of winding rivers and creeks that serve as highways.

Between nesting sea turtles, agro-tourism, welcoming Amerindian villages, a bounty of flora and fauna and striking scenery, this region has plenty to offer visitors but still remains fairly untapped by tourism. The Rupununi have been perfecting their tourism product for a couple of decades now, but in Essequibo and the Northwest, tourism is still young. This can add some kinks to any trip, but with a little patience and understanding, a visit to this area can be as rewarding as any in Guyana.

Essequibo and the Northwest are two distinct areas, notably due to the development and population of Essequibo, but if travelling overland, many visitors will find themselves seamlessly moving from one area to the next with little realisation. While they offer different experiences to the visitor, and it is possible to visit one area and not the other, the ideal trip to this region of Guyana would include a boat trip that finds you meandering through the many rivers and creeks between the main towns of Charity and Mabaruma.

While the landmass of this area is quite large, unless you are seeking out remote villages, timber concessions or mining towns, most visitors will only tap into the northern third of this part of Guyana.

ESSEQUIBO

On Guyana's administrative maps, this area of Guyana is Region 2, Pomeroon-Supenaam, but it is still commonly referred to as Essequibo, a name given by the Dutch to their first colony when they first started producing sugarcane on the fertile land. At its prime, Essequibo was home to roughly 50 sugar estates, but after the abolition of slavery they began to decline. With the increase of indentured labourers from India to the area, came more cultivation of rice. By the early 20th century, rice had all but replaced sugarcane and Essequibo had become Guyana's main rice-producing region.

The coastal road, which runs for 39 miles between Good Hope on the Supenaam River and Charity on the Pomeroon River, is bordered by dozens of small villages

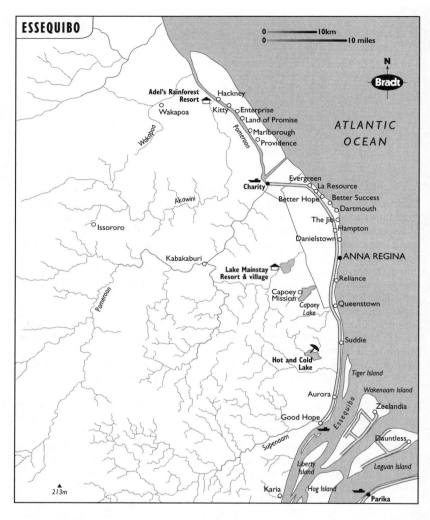

0 ━━━━━ 10km
0 ━━━━━ 10 miles

N

Bradt

ATLANTIC
OCEAN

Adel's Rainforest
Resort
Wakapoa
Hackney
Kitty
Enterprise
Land of Promise
Marlborough
Providence
Pomeroon

Evergreen
Charity
La Resource
Better Hope
Better Success
Dartmouth
The Jib
Hampton
Danielstown
ANNA REGINA

Akawini

Issororo

Kabakaburi

Lake Mainstay
Resort & village
Capoey
Mission
Capoey
Lake
Reliance
Queenstown

Pomeroon

Suddie

Hot and Cold
Lake
Tiger Island
Wakenaam Island

Aurora
Zeelandia

Good Hope
Essequibo
Dauntless

Supenaam
Liberty
Island
Leguan Island

Karia
Hog Island
Parika

▲
213m

and rice fields that stretch into the horizon. There is now just one shabby brick chimney that stands as a physical testament to the sugar estates that once dominated the area.

There are some lakes a short distance off the main road that certainly warrant exploring, for a refreshing swim if nothing else, but many visitors will likely find themselves heading more or less directly from Good Hope, where the boats dock, to Charity, which is the launching pad to the Pomeroon River and all that lies beyond.

In this book, the main villages, towns and places to visit in Essequibo are covered in an east-to-west direction. In most cases, everything is built right on the public road, making just about any place you're looking for hard to miss.

GETTING THERE AND AWAY

By plane There are also a few landing strips in Essequibo, but there are no scheduled flights that make the trip. To charter a plane is a possibility, but with the relatively easy and short journey (about three hours from Georgetown to Charity), there is little reason to add a plane into the equation outside of a medical emergency. Most travel to Essequibo via boat.

By speedboat From the main stelling in Parika there are speedboats that make the 45-minute journey (US$5; see page 154) across the Essequibo to the landing at Good Hope, where the Supenaam River spills into the Essequibo. In Parika the speedboats either go to Supenaam or Bartica so be sure to ask to be certain you're on the right one. There is a constant stream of speedboats that run from dawn to dusk, but they don't depart until they're full, so be prepared to wait.

If you are travelling in a group, or with enough money, it is always possible to rent a boat. The cost for the trip to Supenaam is around US$50.

At its mouth, the Essequibo is 20 miles (32km) wide (comparable to the English Channel) and with the current of the river mixing with the tide of the sea, the boat ride can be a bit rough at times. Sitting in the front of the boat means getting splashed less but feeling the jarring effects of the waves a bit more; nylon tarpaulins are provided and do a surprisingly good job of keeping you dry.

If at first glance the sight of land appears far shorter than 20 miles, that's because it is. The boat journey weaves between and around Leguan, Hog and Wakenaam islands, whose individual sizes are greater than many of the famed Caribbean islands to the north. If you fancy visiting the islands, speedboats will stop at the small village on Wakenaam Island upon request; other islands can be visited by hiring a boat.

By ferry There is also a daily car/passenger ferry that travels the same route in roughly three hours (US$2/person, US$6/vehicle). It also leaves from the Parika stelling but arrives in Adventure, where the Essequibo meets the Atlantic. Departures depend on the tide so are wildly sporadic and often inconvenient. The government sought to reconcile this problem, and cut an hour off travel time, with the purchase of two new drive-on, drive-off ferries and the construction of a new stelling in Good Hope. The stelling has been completed and the ferries purchased, but a series of design flaws and structural concerns led to a series of false openings. At the time of writing, while concerns were still being addressed, the Adventure stelling remained in operation. However as there is an over-abundance of taxis and minibuses that offer transport around Essequibo, there is little reason for the average traveller to worry about using the ferry.

GETTING AROUND
By taxi and minibus Taxis and minibuses ply the route between Good Hope and Charity in plenty. There is little organisation to the trade so you will find yourself being approached by several drivers at once. When getting a taxi it's important to note that there are two different options: *special* and *shared*. Special means that you will be paying the taxi fare yourself (or between your group), while shared is exactly that, you split the fare between four passengers and the taxi often won't leave until the car is full. Shared taxis run the paved road between Good Hope and Charity; hiring an entire taxi allows you to branch off the road and explore some of the hidden roads. Some drivers split the route in half, making it necessary to change vehicles in Anna Regina, but again there are always plenty of vehicles. It is also possible to hail a shared taxi anywhere along the road; if they have an empty seat they will stop.

Minibuses also drive the route but are more apt to stop frequently in many of the small villages that line the road. It's worth it to pay the minor price difference between a minibus and shared taxi for the comfort and convenience. To access Lake Mainstay Resort or the other two lakes in the area, it's necessary to hire a private taxi.

Rates vary with the price of petrol, but those listed below should give you a good idea of what you can expect to pay for a special taxi (divide price by four to get the price of a shared taxi; minibus prices are roughly US$0.50–1.50 cheaper):

Bus 21, Supenaam to Charity, leaves from near the stellings in both Good Hope and Charity and stops at all points in between:

Supenaam–Suddie US$5
Supenaam–Capoey Lake US$10
Supenaam–Anna Regina US$12
Supenaam–Lake Mainstay US$20

Supenaam–Charity US$18
Supenaam–Hot and Cold Lake US$10
Anna Regina–Lake Mainstay US$8
Anna Regina–Charity US$6

By boat Between the rivers, creeks and ocean, boats are as common a form of transportation in the region as road vehicles, especially in Charity, where the road ends and the Pomeroon River begins. Boat travel on the Pomeroon and beyond is covered under Charity (page 184). Also, if you are willing to pay for the use of a boat and the costly price of fuel, it's always possible to find a boatman willing to take you where you need to go.

GOOD HOPE While Good Hope is the name of the village, locals often refer to it as Supenaam after the river on which it sits. This is the drop-off and pick-up point for boats heading to Parika, the Essequibo islands, and further up or down river. There is little reason to spend any amount of time here other than to wait for the boats. A few bars, small restaurants and snack shops can be found on the main road. It is expected that more places of business, including a guesthouse of some sort, will open after the new stelling becomes operational.

SUDDIE Suddie is where the Essequibo Regional Hospital, the High Court, the Magistrate Court, and a police-training centre can be found, but outside of a medical emergency, none offers any reason to visit. If you are passing through on a Sunday or Wednesday the market offers an eclectic mix of goods and decent people-watching.

HOT AND COLD LAKE On the eastern edge of Suddie is a fading sign telling people to turn and visit 'Hot & Cold Fun Landing'. From the public road, it's a roughly three-mile drive on an unpaved and rutted road to the lakeshore. There is an often-unmanned gate at the entrance where you are meant to pay the US$0.50 entrance fee; beeping the car horn or yelling back up the road usually results in somebody materialising from one of the nearby houses.

The lake's name came from certain isolated areas where hot water bubbled up from below mixing with the cooler waters of the lake. Unfortunately, the creek that feeds the lake was damned to create a water conservancy for irrigation purposes and by the time the hot water reaches the surface it has cooled to the temperature of the lake.

It's obvious upon arrival that Fun Landing doesn't earn enough to maintain the property: the thatched *benabs* are deteriorating, the wooden swings are likely a hazard, and any movement on the rickety dock requires caution. Never mind, the sand is fine and white and the setting is beautiful. On a weekday it's likely that the beach will be deserted, and while weekends attract more people, it's rarely crowded.

There is no designated lodging at Fun Landing but intrepid travellers could hang a hammock under a *benab*. Camping is not common here so keep safety precautions in mind, note that the *benabs* are likely to leak, travel with all necessary food and water, and be certain to arrange for taxi pick-up in advance.

QUEENSTOWN This village was once the site of a prosperous sugar plantation, but after the abolition of slavery, it like so many others in the region, fell into decline. A group of freed slaves pooled together enough money to buy the plantation and turn it into a village of their own. Today, while the village is quite sizable, it offers little for the average visitor to do. It is, however, the launching point for a trip to Capoey Lake, and has a good hotel for those not fond of hammocks.

Where to stay
Urbayne Oasis (20 rooms) Queenstown, Essequibo Coast; 771 5387. New & clean hotel with well-appointed rooms; all are en suite, & have AC, phone, TV, & locally made cane furniture. There is no restaurant but meals are made to order & can be enjoyed in the rooftop bar & garden with views of the Atlantic. A salon & gift shop are also on site. **$$**

CAPOEY LAKE AND CAPOEY MISSION The turn to Capoey Lake is as indiscreet as any other dirt road branching off the public road and heading into the rice fields, but it is the first left turn after Urbayne Oasis when heading west. Follow the straight road for roughly two miles and you'll come to the northern edge of the lake where a small wooden building sits advertising Lloyd's Boat Service and Bar (625 2240). Lloyd's bar is sparsely stocked with snacks and drinks, but most people come for the use of his boat.

Lake Capoey is set in the open savanna, the high grasses of which push up along the shoreline, and is lined with alternating white sand beaches and dense flora. Lloyd's main business is running people to and from Capoey Mission, the Amerindian village that sits on the opposite side of the lake (return US$10/person).

When planning a visit, call the village council in advance (774 9288) and alert them. Upon arrival at Capoey Mission (population 400) it's necessary to visit the Captain, or appropriate council member, and pay the US$2.50 visitor's fee. At the mission there is a good white sand beach for swimming, and it's possible to arrange a guide (payment is often in the form of a tip, roughly US$10 per day) that can take you fishing or hiking.

There is no official place for visitors to stay, but if you're travelling with a hammock, you are welcome to use their trees. There is a small shop in the village with basic food supplies but it's always a good idea to travel with your own. Advance notice of visits is always appreciated and can be arranged through Lloyd's. Also, while Lloyd's runs boats daily, it doesn't hurt to arrange a time in advance to make sure someone is at the boat shack. Always remember to arrange for return transportation, both boat and taxi.

ANNA REGINA The government capital of the region, Anna Regina, is the largest town along the coast, but it's still small enough to render lot numbers unnecessary for everything along the main two roads. Again, unless you are in need of a bank, Anna Regina will likely be just a place you pass through or stop to change transportation.

Getting there and away As Anna Regina is more or less the halfway point between Charity and Good Hope, some shared taxis and minibuses start and stop

their route here, resulting in an ever-present congregation of vehicles in the large parking lot directly across from the old turquoise high bridge (a remnant from the 18th-century sugar-producing days). If you find yourself waiting for a ride to leave, shade and cold drinks can be found at the row of snack carts on the south end of the parking lot.

The lot is also located at the point where Market Road connects with the public road. This is the road that leads to Mainstay Village and Lake Mainstay Resort.

🏠 **Where to stay** There is no decent accommodation in Anna Regina, but with its relatively close proximity to Charity and Queenstown, better options are not far away.

🏠 **Arabian Atlantic Hotel** (40 rooms) Henrietta, Essequibo Coast; ✎ 771 4365. The oceanfront location on the edge of town provides nice views & a cooling breeze, but this lumbering building is in need of some renovations. The ageing rooms vary from basic (fan & mosquito net only) to deluxe (AC, TV & mini-fridge); all are en suite & most appear to have worn-out carpet & beds. If you must stay here, request a room with an ocean view. The open-air bar & restaurant are pleasant enough for a meal or drink. **$–$$**

✗ **Where to eat** The restaurant at the hotel above cooks meals to order. There are also several food stalls and small shops selling snacks ranging from curry to hotdogs and (delicious) coconut buns to cheese sticks.

✗ **Cool Off Restaurant & Bar** Public Rd, Anna Regina; ✎ 771 5055; ⊕ 07.30–late Mon–Sat, 16.00–late Sun. The bar is outside with a view of the passing traffic; what the restaurant lacks in ambience it makes up for in friendly service & wide selection of normal Guyanese fare. A small market also sells snacks & newspapers. **$$**

✗ **Kwang Yun Restaurant & Disco** Public Rd, Anna Regina; ✎ 771 4289; ⊕ 09.0–022.00 daily. Chinese food served in a stale & dirty dining room. The upstairs disco is popular on w/ends, but mainly night-time patrons looking for an hour or so of privacy use the grungy hotel. **$$**

Other practicalities
Banks The banks in Anna Regina are the only option in the entire region for changing money or travellers' cheques.

$ **Guyana Bank for Trade & Industry (GBTI)** 2 Public Rd, Anna Regina; ✎ 771 4830; ⊕ 08.00–14.00 Mon–Thu, 08.00–14.30 Fri. Exchanges foreign currency & travellers' cheques & gives credit card cash advances.

$ **Republic Bank** 6 Public Rd, Anna Regina; ✎ 771 4171; ⊕ 08.00–14.00 Mon–Thu, 08.00–14.30 Fri. Exchanges foreign currency & travellers' cheques.

Post
✉ **Anna Regina Post Office** Public Rd; ✎ 771 4200; ⊕ 07.00–16.00 Mon–Fri, 07.00–11.00 Sat

LAKE MAINSTAY On the northern side of this lake is the Amerindian village of Mainstay/Whyaka, and within its boundaries is Lake Mainstay Resort. About five miles from Anna Regina, you will come to Red Lock Creek and the small Feather Beach, which is good for swimming and has two *benabs* for shade. This is also the point where you enter the village, and you must inform the guard at the gate of your intentions, ie: to visit the village or the resort. From here it is roughly two miles to the lake.

Lake Mainstay is a popular destination for daytime swimming excursions and picnics, and for this there are two options. The village has its own beach and *benabs* that can be used for US$1; there are no services here but it's a good opportunity to interact with the local residents. The resort's beach can be used for US$1.50; this includes use of showers and access to the bar and restaurant.

Lake Mainstay Resort (*28 cabins, 5 dbl rooms, 8 sgl rooms;* ✎ *226 2975;* e *lm_resort@mail.com; www.lakemainstayresort.biz; hammock* **$**; *sgl* **$$**; *cabins* **$$$–$$$$**) This resort, now popular with large groups and conferences, was originally built in the 1980s as a government retreat. Due to a lack of funds and maintenance, by the 1990s it had fallen into a state of disrepair. Later that decade, in an attempt to revive the government's original vision, a group of investors leased the 15 acres and remodelled and refurbished everything. In 1999 it reopened with much fanfare, and a fleet of canoes, jet skis, boats and a large selection of watersports. Unfortunately the refurbishments weren't able to do away with the army barrack feel of the cabin layouts, and the advertised gardens are little more than flowering shrubs growing from the white sand that covers the grounds.

All cabins and rooms have air conditioning (a necessity as the sun is relentless with few trees to offer shade), television, fridges and en-suite bathrooms. The cabins are simple, one- or two-bedroom affairs, with a sitting room, small balcony and kitchenette that is rendered useless by a no-cooking policy. The clay bricks plastered on the outside of the buildings took away any charm that could've been gained from the dark hardwoods they are actually built from. The single rooms are cramped and the sanitary white walls are screaming for decorations.

The main building houses a restaurant that offers a very limited selection of options per meal, a small sitting area, pool table and a gift shop that is really a convenience store. The saving grace of the resort is the lake. The beach is wide and the water a welcome relief from the heat. There are a few *benabs* offering shade and a small bar built over the shore of the lake that is perfect for the beautiful sunsets. Unfortunately most watersports are no longer an option as the boats and toys have fallen into disrepair.

There is always talk of once again reviving everything, but if you're coming for the resort advertised in their brochures and on their website, you may want to call in advance and save yourself the disappointment.

Other activities include nature trails across the lake (providing the boat is working to get you there) and tours of the Amerindian village, including the organic pineapple processing plant when in season. Hammock camping on the beach can be arranged with advance notice.

CHARITY Charity is the end of the road, literally. In Charity the paved road runs to the edge of the Pomeroon River and a world of cars and trucks relents to one of canoes and speedboats. Charity is a small village where people come from the outlying riverside villages to sell their produce and buy necessities. And with the two sizeable nightclubs in town, it's also where the same locals come for entertainment and believe it or not excitement. If you're heading further up the coast from here, it's also a good place to buy any essentials, such as batteries and chocolate.

Getting there and away
By taxi and minibus Getting ground transportation from Charity is not a problem as it's where all of the taxis and minibuses sit looking for passengers to fill their vehicles before they head back in the direction of the Supenaam River. To

decrease your waiting time for shared taxis and minibuses, be sure to pick a vehicle nearing departure, ie: with other passengers.

By boat Water transportation is abundant in Charity, and outside of the regular routes listed below, it is always possible to hire a boat and driver for short or long distances; just be prepared to pay high costs. To enquire about a boat ask anybody near the main dock or at the Original Juice Centre (see page 185). Phone numbers are also listed below for the captains.

Charity–Wakapoa Andrew Cornelius (↘621 3466) captains a boat that makes daily return trips between Wakapoa and Charity (one-way US$15; 75 minutes). With advance notice, Andrew will also drop off and pick up anywhere along the route. Andrew leaves Wakapoa between 06.30 and 07.30 and departs Charity around 15.00, but times can be fluid.

Charity–Moruca Dave (↘ 615 4020) and Johnny (↘ 610 0761) oversee the daily boat journey between the Amerindian villages of the Moruca region and Charity (US$15; 80 minutes). Again, with notice it's possible to be dropped off or picked up along the route. The boat leaves Moruca at 05.30 and departs Charity at 11.30. On Mondays there is a second boat that leaves Charity at 15.00.

Charity–Mabaruma/Kamuka On Tuesday around 06.00 a speedboat leaves for the weekly journey from Charity to Mabaruma/Kumaka, in the far northwestern corner of Guyana (US$60/person; 6–8 hours). During the rainy season, the boat will often take an interior route of several different rivers, which can be a wonderful way of seeing the country. Once the rivers begin dropping during the dry season, the route changes and the boats follow the Atlantic coast. This can make for a long, bumpy and wet ride. Whichever route, the boat is often crowded with people and stuffed with baggage, doing away with any notions of comfort.

Advance bookings are recommended, and the best way to guarantee a spot is by coming to Charity on the Monday before departure and speaking with a boatman. Ask around in Charity for which captain will be making the trip; the best point of contact is the Original Juice Centre (↘ 771 4093), which is also the best place to reach a captain on the phone.

Return trips from Kumaka are less scheduled, with the boat normally leaving a day or two after arrival.

🏠 **Where to stay** The two main hotels in Charity are nearly next door to each other and are remarkably similar, from the rooms to the nightclubs and restaurants. Both can be noisy when the nightclubs are open, Friday–Sunday nights and all day Monday.

🏠 **Hotel Purple Heart** (9 rooms) 9 Public Rd; ↘771 5210. The simple & clean rooms are located above the main-floor nightclub & bar. All are en suite & have fans & mosquito nets; rooms with TV & AC are extra. The staff are friendly & the shared patio makes a good perch for people-watching on market day. Restaurant serves all meals. **$$**

🏠 **Xenon Hotel** (11 rooms) 109 Public Rd; ↘771 4989. The rooms (& entire establishment) here are essentially the same as at Purple Heart: above the disco & bar, en suite, fan, mosquito net & TV; AC is extra. Even the balcony is the same. Drawbacks are the slightly higher prices & less friendly staff. **$$**

✖ **Where to eat** All restaurants here serve typical Guyanese cuisine but the seafood is fresh and the locally grown fruits and vegetables are delicious.

✘ **Xenon Hotel** Public Rd; ✆771 4989; ⏰ 11.00–close daily. Small dining room offers b/fast for hotel guests & lunch & dinner to public. Food at restaurant & snack bar is typical Guyanese; served buffet-style on Mon. $$

✘ **Purple Heart** Public Rd; ✆771 5210; ⏰ 07.30–close daily. The small AC dining room offers up a variety of dishes for b/fast, lunch & dinner. The snack bar outside also has a selection of finger foods, curries & rotis. $–$$

✘ **Big Bird & Sons Restaurant** Big Bird & Sons Complex; ✆771 5151; ⏰ 08.00–18.00 daily. Local answer to fast food; serves fried fish, chicken, chips & rice. Dining area is basic but has AC. $

✘ **Channie's Halaal Restaurant** Public Rd; ⏰ 06.30–17.00 Sat–Thu, closed Fri. The red & white chequered tablecloths & colourful murals add a cheery atmosphere to this homely restaurant where the friendly cook & owner treats you like family. The food is said to be Chinese, Indian, English & Creole, meaning it's typical Guyanese-style cuisine cooked fresh. $

✘ **Original Juice Centre** ✆771 4093; e originaljuicecentre@yahoo.com; ⏰ 08.00–21.00 daily. A visit to Charity wouldn't be complete without a visit to the Juice Centre. People come for the fresh juices & varying selection of muffins, buns & fried snacks, but they also come because this is the town gathering spot. If you need to inquire about boats, trips or any other matter this is your place. There are also public phones & phone cards on sale. $

Entertainment Hotel Purple Heart and Xenon Hotel are the places to go for drinking and carousing. Again, their offerings are remarkably similar as both have a few pool tables and a large patio area filled with tables and chairs. Both places also have discos that are open Friday–Monday. Both feature DJs and a liberal use of black lights; Xenon is perhaps a bit larger and more modern; Purple Heart is – big surprise – purple from floor to ceiling.

Market day For the most part, Charity is a sleepy little riverfront town, with not much happening on your average day. However Monday is market day, and every Monday Charity becomes vibrant. People flock to town to buy, sell and catch up on gossip. Boats line the riverbank and taxis and minibuses jostle for space outside town. The public road leading into town is converted into a strip of market stalls selling everything from fresh fruits and vegetables to underwear and fake flowers to toiletries and pirated DVDs.

Market day is as much a social event as it is a day of commerce. By 08.00 the bars and rum shops begin playing loud music; come mid morning the pool tables are filled and empty beer bottles begin to collect on the tables. Everybody seems to know everybody else and it feels as though you've been invited to a festive family reunion that takes place once a week.

If you are passing through and need to stock up on any staples, **Big Bird & Sons Supermarket** (*Big Bird & Sons Complex;* ✆ *771 5151;* ⏰ *06.30–17.30 Mon, 08.00–17.00 Tue–Sat*) stocks everything from food to toiletries to framed pictures.

Other practicalities

Banks There are no banks in Charity; Anna Regina (see above) has the only banks in the region. Money wires and transfers can be done at **Western Union** (*Big Bird & Sons Complex;* ✆ *771 5151;* ⏰ *08.00–15.30 Mon–Fri, 08.00–13.30 Sat*).

Communications
Post
✉ **Charity Post Office** Public Rd; ✆771 4204; ⏰ 07.00–16.00 Mon–Fri, 07.00–11.00 Sat

Email and internet

☒Xenon Broadband Internet Café & Business Centre Xenon Hotel, Public Rd; ✆771 4989; ⊕ 08.00–20.00 daily. Charity's only public internet access usually has at least 3 machines that are working with fairly quick connections for US$2.50/hr. Cheap international calls can also be made using internet phones.

Telephone The Original Juice Centre has phones for public use. They also sell the necessary phonecards. There is also mobile phone service in the area. International calls can be made via the internet at Xenon Hotel (see above).

What to see and do Outside of market day, Charity really has little for you to do other than to get on a boat and explore Pomeroon River and outlying creeks. Tourism in the area is still fairly non-existent but there are a few locations that are doing their best to promote it. The lack of real tourism infrastructure can make planning a trip a bit trickier, but the rewards waiting in the expansive savannas and tunnel-like creeks are certainly pay-off enough for any hassle. Tourism anywhere in Guyana comes with a bit of the pioneering spirit, but this becomes even more evident in this region. Venturing past Charity should be the reason you find yourself travelling through this area in the first place.

POMEROON RIVER

Adel's Rainforest Resort (*10 rooms; Akawini Creek & Pomeroon River;* ✆ *771 5391;* e *zenafred@gmail.com; www.adelresort.com. FB inc all meals & local drinks,* **$$$$**) For those seeking the most comfort and assistance in planning and organising a trip to this area, Adel's is the best option. Located ten miles south (20–30 minutes' boat ride) of Charity where the Akawini Creek meets the Pomeroon River, Adel's is the only place of its kind in the area. The resort comprises three open, colonial-style buildings raised above the ground and connected by small bridges. The main building is an eclectically decorated lounge and dining area with two loft-style rooms above. Another houses the guest rooms and a line of hammocks for relaxing. The rooms are basic but provide everything you need. They have double beds with mosquito nets, and besides the two loft rooms, are en suite. The final building has a bar with a spacious dining/seating area for hosting large groups.

The riverfront grounds are beautifully landscaped with an array of manicured tropical plants. Hummingbirds seem quite fond of the gardens. Behind the lodge is the source of your meals and fresh juice drinks: a large organic farm, where a bit of everything is grown, including bananas, plantains, papayas, coconuts, oranges and a host of vegetables.

Activities can be arranged for an extra charge. Hiking consists of an uneven trail that circumnavigates the farm; fishing can be arranged; dugout canoes can be obtained from riverside neighbours; and boat tours to the nearby Amerindian missions of Wakapoa and Moruca can also be arranged in advance.

For the best bird and animal spotting, explore the stunning Akawini Creek silently in a canoe, but also take a speedboat trip through the tunnel of foliage until it opens into the savannas and Akawini Mission. There are plenty of birds in the area, including herons, egrets, anhingas, kingfishers, parrots and parakeets. Past guests have identified 100 species during a short stay.

Adel's makes a good base for further exploration of the area, and with their own boats, they can organise all aspects of your trip, from pick-up and drop-off in Charity to excursions further afield.

WAKAPOA A visit to Wakapoa gives visitors a chance to experience the traditional lifestyle of Guyana's indigenous peoples. Because of its isolation in the middle of the savannas, getting to Wakapoa involves a beautiful boat ride up Wakapoa Creek. Just shy of where the Pomeroon empties into the Atlantic is a small, dark opening in the trees of the shoreline and as the boat turns in, it's hard not to feel the claustrophobia of the jungle. The trees, battling for their share of sunlight, have created a tunnel of foliage. For the first ten minutes, you wind up the dark creek surrounded by mangroves. As quickly as the tunnel began, it ends and you're shot out into the savannas. From here, the horizon opens up, several species of birds line the banks and calmness begins to settle in.

If planning a visit to Wakapoa, either for an afternoon or overnight, visitors must make contact with the village in advance – showing up unannounced is seen as rude – and always check in with the captain or a council member upon arrival. A good point of contact is the village boat captain Andrew Cornelius (see page 184).

Getting there and away Located deep in the savannas, arriving by water is the only option for getting to Wakapoa, but the boat journey itself is one of the highlights of a visit. See page 184 for information on the daily boat between Charity and Wakapoa. Charters can also be arranged in Charity.

Where to stay Wakapoa has a small guesthouse to host visitors, providing a shelter and bed (**$**). With no running water or electricity, accommodation is basic, but representative of the local lifestyle. It is best to self-cater any trips to Wakapoa, but basic meals can be prepared with advance notice.

What to see and do Wakapoa is proud of its traditional heritage and many of the activities for visitors revolve around this. Activities recommended by the village include paddling a dugout canoe through the savannas while spotting for birds and, if desired, fishing. Cassava is also an important local product and visitors can tour cassava farms, and watch it being processed from straining the cyanide to making casreep.

THE NORTHWEST

This area of Guyana is also called the Barima-Waini, after the region's two main rivers. It is a largely undeveloped area with beautiful waterways, rolling hills, wide savannas and dense forests. Besides Shell Beach, tourism to the area is very limited. But those who visit will see unlimited possibilities in the natural environment. Guyana's northwest region, one can hope, will someday enjoy more tourism infrastructure to host visitors.

In the far northwestern corner, the proximity of the Venezuelan border causes this region to be a hotspot for smugglers running between the two countries. The porous waterways allow boats to transport large quantities of fuel and drugs, mainly from Venezuela to Guyana, but unless visitors are really looking to get involved, they will probably not notice any of the illegal activity. Do note, though, that many of the boats that take passengers from Guyana to Venezuela are involved in illegal smuggling; they need to fill their boats with cargo for the return trip.

This area of the country has long been valued for its rich soils. Today it is the site of a heart of palm factory, organic farms, a palm oil estate and countless other small

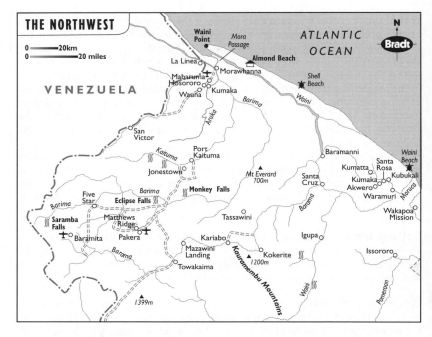

0 ⟞▬▬▬⟝20km
0 ⟞▬▬▬⟝20 miles

N

Bradt

Waini
Point

Mora
Passage

ATLANTIC
OCEAN

La Linea

Almond Beach

Morawhanna

VENEZUELA

Mabaruma
Hosororo

Shell
Beach

Kumaka

Wauna

Barima

Waini

San
Victor

Aruka

Port
Kaituma

Baramanni

Waini
Beach

Kumatta

Santa
Rosa

Kubukali

Kaituma

Jonestown

Mt Everard
700m

Santa
Cruz

Kumaka

Akwero

Waramuri

Moruca

Barima

Monkey Falls

Five
Star

Eclipse Falls

Barima

Tassawini

Barama

Wakapoa
Mission

Saramba
Falls

Matthews
Ridge

Pakera

Igupa

Baramita

Kariabo

Barama

Mazawini
Landing

Kokerite
1200m

Issororo

Towakaima

Kauramembu Mountains

Waini

Pomeroon

1399m

farms. In recent times however, the area has also been growing in popularity for the trade of natural resource extraction, mainly mining and forestry.

Land seems to be handed out with free will and with little monitoring and enforcement; both social and environmental effects are starting to show. With the rich biodiversity in the area, the illegal wildlife trade has also long flourished here. In an effort to combat this, at least in part of the region, work is currently under way to create the Shell Beach Protected Area (see page 199).

HISTORY Guyana's indigenous peoples first arrived in this area some 11,000 years ago. Based on archaeological evidence, the Northwest region is believed to be the area the nomadic hunters first settled of what is now Guyana.

It appears they kept up their hunting ways for many generations, but they slowly began to adapt to their environment and took advantage of the highly fertile soil. Some groups kept up their nomadic ways and ventured further east and south, but those that settled in the Northwest set up permanent camps centred on the gathering of fish, turtles and crabs.

Roughly 4,000 years ago, farmed produce began to grow in importance in Amerindian diets; evidence of cassava-growing communities dates back some 3,000 years. Guyana's long dependence on agricultural products as the main means of survival has a long history that began in this isolated corner of the country.

When the Dutch and Spanish began arriving in the 16th and 17th centuries, they traded heavily with the Amerindians who had valuable items including meat, fish, natural medicines and canoes.

INDIGENOUS PEOPLES The main Amerindian groups that populate the Northwest today are the Arawaks (population 16,000), Warraus (population 5,000) and Caribs (population 3,000). While the different groups are located throughout the region, for the most part, they have each remained centred around a general environment: Arawaks, the coastal white sand plateau; Warraus, coastal swamps; and Caribs, coastal riverheads and lowland forests.

MORUCA Besides being the name of a river, Moruca is also the name given for a cluster of small Amerindian villages that, during the rainy season, are essentially islands in the savanna. Moruca is isolated – the trip from Charity takes about 80 minutes and passes over the Pomeroon River, the Atlantic Ocean and the Moruca River, which winds endlessly through narrow mangroves and wide-open savannas – but is much more developed than many Amerindian villages.

Large wooden boats have allowed modernity to be shipped in, and in Kumaka where most boats land – visitors are greeted by cement houses, vehicles, power lines, and shops selling DVDs and imitation designer clothes. However while some aspects of the traditional lifestyle have been replaced, many still remain, including morning traffic consisting of children paddling themselves to school in their dugout canoes. In Moruca, with access coming only from chartered flights and a fleet of boats, island life prevails: the people are welcoming, the atmosphere is relaxed and time slows down.

In the heart of Moruca are the closely clustered Kumaka, Santa Rosa and Kabukali villages. Separated by a couple of miles to the southeast is Waramuri; to the northwest is Kumatta.

Getting there and away The boat trip to Moruca will likely be remembered as a highlight of the whole visit. When coming from Charity, the ride consists of roughly 30 minutes on the Pomeroon River, followed by ten minutes on the Atlantic, allowing you to look back on the coast of South America before dipping back into the narrow Moruca River. At first the Moruca is little more than a tunnel through mangrove trees growing out and up in search of sun, their roots branching out everywhere to support the struggle to survive. Sunlight is a sparse commodity, barely making it through the trees to glassy black water.

Then, like a carnival ride cut short, the tunnel ends and the wide-open lands, dotted with palm groves, vanquish any sense of claustrophobia. One paradise leads to another. Along the way there are flowers floating in the reed beds and birds – herons, egrets, hawks, vultures, scarlet ibis, kingfishers – dot the sky.

By plane There is an airstrip on the edge of Kumaka mission, but there are no scheduled flights to the area. Unless you have the money to charter a plane, access to Moruca is going to involve a boat.

By boat Unless otherwise requested, boats will dock near the pedestrian bridge in Kumaka. Upon arrival every visitor must register at the police station and at the village council office.

When coming from Charity or the Pomeroon, the cheapest option is to use the daily boat that Johnny and Dave run between Moruca and Charity (see page 184). Using this service will require an overnight stay. Adel's Rainforest Resort (see page 186) can arrange day trips to Moruca.

The weekly boat that runs between Charity and Mabaruma (see page 184) takes an overland river route when the rivers are high, mainly during the rainy season. This route passes through Moruca and, space permitting, will pick up or drop off passengers. Priority is given to those paying full fare to travel the entire route.

Private boat hire is also an option, albeit one that can be prohibitively expensive unless you're travelling in a group. On the docks in Charity (see page 184) and in

Kumaka (the village near Mabaruma; see page 191) one can hire a boat to make the trip. Moruca is also inundated with boats, many available for hire; ask Johnny or Dave (see page 184) or at the landing.

Getting around While there are a couple of vehicles in Kumaka, your main means of getting around Moruca will involve a combination of walking and boats. In the dry season, it's possible to walk between the villages of Kumaka, Santa Rosa and Kabukali, but in the rainy season the villages become small islands in the midst of wetlands. When the area is flooded (and to get to the outlying villages), boats are readily available for transportation. Options range from faster boats with outboard motors to dugout canoes; prices vary accordingly. Boats can be organised by asking at the docks in Kumaka, or just about anybody you meet.

Where to stay There are two guesthouses in Kabukali that provide good accommodation and meals.

Savannah View (3 rooms) Kabukali. The friendly proprietor prides herself on cleanliness & it shows in the basic rooms & shared lounge. The bathroom is shared but each room has a sink. A generator provides electricity at night. Meals are extra ($) but freshly prepared. **$**

Sweet Home Resort (3 rooms) Kabukali. While resort it's not, your basic necessities will be looked after as there's friendly service, clean rooms, mosquito nets & home-cooked meals ($). The bathroom is shared & there's no electricity, but lanterns provide atmosphere.**$**

Where to eat There are no restaurants in Moruca. The guesthouses listed above prepare meals for guests and sometimes do so for non-guests with advance notice. In Kumaka there are small stores selling cold drinks and snacks, ranging from bread and buns to chips and cookies. Limited fresh fruits and vegetables are also usually available from the market stands in Kumaka.

If it's liquid nourishment you're after, there is a rum shop on the river's edge in Kabukali, just up the trail from the guesthouses.

What to see and do When checking in with the village council, make clear what it is you'd like to do while in Moruca and they can help to arrange appropriate guides for your desired activities. It's likely that there will be no system of set fees, leaving payment up to the discretion of the visitor. Figure about US$10 per day, per guide, adjusted for number of hours and quality of service.

A good activity is to explore the villages by foot, stopping to talk with the friendly and curious locals along the way. A good guide for this is Clarence 'Vaughn' James, who can almost always be located at the Santa Rosa Mission. He is always smiling, quick to laugh and knows everybody. He's also very religious, but won't try to convert you to Catholicism. Besides, a tour with Vaughn is also a good way to ensure that you see each and every shrine to Mary that's scattered throughout the area.

Be sure not to miss the **Santa Rosa Mission** (if you're with Vaughn, you won't), which was established in 1813 by the Spanish who had fled to Guyana from Venezuela during the Simón Bolívar revolution (the reason so many residents have Spanish family names today). The church remains a beautiful, simple wooden building, whose beauty lies in the realisation of how little has surely changed in the area since its inception. There is also something to say about its hilltop location with views of the river and far-reaching savanna.

Also in Santa Rosa is the small **Mariaba Crafts**, owned by Uncle Basil and Delores Rodriguez. From here you can buy locally crafted baskets, hammocks, hats, jewellery, children's toys and traditional tools used in processing cassava. Much of it is made from tibisiri, the local straw used in many products. While they don't have a formal guesthouse, Uncle Basil and Delores can always find space to hang a hammock for the night. The nominal fee charged also includes breakfast.

Uncle Basil is himself a local character, known for writing several books and poems on Moruca and Amerindians. His books are on sale at his shop, but it's worth finding some extra time for an extended chat with him, as he is a respected oral historian in Guyana.

Kumaka village is where the police station, village council office, health centre, secondary school and several small shops are located. Each visitor is required to visit the police station and village council, but other stops will hold little of interest unless you need some basic supplies for your stay.

Kumaka is also where the good-sized Saturday market takes place. Boats come from all over Moruca to sell and buy coveted fresh fruits and vegetables, among other items. Be sure to take some time on the riverfront to watch the endless families come and go in their dugout canoes, loading and unloading their supplies.

After a walking tour, activities mainly revolve around the water. Locals say the best time to visit is during the rainy season as that's when the river is high, the savannas are flooded and a boat can get anywhere. It is true that access by boat is much easier in the rainy season, but when the savannas are flooded it also makes getting from one village to another much more difficult. The dry season paths are flooded, often making boat transportation necessary for even short trips. It's also important to note that mosquitoes and kaboura flies are worse during the rainy season.

No matter the time of year, a trip to Moruca will always involve a boat, and from Kumaka it's easy to arrange either a traditional dugout canoe or modern speedboat to take you around. The dugouts are good for trips close by the main villages of Moruca. Their silence and slower speed make them ideal for birdwatching trips into the back dam. Speedboats are more expensive but make travel to places further away much more convenient. With the help of an engine, outlying villages, rivers, creeks and beaches can be accessed much more easily.

There are also plenty of places to swim along the Moruca River and fishing trips can be arranged. Ask around for a recommended fishing guide and then have them take you out, preferably with a dugout canoe. If you don't have a pole, you can always use the time-honoured hand line.

MABARUMA, KUMAKA AND HOSORORO These small towns located about ten miles from Venezuela in northwestern Guyana are close enough together that they are often collectively referred to as just Mabaruma, but each is distinct from the others.

Mabaruma is the administrative capital of the region, and home to the airstrip, hospital, police station, post office, regional chairman's office and several other government outposts. The town is built on top of a narrow hill to protect it from any flooding and the single road running its length is lined with stately rubber trees (unfortunately, at more than 150 years old, some are rotting and being cut down). From the hilltop town there are beautiful vistas in both directions.

With its location on the Aruka River, Kumaka is the port town. The river connects to the region's other large rivers – Barima, Waini, Kaituma – and out to the Atlantic so If you are arriving or departing by boat, be it large or small, it will be from the wharf in Kumaka. Around the wharf there is a small collection of market stalls, small shops and a few rum shops masquerading as snackettes. The rest of the small town is composed of houses.

The small Amerindian village of Hosororo, with its simplicity and stunning views, is perhaps the most beautiful of the three. Accessed by a steep, winding road the hilltop village is little more than a collection of houses, a disproportionate number of missionary churches, and agriculture projects. But from the moment you start ascending the hill, your surroundings begin to unfold beneath you. To the west is Venezuela, in every other direction is Guyana; the panoramic landscape is all a blanket of trees rising and lowering around numerous rivers and creeks.

Getting there and away

By air TGA has flights from Georgetown's Ogle Airport to the Mabaruma airstrip on Monday, Wednesday, Friday and Saturday (one-way adult/child US$80/40, return US$155/78). Flights depart Ogle at 07.00 and Mabaruma at 08.30 (some Saturday flights leave earlier; double-check the times). Total flying time is 50 minutes and the scenery is beautiful.

By boat Boats are the other option for getting to this far-reaching corner of Guyana and, while they aren't as quick or convenient as flying, the journey is often more memorable. There are essentially two routes by boat: the Atlantic or a series of mainland rivers. Going via the Atlantic is a long trip over rough seas best left to the hardiest of travellers.

The 'overland' journey, however, winds through beautiful savannas and thick rainforests and rivers often smooth as glass. At the right time of year, this trip is highly recommended and can always be combined with a one-way plane ticket.

Many boats travel between Mabaruma and Charity; see page 184 for information on all routes between the two towns, including the weekly public speedboat and private hires.

From the wharf in Kumaka it's possible to charter private boats going to Shell Beach (return US$250), Moruca (return US$450), Charity (return US$600), Red Hill (return US$350) or to any other destinations around the region. Prices above are estimates and fluctuate regularly with the cost of gasoline. When hiring a private boat, prices are almost always given for a return trip, because even if you plan on a one-way trip, the captain and boat must return.

There are also frequent boats that go to Venezuela. While many of these offer to take passengers (US$100), use the utmost caution in choosing a captain if you plan on continuing overland to Venezuela. Many of the boats cross into Venezuela illegally in pursuit of returning with cargo that is equally illegal (gasoline and drugs). Note also that without proper immigration, you will be leaving Guyana illegally.

A reliable area boat captain, especially for Shell Beach, is Basil Ah-Lam who can be reached through the Education Department (✆ 777 5092). If he is not available he will be able to make a good recommendation, as can the tour guide Mr Chung (✆ 777 5021).

By ferry A passenger and cargo ferry travels between Georgetown's Kingston wharf and Kumaka's wharf on a fortnightly basis (adult/child US$10/5). The long, arduous and seasick-inducing journey takes 24 hours by way of the Atlantic, but it's the cheapest way of getting from Georgetown to the Mabaruma area. Don't come expecting any sort of nice accommodation (benches or chairs) and travel with all necessary food and water.

At the time of writing, the ferry left Georgetown on Wednesday afternoon, arriving in Kumaka on Thursday afternoon. The boat is typically docked in Kumaka for five to seven days before returning to Georgetown. Schedules and departure times can vary greatly depending on weather and other unforeseen circumstances. For updated departure times and days call the Transport and Harbours Department's Georgetown ferry stelling (✆ 225 6471).

Getting around

By taxi and minibus Rather unexpectedly for such an isolated area of Guyana, there are plenty of minibuses and a few taxis that shuttle people from village to village. The majority of minibuses make a constant trip between Mabaruma and Kumaka; all are aware of the plane schedule so there is always a handful waiting at the airstrip, which is a short distance outside of Mabaruma.

Minibuses also drive from Kumaka to Hosororo, although much less frequently. Ask near the wharf for any buses heading in that direction.

A few industrious residents also make their cars available as taxis; ask locals for current recommendations.

Highly recommended for road transportation is Mr Chung (✆ 777 5021), a local tour guide and minibus driver. Besides providing regular transportation to and from the airport, Mr Chung is mainly available for private hire and is an excellent guide (see page 194).

On foot This is a good way of getting around for those who don't mind hills and heat. On foot, transportation around the area can be broken up into chunks of 15–20 minutes: to walk from the airstrip to Mabaruma; to get from one end of Mabaruma to the next; another hilly leg (downhill from Mabaruma) will get you to Broomes Guest House; and another shorter and flatter section leads to Kumaka. Hosororo is further off and involves a good climb on the way there. Allow at least an hour for this trip and more if it's peak afternoon heat. Always carry sunscreen and water.

Where to stay
As tourism in the area is still very limited, there are only a couple of lodging options; hopefully one of them will suffice for all but the pickiest of travellers.

🏠 **Broomes Guest House** (16 rooms) ✆ 777 5118. The simple self-contained rooms at this ageing wooden guesthouse have everything you need to be comfortable – dbl bed, fan, mosquito net, table & chair – & little more. They could use some fresh paint & perhaps be cleaner around the edges, but the saving grace is the location. Broomes sits on a hill overlooking Kumaka & the Aruka River & each room has a small private balcony (request rooms 1–8 for best view; the higher the number the further away you'll be from the noise of night-time TV). There's satellite TV at night, the staff are friendly & the meals good. **$**

🏠 **Mabaruma Guest House** (8 rooms) ✆ 777 5091. Located in the administrative section of Mabaruma, this guesthouse is often filled with government officials. 2 rooms are self-contained, while the others share bathrooms. There are mosquito nets but the fans stopped working some time ago. Meals are offered but the kitchen could be cleaner, just as the staff could be friendlier. Use only as an alternative if Broomes is full. **$**

Where to eat
Dining at a restaurant, per se, isn't really an option here. There are a few rum shops and snackettes in Mabaruma and Kumaka that sell a limited selection of typical Guyanese fare, but the quality is often hit or miss. Guesthouses prepare all meals and it's best to have your meals there. Guesthouses will also often prepare food for non-guests with advance notice. Prices are low.

There are a few small shops selling an assortment of basic foodstuffs, toiletries and drinks. These are good for purchasing snack items, but it would be hard to scrape together a meal without cooking facilities. Fresh fruits and vegetables are also normally available, but become more abundant on Tuesday and Saturday, which are market days.

Entertainment Unless your idea of fun is going to generic rum shops and bars that accompany their beverages with blaring music, don't visit Mabaruma for the entertainment options. On weekends there are sometimes organised dances, concerts and the like but they are nothing to plan your trip around. By and large, the towns are quiet, which should be welcomed as a refreshing change.

Other practicalities Mabaruma has few services to offer visitors.

Bank There is no bank or official place to change money. It's best to travel with Guyana dollars, but it's often possible to find somebody who will buy or accept US dollars.

Communications
Post
✉ **Mabaruma Post Office** ☏ 777 5011;
🕐 07.00–16.00 Mon–Fri, 07.00–11.00 Sat

Email and internet At the time of writing there was no public access point for internet. Broomes Guest House offers access to guests.

Telephone Mabaruma has landline service and widespread mobile phone service from Digicel and GT&T. Public phones are located at Broomes Guest House and in front of the GT&T office in Mabaruma. They work with phonecards, which can be purchased at GT&T and a few of the small shops.

What to see and do The beauty here is truly magnificent, and all of it, from the undulating hills to the meandering rivers, is aching to be explored by whatever means possible – hiking, canoeing or driving. Unfortunately, this is an area of Guyana where tourism is in an infancy stage. Most visitors only use Mabaruma as a launching or landing pad when going to or returning from Shell Beach.

It's hard to recommend Mabaruma as a destination in itself. For the time being it's best combined with another trip, be it to see the turtles or to take an overland boat trip through the Northwest.

Tourism must start somewhere and Mabaruma definitely has a beginning. The problem is that the established sights around Mabaruma take all of a day to visit, hence the reason for it being best to add them to another trip.

If you enjoy visiting markets, Kumaka has a waterfront market every Tuesday and Saturday, Tuesday's being the larger of the two.

The best guide for showing you around on your trip is, again, Mr Chung (☏ 777 5021). He has been involved with the growth of tourism in Mabaruma since the beginning and he understands the importance of being punctual, reliable and easy to laugh.

Depending on how much time you spend at each location, the two trips below take a few hours each. The trips are priced separately (US$40) as they are in two different areas, but all sites can be visited in one day.

The Hosororo trip could be done on your own, either with a lot of walking, or with a taxi or minibus. The road to the falls is just before the primary school; follow this to the National Agriculture Research Institute (NARI) cocoa nursery. From here there is a well-trodden trail leading downhill to the left. The cocoa plantation is right on the main road in Hosororo.

Hosororo Falls and Hosororo Cocoa Plantation This tour gives visitors a brief insight into an agricultural history in Hosororo that dates back thousands of years. Farming aside, one of the highlights of this trip are the views provided by Hosororo Hill

The Hosororo ('running water' in an Amerindian dialect) Falls are reached after an easy ten-minute walk past a small plantation of cocoa trees. The falls are just a series of rapids running down a steep hill shaded by the trees growing along the banks. They are nothing spectacular but the peaceful location is pretty enough and the banks of Hosororo Creek are good for exploring and swimming.

The cocoa plantation is a small farm on the edge of Hosororo Hill run by a collective association. Those expecting to walk through rows of cocoa trees may be a bit disappointed, but a visit provides an interesting behind-the-scenes look into the small organic farms in developing countries that are so often used to sell products in Westernised countries.

Cocoa plantations used to be common in this area of Guyana and brought a considerable amount of income in the 1950s and 1960s. For various reasons the plantations slowly closed throughout the 1970s. In 2000, Prince Charles paid a visit to Guyana and encouraged the president to start producing cocoa again. For a period of time, the majority of the cocoa seeds produced at Hosororo are exported to the UK and turned into organic chocolate sold under Prince Charles's Duchy Originals brand. Now the cocoa produced is sold through the local Northwest Organics line, which is a project developed by the Guyana Marine Turtle Conservation Society.

On the ad hoc tour visitors are shown the cocoa trees, pods and seeds and the basic, and still very traditional, process they go through before being exported. Some seeds remain in Guyana and are made into cocoa sticks sold locally. The most interesting visit is during one of two main harvesting seasons in May–June and November, which are also unfortunately rainy seasons. Even during peak harvest, the tour is nothing to plan a trip around; there are also smaller crops throughout the year and if you're lucky your tour will end with a cup of hot cocoa. And the views from the plantation leading deep into Venezuela are there year-round.

Kissing Rocks and Tiger Caves This tour takes place in smaller villages located behind Mabaruma and the locations are harder to find without a good guide. Both sites are focused around the hard granite rock of the area from which Mabaruma derives its name. Small pieces of granite were placed in wooden boards by Amerindians and used to grate cassava when making bread and casareep. Hence Mabaruma, or 'my grater'.

The Kissing Rocks are two touching rocks, and little more. It appears that at some point in its long history a behemoth rock toppled and landed at a slight angle on the other massive rock to its side. Or maybe to romantics it appears that papa rock leaned in to give mama rock a kiss and was forever frozen in time. Either way, they are nothing impressive. You can stand under them for a photo, which people will likely gaze at and ask what is significant about the foliage-covered rocks. The story is up to you.

The rocks are also near a muddy creek with large granite slabs that would be good for sitting on only it feels like you're in somebody's garden as there is a house built alongside the creek. The kissing rocks could be skipped and the extra time spent at Hosororo.

Tiger Caves are a bit harder to access and as the trail leading to them isn't much of a trail at all, a guide is necessary. Depending on the vehicle and the condition of the road leading in, the walk to the first, upper cave takes about 15–25 minutes through secondary forest that isn't particularly stunning as far as jungle scenery goes.

The caves get their names from the jaguars (locally called tigers) that are said to sleep there at night. From time to time fresh paw prints and scat will affirm their presence but sightings are rare.

The upper cave is the easiest to get to but it is also the least interesting of the three, being little more than a rock overhang. The two much larger caves are located at the bottom of a very steep hill without a trail. Going down involves doing a sideways shimmy while grabbing onto any vine or tree within reach and hoping it holds. It's not a particularly long hill but coming up it may find some on their hands and knees. It will either be considered good fun or a horrible experience.

The lower caves appear to lead back some way but exploring them would involve crawling over quite a bit of bat guano, the smell of which will likely cut your visit shorter than you'd like for the effort put in to reach the caves in the first place.

Wear a decent pair of trainers for this trip, which is best for those who like a short trek through the forest.

FURTHER AFIELD As mentioned earlier, tourism in this region is developing slowly, but is doing so with a concentrated effort. Several residents from villages in the Northwest have been trained as guides and are developing tours and attractions to generate much-needed income from tourism. The main constraints for the growth of tourism in this area are a lack of development and limited and costly transportation to and from the locations, many of which are fairly isolated.

At this early stage of development, planning a trip to the Northwest can be frustrating. Expect to be put on to several different people, receive multiple different answers to the same question and have things not always work out as planned. At the same time, those who put in the effort can expect a memorable trip filled with pristine rivers and rainforests, a bevy of flora and fauna and welcoming villagers whose warmth and genuine hospitality is sincere, not a practised routine for a constant stream of tourists.

Shell Beach (*With information provided by Michelle Kalamandeen, of the Guyana Marine Turtle Conservation Society, www.gmtcs.org*) This 90-mile stretch of beach is the main reason people find themselves planning a trip to this region of Guyana, but visitors don't just come for the endless expanse of unspoiled Atlantic coastline; they come hoping to see a prehistoric sea turtle crawl ashore and lay her eggs.

From March through August, Shell Beach becomes the nesting ground for four of the world's eight endangered species of marine turtles: leatherback, green, hawksbill and olive ridley (see *Sea turtles*, page 47 for detailed information on the different species). Most of the world's sea turtle nesting sites are visited by only one or two species, adding to the exceptionality of Shell Beach.

Shell Beach stretches from the mouth of the Waini River, along Guyana's northwestern sea coast to the Pomeroon River's mouth, a distance of roughly 90 miles. It is a rare swathe of undeveloped tropical coastland that, for the most part, remains ecologically undamaged.

The entire area is broadly referred to as Shell Beach, but nine sections of beach have been given separate names, such as Almond, Kamwatta, Tiger and Gwennie. While largely unpopulated by permanent inhabitants, nearly 150 inhabitants occupy Almond Beach, near the Waini River's mouth; roughly 180 people reside at Gwennie Beach, near the Pomeroon River.

While the name Shell Beach may sound like a romanticised appellation, it's actually utilitarian. Shell Beach is a beach composed entirely of seashells, from perfectly intact to crushed bits the size of sand.

GUYANA PROTECTED AREA SYSTEMS

Roughly 80% of Guyana remains covered by forests, but as time marches onwards this number is surely going to continue declining. As Guyana struggles with economic development, increasing pressure is being put on the country's natural and biological resources. As Guyana's foreign debt grows and poverty remains, the government is more apt to yield larger areas of the forest for timber and mining concessions (depending on how the LCDS pans out; see box on pages 20–1). Also, with the completion of the bridge over the Takatu River on the border of Brazil, and the eventually inevitable paving of the Linden–Lethem roadway, environmental pressures will only increase.

There has been pressure on the government for more than a decade to create a system of protection for large tracts of some areas of Guyana's mostly-intact pristine environment. In 1999, five sites were identified as priority areas for protected area status: Shell Beach; Kanuku Mountains; Orinduik; Mount Roraima; and southern Guyana region. (Kaieteur National Park and Iwokrama International Centre for Rain Forest Conservation and Development were already protected areas.)

In 2003, the government of Guyana officially launched the Guyana Protected Area System (GPAS), which sets out to protect and sustainably manage select ecosystems. The GPAS seeks to promote conservation initiatives while protecting traditional ways of life (the proposed Protected Areas are largely on Amerindian lands), support socio-economic advancement and sustainable development.

Of the five original sites, two – Shell Beach and the Kanuku Mountains – were chosen to serve as pilot projects to help establish a national process in establishing Protected Areas. Each pilot protected area has a lead agency to oversee the project: Guyana Marine Turtle Conservation Society for Shell Beach and Conservation International for Kanuku Mountains.

With help from a World Bank grant, each lead agency is working towards setting goals in establishing the protected areas, including education and community awareness activities for those living in or near the proposed protected areas (nearly 40 communities are impacted by the two pilot projects); creation of management plans; and identifying conservation-based, alternative activities (outside of timber, mining, wildlife trade, etc) that will generate income.

In today's modern world, the global benefits of protecting large swathes of biodiversity are obvious, but the Protected Areas would also help to protect Guyana's indigenous communities from encroaching developments that are making them change their very way of life. Progress has been slow, but hopefully funding and legislation will accelerate as Guyana continues to look at conservation as a new means of economic development.

Essequibo and the Northwest THE NORTHWEST

8

Ecosystem The main ecosystem of Shell Beach is a collection of mangrove forests, inland swamp forests and flooded ité palm savannas, all of which are greatly influenced by the Atlantic Ocean to the north. The relentless rising and falling of the ocean causes a never-ending cycle of erosion and accretion, death and renewal. After a prolonged change in the tides and currents, excess salinity wipes out mangrove forests causing shoreline mudflats to undergo a constant rearrangement. Nevertheless, the area supports nearly 1,500 species of plants.

Two large estuaries – the Essequibo River to the southeast and the Orinoco Delta to the northwest – flank the area and greatly affect the biological diversity found along the shores.

Biodiversity The waters near Shell Beach are home to great populations of fish and crustacean species, including the intriguing mud skippers. Other turtles found in the area include yellow-foot tortoise and scorpion mud turtles. Giant river turtles and matamata turtles are also very occasionally spotted in the area.

More than 250 species of birds have been identified at Shell Beach, including scarlet ibis, herons, egrets, ospreys, frigatebirds, muscovy ducks, harpy eagles, roseate spoonbills, pelicans, greater flamingoes, kingfishers, antbirds, toucans, parrots, macaws and tanagers.

Mammals include jaguars, tapirs, deer, sloths, primates such as red howler, squirrel and capuchin monkeys, giant river otters, tamandua, river dolphins and manatees. The limited research that has been done on further reptiles and amphibians has identified around 30 species.

Turtle wardens Area Amerindians have been turning to Shell Beach's varied biodiversity as a source of food for thousands of years. They come to fish the waters, hunt the birds and mammals and round up coveted sea turtles and their eggs.

Because much of the coast is inaccessible and inhospitable, hunters and their families come for periods of time to stock up on meat and then return to their village. The lack of settlements has largely left the ecosystem intact, but the hunting and fishing was taking a toll on species whose numbers were already in decline.

While Dr Peter Pritchard, a leading turtle biologist, first began studying the biology and conservation of marine turtles in Guyana in the 1960s, it wasn't until the 1980s that he began doing so in earnest.

Initially the research only documented species present, their numbers and their fate. The specimens collected were mainly skulls remaining from turtles killed by hunters.

Over the years Dr Pritchard noticed that the numbers of marine turtles were declining drastically. This was due to unsustainable harvesting, habitat loss, commercial fishing, pollution of the oceans and overall climate change.

In 1988, Dr Pritchard realised that the threats to sea turtles were likely only going to keep increasing and he decided to take action on the areas that he could impact. He recruited Audley James, a converted turtle hunter, and together they launched a pilot project that sought to protect the endangered species by working with the local communities.

They urged fisherman to stop hunting sea turtles and to leave the eggs undisturbed. It is difficult for a person to turn their back on their livelihood and in the beginning Dr Pritchard and Audley would buy the turtles and eggs from the hunters.

The men went on turtle patrols, walking along stretches of beach to make sure no harm would come to the nesting turtles. Slowly, more members of Audley's family joined the cause and soon more indigenous turtle hunters were being converted and began protecting the species they used to kill. The people who patrol the beaches are called turtle wardens.

The wardens and researchers at Shell Beach began tagging the turtles and keeping track of return visits and sightings at other beaches and faraway feeding grounds. They also began holding seminars and classes to educate the indigenous population of the area. The work continued on a very grassroots level throughout the 1990s. Because of limited resources, manpower and funding, only about 20 miles of the shoreline is regularly patrolled during the nesting season.

Conservation The Guyana Marine Turtle Conservation Society (GMTCS) was established in April 2000 to focus on the acquisition of grants to allow for a more concentrated effort in the continuation of sea turtle monitoring, research, education and awareness. Their goal is to have 'community-based conservation of Guyana's marine turtle population'.

Fully aware that enforcing any set of conservation rules often involves an attempt at banning practices, areas and other components of daily survival for indigenous cultures, GMTCS has always focused on community development and alternative forms of livelihood.

This has involved several different projects that teach locals alternative means of generating money, the most popular being the North West Organics line, which sells casreep, cassava bread, crabwood oil and cocoa sticks that are produced by Amerindians in the area. Tourism has also been identified as an alternative form of income. If the indigenous can realise that visitors will pay to see aspects of their surroundings that they often take for granted, they'll have motivation for not over-hunting birds and mammals, or over-fishing the rivers and ocean, and not killing turtles for their meat.

In May 2011 a new turtle conservation field station was commissioned at Almond Beach. The field station brings much needed technology and research materials – solar power, satellite internet and library – to the ongoing conservation efforts of the GMTCS. The field station will also feature a guesthouse that will accommodate visitors and host workshops.

Protected area (For information on the Guyana Protected Area System, see box, page 197). Along with the Kanuku Mountains in the Rupununi, Shell Beach has been identified as a pilot project for creating a process under which protected areas will be set up. GMTCS is now working to establish Shell Beach as one of Guyana's few protected areas. They seek to protect not only rare and endangered species and habitats, but also the lifestyles of the indigenous, whose rights and traditions are often negatively impacted by the establishment of a protected area. In 2010, a Community Representative Group from the 12 area indigenous communities helped finalise the deliniation of the Shell Beach Protected Area; hopefully it won't be long before it is recognised as such by the government.

Tourism Visitors have always been a necessary component of the project's success and thus are always encouraged to visit Shell Beach. To better facilitate hosting visitors, at the time of writing a new guesthouse was being constructed at Almond Beach. Expected to be completed by the end of 2011, it will be connected to the new conservation field station. With solar power and internet access, it will bring major upgrades to the current camping. Call Romeo de Freitas (see page 200) for current information on the lodge.

Until the lodge is finished, visitors must come fully aware of the facilities and conditions that are present at the camps used by the turtle wardens. The camps

– lodging is in tents set up under thatch shelters – are working camps. Meals are prepared over wood fires and it's preferable that guests bring their own food and drinking water. During the nesting season, the mosquitoes are dreadful. Visitors are woken up at all hours of the night to walk the beach and search for turtles. Besides limited rainwater there's no source of fresh water; showers are non-existent.

It's not Club Med and there are no blended alcoholic drinks served on platters, but there's some good juice made with rainwater and you can bet that your treatment will be friendlier and more genuine than at any expensive resort. For travellers who enjoy camping, don't mind roughing it a bit and don't expect to be pampered or doted over, and instead be seen as a member of the team, it can be a memorable experience.

The beach is a remote South American tropical paradise; miles of uninterrupted shoreline complete with an endless army of coconut palms. Sunrises and sunsets are stunning. The birds are plentiful, the millions of seashells mesmerising. And then there are the turtles.

If you're lucky (sightings are never guaranteed) you'll get to see a creature that has been in existence for millions of years, lumber onto a shoreline seemingly in the middle of nowhere, and deposit a clutch of dozens of eggs. For that moment, everything is antediluvian except for the humans and their elements of modernity – cameras, torches, microchips. It's a clash of worlds; one doing the only thing it knows to do, the other respectfully watching in awe, likely with a tinge of guilt for having a hand – direct or not – in what is responsible for slowly killing the ancient world.

The trickiest part of visiting Shell Beach can be arranging a trip. If you want to leave the arrangements to somebody else, call around to Guyana's tour operators (see page 58). However, you pay a premium price to have a tour operator arrange either the combined flight and boat trip (3 days, FB US$700/person) or the overland Atlantic route through Charity (3–4 days, FB US$300/person, minimum 8–10).

Sea Turtle Monitoring Manager Romeo de Freitas (☏ 260 2613 or 686 8951; e romeodefreitas@yahoo.com) organises tours with the Marine Turtle Project in collaboration with Almond Beach. When Romeo is at Shell Beach, which is most of the time during turtle season, someone else handles the phone calls (same number; email response can be slow) and will be able to take your booking and inform those at camp via the radio of your reservation. Romeo offers an overland trip from Georgetown to Almond Beach (3 days, FB $380/person). Transport and accommodation details are outlined in the following sections.

Getting there and away There is no option other than using a boat to get to any location along Shell Beach, but different routes allow for varying lengths of time spent on the water, and on the often rough Atlantic seas.

When using any form of public transport beginning in Georgetown, you will likely end up making your way to Mabaruma and then chartering a boat from there. The easiest and fastest route is to take the TGA flight to Mabaruma (50 minutes; see page 84); a cheaper option is to take the weekly speedboat from Charity to Mabaruma (5–6 hours; see page 184); the cheapest (and some say most miserable) alternative is the fortnightly steamer from Georgetown to Mabaruma (24 hours; see page 103).

There are obvious kinks to each route, except perhaps for the aeroplane. Taking the public speedboat or steamer would involve a quick turnaround time, but both options would still allow enough time to squeeze in a trip to Shell Beach.

Once in Mabaruma, you will need to hire a boat from the Kumaka wharf to Shell Beach (1 hour 15 minutes; return US$200–250). Prices vary depending on length of trip (day trips are cheaper than overnight stays) and can often be negotiated. A good captain for the trip from Kumaka is Basil Ah-Lam (✆ 777 5092).

One final option is available if the speedboat from Charity to Mabaruma will be travelling via the Atlantic versus the inland rivers. If the boat is taking the Atlantic route it's possible to have them drop you at Shell Beach along the way. Be sure to arrange for them to pick you up on their return voyage and have somebody from Shell Beach radio Kumaka to reconfirm your return passage.

Where to stay The main turtle nesting season is March–August. It is during these six months, when turtle wardens are posted along Shell Beach, that the area sees the most visitors. The wardens typically leave Shell Beach during the off-season, although some reside at Almond Beach year-round. A visit to Shell Beach outside of nesting season is little more than a camping trip on the coast, which is still a great trip. All necessary gear, food and water would have to be provided and it's always worth contacting turtle warden Romeo de Freitas (see above) for information or assistance in organising a trip anytime of the year.

At the time of writing work on a new guesthouse at Almond Beach was underway. The new lodge should be ready for visitors by 2012. Details on the accommodation were still sparse, but expect beds, kitchen facilities, internet access and solar power. How this will change the way tourism is handled at Shell Beach is yet to be seen, but visitors can expect a much more comfortable stay. Contact Romeo de Freitas (see page 200), or visit www.gmtcs.org, for current information on the lodge.

While writing this edition, the only place to stay remained at the camp where the turtle wardens happen to be (**$**). While the lodge at Almond Beach can be expected to become the main base for the researchers and guests, visitors may still have to camp during their visit. To patrol effectively as much of the coastline as possible, and depending on where turtles are coming ashore, they move between different satellite camps spaced out along Shell Beach. When you are arranging your trip, details will be provided as to which camp the team will be at during your visit.

The camps are all more or less the same. Lodging is provided in a tent under a *benab*; if you don't have your own, one will be provided. Hammocks could be used as well, but tents provide more space to move about in when the mosquitoes come out in force and a hasty retreat is made to shelter.

There are pit toilets only. There is no running water and the only freshwater source is rain. Unless there is plenty of rain during your visit, bucket baths are taken with salt water.

As stated earlier, these are working camps, not tourism sites. They are not set up to cater to visitors. Guests are treated like one of the team and this is nearly akin to being treated like family, but this is not like visiting a resort.

The beach is isolated and supplies are limited so if you are booking on a more ad-hoc basis, it's preferred that you travel with your own food and drinking water. If you are coming with a larger group, it is necessary to bring your own food and water (if booking with a tour operator or with Romeo, this will be taken care of). It's always appreciated if you show up with some extra fruits, vegetables and sweets to share with the hosts as they can go long stretches with only tinned food.

Those travelling alone or in smaller groups will likely have their meals prepared for them and eat with everybody at camp (donating your supplies to the pot works well), but larger groups should plan on cooking for themselves. All necessary utensils are at camp.

Unfortunately, but perhaps understandably, the so-called Jonestown Massacre, during which 913 men, women and children lost their lives in a mass murder-suicide on 18 November 1978, remains one of the most memorable events in Guyana's history.

Jonestown was a communal settlement in the jungles of northwestern Guyana, roughly seven miles from Port Kaituma. The community was inhabited by members of the People's Temple, a cult that was founded by American Jim Jones in the mid-1950s.

The People's Temple began in Indianapolis, Indiana, as an inter-racial congregation – a rarity at the time. It's said that Jones recruited followers through claims of having cures for cancer, heart disease and arthritis; in Indiana his congregation of approximately 900, consisted of many who were sick, homeless, poor or jobless.

Jones initially preached of social equality, freedom and love for all, but over time his beliefs became increasingly socialistic and communistic, while warning of a pending doomsday from nuclear fallout. In 1965, Jones moved his group to northern California, because he believed the area to be safe in the event of nuclear attack on the USA.

In the early 1970s, Jones expanded the People's Temple and moved his congregation to San Francisco, while also opening a second church in Los Angeles. In San Francisco Jones began spotlighting himself in the public eye, especially through his socialist political beliefs.

While the notoriety brought Jones more members, and ultimately more wealth, it also led to public scandals and investigations into illegal activities within the Temple, including tax evasion. Planning his escape, Jones looked to relocate the People's Temple yet again. He decided on the isolated tropical jungles of Guyana – a country whose then government had strong socialist beliefs similar to those of Jones.

In 1974, Jones leased nearly 4,000 acres of land from the Guyanese government and a team of followers began constructing Jonestown. In 1977, People's Temple members began moving to Jonestown to work on an agricultural co-operative called the 'People's Temple Agricultural Project'. The group raised animals and grew fruits and vegetables for consumption and sale in nearby markets.

Members of the People's Temple were lured to Guyana by promises of life in a utopian community. It wasn't long, however, before they realised life was far from the paradise they were promised.

Reports from survivors say that members were forced to work long days in the fields and were often given little more than rice and beans to eat, while Jones dined on meats, salads, fruits and soft drinks kept cold in his private refrigerator.

Tropical maladies were common within the group, and to keep his followers in an artificial state of contentment while controlling their behaviour, Jones administered sedatives and other drugs to those living in Jonestown. Those who attempted to leave Jonestown were often drugged to the point of incapacitation.

Those who did manage to leave Jonestown brought with them stories of people being held against their will (the compound was patrolled by armed guards), harsh punishments for both adults (beatings and being sent to 'The Box,' essentially a six-by-four-foot underground hole) and children (being dangled head first into a well said to house a monster late at night) and a controlling and paranoid leader (Jones's voice was constantly booming out of loudspeakers; he was addressed as 'Father' or 'Dad' by all members; children had to be surrendered to communal care; and all welfare payments collected by residents had to be given to Jones).

Jones also preached what he called *Translation* – an act where he and his followers must commit suicide to move on to a different planet that offered bliss. He tested loyalty by rehearsing mass suicides in an event termed 'White Night' during which he would hand out liquid said to contain poison to all followers, including the children. Only after everybody drank would they be told it was just a test and there was no poison present.

As tales of human rights violations in Jonestown reached the States, concerned family members made their stories public. In November 1977, the *San Francisco Examiner* ran a story that made many allegations against the People's Temple; one of the people it disturbed was Congressman Leo Ryan. Over the subsequent months, Ryan began researching People's Temple and spoke to ex-members and family members of current followers.

Wanting to personally investigate the situation, Ryan planned to visit Jonestown in November 1978. Interest in joining him was high, and the final group that went to Guyana on 14 November consisted of 18 people representing the government, the media and a group called Concerned Relatives.

Ryan met with Temple members at their Georgetown headquarters and he was told they would not be allowed to visit Jonestown. On 17 November, Ryan decided to fly to Port Kaituma regardless of what he was being told. Members of the group were eventually allowed in to Jonestown later that day and were greeted by a rehearsed reception and concert. That night a member of the Ryan party was slipped a note by two members of People's Temple who wanted help in leaving.

The next day the media and government officials were given a tour of Jonestown. When the group met Jim Jones, he was confronted with the note. During the ensuing discussion more Temple members stepped forward and asked to leave with Ryan. Jones eventually consented and wished them luck.

Shortly before Ryan's party and 15 Temple members left Jonestown to return to the Port Kaituma airstrip, one more follower – Larry Layton – asked to leave with them. Suspicions were raised by other members but Ryan consented.

The group needed two planes, and just before the first, a small Cessna, was set to take off with six passengers, Layton took a gun from his waistband and began shooting at those on the plane with him. At this same time, Ryan and others were boarding the second plane when Temple members driving a tractor appeared near the runway.

They opened fire on the group, killing Ryan, three members of the media and one People's Temple defector; six more were seriously wounded. The Cessna was able to take off during the attack, but the larger second plane was disabled. Those who carried out the shooting returned to Jonestown.

After the shooters returned to Jonestown, a meeting was held and it was decided to hold another 'White Night', only this time the nurse was told to mix cyanide and sedatives into the grape Flavor Aid (not the Kool Aid of lore). All members, including the children, lined up for their poison and then went to lie

continued overleaf

down. Those who refused to drink the juice were believed to have been injected with the poison using needles. Jones either shot himself, or had someone do it for him. A small handful of members were able to escape the murder-suicide by hiding in buildings or in the surrounding jungle.

In the end, 913 members, including more than 270 children, died at Jonestown on the night of 18 November 1978. There are many rumours and conspiracy theories surrounding the tragedy (most involving the CIA), but nothing has ever been proven. Jonestown was largely left deserted after the tragedy, and many of the buildings were destroyed by fire in the mid-1980s.

Today, the area has largely been reclaimed by the jungle and there is little sign left of any sort of the settlement. If you would like to visit the jungle that was once home to Jonestown, which is located outside of the small logging and mining village of Port Kaituma, you can arrange boats at Kumaka and overland travel in Port Kaituma. Some travel agents in Georgetown also offer the trip (either overland or via aircraft); Captain Gouveia at Roraima Airways (see page 84) was there on the fateful day and makes a passionate guide.

What to see and do The obvious draw of Shell Beach is the sea turtles. Visitors are invited to join the wardens on their monitoring duties, which essentially means visitors join wardens as they walk the beach looking for nesting turtles.

Most sea turtles arrive to lay their eggs at night with high tide. The entire process of coming ashore, building a nest, laying eggs and covering the nest takes one to three hours. So, in keeping with the schedule of the tide, and the average length of nesting, there are usually two times during the night when wardens stroll the beach.

The night-time, turtle-spotting aspect of the visit entails waking at odd hours and walking for a few miles along the beach while looking for sea turtles. Keep in mind that turtle sightings are never guaranteed. The best way to ensure that you get to see one of the 500–700 turtles that nest there annually is by staying for at least two nights. It often boils down to the luck of your timing.

Daytime activities are much the same as in the night, without a focus on the turtles. As it goes on an isolated beach, there's not much to do. The area is great for long walks, collecting seashells, birdwatching, reading a book, sunbathing, but swimming is an activity best done only in the shallow waters. The ocean can be rough and the tidal currents strong.

During the day is also the time when there are no mosquitoes to contend with. 'Heaven and Hell', is how those that live on the beach compare the difference between daytime and night-time regarding mosquitoes. During the rainy season (which is peak nesting season) the mosquitoes are truly horrendous. Clouds of them come from the mangroves and the only escape is by retreating to your tent and then slapping all of the ones that entered with you.

March and the very early part of April has the fewest mosquitoes (sometimes none will be seen) as the rains normally haven't begun to fall. The only drawback is that your chances of seeing turtles decrease at this time of the year.

9

Central Rainforests

Central rainforests is not an official name for this region of Guyana; instead it is a broad description of the relatively large area covered in this chapter, which mainly focuses on Guyana's Pakaraima and Iwokrama mountains. Much of this area, like a lot of Guyana, remains largely inaccessible to the average visitor, but the range that has been developed for tourism is certainly enough to keep most busy.

Highlights of this chapter include Kaieteur Falls – Guyana's tourism pride and joy – and Iwokrama International Centre for Rainforest Conservation and Development, certainly one of the most interesting projects taking place in the world's rainforests today, and a Mecca for ecotourism.

Linden is not really geographically located in the central rainforests of Guyana but it serves as a frontier town of sorts. For those who are driving south it is the last truly developed town for hundreds of miles; when coming north, it serves as a welcome back to reality as you bid farewell to the depths of the jungle and the space of the savannas.

GETTING THERE AND AWAY

This section provides transportation information for accessing the most visited area of Guyana's interior, namely from Linden south through the Iwokrama Forest and on to the Rupununi Savanna. All information here is based on travelling from Georgetown and heading south to Lethem, where the main road and scheduled flights end. (For information on heading north from the Brazilian border town of Lethem, see page 278).

While transportation forms covered here emanate from Georgetown, they follow one main route southwards and can be used to pick up and drop off at several locations along the way. Specific transport information is given for each village, lodge or other interior destination in its respective section in this or the following chapter.

Without your own vehicle, organising transportation around the interior can be a tricky and costly experience. Local tour operators and interior lodges are very helpful in arranging logistics and should be consulted for assistance.

Transport options range from scheduled and chartered flights, minibuses, larger coach buses and private 4x4 vehicles. Boats, which are relied upon at many destinations, but not used when travelling to or from Georgetown, are covered in other relevant sections.

From Georgetown the road heading to Linden is paved, but south of Linden there are no paved roads until you reach Lethem, which is starting to pave areas block by block. The Linden–Lethem road into the interior is rutted and full of pot-holes. The journey involves driving over wooden bridges in various states of repair and it can be impassable during the worst of the rainy season. However, it's also

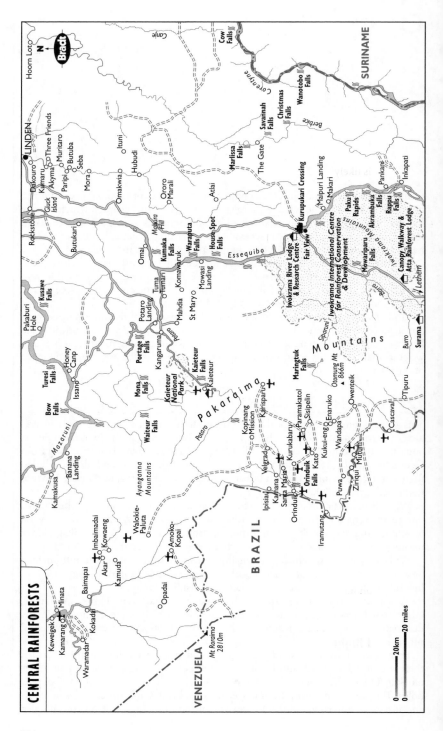

CENTRAL RAINFORESTS

a stunningly beautiful path that slices through the heart of Guyana's jungle and meanders lazily through the wide-open savannas. It will make you realise just how isolated interior locations are away from the coast.

Travel on the road has been much improved in recent years. Travel between Georgetown and Lethem used to take a matter of days not much longer than a decade or two ago, but now when the road is good it can be done in 10–12 hours with a 4x4.

There are occasional hazards. Trees sometimes fall across the road (many travellers, including the Intraserv buses, travel with chainsaws) and sometimes the wooden bridges that line the trail will crumble under the pressure of too many overweight trucks. People can be trapped on either side for days.

All that is likely to change much sooner than later. The Brazilian-funded Takatu River bridge opened in 2009, connecting Lethem to Bonfim, Brazil. The completed bridge is now a pillar of support for the many meetings and much discussion between Guyana and Brazil about building a proper road between Lethem and Linden. Guyana does not have the funds for this, but the landlocked northwestern corner of Brazil is interested in having access to Guyana's coast and the Caribbean markets just beyond the shores. The impact the road will have on Guyana's interior when (it's no longer a matter of 'if') this happens remains to be seen.

BY AIR All flights within Guyana are in small prop planes, most with a maximum capacity of 13 passengers. Flights can get booked weeks in advance and reservations are recommended. As Lethem continues to grow, demand for flights is increasing and many of Guyana's airlines are looking at adding scheduled flights. If flights can't be booked with the companies listed below, try enquiring with those listed on page 84.

Scheduled flights TGA (see page 84) has regularly scheduled flights that travel between Georgetown's Ogle Airport and Lethem. This flight will also stop at other airstrips along the way, including Annai and Karanambu (at the time of writing, the newer airstrip at Fair View in Iwokrama was not an option for scheduled flights, but that may change so it doesn't hurt to enquire upon booking). Keep in mind that flights, and additional stops, depend on weather conditions. Depending on payload, number of passengers and scheduling, drops at additional airstrips are made either on the outward or return trip.

The flight is operated twice a day, seven days a week. On Monday, Wednesday, Friday and Sunday it leaves Georgetown at 10.30 and 13.00; on Tuesday, Thursday and Saturday it leaves at 07.30 and 13.00. Flying time to Lethem is about 1½ hours and the flight does an immediate turnaround. One-way tickets (adult/child US$130/65) and return (adult/child US$245/125) are available.

Maximum baggage allowance is 20lb. Extra baggage is roughly US$0.75 per pound and can be booked in advance, but excess space is not always available so don't plan on it.

Air Services (see page 84) offers three scheduled flights per week from Ogle to Kaieteur at 09.00, Sunday, Wednesday and Friday (return US$210).

Chartered flights It's not cheap to charter an entire plane, but if you have a big enough group it can become more affordable. For a list of airlines in Guyana see *Getting around*, page 84.

BY LAND The cheapest option for overland travel is found with the minibuses that travel along the road, but these can make for a crowded and cramped experience.

Intraserv buses aren't much more expensive and, while they travel a bit more slowly, they are much more comfortable. Private 4x4 is probably the ideal way to travel, but hiring a vehicle to transport you into the interior is very expensive.

Bus With their coaches that can hold around 40 passengers, Intraserv (*177 Water St, S Cummingsburg;* ✆ *226 0605;* e *commercial61@live.com*) had greatly improved transportation in the interior. While they aren't first-class buses nor do they make the journey as quickly as 4x4 vehicles can, they were the best option for cheap travel to Guyana's interior. However, they have currently ceased all services until road conditions improve.

If services resume the buses travel on Sunday, Monday, Tuesday, Thursday and Friday, leaving from Jerrie's/The New Tropicana Hotel (*177 Water St*) in Georgetown at 19.00. If all goes well, the trip takes 12–15 hours. One-way fares vary according to stops along the way, including the Kurupukari Crossing (US$40), Annai (US$45) and Lethem (US$50). Space permitting, you could also use the bus to go shorter distances within the interior such as Kurupukari–Lethem (US$15) or Annai–Lethem (US$10). Contact the Correia group on ✆ 222 2525 for an update on services.

Free baggage allowance is 50lb; excess is US$0.25 per pound.

Minibus This form of travel is for the more intrepid traveller. The journey is dusty, loud and cramped, but popular as more and more minibuses are travelling this route. From Georgetown, buses depart from P&A Ice Cream and Transport Service (*75 Church St, Georgetown;* ✆ *225 5058*) at 19.30 and charge US$50 for the trip to Lethem. Arrive an hour early for check-in. It's possible to go shorter distances, but you'll likely have to pay full fare as preference is given to those paying the full amount.

4x4 Hired 4x4 vehicles are a great way to travel to the interior as they allow for the most flexibility; you can stop along the way and choose your own departure times. The problem is the cost. Hiring a vehicle and driver can cost hundreds of dollars. It is also not wise to go with just anybody; driving conditions on the road are hard on vehicles and if you break down on the way, you're likely to be in the middle of nowhere. Contact local tour operators for recommendations on reliable vehicles and drivers who journey into the interior.

Prices for vehicle hire within the interior (transfers between villages and lodges) is covered on pages 243 and 280.

If you are driving in your own vehicle (rented or personal) be sure to carry extra petrol or diesel and emergency equipment such as a tow rope, jump leads, extra water, torch, spare tyre and jack.

LINDEN

For most people who visit Guyana, Linden is a town they pass through only if they head into Guyana's interior overland via the main Linden–Lethem highway, or trail, as it is more affectionately known. Linden is the gateway to the pristine forests that lie directly to the south, and many who are excitedly toying with images of what awaits them in Guyana's interior – soaring macaws, towering trees, mischievous monkeys, remote villages – are a bit taken aback, and often turned off, by the industrial smokestacks and mined-out hillsides that Linden is best known for. When judging the book by its cover, there appears to be little reason to stop except to buy fuel so the journey can continue south.

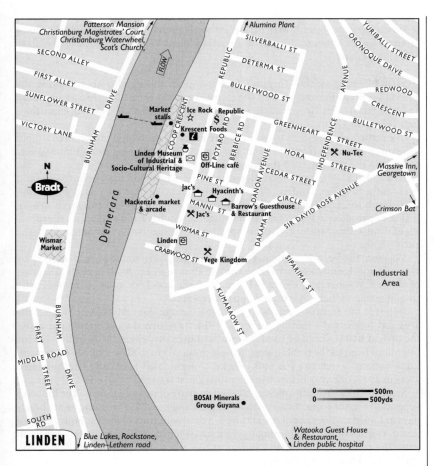

There is no denying that Linden is an industrial town. The mining and timber companies that boomed here in the 19th and early 20th centuries did much to support the entire country. Lindeners aren't ashamed of their industrial past; the money that was dug up and cut down was responsible for great prosperity in the region. If a visitor turns their nose up at the activities, they should remember all of the products they use in their daily lives that rely on these very mines. Lindeners like to ask if the visitor enjoyed Georgetown's beautiful colonial buildings, and then ask where they think the wood came from.

Regardless of your feelings, the industrial boom that the region experienced has largely collapsed and lately Linden has been looking to other sectors to bring in money, tourism being one of them. And while Linden may have a tough time selling itself as Guyana's next ecotourism destination, it serves well as an overnight stop before heading into, or after coming out of, the interior. There is no doubt that Linden will experience another transformation with the building of a proper highway to Brazil that now seems inevitable sooner than later.

How Linden adapts, and what changes this will bring to its tourism offerings can only be guessed at, but for now those visitors who take a moment to peer beyond Linden's smoky façade will find friendly locals and some charming reasons for a stopover, however brief it may be. Recommendations include the Watooka Guest House; Linden Museum; Irene's Creative Handicraft Workshop; Rockstone Village and Gluck Island.

HISTORY Seeing as how Guyana's first European immigrants settled along the Essequibo River, the area around the Demerara River wasn't largely explored until Laurens Storm Van Gravensande was granted permission to seek out lands for a new colony in 1742.

The settlers created plots to use as sugarcane plantations and this secured a rapid growth for the new colony. In 1746, the Dutch began allowing British immigrants to settle in the area; by 1769 the colony had more than 200 plantations.

In 1759, LL Bercheych completed the first survey of the lands that would eventually become Linden. The first settlement in the area was Plantation Christianburg, a sugar producing estate. The success of the settlement saw an influx of people seeking to cash in on sugarcane cultivation and balata bleeding. Plantation Christianburg also became home to the Patterson Sawmill in the early 1800s.

Wismar, the second settlement in the region, was founded and named by German immigrants who arrived to work in the sugarcane fields after the abolition of slavery. Wismar was also a hub for the pork knockers, or local miners, who sought gold and diamonds on the upper Demerara.

In 1913, the Scottish-American geologist George Bain Mackenzie, visited the area and conducted a mining survey. In 1914, he returned and bought land under the pretext that it would be used only for farming. The sellers didn't realise that his intentions from the beginning were to mine the newly named Mackenzie settlement. Linden's bauxite industry was built on a lie. Unfortunately for Mackenzie, he passed away in 1915, one year before bauxite mining first started.

Since then, the bauxite industry has had its share of ups and downs. The industry supported a lot of economic growth in Guyana and provided for some pretty heady days in Linden. Mines opened and closed, a costly alumina plant was built and shut down, control of bauxite mining operations switched from Canada to Guyana to Australia to Guyana to Canada and most recently to China, but the digging still continues, although at a slower pace.

On 29 April 1970, Mackenzie, Wismar and Christianburg were collectively renamed Linden and formally declared a town.

Today, different sections of Linden are still referred to by the old plantation names. The Demerara River splits the town in half, with much of the business development being centred along Republic Avenue in Mackenzie.

GETTING THERE AND AWAY From the north, Linden is easily accessed by the paved Soesdyke–Linden highway, but to the south is the unpaved Linden–Lethem road. Getting to Linden from this direction involves using a 4x4 vehicle, the Intraserv bus or one of the minibuses that travel the route.

Linden is approximately 64 miles south of Georgetown, a trip that takes roughly 1½ hours. To the south, it is approximately 300 miles, or an average of ten hours (depending on the road and mode of transportation) to Lethem.

By taxi Any of Georgetown's major taxi companies will drive to Linden (one-way US$40), but none will go much further south. In Linden, the main taxi companies are **Double Team Taxi Service** (✆ 444 6633) and **Odki Taxi Service** (✆ 444 2500); both will make the journey to Georgetown (US$45).

By bus Minibus number 43 travels the route between the bus park at Georgetown's Stabroek Market and Linden's bus park on Republic Avenue (US$4; less for stops in between). As always, they drive recklessly fast on the Linden highway, which doesn't have a reputation as the safest road in Guyana.

Another option is to take one of the bigger buses (US$3), which leave from the same bus parks. They don't depart as often, and their slower speeds add roughly 30 minutes to the travel time, but they are much safer.

If you are coming to Linden from Lethem, minibus number 72 leaves from the T&M Restaurant & Bar (US$50; for details see page 280). Making the trip in a minibus is an uncomfortably long, dusty, bumpy and cramped ride that only the hardiest of travellers will wish to undertake.

There is little reason for passengers to use Intraserv as transportation coming from Georgetown, but when travelling from the south, this was the main, and recommended, mode of public transportation. At the time of writing all services have been cancelled. See page 208 for further details.

GETTING AROUND The central part of Linden is easy enough to manoeuvre on foot, but to reach destinations a bit further out, you'll have to use transportation.

By taxi While not as prevalent as in Georgetown, you still won't have any trouble finding a taxi in Linden. Two of Linden's main taxi companies are listed above; rates for drops around Linden are US$1.50–3.00.

By minibus The Republic Avenue bus park in Linden is where minibuses can be found for local destinations; ask around to make sure you board the correct bus.

By boat The easiest way to cross the Demerara River, which effectively splits Linden in half, is with the picturesque covered wooden boats (US$0.30). On the Mackenzie side, they dock near the market stalls on Coop Crescent Street; on the Wismar side, they dock at several locations along Burnham Drive.

WHERE TO STAY With Linden's new push for tourism to the area, there are a surprising number of decent hotels and guesthouses for a city of its size. All rooms at the establishments below are self-contained and equipped with fans and mosquito nets (except where air conditioning makes them unnecessary); extra amenities are outlined in each entry.

⌂ **Massive Inn** (9 rooms) 153 Frasier Rd, Kara Kara; ☏ 444 6383. While the location may be inconvenient for travellers without a vehicle, this new guesthouse offers nice rooms in a quiet residential area. They are fully outfitted with AC, TV, DVD, ironing board, stocked minibar & tables & chairs & still have space to move around in. Meals prepared on order or guests can use the kitchen. The 2 family rooms are sprawling suites with their own kitchens. **$$$**

⌂ **Barrow's Guesthouse** (3 rooms) 82 Dageraad Av & Manni St; ☏ 444 6799. The upper-level rooms all have AC, TV, 4-poster bed, desk & chairs & are neatly arranged with plenty of space.

The only drawback to these rooms is that they are above the popular downstairs restaurant & bar, & the smell of food & sounds of revelry tend to waft up. **$$**

⌂ **Hyacinth's B&B** (3 rooms) 94 Manni St; ☏ 444 6350; e katabullic@yahoo.com. Immediately after walking past the flowering bushes & through the gate you feel transported out of Linden. The proprietor has transformed the upstairs of the home where he grew up with 11 siblings into a stylish & welcoming B&B. The spotless AC rooms are spacious, full of light, brightly painted & tastefully decorated; the back room has a private balcony overlooking the garden while the front room has a window seat above the street. The TV lounge, dining room & kitchen are shared. On the ground floor is an additional 1-bedroom garden apartment with veranda. Guests can also access free internet. The owners also help arrange trips in & around Linden & mountain bikes are available for rent. **$$**

🏠 **Jac's** (10 rooms) 91 Republic Av; ☎ 444 6461. There is nothing special about these rooms, but then there's nothing wrong with them either. They are well appointed with AC, TV, fridge, bath & they are pretty clean, but the wooden building is showing its age. It's worth paying slightly more for the rooms with extra space. **$$**

🏠 **Watooka Guest House** (15 rooms) Riverside Dr; ☎ 444 2162; e info@watookahouse.com; www.watookahouse.com. Originally built c1920 by Demerara Bauxite Company (DEMBA)

as a company guesthouse, this grand wooden colonial building hosted a fair share of esteemed guests during Linden's glory days, including British royalty. Now government-owned, it has only recently been opened to the public as a guesthouse, restaurant & bar, providing a chance to see how the other half used to live. Set on the shores of the Demerara River, the beautiful grounds are spacious & include a swimming pool. There are 8 very basic sgl rooms with shared bathrooms in a separate building, but you'd be foolish not to pay extra for the expansive suites. These are preserved time capsules with Art Deco furniture, classic fixtures, TVs & mini-fridges; some even include little bonuses such as a waterbed or sweeping veranda. It's the perfect place to role-play a life you'll never really live, mainly because its time has come and gone. *Sgl* **$**; *suites* **$$**.

✗ WHERE TO EAT AND DRINK

✗ **Barrow's Restaurant & Lounge** 82 Dageraad Av & Manni St; ☎ 444 6799; ⏰ 11.00–23.00 daily; outdoor canteen open late. The outdoor patio serves cold beer & a range of snacks, but the place to eat your meal, chosen from the daily selections including meat, seafood, vegetables & rice, is in the quiet restaurant. The small bar, with its warm woods & one of the widest selections of alcohols in Guyana, is also inviting. **$$$**

✗ **Jac's** 91 Republic Av; ☎ 444 6312; ⏰ 10.00–19.00 daily. The AC dining room of Jac's, with its plain walls & tiled floors, is cosy only in a sterile hospital cafeteria kind of way, but it is new, clean & they slowly serve up good, basic meals. **$$**

✗ **Watooka Guest House Restaurant** Riverside Dr; ☎ 444 2162; ⏰ 08.00–19.00 daily.

The restaurant here serves typical Guyanese fare that is pretty good, but the real reason to come is for the large open dining room, the grand building, sweeping riverside grounds & free use of the pool for customers. **$$**

✗ **Nu-Tec** 245 Greenheart St; ☎ 444 2010; ⏰ 08.00–20.00 Mon–Sat. This nondescript restaurant, with crowded outdoor seating, is said by locals to make some of the best Creole food around. Everything is homemade & fresh, including the bread, pastries & ice cream. The attached Star Chinese Restaurant is also good. **$**

✗ **Vege Kingdom** 313 Dageraad Av; ☎ 444 2056; ⏰ 08.00–21.00 daily. This funky Rastafarian *ital* eatery serves up excellent veggie & tofu dishes & fresh juices. The bright colours & Bob Marley music recalls Guyana's Caribbean connections. **$**

ENTERTAINMENT AND NIGHTLIFE Linden used to carry a reputation as quite the party town, and while it has moved past that, the town's many bars, rum shops and clubs still show an appreciation of merrymaking.

☆ **Barrow's Restaurant & Lounge** 82 Dageraad Av & Manni St; ☎ 444 6799; ⏰ 11.00– late daily. The outdoor patio is popular late into the night, but don't miss the inside bar's cosy atmosphere & impressively stocked bar.

☆ **Crimson Bat Discothèque** 633 Industrial Area; ☎ 444 6221; ⏰ 24hrs daily. Linden's long-time favourite for drinking, loud music & general carousing.

☆ **Ice Rock** Lot 8 Coop Cr; ⏰ 19.00–late Fri– Sun. Linden's newest nightclub is also reputedly the largest in the country. With AC, digital surround sound, motion-sensor disco lights, dress codes & separate VIP levels, Ice Rock is a self-acclaimed New York-style club. If you leave the New York expectations at home, you might have an OK time.

SHOPPING Linden is home to some people very talented in handicrafts, which can make for good shopping opportunities. While much of the better items produced in Linden can be purchased in Georgetown's souvenir shops, in Linden visitors have a chance to see a couple of the artisans at work and purchase their crafts direct from the production facility.

The **Mackenzie Market** and adjacent Mackenzie Arcade is the place to find cheap, imported goods mingling with not-so-cheap Guyanese gold and diamond jewellery. The buying of expensive jewellery from these stalls is best left to those who are personally able to suss out good quality from bad. The **Wismar Market**, on the other side of the river, is also stuffed full of more typical market goods.

The best place for grocery and toiletry items is **Krescent Foods** (*Lot 2, Coop Crescent;* ☎ *444 6014;* ⊕ *Mon–Sat 07.00–17.30*). The market stalls in front of the supermarket sell a wide range of fresh vegetables and fruits.

Irene's Creative Handicraft Workshop 248 Kara Kara; ☎ 444 6637; e amazonauthentics@ gmail.com; www.amazonauthentics.com; ⊕ 09.00–16.00 Mon–Fri. Irene's beautiful wooden pieces are works of art posing as functional bowls, boxes, vases & the like. Some are enhanced with designs imprinted through pyrography, & all are made with scrap wood from Guyana's timber industry. While her work is sold throughout Guyana, it's only at her workshop that you can watch them being made; call before visiting, especially if you have a certain item in mind to purchase.

OTHER PRACTICALITIES
Bank
$ **Republic Bank** 101 Republic Av; ☎ 444 6951; ⊕ 08.00–14.00 Mon–Thu, 08.00–14.30 Fri. Foreign currency & travellers' cheques can be exchanged.

Communications
Post
✉ **Mackenzie Post Office** 15 Republic Av; ☎ 444 6576; ⊕ 07.00–16.00 Mon–Fri, 07.00–11.00 Sat

Email and internet Rates average US$1 per hour for internet and US$0.10 per minute for calls to the US, Canada and UK.

Linden Online 62 Republic Av; ☎ 444 6293; ⊕ 08.00–23.00 Mon–Sat, 15.00–23.00 Sun

Off-Line Café Region 10 Business Centre, 9798 Republic Av; ☎ 444 4057; ⊕ 07.00– midnight daily

Hospital The new **Linden Public Hospital** (*Riverside Dr, Watooka;* ☎ *444 6127*) is vastly better than the old facility, but for serious medical attention the best option is to transfer to Georgetown (see *Hospitals, doctors and pharmacies,* page 119).

Tourist information The Region Ten Tourism Development Association (RTDA) is the local body that has made many recent strides in injecting life into a tourism industry in and around Linden. Its home, the Linden Office for Visitors, or LOV as the friendly staff members like to call it, is located in the Linden Museum of Industrial and Socio-Cultural Heritage (*Lot One, Coop Crescent;* ☎ *444 2901;* e *info@lindentourism.com; www.lindentourism.com*). The staff at LOV also arrange tours for visitors, be it historical, industrial or river based.

WHAT TO SEE AND DO Every visit to Linden should begin with a stop at the **Linden Museum of Industrial and Socio-Cultural Heritage** (*Lot One, Coop Crescent;* ☺ *09.00–17.00 Mon–Fri, Sat–Sun by special request; adult/child US$0.50/0.30*) Don't let the long-winded name turn you off as this is one of Guyana's better historical museums. Tucked into half of the old Mackenzie Recreation Hall, which dates back to 1925, the Linden Museum has an impressive collection of historical artefacts from the region, ranging from early Amerindian fish traps to Dutch gin bottles. The knowledgeable guides also do a wonderful job of highlighting Linden's glorious past while explaining the bauxite industry. After seeing the products that bauxite is used in, for example aluminium and anti-diarrhoea medicine, it's harder to turn your nose up at the scarred hillsides surrounding the town.

Linden's foundations grew from the logging and mining industry, resulting in present-day historical sites that mainly involve hulking metal forms and towering smokestacks. They don't create the prettiest skyline, and aren't aligned with the nature that most seek out on a visit to Guyana, but for those who like big machines, stagnant conveyor belts and rusting storage tanks, the industrial tour may prove captivating.

Burnham Drive in Christianburg, on the west bank of the Demerara River, is home to a few surviving historical landmarks. The diminutive wooden building that is **Scot's Church**, c1850, was the area's first. Just past here is the bright red **Christianburg Waterwheel**, which was installed in 1855 and harnessed the energy of the Katabulli Creek to power the Patterson sawmill operations. It revolutionised the industry and much of the wood that was processed here got shipped to Georgetown and was used in many of the colonial buildings that still stand today. Just adjacent is the old **Patterson Mansion**, which, in the 1830s when it was constructed, was one of the largest homes in British Guiana. The wooden building is now the rundown site of the Christianburg Magistrates' Court. A better-preserved example of the celebrated wooden architecture of the time can be seen at **Watooka House** (see page 212).

Furthering on Linden's industrial past is the now defunct **Alumina Plant** that was completed in 1961. Having closed in 1983, it is little more than a series of rusty, oversized buildings, storage tanks and tubes standing as a testament to better economic days. The Linden Museum has some good photos of the plant in full operation.

The most striking site of Linden is the current **BOSAI Minerals Group Guyana bauxite plant** whose billowing smokestacks welcome visitors to town. (It's claimed that it isn't smoke pouring forth into the air, but bauxite dust resulting from the baking process, which hardens the bauxite at 1,700°C.) The plant is impossible to miss, and if the big machinery (including trains running on Guyana's last functioning railroad) transporting crushed bauxite from the mined-out hills to the factory intrigues you, tours can be arranged with advance notice through LOV (see page 213).

On the flip side are Linden's nature offerings, but the best-known sites aren't so far removed – or removed enough – from the mines. Located in the remains of several old mined-out holes are **Blue Lakes**, or Linden's Caribbean. Indeed the bright turquoise water filling the holes and the pure white sands lining the banks are little patches of paradise. However, these unnatural pools that develop in old mining sites make many concerned about the quality of the water and the chemicals that remain, and likely for good reason. Many others, however, claim the water is fine, and swim in the Blue Lakes often.

Even though many are rightfully cautious about swimming in the ponds, the Blue Lakes are worth a visit, for their unnatural beauty if nothing else. There is one main Blue Lake, located roughly two miles from Linden in the Wisroc area, which is slowly being developed into a functional beach. The water here is considered the safest as it experiences run-off as opposed to other stagnant pools, but swimming is at your own discretion. The surrounding sand dunes make for fun slides and the beach is good enough for a picnic. Local taxis will make the trip.

River-based trips can also be arranged. These take visitors up and down the Demerara River to locations such as Kara Kara Creek, Coomacka Beach, Great Falls and Butooba village. The boat trips are a pleasant way to pass a morning or afternoon and can be arranged through LOV; prices vary according to distances and number of people.

EVENTS

Linden Town Week This event, which is an expanded form of the original Linden Town Day, celebrates all things Linden and is mainly geared towards local Lindeners and those returning from outside countries. The event is usually held the final week of April so as to coincide with the anniversary of Linden's founding. Activities include sporting competitions, bodybuilding competitions, dances and special historical and nature-based tours.

The Annual Kashif and Shanghai Soccer Tournament What started as an ad hoc football tournament for local Linden clubs in 1989 has since grown into one of Guyana's largest annual sporting events. The tournament begins in mid-December with games throughout Guyana and culminates on New Year's Day. Historically, the final game always drew visitors from all over Guyana to Linden to watch the final match and participate in the many parties that accompany it, but it is now held at the Providence Stadium in Georgetown.

ROCKSTONE

Rockstone is a small Amerindian village located roughly 20 miles west of Linden on the Essequibo River. Its proximity to Linden has resulted in its being billed as the region's new ecotourism destination. In late 2006, to further tourism growth in the village, the Rockstone Tourism Association (RTA) was founded. Rockstone has long been visited for the legendary fishing in the area, but with a newly built guesthouse, a few good nature trails and the magnificent Gluck Island, it will surely become a popular destination for nature lovers as well.

As tourism is still a relatively new business for Rockstone, at the time of writing the RTA was still working out many of the details, such as pricing for trips offered; call for a quote. Also, before making any visit, advance notice should be given to the villagers. This can be done through the RTA (✆ 444 9288) or LOV (✆ 444 2901).

GETTING THERE AND AWAY Rockstone is only 20 miles from Linden, but the trail in can be rough, causing the short journey to take about one hour. To self-cater, taxi companies in Linden make the trip (one-way US$25, same-day return US$40), otherwise it's possible to arrange an entire trip through the RTDA (see page 213; prices vary according to number of days and people).

Avid birdwatchers and nature lovers may want to enquire with Guyana Feather Friends (see page 59), the tourism offshoot of Guyana Amazon Tropical Birds Society (GATBS). It was GATBS members who did the birding assessment at Gluck Island that found it to be a first-class birding location, and they make the best guides.

GUIANA SHIELD

The Guiana Shield is 2.5 million km² of tropical forest covering Guyana, Suriname, French Guiana and parts of Colombia, Venezuela and Brazil. The massive granite dome, or *craton*, underlying the Guiana Shield formed some two billion years ago during the Precambrian period. Covering the craton are sandstone, quartzite, shales, conglomerates and boulder beds that support the world's largest remaining tract of mostly undisturbed tropical rainforest (one of only four such forests left in the world).

While the Guiana Shield is primarily covered in tropical forest, the area also supports large savannas, wetlands and a series of *tepuis* (tabletop mountains) that dot the higher elevations, known as the Guiana Highlands. These tepuis, the most famous of which is Mount Roraima (see box, page 223), also create some of the world's tallest and most stunning waterfalls, including Venezuela's Angel Falls.

The Guiana Shield has been preserved because the area has low human population densities, remains largely inaccessible and has limited agricultural potential. The low demands on the natural resources have allowed the Guiana Shield the rare luxury of keeping its forest ecosystem largely intact.

In today's world the importance of the region seems obvious –the Guiana Shield contains 10–15% of the world's freshwater resources, it supports one of the highest concentrations of biodiversity on the planet and there are more than 5,000 medicinal plants also found here – but it has not been able to escape the attention of large-scale investors who seek to gain by exploiting natural resources.

Timber harvesting, mining and oil drilling have been slowly expanding through the region, and have been leaving their marks on the pristine habitat. And as the Western world seeps into many of the local communities, the residents often try to survive the economic shifts by turning to small-scale enterprises such as gold mining, chainsaw logging and wildlife trading.

In an effort to protect and preserve the ecosystems of the Guiana Shield, and turn the focus away from short-term gains, a few organisations are working with communities, government bodies and researchers of the region to create financial stability through activities that encompass sustainable activities and conservation.

In Guyana, organisations such as Conservation International (CI) and the Iwokrama International Centre are leading the way by protecting large swathes of pristine forest and working with local communities in creating innovative ways of netting financial gains from their natural surroundings without destroying it, such as ecotourism projects.

WHERE TO STAY AND EAT If you have the necessary gear, tent or hammock camping is a good option. If you are planning on making a trip to Gluck Island, special arrangements can be made to camp on one of the sandbanks. A nominal fee may be charged in both cases.

The other option is the new **Arawana Lodge** (*444 9288*; **$**). Built on stilts, and overlooking the river and Gluck Island, this simple cabin has four rooms with shared bath, a kitchen for use and a nice veranda for relaxing. Hammocks are also available to rent.

When staying over, it's often best to self-cater, but with advance notice, meals can be provided ($$).

WHAT TO SEE AND DO The main reason to visit Rockstone is to make a trip to beautiful Gluck Island, but there are other activities as well.

Fishing This has long been a popular pastime in the area; a few species found nearby include perai, piranha, arawana, haimara, lukanani, patois and hassar. Catch-and-release fishing is encouraged; rods are available for rent.

Nature trails There are several nature trails of varying length around the village perimeter; guides are provided. More are located on Gluck Island.

Swimming During the dry season, the waters of the Essequibo drop and expose numerous sandbanks perfect for swimming.

Boat trips Destinations include Teperu Lake for fishing, Ariwani Creek, Golden Beach and Aharo Rapids for swimming and Gluck Island for bird and wildlife watching. With a group, prices range from US$5 to 15/person, more for destinations further away.

Gluck Island In 2006, the Guyana Amazon Tropical Birding Society completed a four-day rapid assessment programme at Gluck Island, gathering some impressive data. The team identified 140 different species of birds, including a healthy population of blue-headed parrots and blue-and-yellow macaws, as well as antbirds, antwrens, tanagers, the nocturnal agami heron and several other species of waterbirds. Other fauna on the island includes giant river otters, long-nosed armadillos, red howler monkeys, black caiman and giant river turtles. There is also a pond where the impressive *Victoria amazonica* grows in abundance.

While trails have been developed, including one to a viewing platform over the lake with *Victoria amazonica*, there remains much discussion about how to best further develop it as an ecotourism destination, complete with lodge, without disturbing the natural setting.

Rockstone Fish Festival In October of every year (call for exact dates), Rockstone hosts a fish festival. Many of the activities listed above are included with extra events such as a mountain bike race and a fishing competition. It's an overall festive time that serves to boost recognition of Rockstone as a tourist destination, but for those who truly want to experience the area, it's not the best time to visit. Crowds of people can take away from the nature experience and often the wait for boat tours and guided hikes reaches into the hours.

PAKARAIMA MOUNTAINS

The Pakaraima Mountains are found in central and western Guyana along the border with Venezuela and Brazil. The range, which covers a distance of roughly 500 miles (800km), is part of the Guiana Shield's highlands and is dotted with *tepuis*, or flat-topped mountains. At 9,222ft (2,810m), the largest of these tepuis is the famed Mount Roraima. The crown of the ancient mountain range is Guyana's highest point and the meeting spot of Guyana, Brazil and Venezuela.

The Pakaraima Mountains are also home to Guyana's grandest waterfall.

Within Kaieteur National Park is Guyana's most celebrated, and highly touted, natural wonder: Kaieteur Falls. Since it was discovered in 1870 by the European explorer, Barrington Browne, Kaieteur Falls has been recognised as the crown jewel of Guyana's vast ecosystem. During its peak, some 30,000 gallons of water cascade over a 741ft-sheer drop, making Kaieteur Falls one of the world's largest and most powerful single-drop waterfalls (the falls measure 822ft to the bottom of the gorge; five-times the size of Niagara Falls).

In 1929, the British Colonial Administration designated 45 square miles surrounding the falls as a National Park. It was a groundbreaking step for conservation, as it was one of the first such acts in Latin America and the Caribbean. In the 1970s, all glory was lost when the park was downsized to allow for expanded mining concessions in the area. Two decades later, in what must surely have been an embarrassing moment of retrospection for those involved, the boundaries of the park were expanded again to protect it from the damaging mining practices. The good news is that Kaieteur Park now consists of 224 square miles (580km²) of protected lands; unfortunately it remains Guyana's only national park.

Legend has it that the waterfall draws its name from a selfless Patamona Amerindian chief named Kai. In an effort to appease the Great Spirit Makonaima, Kai sacrificed himself to save his tribe from the vengeful Caribs. Appeasing gods takes bold acts and Kai outdid himself by paddling over the point where the Potaro River tumbles into the gorge below. If nothing else, he succeeded in getting a natural wonder named after him (*teur* means 'falls' in a local dialect).

The beauty of Kaieteur Falls lies in its sheer size and power – during the rainy season, watching 30,000 gallons of water per second flow over the nearly 400ft-wide edge is a stunning sight and sound – but also in its raw state. The isolated location of the falls has kept much development at bay. There are no guard rails, let alone kitschy tourist shops (or any tourists really). Nature, by and large, is left undisturbed and the place surely looks remarkably similar to the day it was 'discovered' by Mr Brown.

LOCATION Kaieteur National Park is located roughly 150 miles southwest of Georgetown, within the Pakaraima mountain range. In a larger picture, it sits within the vast Guiana Shield, an ancient plateau watershed between the Amazon and Orinoco river basins that is around two billion years old (see box, page 216).

The focal point of the park is the location where the plateau that the Potaro River follows makes a sudden drop in to lowlands. From the falls, the river travels for some 50 miles through a deep gorge and then makes its way towards the Essequibo River.

BIODIVERSITY The Guiana Shield is one of the most biodiverse areas on earth, and when combined with the unique conditions created by the spray of the falls, Kaieteur National Park supports a fascinating microenvironment.

There are hundreds of species of birds within Kaieteur Park, but a few of them garner the most attention. Guianan cock-of-the-rocks (see page 44) have a few *leks* alongside the trail, and are spotted on a fairly regular basis. The white-chinned and white-collared swifts, or Makonaima birds, roost under the vast shield of rock hidden behind the falls; at dusk thousands of swifts return to their home and carry out an acrobatic insect-feeding frenzy before darting behind the curtain of falling water for the night. Beautiful red-and-green macaws are also frequently seen soaring overhead.

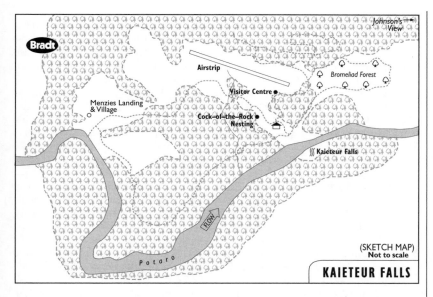

Two of the more fascinating creatures at the park are the prehistorically large tank bromeliads and the tiny golden rocket frogs (see page 40) that spend their entire lives inside the base of the bromeliads' leaves. The terrestrial tank bromeliads, which in extreme cases can grow to nine feet in height, collect water in the natural tanks formed at the base of their upturned leaves. The microenvironment that results proves to be the perfect habitat for the brilliant golden rocket frogs (*Anomaloglossus beebei*), which are endemic to and easily seen at Kaieteur Park.

Among the several butterfly species present in the Kaieteur gorge are the brilliant morphos. Among these are the morpho hecuba, whose eight-inch wingspan makes it South America's largest butterfly, and the blue morpho, with their striking, iridescent blue wings.

While sightings are considerably more rare, especially on day trips, visitors can also hope to see the more elusive ocelot, tapir, bush dog, giant river otter and red howler monkey, which will likely be heard.

GETTING THERE AND AWAY Kaieteur Falls is accessible by either land or air. Flying time from Georgetown is one hour; the overland route, which is a combination of minibus, boat, trekking and return flight, takes a minimum of five days.

By air When flying to Kaieteur, the majority of visitors go with a day-trip package, but there is a scheduled flight to Kaieteur Park three times per week.

Day tour Kaieteur Falls is most often visited as part of a day tour. Some trips visit only the falls (US$220), but most combine it with another location such as Orinduik Falls (US$270), Baganara Island Resort (US$255) or Arrowpoint Resort (US$235). At the time of writing there were also discussions about arranging a day trip that would possibly visit Kaieteur Falls and Iwokrama; contact a local tour operator for details.

A trip to Kaieteur Falls can be booked through most tour operators in Georgetown (see *Tour operators*, page 56). As the trip involves chartering a plane, there is a minimum number of people required (usually five) for the trip to take place. While tour operators often work together to collect enough passengers for a trip, it isn't uncommon for planned trips to be cancelled due to a lack of passengers.

It's best to try and schedule a trip to Kaieteur on a weekend and allow for at least one or two optional dates. It may also be that you will have to make compromises on your trip; if you want to go to Kaieteur and Orinduik, but the majority of passengers want to go to Kaieteur and Baganara, the trip will go to the latter. Either way, it's Kaieteur Falls that is the highlight of any trip.

In some cases, if there are scheduled trips that are not at maximum capacity, it's possible to plan an overnight stay using Kaieteur flights booked by tour operators. More information can be provided by the operators and be sure flights are confirmed or risk being stuck at Kaieteur for longer than planned.

Scheduled flights Air Services Ltd (see *Airlines*, page 84) offers three scheduled flights per week departing from Ogle at 09.00, Sunday, Wednesday and Friday (return US$210). This is a good option for those who wish to overnight at the falls without undertaking the overland trek.

By road This challenging trip is for those who like a sense of accomplishment with their scenery. While this trek is offered by several tour operators, it is the speciality of Frank Singh at Rainforest Tours (5 days; US$795 FB; see *Tour operators*, page 56) and over the years he has established good trails and campsites along a route that provides insight into what the early European explorers went through more than a century ago.

The trip begins with an eight-hour minibus ride that takes you through Linden, along the interior trail and past the mining town of Mahdia until you reach Pamela Landing on the Potaro River. From here it's a 2½-hour boat ride to a camp at the base of 170ft Amatuk Falls.

The following two days consist of short boat rides and longer treks up the Kaieteur gorge. The trek culminates with the four-hour climb up 'Oh My God' mountain, which takes you to the top of Kaieteur Falls. One night is spent at the Kaieteur Guest House before returning to Georgetown by plane the following day.

The trip is rugged. It involves trekking through thick jungle, over and often through rivers and creeks and you can plan on battling bugs and spending a good amount of the day in wet boots and clothes. The level of hardship involved depends on the season, with dry season being the easiest.

The trip is offered year-round, except for the wettest months of May and June. It can never be considered easy, but it can be customised for different difficulty levels. Those who want an easier trip can spend more time moving up the river in boats instead of trekking. A porter can also be hired to carry your rucksack up the last climb to the top of Kaieteur Falls. If you want it to be more difficult, less time can be spent in the boats and more on your feet. The trek can also be extended in length to provide more time at Patamona villages along the way.

Participants must have their own rucksacks and some other supplies common for a rainforest trek (see *www.kaieteurpark.gov.gy* for list). Hammocks, nets and sheets can be provided.

The overland trek has a minimum capacity of four persons and maximum of 20. For those looking to truly experience Guyana's vast rainforest, this trip comes highly recommended by the adventurous who have completed it.

WHERE TO STAY There is a basic guesthouse for those who plan an overnight visit. If you overnight in conjunction with the overland trip, all planning will be taken care of. If you are arriving on a flight, staying at Kaieteur is a self-catered trip that involves bringing all necessary supplies, food and water (or water purification tablets).

Kaieteur Guest House c/o National Parks Commission, National Park, Thomas Lands; 226 7974; e natpark@networksgy.com; www. kaieteurpark.gov.gy. Offers basic lodging a short distance from the falls. Each bedroom has 2 beds; one self-contained bedroom, the second shares the main bath. Hammocks are also provided & there is space throughout the house to hang them. The house has limited solar power (110V), running water & the kitchen has a gas stove, fridge & all utensils. A cook is available to help prepare (self-catered) meals on request. The guesthouse is often shared with employees of the park & visiting researchers. It's not luxury but it's perfectly suitable, especially considering its surroundings. The guesthouse is very cheap but visitors arriving outside of an arranged tour must also pay a park entrance fee (US$12 pp) & a negotiable guide fee. Arrangements to stay at the guesthouse must be made in advance with the National Parks Commission in Georgetown. **$**

WHAT TO SEE AND DO Kaieteur is still very much an isolated wilderness area. There are no hotels, no restaurants, no convenience stores and not even any guardrails to prevent visitors from plunging from overlooks. However, this lack of development is one of Kaieteur's greatest assets. How many of the world's natural wonders haven't become a bit overshadowed by tourism facilities? At Kaieteur, the only distractions come from nature. It's entirely possible that on any given day you, along with your group, will be the only visitors at the park, giving the sense of having an entire national park all to yourself.

How long this lack of infrastructure will last remains to be seen, as there has been talk about building a proper lodge in the area for some time now. In 2010, work on a new visitor centre was completed, replacing the old covered patch where groups gathered for a safety talk. At the time of writing, toilets had been completed but finishing touches were still being put in place, and how long each stage takes to be realised will only be told in time, but plans for the solar-powered building include craft store, waiting areas, a restaurant and even internet. The building's design and placement away from the falls was well thought out and the National Parks Commission continues to place the importance of biodiversity conservation ahead of infrastructure development.

The best time to see Kaieteur Falls is during or just after the rainy season when they are fullest. While they're spectacular any time of the year, the width of the falls varies greatly from 75 to 400ft.

How much of the park you get to explore will depend on the length of your stay. As part of a day trip, visitors typically have two or three hours to explore the falls. Experienced guides lead groups on a circular tour of the upper plateau that provides many stunning vistas of Kaieteur Falls.

All biodiversity of the area is explained, and much of it is seen on the tour. Along the route, you slowly make your way towards the roaring falls; from each of five successive viewing points, less and less zoom is required for photos.

The final stop is at the top of the falls. Visitors can step in the Potaro River just feet before it tumbles for 741ft. This is also the site of the much-photographed rock overhang. For some stunning photographs, guests can slowly inch their way out on an unprotected rock that hangs right over the canyon below; for a true experience, lie on your stomach and stare over the edge. The views of the gorge are equally impressive.

Those who overnight at Kaieteur get to experience the same as day trippers, but also see the many different faces of Kaieteur. Being at the falls in the early morning and at sunset allows you to see the thousands of swifts emerging from, and descending into, their roosts behind the falls. It's a beautiful sight that has led to much speculation, and many myths, as to what lies behind the torrent of water.

Staying overnight also provides an opportunity to see the fog that covers the falls in the morning and the river at night, as well as some spectacular sunsets and great views of the falls by moonlight. Also, as most day trips are conducted during peak daytime hours when much of the wildlife seeks shelter from the sun and remains hidden, staying longer allows for more time for birdwatching and animal spotting.

ORINDUIK FALLS

While Kaieteur Falls is the elegant grandfather falls best admired from a distance, Orinduik Falls is the playful child best enjoyed while wading under its tumbling waters. The combination works perfectly for one of the most popular day trips in Guyana, which flies visitors to Kaieteur in the morning and Orinduik in the afternoon.

The setting of Orinduik Falls also couldn't be any more different from Kaieteur. Orinduik Falls are on the Ireng River, which forms the border with Brazil for many miles. They are located in the grassy savannas of the Pakaraima Mountain foothills. When flying from Kaieteur the change from the endless treetops of the jungle to the wide-open savannas is sudden and stunning.

Orinduik, which is a local name for the vegetation growing around the falls, is a series of drops where the water rushes over smooth red jasper. Swimming is best at its base where sitting under the falls is a good way to get a massage. Those with good river shoes can climb up the different levels of the falls but note that it is very slippery. Lose your footing and you can easily slide over the roughly 30ft drop.

Due to its location in the savannas, Orinduik has a lot of kaboura flies. Bring plenty of insect repellent, but expect to get bitten; the nearly invisible bugs are ruthless.

GETTING THERE AND AWAY Due to the remote location of Orinduik Falls, access is mostly by air and typically involves going on an organised day trip that stops at both Kaieteur and Orinduik falls. These can be booked through most of the tour operators in Guyana (see *Tour operators*, page 56).

For the very adventurous there are two more options – an overland trek and an overland 4x4 safari – that only occur once or twice per year. Contact Rainforest Tours (see page 59) for more detailed information.

Bushmasters (see page 59) also do a good job of catering trips to the desires of their clientele and can organise overland trips to Orinduik Falls.

Overland trek: Kaieteur to Orinduik (7 days; US$900 FB; *www.rftours.com*) Offered only in the driest month of September, this arduous trek is billed as hard adventure. In one week you cover the 70 miles that separate the two falls. The terrain is rugged, but there is no better way to see the pristine, and little-visited, jungles of the Pakaraima Mountains, their lowland savannas, and stay at very remote Amerindian villages. The area is often regarded as one of Guyana's most beautiful.

The trip is a combination of boat rides and trekking; the terrain varies from dense rainforests to sun-scorched savannas. It begins with a flight to Kaieteur Falls, where you overnight. The next day it continues to Menzie's Landing and Chenapou, an Amerindian village where you spend the night. From there you continue up the Potaro River and camp along the Kopinang Creek one night and spend two others at the Amerindian villages of Kopinaang and Kamanaa. The final day ends at Orinduik, where you overnight at the guesthouse. The following day you fly out to Georgetown. There is a minimum requirement of five persons and maximum of 12 for this trip.

Pakaraima 4x4 Safari (5 days; US$1,700 FB; *www.rftours.com*) The Pakaraima Safari began in 2003, but only recently has it become a tourism offering. The off-road safari begins in Georgetown and ends at Orinduik. That is, providing the vehicles can reach their destination. Once the safari leaves the main Linden–Lethem road, the vehicles drive on a very rough, and often muddy, trail that leads through creeks and up and down steep mountains, all in a very remote area of Guyana that is rarely visited with vehicles.

Participating vehicles must be completely off-road ready, as the going is far from easy and much time is spent winching vehicles up steep hills or out of rushing streams that cover the bonnet. It's a bumpy, muddy, tiring and bug-laden journey. Nights are spent camping at some of the 14 different Amerindian villages that are visited on the safari. The vehicles also carry in medical and other necessary supplies for the villages and deliver them along the way.

Because of the remote areas visited and the presence of malaria and other tropical diseases, participants must have all necessary vaccines (see *Health*, page 64) and be in generally good health.

Due to fluctuating weather patterns, the actual dates of the trip change from year to year but it typically takes place around the end of February to the beginning of March. Tourists who ride in as passengers return to Georgetown via a flight from Orinduik. The trip cost includes all vehicle transport, lodging (camping), meals, and flight.

MOUNT RORAIMA

Some two billion years old, nine miles (14 km) long and 9,222ft (2,810m) at its highest point, Mount Roraima is the granddaddy of the *tepuis*, or tabletop mountains, found in the Highlands of the Guiana Shield. The towering sandstone plateau that rises sharply from the surrounding savannas and forests also marks the point where the three national boundaries of Guyana, Brazil and Venezuela meet.

The strange and unique ecosystem found on top of Mount Roraima is widely believed to have provided inspiration for Sir Arthur Conan Doyle's, *The Lost World*. With nearly daily rains that often come in torrents, and a surface that is almost entirely bare sandstone rock, conditions for supporting life on Mount Roraima are extremely harsh.

Any nutrients that are present in the soil are often washed over the edge during the rains and many of the plants that are present – roughly a third of them are believed to be unique to the mountain – are carnivorous.

As a result of the near constant rain and wind, the top of the mountain is covered in strange geological formations that have been eroding and changing since the Precambrian area. Water runoff from Roraima feeds a significant portion of the Guyana, Amazon and Orinoco river systems.

Access to most of Mount Roraima is limited to say the least. Much of the upper portion of the mountain is little more than sheer cliff walls, and nearly impenetrable forests ring its base. Nearly all of those who reach the top of Mount Roraima do so on organised treks, which access it from Venezuela.

In Guyana, an elite few have used professional rock climbing skills and equipment to scale the sides, but this is hardly an option for normal travellers. It is possible to organise specialised treks to the base of the mountain in Guyana (see page 59), but even this trip is arduous.

Those who have their own 4x4 vehicles in Guyana are also invited to join. Vehicles must pass an inspection and participants then are required to cover their own costs (fuel, food, village fees, etc).

IWOKRAMA

Iwokrama International Centre for Rainforest Conservation and Development (*77 High St, Kingston;* ℡ *225 1504;* e *tourism@iwokrama.org; www.iwokrama.org*) encompasses nearly one million acres (371,000ha) of pristine Guiana Shield rainforest that serves as a living laboratory for scientific research, ecotourism, and sustainable tropical forest management. Located in the heart of Guyana, the Iwokrama Forest has an amazing cross-section of Guyana's biodiversity, including 1,500 species of flora, 200 mammals, 500 birds, 420 fish and 150 species of reptiles and amphibians.

The Government of Guyana and the Commonwealth Secretariat established Iwokrama in 1996 under a joint mandate to manage the Iwokrama forest 'in a manner that will lead to lasting ecological, economic and social benefits to the people of Guyana and to the world in general.'

Since then, Iwokrama has become internationally recognised for its unique and ambitious conservation and development practices that seek to show that rainforest resources can be used sustainably to generate economic benefits for communities through traditional and scientific resource-based knowledge and management.

Iwokrama is home to some of the Americas' and world's largest species – black caiman (alligator), capybara (rodent), arapaima (freshwater fish), anaconda (snake), giant anteater, giant river otter, giant river turtle (freshwater turtle), bushmaster (pit viper), false vampire bat (South America's largest bat), harpy eagle (the Americas' largest eagle) and jaguar (largest cat in the Western Hemisphere).

Of course all these species are living in some very dense forest and can be hard to spot, but there are a number of good activities to increase visitors' chances. Any visit should include a walk on some of the nature trails, a night-time boat ride to spot caiman and other nocturnal wildlife, a trip up the 1,000ft-high Turtle Mountain and a boat ride to Kurupukari Falls to see ancient petroglyphs. Lodging at the beautiful River Lodge goes without saying, but the more adventurous should spend at least one night at one of the hammock camps.

GEOGRAPHY The Iwokrama Forest, sometimes called 'The Green Heart of Guyana', is located in the centre of the country, some 200 miles (320km) from Georgetown. For GPS enthusiasts, it lies between 4° and 5°N latitude and 58.5° and 59.5°W longitude. Its nearly one million acres are surrounded by a boundary of 274 miles (442km) with the widest point being 53 miles (85km) and the longest point being 45 miles (72km). Almost the entire boundary of Iwokrama is set by waterways, the most significant being the Essequibo River to the east and the Siparuni to the north. The Iwokrama Forest is bisected by the Linden–Lethem road, which cuts directly through the centre heading north–south for roughly 45 miles (72km).

From its lowest point of 98ft above sea level, the rolling forest reaches a peak at 3,281ft within the Iwokrama Mountains, which are in the southeastern corner of the forest.

Rainfall to the area varies between 55 and 118 inches per year, most of which falls during the rainy season of May–August.

HISTORY While the history of the centre goes back only about 20 years, the Iwokrama Forest and Mountains have a much longer past. Guyana's indigenous

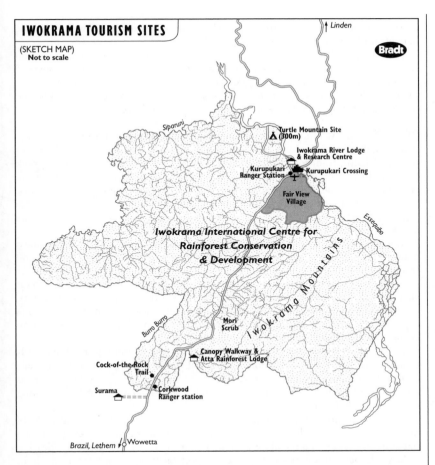

(SKETCH MAP)
Not to scale

Linden

Siparuni

Turtle Mountain Site
▲ (300m)

Iwokrama River Lodge
& Research Centre

Kurupukari
Ranger Station

Kurupukari Crossing

Fair View
Village

Iwokrama International Centre for
Rainforest Conservation
& Development

Essequibo

Iwokrama Mountains

Burro Burro

Mori
Scrub

Canopy Walkway &
Atta Rainforest Lodge

Cock-of-the-Rock
Trail

Surama

Corkwood
Ranger station

Brazil, Lethem

Wowetta

people, mainly the Makushi, have been living in the Iwokrama Forest for thousands of years.

Archaeological evidence shows that groups of hunter-gatherers migrated to the area some 4,000 years ago and there are petroglyphs that point to settlements around Kurupukari Falls and Sharples Island.

In search of the fabled city of gold, Europeans began exploring Guyana's interior via the Essequibo River in the 16th century. Sir Walter Raleigh (see page 5) is said to be the first European explorer to come into contact with the Makushi. His writings on his travels in search of El Dorado caught the imagination of Europe and compounded future exploration of the area.

Unfortunately, along with European colonisation came the Amerindian slave trade, which was continued until the late 18th century. By the time the Europeans began pillaging the Makushi lands, they had grown used to raids by rival indigenous groups that came from Brazil. However, the Makushi had long retreated to the surrounding mountains, hence their name, Iwokrama, meaning 'Place of refuge'.

In 1989, at the meeting of the Commonwealth Heads of Government in Malaysia, Guyana's then president offered to set aside this place of refuge so the international community could use it to study a tropical rainforest in an attempt to show how it can be used without destroying it, yet while still increasing social and economic benefits for local communities.

It took several years to draw up suitable guidelines. In 1994 a field station was established; in 1995 an agreement laying out the objectives, functions and organisation of Iwokrama was signed; in 1996 Guyana's Parliament passed the Iwokrama International Centre for Rainforest Conservation and Development Act, which was later signed into law by then president Cheddi Jagan.

BUSINESS The Iwokrama International Centre (IIC) has become internationally recognised for its unique and ambitious conservation and development practices using traditional and scientific resource-based knowledge that seek to show how rainforest resources can be used sustainably while generating economic benefits for local communities. At Iwokrama, scientists, researchers, sustainable timber experts, ecotourists, and indigenous communities all come together to both preserve and use a rainforest to the benefit of local, national, and global populations.

The many different ways that the IIC uses the rainforests in their overall business plan includes ecotourism, sustainable forestry, ecosystem services, research and training.

In Iwokrama's early days there was much talk and many promises of donor agencies contributing large sums of money to the worthy cause. Indeed, huge sums of money have been given to Iwokrama over the years. However, in 2003 Iwokrama began to see a decline in forthcoming grants and the board decided it was time to become more business savvy.

Iwokrama's main business initiatives are heavily touted amongst the buzzwords of sustainability and conservation. Additional funds are brought in by the sale of merchandise, consultancy services and non-timber forest products such as aquarium fish, honey, crabwood oil and nibbi and kufa vines used in making furniture and handicrafts.

From the beginning Iwokrama has been effectively split in half, with 50% of the land designated as the Sustainable Utilisation Area, for the money-generating pursuits, and the other 50% set aside as the Wilderness Preserve, where the clearing of land, timber harvesting, mineral extraction, construction of tourism facilities outside of low-impact camps and hunting or fishing for commercial purposes are all prohibited.

Iwokrama's logging initiative came as a shock to some, as it seems at odds with the conservation bit of the official title. However, Iwokrama Timber Inc (ITI) has been receiving accolades as a model for a sustainable forest management programme and it is Guyana's only Forest Stewardship Council (FSC) timber concession. ITI remains on track with its mission of being a model to show the world that timber harvesting can occur in a protected area while demonstrating environmental sustainability, social sensitivity and (of course) economic viability.

The 'Reduced Impact Logging' project provides numerous jobs in local communities and is highly selective. The average number of commercial trees in each hectare of Iwokrama's sustainable utilisation area is 307, but only three or four trees are cut in each hectare. Also, each harvested hectare will not be revisited for 60 years. Annual harvesting will never be more than 20,000m³.

Iwokrama also recently launched a new integrated research framework to help the world find new ways of using a rainforest without losing it. The framework is spearheading a new cross-disciplinary science agenda designed to support the development of a sustainable future for tropical forest communities in the face of climate change. The Iwokrama Science Committee will undertake a range of research projects that fall in line with the overall mandate of Iwokrama, while evaluating the contribution of ecosystem services to the forest's overall monetary value.

Natural ecosystem services that tropical forests provide include watershed protection, water flow regulation, rainfall generation, large scale nutrient recycling and the natural capture and storage of carbon. It is estimated that the world's remaining rainforests capture an estimated 1.3 billion tonnes of carbon per year; Iwokrama alone captures 1.3 million tonnes annually. By working with UK investment house Canopy Capital and the Government of Guyana's Low Carbon Development Strategy (see box, page 20), Iwokrama is seeking to use innovative financial mechanisms to place a greater value on the global importance of rainforests, including water production, biodiversity protection, provision of medicines and reduction of global emissions.

With this fascinating backdrop of different business ventures, ecotourism is still Iwokrama's most developed business initiative. The good news is that visitor numbers have been growing every year and bringing in the greatest number of profits.

With everything going on within this giant research project, of utmost importance is that Iwokrama is still a rare place of beauty. When you're in the midst of its tangled trees – macaws screeching overhead, caiman lurking in the water – you'll swear you've found a paradise. You have.

If Iwokrama were in almost any other country, it would most likely be overrun with tourists and overly developed. That is not the case here. Guyana's only road that runs north–south through the country and cuts right through Iwokrama sees an average of 40 vehicles per day. Of course this lack of visitors causes a catch-22 situation, but as long as the timber business remains low-impact, the sight of a lone logging truck may not be as bad as hundreds of cars queuing up in anticipation of a jaguar crossing the road, which also still happens.

BIODIVERSITY The rich biodiversity of the Iwokrama forest that has been supporting indigenous populations for generations is now attracting renowned scientists and researchers as well as adventurous tourists. Iwokrama's location within the Guiana Shield places it within one of only four remaining pristine tropical forests (the others are the Amazon, Congo and Papua New Guinea), which effectively means the flora and fauna are living representations of a history that reaches back thousands of years.

The forest is also located in an area of South America that sees an overlapping of flora and fauna from the Guiana Shield and Amazon Basin. During the high-water season floods, the Amazon Basin becomes linked to the Rupununi Wetlands (see *Biodiversity*, page 240), located southeast of the Iwokrama Forest. This convergence results in an ecosystem that is a wealth of flora and fauna.

While populations of most fauna within Iwokrama have healthy numbers, due to declining numbers in other parts of the world, some 30% of the mammal species (and a host of other animals) are listed as threatened or endangered under the International Convention of the Trade in Endangered Species (CITES).

Roughly 75% of the northern part of Iwokrama is classified as tropical moist forest, with the remainder in the deep southern portion being tropical dry forest. Within this there are 12 different forest types that support more than 1,500 species of plants. Within this range of mini ecosystems no particular plant species seems to dominate; instead they are spread out over different sections of the forest.

To collect more information on the Iwokrama Forest, the business of Iwokrama or general ecology and biodiversity of Guyana, visitors are encouraged to visit the small library at their main office in Georgetown; their website is also informative.

FOREST RANGERS In an effort to combat illegal wildlife trapping and poaching, and to monitor traffic through the area, there is a gated ranger station on the main road at the north and south entrances to Iwokrama. Corkwood Ranger Station is located at the southern entrance; Kurupukari Ranger Station is located at the northern entrance. Each station is outfitted with an Iwokrama ranger and police officer and every vehicle passing through the area is required to stop at both stations. The road through Iwokrama is also closed at the ranger stations every night at sunset and reopens just before dawn.

Strangely a few of the best-trained and most skilled of Iwokrama's guides and rangers spend much of their time counting cars and opening gates.

TOURISM As should be expected, to see all of Iwokrama during one visit would entail covering a lot of terrain. In fact, considering how inaccessible most of Iwokrama remains, visitors should be satisfied to see only a fraction of it. The tourism activities that are offered by Iwokrama do a good job of providing visitors with a range of options that exhibit many different features of the rainforest, including the rivers, the mountaintops, the treetops, the forest floor and many of the creatures found in between. But don't expect to have a chance to do everything unless you have several days to spend.

Keep in mind that Iwokrama is not just a place set up to host tourists. It is an ongoing case study in sustainable tropical forest management. Your visit is likely to be educational and eye opening. Researchers, guides, rangers, staff and scientists share the same grounds and being able to openly interact with them is one of the benefits of visiting Iwokrama.

For a normal visit to Iwokrama, guests buy an all-inclusive package for their desired length of stay (prices are slightly cheaper for multiple nights). The package includes full board and accommodation, experienced guide, different activities each day, transfers to/from Kurupukari crossing (if necessary), River Lodge and Research Centre orientation and the forest-user fee. Prices range from US$500 to 1,000 for one to three nights at double occupancy.

Transportation arrangements to and from Iwokrama will be left up to individual parties and have an added expense. Options are covered later in this section.

If money is a concern, the cheapest way to visit Iwokrama is to arrive and leave using the bus, and stay in a hammock while you're at the River Lodge (US$10/night; meals US$30/day). Activities are then organised and charged according to what you would like to see and do.

Trips to Iwokrama can be arranged through Iwokrama's tourism division or with many of the tour operators in Georgetown. There is a one-off US$15 forest-user fee implemented by Iwokrama on all guests staying overnight. The fee is included in all package trips but individual tours will be required to pay.

Iwokrama prefers to have advance notice of any visit, but if you decide to stop on a whim, make contact at one of the ranger stations to arrange transport to the River Lodge.

VOLUNTEERS Iwokrama also accepts people willing to volunteer their time and expertise to one of Iwokrama's fields of research. Volunteer terms typically run from one to six months, but could be extended, or in rare cases, shortened.

Volunteers receive no salary or compensation and are required to pay for their own lodging, meals and transportation to the River Lodge and Research Centre. The rates however, are much less than those charged to normal visitors.

If you have a skill or knowledge that applies to any of Iwokrama's current projects, contact Nadia Salick (*nsalick@iwokrama.org*) about the application process. Volunteers are placed according to their experience.

GETTING THERE AND AWAY Visitors to Iwokrama have two transportation options: the Linden–Lethem road or by scheduled or chartered flight. Access to the River Lodge and Research Centre is by road or a five-minute boat ride from the Kurupukari Crossing; pick-up will be arranged when you plan your visit.

By road For detailed information on accessing Iwokrama from the north (ie: Georgetown) using either the Intraserv bus or a minibus, see the *Getting there* section at the beginning of this chapter, page 205. If you will be arriving on a bus or minibus from the south (ie: Lethem), see the *Getting there* section on page 278. The section also has helpful road information for those who will be driving their own vehicle.

From Georgetown to the Kurupukari Crossing is a distance of 200 miles (320km), a trip that takes an average of six hours in a 4x4 and about eight in the Intraserv bus. The cheapest overland option is the Intraserv bus (if it has started running again), but if you wish to organise a 4x4 vehicle, this can be arranged when booking through Iwokrama or a tour operator. Tour operators will likely be able to arrange 4x4 transportation at a cheaper rate; through Iwokrama vehicles can be hired for the return trip at a cost of US$500 (4 seats) or US$700 (6 seats).

It's also possible to arrange transportation using Iwokrama vehicles to access destinations throughout the North Rupununi. Prices vary; arrangements should be made with Iwokrama.

If you will be arriving with your own vehicle, it can be parked at the River Lodge. The access road is adjacent to the Kurupukari Ranger Station.

By air In 2007, Iwokrama's airstrip in Fair View village was officially opened. Unfortunately it is not a stop on TGA's scheduled flights. While it makes access via charter planes more convenient, at the time of writing the only way to access Iwokrama by scheduled flights was by landing in Annai with TGA (see page 207), 2½ hours to the south, and driving there. Hopefully the status will change; it's worth contacting Guyana's airlines to enquire.

Using TGA's scheduled flight also allows you to have a different drop-off and pick-up destination (ie: Annai, Karanambu or Lethem).

Chartered flights can be arranged through any of Guyana's local airlines (see page 84). Most local tour operators (see page 58) can also arrange chartered flights and (hopefully someday) day trips to Iwokrama.

WHERE TO STAY The main accommodations within Iwokrama are at the River Lodge and Research Centre and Atta Rainforest Lodge, although there are a few other choices for those who don't mind spending the night in a hammock. It's understandable if you're hesitant about camping in the jungle with little more than a hammock and mosquito net as your protection, but it's a great way to have the full experience. If you're worried about back pain, ask a local to show you the proper way to lie in one (at an angle).

River Lodge and Research Centre (*8 cabins: hammock* **$***; hammock FB* **$$***; cabin FB* **$$$$$**) The lodge is located on the west bank of the Essequibo River near the Kurupukari Crossing. The centre's open grounds consist of nicely landscaped and well-manicured lawns leading to lush rainforest.

The epicentre of the lodge, the Fred Allicock Training Centre, otherwise known as the Round House, serves as the hub not just for visitors, but for researchers, scientists, rangers and local staff as well. The 9,000ft^2 octagonal building houses a shop, scientific labs, business centre (free Wi-Fi), library, offices, and an upper-level, open-air dining hall, bar and gift shop that offer spectacular views of the river, and a perfect perch for birdwatching.

Lodging is in eight guest cabins that are all built in a traditional style (although thatch is being replaced with shingles) and face the river. Each cabin has one double and one single bed (extras can be added) and en-suite bathrooms. The cabins are comfortable and basic, yet have extra touches like window screens (nets are also on each bed) and internet access. The hammocks on the spacious verandas are easier to get into than out of.

All meals are taken in the Round House and the food is often a hearty combination of fresh vegetables and fruit from the garden accompanied with meat and fish bought from local communities. During meal times at Iwokrama staff and researchers are typically separated from guests, in what can seem like an awkward form of segregation. Guests should use every effort to ignore this and use dinnertime as an opportunity to mingle with the staff, guides and researchers who dine at the same time.

The field station has solar power (110V) throughout the day and night.

Turtle Mountain Camp (*FB & transport* **$$$$$**) Located at the foot of Turtle Mountain (see page 235) is this hammock camp that has a nice jungle setting and just enough conveniences to make a stay here a step above roughing it.

The three hammock *benabs* at camp are just that: round wooden structures with zinc roofs and enough hooks in each to hold ten hammocks. They provide protection from the sun and rain but their open sides don't keep out the bugs or noises of nature – how it should be when you're camping in the jungle.

The camp also has running water, showers and flush toilets. There's a dining hut where the meals are prepared and served. When staying at Turtle Mountain Camp, there is always at least one guide and one cook on site.

A short walk from camp is Paddle Rock Creek, which at night becomes a good place for a chance of spotting wildlife, including tapirs, peccaries, agoutis, pacas and a rare jaguar.

Atta Rainforest Lodge (*c/o Wilderness Explorers, 176 Middle St, Cummingsburg;* ⟋ *227 7698;* e *info@iwokramacanopywalkway.com; www.iwokramacanopywalkway. com; FB* **$$$$$**) While located within Iwokrama, this lodge, along with the nearby Iwokrama Canopy Walkway, is managed by Community & Tourism Services (CATS), which is a unique partnership between Surama village, Wilderness Explorers and Rock View Lodge.

The lodge derives its name from the Makushi word for hammock, *atta*, because it was originally built as a hammock camp. Thankfully, after much demand from visitors who wanted to stay at the base of the Canopy Walkway, but didn't want to do so in a hammock, the camp was converted into a lodge consisting of eight rooms. Atta Rainforest Camp is located 500m from the Canopy Walkway (see page 235), and roughly a mile off the main road. The camp is surrounded by jungle on all sides. This location is ideal for observing the changes in jungle activity between day and night.

The two new buildings have four rooms, each with two singles (or one double if pushed together) and while there are plans to make them all en suite, at the time of writing, there remained four beautiful shared bathrooms, which are tastefully decorated, spacious and feature outdoor showers.

The main building, which is also beautifully designed, houses the dining area and bar. All meals are prepared on site from fresh meat, fish and vegetables. Considering the location, the bar offers an OK selection of beer and spirits as well as some good souvenirs. There is also free Wi-Fi when the generator is running.

A guide is always on site with visitors. By spending the night you have the chance to explore the canopy walkway at all hours – sunset, sunrise and in the middle of the night when the forest is alive with nocturnal creatures.

Outside of the canopy walkway and surrounding system of trails, the area offers little to do beyond experiencing the jungle. Unless you're an avid birdwatcher, entomologist or anything else along those lines, it's likely that one night at the camp will be enough. During the afternoon, when the forest is at its hottest and wildlife at its quietest, there is little to do other than take a siesta, which is welcomed after the early mornings.

Satellite camps In addition to Turtle Mountain, Iwokrama has a few satellite camps scattered throughout the forest. These hammock sites are more remote and consist of open-sided buildings with zinc roofs, a basic cooking and dining area and pit latrines. The camps are located near a waterway to provide a source of drinking water (if purified) and bathing.

One of the more established rustic satellite camps is the **White Water Campsite** located in the primary forest along the Burro Burro River. Travel to the camp, which is 31 miles from the River Lodge, entails a two-hour boat trip down the Essequibo River and up the Siparuni and Burro Burro rivers. The camp is roughly five miles from the Burro Burro River's mouth.

The area around the camp has a high diversity of bird species, including the Guianan red cotinga, scarlet macaws, Guianan toucanette, capuchinbird, as well as a rich population of reptiles and mammals.

There is a series of shorter trails around the campsite, as well as a 7km trail that leads to an old Dutch settlement.

Fly camps Even more remote and more rustic, these provide options for the truly adventurous who wish to trek further into the depths of Iwokrama. The guides usually build these on the spot; the rough frame is made from trees and the top is covered with a tarpaulin. Cooking is over an open flame and toilets are where you dig them in the woods.

The **Water Dog Camp** is located on the Burro Burro River, about four miles further up from the White Water camp. The 35-mile boat trip from the River Lodge takes roughly 2½ hours and follows the Essequibo, Siparuni and Burro Burro rivers. The primary forest setting is similar to White Water, also making for excellent birding.

As this camp isn't established a visit entails watching or helping the guides to construct camp. There also aren't as many established trails, but with a guide and a machete you can go anywhere. This area of the Burro Burro is also great for sport fishing.

Another fly camp is located on the Iwokrama Mountain trail (see page 236).

Satellite and fly camps are rarely used so a bit of maintenance (cleaning up some bush) may be required for your stay. Trips are typically offered as an inclusive package (**$$$$$**), including transportation, guide, cook, meals, hammocks and nets.

WHAT TO SEE AND DO How much you will get to see and do at Iwokrama will depend largely on how much time and money you have to spend. The package trips offered by Iwokrama include two select activities per day. Activities included in the package are nocturnal wildlife spotting; guided nature walks (day and night) and birdwatching (at the River Lodge); Indian House Island boat tour; Fair View village, Kurupukari Falls and the petroglyphs; canoe ride; and Amerindian archery.

There is more time in the day for extra activities, which are on offer for an additional fee. The established fees are per person based on a minimum of four people. If you are travelling with fewer, Iwokrama tries to organise trips for all interested guests at the same time. If there are not four people, and you still want to go, you will be required to pay the cost of four persons. Optional activities and related charges are outlined in the following pages.

Spending at least one night in the jungle, either at Turtle Mountain Camp, Atta Rainforest Camp or somewhere even deeper in the bush should be considered a must for anybody without an aversion to sleeping in hammocks or the jungle.

Besides the activities outlined below, Iwokrama can also help to organise trips to locations in the North Rupununi, including Wowetta (see page 254), Aranaputa (see page 256) and Rupertee (see page 259).

River Lodge and Research Centre
The River Lodge serves as the home base for many people's visit to Iwokrama and you will come and go from here while exploring other areas of the forest. During the down time, when you can manage to pull yourself out of the hammock, there are a few things to do on your own.

In the heat of the afternoon, the jetty is a good place to swim from. You may even get to spot Sankar, the resident black caiman that often hangs around offshore. Sankar normally keeps a safe distance from shore, and visitors should always remember that in no way is Sankar a tame black caiman.

If there is a dugout canoe near the landing and any locals around, ask them to take you on a paddle. There is also an impromptu archery range set up that allows you to try shooting the traditional bows and arrows used by the Amerindians when they hunt. If nothing else, you gain more appreciation for their skills.

The resource library in the Round House has a good selection of field guides, research papers, maps and a slew of other books that can be borrowed during your stay. Also in the Round House are preserved specimens in the scientific labs. By asking any of the staff you can have a tour; if you're lucky there will be a friendly scientist conducting some research.

Upstairs in the dining hall, you can even kill a few minutes (or hours) at the gift shop and bar. Also take some time to explore the open grounds of the River Lodge; those who walk with open eyes will find an amazing number of creatures.

Nocturnal wildlife spotting
(*US$30/person*) For this trip, once it is sufficiently dark, you climb into a small boat at the River Lodge and motor into the blackness of the Essequibo River. At first it will likely be the stars overhead that command your attention but as soon as your guide starts illuminating the river with the spotting torch your focus will probably change.

The torch creates eye shine in animals both in the river and along the shore. Black caiman are frequently spotted, and if you're really lucky it will be one of the larger ones measuring around 15ft in length. If the caiman are small enough, the more daring and experienced guides like to show off by capturing them barehanded, giving wary passengers a closer look.

Other sightings often include various tree boas (which the guides will also catch on request), tree frogs, nightjars and large rodents such as pacas and agoutis.

Jaguar spotting (*US$50/person*) Similar to the night-time boat ride, this trip entails spotting nocturnal animals along the main road. This is done in the early morning or late afternoon and provides a chance to see many of the same creatures, without the caiman and with a (slim) chance of seeing the jaguar (it comes down to luck and timing). No promises are made, but sightings do occur along the road, and this excursion takes visitors to the areas where jaguars are most frequently seen.

Indian House Island boat tour (*US$30/person*) An early morning boat tour around this island, located directly across from the River Lodge, is a great way to experience the dawn chorus of the jungle. As the sun begins to burn away the mist over the treetops, macaws, parrots and toucans greet the day with loud screeching, pileated woodpeckers pound and the guttural rumblings of red howler monkeys fill the air. Giant river turtles also nest in the area and during the dry season months of February–March and September–October they can often be observed.

Fair View village: Kurupukari Falls, petroglyphs and butterfly farm
(*US$43/person*) Fair View is the only village located within the Iwokrama reserve's boundaries. It's on the northern edge very near the Kurupukari Crossing and River Lodge.

Kurupukari, as the village was previously known, played an important role in Guyana's booming cattle and balata trade during the early 20th century. It was an important stopping point along the cattle trail that led from the Rupununi to the coast, as it was here that the Essequibo River would be crossed. The village also experienced a small boom during the profitable balata trading days.

However, when the market fell out of both the cattle and balata businesses, the bottom fell out of Kurupukari. Most families moved on, leaving very few inhabitants. Towards the end of the century the Linden–Lethem road was improved and with increased traffic to the area around the crossing, the village experienced a rebirth. After the establishment of Iwokrama, which provides work for many locals, the village was revived and renamed Fair View.

Fair View is a small village with a population of roughly 200 persons, mostly Makushi Amerindians. While a visit to Fair View often involves a quick village tour that provides insight into the traditional way they live, be it through cassava production or hunting, the main reason to visit is for the Kurupukari Falls and butterfly farm.

The falls can be reached either by a ten-minute walk from the village (which can be part of the tour) or by boat when the water is high enough. The best time to visit is during low water because that is when the many petroglyphs dating back more than 6,000 years are exposed.

Fair View is now the site of Iwokrama's airstrip, making the village the welcoming point for some visitors to the forest. Because of this, the village councillors have many plans for future tourism offerings including new nature trails, a resting place by the falls, a new snack and craft shop and offerings for birdwatchers.

One such tourism offering is a butterfly farm, built with funding provided by the Darwin Initiative. This community-based project breeds butterflies for export and visitors are invited to tour (US$8) the large breeding house that is home to several species of butterfly, including the magnificent morphos and heliconias. The tour also includes up-close encounters with different caterpillars and chrysalises.

Michelle's Island This small island in the middle of the Essequibo River features a bar (run by the island's namesake, Michelle), great swimming spots and excellent views of the Kurupukari Rapids and glowing sunsets. The island is perfect for a cold drink (request rum and juice served in a coconut) and bar snacks at the end of a river trip. One side of the island is a good spot for swimming in the river: always friendly and helpful Michelle knows all the best and safest places to swim depending on the height of the river, so ask for directions.

Nature trails When at Iwokrama, several of the activities involve hiking for short or long periods (ie: Turtle Mountain, Canopy Walkway, Iwokrama Mountain Trail) but there are also some great trails that have been designed specifically for just walking and exploring the forest. Three of these are at the River Lodge and two are located just across from the Corkwood Ranger Station.

River Lodge (*US$20/person*) Located near the River Lodge are the Screaming Piha, Woodcreeper and Bushmaster trails. The Screaming Piha Trail is the most extensive and it also connects with the Bushmaster Trail; none is incredibly long (1–3km) and how much time you spend depends on your interests. The trails are great for basic botany lessons and birdwatching.

The **Screaming Piha Trail** is 1,500m long and winds through a forest of mora trees, which have massive buttresses and reach heights of 45–55m. Other trees include wallaba (used for shingles and poles), manicole palm (source of heart of palm), lu palm (fruits used in local juice), sand baromalli (used for plywood), tonka bean (seeds used in producing cosmetics), trysil (used to make paddles), wamara (a species endemic to Guyana), haiawa (used for incense) and Congo pump (used for making a tea).

The **Bushmaster Trail** also winds through mora forest and features many of the same species of trees. The trail derives its name from a bushmaster snake that was captured within the trees.

The **Woodcreeper Trail** is filled with lianas, which are used to make local cane furniture. There is also a high number of fungi and orchids that grow on the trunks of trees, many of which are similar species as the other two trails.

There are many red-and-green and blue-and-yellow macaws and black-necked aracari birds, in addition to several primate species, that can be seen feeding on the fruits of the palm trees.

Corkwood Ranger Station Directly across from the ranger station on the southern border of Iwokrama are two interlinking trails that provide amazingly easy access to a Guianan cock-of-the-rock lekking ground.

The **Prince Charles Nature Trail** (*US$20/person; US$55/person with transport from River Lodge*) was created and named in honour of the prince's visit to Iwokrama in 2003. It's an easy, level walk of roughly 800m through a beautifully varied forest. The trail connects with the 400m-long Cock-of-the-Rock Trail to form a loop.

The **Cock-of-the-Rock Trail** leads past a virtual forest of towering boulders that create small caves. In these caves are pottery shards from long-ago inhabitants and peccary skulls from not-so-long-ago inhabitants (jaguars). The *lek* is most active in January, but sightings of the birds are fairly common year round. Around April the new chicks are born.

Flora seen along the one-hour walk includes bulletwood tress still bearing balata-bleeding marks from the early 20th century, a towering Brazilian cedar, groves of the kokorite palms that are used in thatching roofs, manicole palm trees and massive mora buttress trees.

Mammals in the area include a lot of spider, red howler and wedge-capped capuchin monkeys, agouti, peccary, deer, tayra and an occasional jaguar. The area is particularly good for birdwatchers. Besides the coveted Guianan cock-of-the-rock the forest is also great for spotting antbirds, cuckoos, trogons and other cotingas, in addition to the macaws and parrots that feed on the kokorit palms.

Transportation costs could be saved for these trails by combining them with a trip to Canopy Walkway, which is nearby, or by stopping on your way in or out of Iwokrama by road.

Turtle Mountain (*US$50/person*) This 950ft (300m) mountain draws its name from Turtle Pond, which sits at its base. Turtle Mountain provides some of the best, and certainly most accessible, panoramic views of the Iwokrama Forest.

The trip begins with a 30-minute boat ride down the Essequibo River to the trailhead at the base of the mountain. Depending on your level of fitness and the amount of time spent studying the flora of the forest on the way up, the trek to the top takes 45–90 minutes. The trail is mostly uphill and there are some fairly steep inclines along the way, but the path is decent and there are handrails at the steepest points. Most should make it just fine after a few rests. Besides the reward of the view at the top, there are plenty of opportunities for birdwatching along the way, as well as a jungle vine for some Tarzan-style swinging.

From the peak, there are views of the forest in all directions. The treetops form a green carpet rising and falling with mountain ranges and interrupted only by the winding Essequibo. Macaws are frequently spotted soaring above the treetops and sightings of red howler, black spider and wedge-capped capuchin monkeys are fairly common.

There are also 7km of trails that wind around the Turtle Mountain camp and lead to the often-flooded Turtle Pond. During the dry season many turtles can be observed sunning themselves on the rocks along the pond.

The hammock camp at the base allows for overnight stays (see page 230).

Iwokrama Canopy Walkway (e *info@iwokramacanopywalkway.com; www. iwokramacanopywalkway.com; US$24, US$52/person, with transport from River Lodge*) One of the highlights of Iwokrama is the canopy walkway, a series of suspension bridges and viewing decks up to 100ft (30m) above the rainforest floor and 450ft (154m) in length. It's a unique opportunity for visitors to immerse themselves in the mid-level canopy of the forest.

The canopy walkway is an engineering marvel consisting of a series of adjustable cables and braces that support the aluminium walkway and allow the anchor trees to grow normally. Maintenance and upkeep are constant.

Visitors access the walkway by an easy 20-minute jungle hike that showcases some beautiful flora such as the bullet wood, greenheart, strangler fig and waramadan (endemic to Guyana) trees all twisted and covered with a series of vines. The path also has a rock with ancient petroglyphs and an optional extension that allows visitors to have a bottom-up view of the walkway.

Visitors should come for the experience of tiptoeing through the top of the forest, for having a monkey's-eye view of the forest below, for the scene of the Maipa Mountains in the distance and for the utter serenity of it all.

As the walkway is located in the heart of Iwokrama, visitors also come with hopes of spotting an endless array of birds and wildlife. Chances are you won't be disappointed, but remember that the jungle can be finicky and sightings are often a matter of luck, of two beings crossing paths in the middle of nowhere.

The birdwatching from the platforms is excellent and avid birdwatchers will have a good chance of seeing some star species, including Todd's antwren, sooty-headed tyrannulet, waved woodpecker, long-billed starthroat, dusky purpletuft, rufous-throated sapphire hummingbird, Guianan toucanet, green aracari, spot-tailed antwren, Guianan red cotinga, pompadour cotinga and Guianan puffbird.

However those who come to see the archetypal jungle birds also likely won't walk away disappointed. The forest is often filled with several species of hummingbirds, toucans, macaws and parrots.

Most mammals spotted will be primates, including families of red howler, black spider, capuchin and squirrel monkeys. Lucky visitors may get a chance to see tapirs, peccaries, deer or large rodents on the forest floor. On very rare occasions jaguars have been seen on the trails below the walkway.

The best time to visit the walkway is when the forest and the birds are most active in the very early morning, just before and after sunrise, and late afternoon, just before sunset. The walkway is located at Mauisparu, near Iwokrama's southern boundary. From the River Lodge it's about an hour's drive. The ideal way to visit the walkway is by spending the night at the Atta Rainforest Lodge (see page 230), otherwise plan on a very early morning or mid-afternoon drive to the walkway. Another option is to access the walkway from Rock View Lodge (see page 248), which is 45 minutes to the south.

Turu Waterfall and Reservoir (*US$15/person; US$35/person with transportation*) The Turu Waterfall trip is one of Iwokrama's newest tourism offerings, but the history of the location goes back centuries. Local legend has it that when the Makushi tribes sought refuge in the Iwokrama Mountains during the 18th century, Turu Waterfall and the deep pool at its base kept them supplied with water, even during dry spells. The deep pond was named the Reservoir.

The falls are located just south of Fair View village and about five miles (8km) in from the main road. They're 30ft (10m) high and the clear water pool is ideal for swimming and provides a refreshing change from the tepid brown waters of the Essequibo.

Iwokrama Mountain Trail (*FB $$$$$*) This rarely used trail is the perfect way for avid hikers to push deep into the jungle, but it is only for serious hikers in good condition who have had a couple of days to acclimatise to the tropical climate.

The trail is eight miles (12.5km) each way and it mainly follows a creek straight up the Iwokrama Gorge. After roughly six miles (10km) the gorge narrows and the Iwokrama Mountains close in on both sides. Here the creek forks, each route leading to a different waterfall, one with a deep cold pool perfect for swimming.

Until this point the trail isn't overly strenuous as it gradually climbs with only a few steep inclines where it's necessary to bypass the river or other obstacles. For the most part the challenges come from fallen trees, thick vegetation, slippery creek crossing and swarms of angry ants. From here it's straight up the mountainside.

The last section of trail averages a 45° slope, with some sections where you literally pull yourself up using trees. Because this area is visited so rarely, to say the route has a trail would be stretching it. You basically scramble up a steep and slippery mountainside.

At the top all pain resulting from burning legs, lungs and ant bites disappears with the view. From nearly 3,000ft (1,000m) the vista through one opening in the trees is endless. It's a stunning sight that unveils mountain ranges and thick forest stretching deep into southern Guyana.

Everything about the hike is beautiful. It provides a true sense of isolation, as even at the trailhead, which is off the road in southern Iwokrama, it feels like you're in the middle of nowhere. As the trail is so rarely used the guides have to keep a constant chopping motion going with their machetes to clear a path.

Coming from the mountains, the creek water is crystal clear and cold. There are many animals and birds in the gorge, including beautiful orange-and-black and yellow-and-black poison dart frogs, peccaries, tapir, howler monkeys, squirrel monkeys, capuchin monkeys, jaguar and agouti, and a large population of the magnificent blue morpho butterfly. There is also a large petroglyph along the banks of the creek that has likely been seen by very few since it was carved thousands of years ago.

There is one established fly camp about two miles (4km) from the start of the trail. It's near the creek and is a perfect place to spend the night in the jungle. Additional hammock camps can be placed further up the gorge if desired.

This trip is for those who are looking for a true jungle immersion experience and have the necessary camping and trekking equipment to do it. Bushmasters (see page 59) periodically offer an Iwokrama Gorge trip, and they have jungle kit as well.

Birdwatching The activity of birdwatching either seems to bore people terribly or excite them to the point of obsession. No matter which side of the fence you're on, you can be sure that birdwatching on some level will be a part of your visit to Iwokrama.

Those who have never entertained the idea of birdwatching as an activity could find themselves with their neck craned skywards in an attempt to identify archetypal jungle birds such as colourful macaws, parrots and toucans. And the more dedicated birdwatchers have roughly 500 different species to check off.

Birdwatching entwines itself within every other activity at Iwokrama, whether it is hiking to the top of Turtle Mountain, boating down the Essequibo River, eating breakfast at the River Lodge or driving down the road. Wherever you go within the Iwokrama Forest, birds will accompany you; how many you identify depends on your level of interest. More serious birdwatchers should inform Iwokrama of their passion upon booking so an appropriate guide can be arranged to assist in finding particular birds.

For twitchers, the following outlines some of the highlight birds that can be seen in different areas of Iwokrama. Along the Essequibo River, species include black curassow, capped heron, tricoloured heron, green-and-rufous kingfisher, semi-palmated and collared plover, black skimmer, large-billed tern and many blue-headed and orange-winged parrots along with red-and-green macaws.

Along the forested trails, birders often sight great jacamar, golden-sided euphonia, violaceous trogon, spotted antpitta, white plumed and rufous-throated antbirds and buff-throated woodcreeper.

In Iwokrama, keen birdwatchers will even be thrilled with the birding along the main road corridor. Species include great jacamars, black-necked aracari, Guianan red cotinga, gray-winged trumpeters, spangled cotinga, white-crowned manakin, yellow-tufted woodpeckers, purple honeycreeper, marail guan, black curassow, king vulture, green oropendola, painted parakeet, black-headed parrots, paradise jacamar, great black hawk, double-toothed kite, and rufous-crowned elaenia. Really lucky visitors may even spot a prized harpy eagle, crimson topaz, hoatzin and crimson fruitcrow.

Sport fishing Avid fishermen can arrange fishing trips that visit locals' favourite fishing holes along the Essequibo, Burro Burro and Siparuni rivers and connected ox-bow lakes. Trips are catered to meet specific wishes of the clients and lodging is at satellite and fly camps throughout the forest.

The client must provide all gear including tackle, rod and reel, and fishing in Iwokrama is strictly on a catch-and-release basis, but the fishing can be spectacular.

Most sport fishermen come to catch a fighting peacock bass, or lukanani (*Cichla ocellaris*), but other large species include 350lb piraiba or lao lao (*Brachplatystoma filamentosum*), 110lb jau (*Zungaro zungaro*) and 90lb banana fish or skeete (*Phractocephalus hemiliopeterus*).

Trips are costed and organised according to specific client desires. Contact Iwokrama for details, and request one of their guides from Fair View to accompany you.

For more information on fishing in Guyana, see page 27.

10

The Rupununi

Guyana is renowned for the pristine, dense claustrophobia-inducing rainforest that covers much of the country. In the jungle, the sun is rarely seen and the world is restricted to your immediate surroundings of twisting greens and browns and a host of unlimited creatures all fighting for the limited space. It can cause one to dream of wide-open land and endless vistas baked by the sun's rays. This is exactly what the Rupununi offers.

The change is dramatic. In an area of the south, Guyana's forest ends, and does so abruptly. One moment you're driving through (or flying over) a sea of green that surely stretches into eternity, and the next moment it stops and spits you out into vast savanna lands that resemble east Africa without the big game. Welcome to the Rupununi, the other half of Guyana and one of the most untouched areas in the world.

The Rupununi Savannas encompass roughly 5,000 square miles and cover a significant portion of southern Guyana and parts of northern Brazil. They are one of the world's largest open ranges of savanna lands, but the terrain here is far from being solely flat grasslands (although there is plenty of that); within the Rupununi Savannas there are some of the world's most biodiverse wetlands, rainforest-covered mountains, endless freshwater river systems marked by strands of palms in the middle of grasslands, Dr Seuss-like termite mounds, sprawling Amerindian villages and cattle ranches steeped in history.

The savannas are named after the Rupununi River, which flows into the Essequibo River just southeast of the Iwokrama Mountains. Its source begins in South Rupununi and as it twists and turns its way northwards it moves through a variety of terrain, including open savannas, dense jungle and the Kanuku Mountains.

The savannas are flanked by the Pakaraima Mountains to the north and the rainforests surrounding the Essequibo River to the south and east; to the west they continue past Guyana and into Brazil. The Kanuku Mountains (see box, page 273) – a range home to 70% of Guyana's known mammal species and more than 50% of Guyana's avifauna – act as the dividing point between North Rupununi and South Rupununi.

The Rupununi Savanna experiences extreme seasonal changes between wet and dry seasons. The typical wet season is from May through August, but some years it can extend or shorten by a month or two on either side. There is also a short period of rain known as the cashew rains, which fall around the Christmas season, but these rains are usually much lighter and are often just a welcome relief from the day's heat.

Annual rainfall in the Rupununi is about 70 inches per year, although most of this occurs during the wet season, with peak months being June and July when it can rain more than 15 inches a month. During the wet season much of the Rupununi turns into floodlands. Rivers rise as much as 30 or 40ft above their dry season levels and water covers much of the savannas.

During the dry season, the water levels drop drastically. Roads become passable and the rivers become lined with sandbanks. During high water level, the wildlife recedes deeper into the forests, but as it drops they become more concentrated in smaller areas, and thus more visible.

The rainy season is good for birdwatching (high water levels mean you can boat right up to nests); for reptiles such as snakes and frogs; for botany, including many orchid species; and for butterflies. In the dry season you'll more likely see caiman, otters, capybara and other mammals, and the fishing is better. But the rainy season is also when the insects are out in droves. The mosquitoes and kaboura flies can try the patience of the most arduous of travellers.

BIODIVERSITY

The relatively limited research that has been undertaken throughout the Rupununi has found there to be approximately 1,500 different plant species, more than 400 species of fish, 120 species of snakes, lizards and frogs, 105 mammal species and at least 500 species of birds. It's also believed that roughly 5% more bird, 10% more mammal, 30% more reptile and amphibian species and 50% more fish species remain unidentified.

This impressive number of different species in the Rupununi reflects the rich ecosystem of the area, partially created by the fact that during the rainy season, when the Amazon and Essequibo rivers overflow (along with their tributaries), the flooded Rupununi becomes linked with the Amazon Basin.

The area of the North Rupununi where the Rupununi, Rewa and Essequibo rivers (and their tributaries) overflow is referred to as the Rupununi Wetlands. The wetlands play an important role in the overall ecology of the area. As mentioned, so far more than 400 species of fish have been identified, but it's estimated that with more research another 200 will be added to that number. These fish play an important role in the region's food chain, including nourishment for the local population and for many endangered species, including jaguar, giant river otter, black caiman and harpy eagle.

PEOPLE

The Rupununi region is home to three of Guyana's Amerindian tribes: the Wapishana, Makushi and Wai Wai. For the most part, the Makushi live in the north and the Wapishana inhabit the south of the Rupununi. In Guyana's far south, some 200 Wai Wai inhabit the area where the land once again becomes jungle around the Essequibo River. The entire area has some 15,000 Amerindian inhabitants in about 60 villages. They are mostly subsistence farmers, fishermen and hunters that often live without running water, electricity, medical care and modern forms of communication.

The rest of the population consists of coastlanders who have settled in the area and descendants of the original Europeans who homesteaded the area in the late 19th century, building large cattle ranches in the process. While the cattle industry's heyday has passed, ranch life still rules in much of the area.

TOURISM

When comparing the north and south regions of the Rupununi, the tourism product of the north is much more developed. Tourism staples such as Karanambu Lodge, Rock View Lodge and Surama village (in addition to the Iwokrama River

Lodge, which is just to the north) are the anchors on a lightly trod tourism trail in Guyana. There are also several Amerindian villages in the area that have recently been developing their own tourism products.

However, the South Rupununi should not be overlooked. It's a place of stunning beauty that is often regarded as Guyana's best-kept secret amongst locals. The reason the south remains largely untapped by tourism is because it's not as easy to access as the north.

The main Linden–Lethem road runs through the North Rupununi; the area can be easily accessed by 4x4, bus, minibus and scheduled flights. However, the range of transportation options diminishes south of Lethem. The administrative capital of Region 9, Lethem, sits on the border with Brazil. For many who have come south from Georgetown, Lethem is the turnaround point; for those entering Guyana from Brazil, it is the point from which they begin moving northwards. Lethem is a frontier town, and the perfect hopping-off point for trips deeper into southern Guyana.

From Lethem, transportation can be easily (although not cheaply) arranged to visit locations in the South Rupununi. The best, and most well-known location in the south is Dadanawa. Once the world's largest cattle ranch, Dadanawa has a long and rich history in the area and the hospitality is legendary.

Both north and south have rich biodiversity. All of Guyana's great bird and animal species are found throughout the Rupununi. Black caiman, giant river otters, giant anteaters, jaguars, harpy eagles, capybara and many more are seen with some frequency. Of course nothing is guaranteed, but a trip to the area is sure to entail plenty of animal and bird sightings.

Besides the wildlife, visit for the people and the culture. In many places it's as if you are stepping back in time; due to the relative isolation of many of the lodges, little has changed in decades, and in the case of some of the most remote villages it has been much longer than decades since lifestyles have changed. All over the Rupununi the nostalgic talk of the old days still strongly resembles the present.

The Rupununi is home to a dying form of tourism, and one that visitors are privileged to experience. At the lodges you are called by your first name, often upon arrival. The different lodge owners form a sort of family, a dysfunctional one of course but it should be no other way. To truly experience the Rupununi, it's best for visitors to bounce from one established lodge to the next, stopping at a few Amerindian villages along the way.

Arrival and departure – on boat trips and Land Rover rides – will be organised by a combination of the modern (email and Skype) and the reliable (short-wave radio). There will likely be hiccups along the way, but in the end you'll be seamlessly passed from one family to the next, always being welcomed as friend.

THE NORTH RUPUNUNI

While there are no strict boundaries, the North Rupununi is loosely identified as the part of the Rupununi Savanna that lies north of the Kanuku Mountains, and south of the Pakaraima and Iwokrama mountains. The North Rupununi is one of Guyana's most popular tourism destinations and, as with all of the Rupununi, visitors to this area can effectively choose from a host of activities ranging from river expeditions and birdwatching to rainforest treks and 4x4 savanna rides.

Many Amerindian communities are slowly beginning to create tourism offerings of their own. They range from simple hikes to beautiful eco-lodges and all provide yet another unique tourism opportunity for visitors.

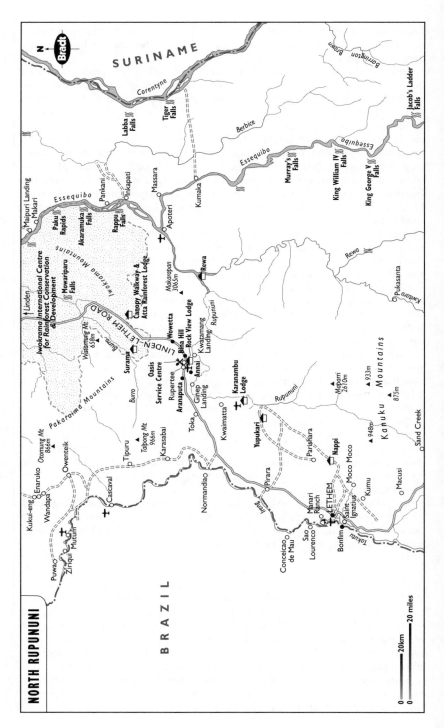

NORTH RUPUNUNI

SURINAME

Corentyne

Borrington Brown

Jacob's Ladder Falls

Labba Falls

Tiger Falls

Berbice

Essequibo

Murray's Falls

King William IV Falls

King George V Falls

Maipuri Landing
Makari

Essequibo

Pankani

Inkapati

Massara

Apoteri

Kumaka

Paku Rapids

Akaramuka Falls

Rappu Falls

Linden

Iwokrama Mountains

Iwokrama International Centre for Rainforest Conservation & Development

Mowariparu Falls

Rewa

Pukasanta

Kwitaro

Makarapan 3065m

Rewa

Canopy Walkway & Atta Rainforest Lodge

Waratama Mt 658m

Burro

Surama

Wowetta

Bina Hill

Rock View Lodge

Kwatamang Landing

Rupununi

Kanuku Mountains

LINDEN–LETHEM ROAD

Oasis Service Centre

Rupertee

Aranaputa

Annai

Ginep Landing

Karanambu Lodge

Maparri 2610m

933m

Toka

Kwaimatta

Rupununi

875m

Sand Creek

Pakaraima Mountains

Talpong Mt 966m

Tipuru

Karasabai

Yupukari

948m

Moco Moco

Parishara

Nappi

Kukui-eng

Enaruko

Otomung Mt 866m

Owenteik

Wandapa

Castaval

Normandiao

Pirara

Ireng

Manari Ranch

LETHEM

Saint Ignatius

Kumu

Macusi

Puwao

Ziriqui

Mutum

Sao Lourenco

Conceicao de Mau

Bonfim

Takutu

B R A Z I L

N

Bradt

0   20km
0   20 miles

GETTING THERE AND AWAY For information on getting to the North Rupununi from Georgetown or other locations to the north, see page 205. For coming from Lethem, or places to the south, see page 278.

Once you are in the North Rupununi, getting from point to point can take some organising. Locations are quite spread out, the roads can be in any state of repair and sometimes you must rely on boat travel.

If you have booked a trip through a tour operator then your transportation logistics should be taken care of. This can make your trip a whole lot easier. If you aren't using a tour operator but have a rough idea of your itinerary it's a good idea to inform locations in advance when and where you'll be going so that transportation between places can be booked and planned. There are several vehicles in the North Rupununi but it's possible that on a given day none will be available.

This section gives visitors a rough idea of what's available for transportation options in the area and how much you can expect to pay (keep in mind that prices can change rapidly and drastically with the cost of fuel). Whenever hiring a vehicle or boat, a driver or captain is always provided.

As a bit of rough background, when going to or coming from locations further up the Rupununi River (Karanambu, Yupukari) boats often leave from and drop off at Ginep Landing; when going to locations down the Rupununi (Rewa), boats typically leave from Kwatamang Landing.

Locations in the North Rupununi are said to have made all transportation prices the same throughout the region, but with everybody coming from different locations and using different types of vehicles, it's hard to surmise if this is the case. Prices listed below give a good average but expect fluctuations.

Locations with modes of transportation (vehicles, motorbikes, boats, etc) for hire that are covered in this section include Surama (see page 244), Bina Hill (see page 253), Rock View (see page 248), Karanambu (see page 264), Caiman House (see page 270) and Ashley Holland in Yupukari (see page 273). Vehicle hire is also widely available in Lethem and through Iwokrama (see page 224).

By road

4x4 Vehicles here range from minibus (Surama) and Hilux pickups (Bina Hill and Rock View) to converted Bedford trucks (Surama and Rock View). Rock View will hire out a vehicle with driver for US$60/day but you must pay US$6 per mile.

When hiring a vehicle to go from one point to another, rates vary from US$5 to 7 per mile. The rate is the same regardless of whether you are making a one-way or return trip because the vehicle must drive both ways. There is sometimes an extra charge for the vehicle to wait at a destination.

Rock View also has a large Bedford truck for hire at US$120 per day and US$8 per mile.

To give an idea of mileage, examples are shown below from Rock View (Bina Hill is just two miles away): Lethem 69, Karanambu 31, Ginep Landing 13, Kwatamang Landing 4, Wowetta 7, Surama 16, Iwokrama Canopy Walkway 26, Kurupukari Crossing 63.

Motorcycle Bina Hill hires out motorcycles with drivers for US$40/day.

Bicycle Rock View hires out bicycles for US$20/day. Bina Hill charges US$10.

Horse Rock View has horses available for US$20/half-day with guide.

By river

Boat Bina Hill hires out a boat, engine and captain for US$50/day, not including fuel charges. They also hire out canoes for US$15/day.

Rock View hires out a boat, engine and captain for US$200/half-day, not including fuel.

Karanambu and Ashley Holland provide boat transfers to/from Ginep Landing for US$200.

On the Rupununi, Ashley Holland also has boats for hire at a rate of US$70/day, not including fuel and oil.

SURAMA (1 347 487 8723; e *info@suramaecolodge.com; www.suramaecolodge. com*) Surama snapshot: five square miles of open savanna lands surrounded by the jungle-covered Pakaraima Mountains. A small Amerindian village where the 300-odd Makushi inhabitants rely mainly on farming, hunting and fishing for sustenance and have lifestyles and customs that have changed little in many generations. Most homes are simple buildings of clay brick walls and thatched roofs. Locals manoeuvre through the surrounding jungle with an innate sense of direction that borders on the uncanny. Most trees and plants have a use, be it as a source of fresh water, medicine for snakebites, or food. Howler monkeys often beat roosters in announcing the start of a new day, macaws screech in seeming disapproval, packs of peccaries roam the forest, the river is teeming with piranha, and jaguar have been known to steal into the village at night and kill a horse.

One might expect Surama to be just another ecotourism cliché, little more than local guides offering mountain treks, jungle walks and dugout canoe trips in a remote village where the culture is preserved and they put on a display for the sake of visitors' dollars.

Surama could indeed be called an ecotourism destination; there is even an eco-lodge in the village. It's remote, plus there's a mountain to climb, jungles to explore and dugout canoes on the river. The word 'sustainable' is also a popular way to describe the activities here, but Surama's charm comes with its own unpretentiousness.

The guides are genuine and their knowledge of the jungle stems from the fact that they rely on it for survival in their daily lives, not because they studied it in a book. The meals are made with local vegetables and meats because that's what's available, not because they are trying to fulfil the expectations of foreigners. And the ecotourism possibilities of their village and surroundings were initially explored to create a source of income close to home; too many of the men were leaving in search of jobs at mining or logging camps elsewhere in Guyana and Brazil.

Surama's location just south of the Iwokrama International Centre for Rainforest Conservation and Development (they share a border along the Burro Burro River) and north of Rock View Lodge (see page 248) helped to initially attract visitors to the village. Now, several years later Surama has become the award-winning role model for community-based ecotourism in Guyana; all other villages building a tourism product look to Surama as their guide.

However, that's not to say that all is perfect at Surama, and it's far from an haute ecotourism destination, which of course creates its charm. There is limited electricity, the lodge is a collection of basic wooden *benabs* that are mostly open to the flying bats and mosquitoes and a less charming building of smaller rooms, and getting from A to B can entail a lot of walking. But the setting is truly idyllic, the guides are virtual walking jungle encyclopaedias and the villagers welcome visitors warmly.

Tourism The Surama Eco-lodge and all tours in and around Surama are managed and operated solely by the local Makushi Amerindians. More than 70 people in the village are employed either directly as hospitality staff, guides, cooks, artisans and drivers, or indirectly as farmers, hunters, fishermen, tailors, and construction and maintenance workers. Roughly 60% of the community's income is now sustainably generated through tourism-related activities, with 75% of village households reporting tourism as a source of income.

Surama's residents – especially the children – are also personally involved in the preservation of the biological diversity that surrounds the village. They lead visitors on hikes, enforce a ban on wildlife trapping, protect groves of endangered bullet, letter, greenheart and waramaden trees, and introduce visitors to medicinal properties of the rainforest.

In Surama, ecotourism helps support the conservation of the Makushi culture, and this is exhibited in several village activities. Within tourism in Surama there is a rotation of staff so that the traditional community lifestyle is not significantly affected and there is still time for necessary things such as farming, fishing and hunting.

Surama also has a cultural group that was formed to help motivate and preserve the culture of the Makushi people. Children and adults in the group compose and perform dances, songs, poems and skits that enlighten tourists about the Makushi way of life. A women's cassava-making project also supplies an interesting tour and a taste of local industry, and the Women's Activity Centre is a place for women to gather for craft making, sewing, embroidery, and to sell the items.

Getting there and away The access road to Surama is five miles (8km) south of Iwokrama's Corkwood Ranger Station. From the main road the village is three to four miles in on a rough road. The closest airstrips are in Annai to the south and Fair View to the north.

By road For detailed information on getting to Surama village from the north (ie: Georgetown) using either the Intraserv bus or a minibus, see page 207. If you will be arriving on a bus or minibus from the south (ie: Lethem), see page 280. The sections also have helpful road information for those who will be driving themselves.

When taking a bus to Surama, you will have to ask to be dropped at the Surama trail; any driver should know where it's located. From the road you can either walk to Surama or arrange transportation with Surama to drive you in.

Surama has vehicles that are used for transfers around the region and also to move visitors around the village. For more information on moving around the North Rupununi, see page 243.

By air Surama does not have its own airstrip but there are two nearby that greatly shorten the driving time required to reach the village. The nearest airstrip to the south is at Rock View Lodge in Annai (16 miles; 45 minutes). To the north, Iwokrama's airstrip is located at Fair View village (45 miles; 1 hour 30 minutes).

There are scheduled flights to Rock View (see page 249) and ground transportation can be arranged from either place to Surama.

Where to stay Lodging at Surama is provided at an eco-lodge located within the village and at a hammock camp along the bank of the Burro Burro River. Surama packages trips that combine all lodging, meals, guides and activities. Based on double occupancy the rates range from about US$100 to 125/person.

Surama Eco-lodge   Built in a traditional style and perched on a hill on the edge of Surama, this basic lodge has great views of the surrounding savannas and mountains.

Lodging is in one of four small *benabs*, whose rough wooden construction and thatched roofs could be considered unfinished or rustic, depending on your outlook. Either way, they provide the necessities of cold showers, flush toilets and three single beds covered in mosquito nets, which become necessary at night as bats chase mosquitoes through the partially open walls. There is no electricity but kerosene lamps are lit at night.

A new cabin-style lodge has four additional en-suite rooms that are more cramped and lack the ambience of the *benabs*. While the building's balcony provides stunning views, the rooms are backpacker-style.

There is also a large round dining *benab* where meals are prepared and served (unless they're eaten on trail). In an effort to further support the community, the meals are made with produce that's been bought from villagers.

The second level of the dining *benab* is great for a breezy afternoon nap, a lingering sunset or stargazing; the bar is one of the most scenic in Guyana.

The lodge is located on top of a small hill on the edge of the village. The location was chosen both for the stunning views and to ensure that it was removed enough from the village so that regular visitors wouldn't interrupt daily life. The drawback for some is that when Surama's vehicles aren't available, a decent walk is required to get anywhere else.

Carahaa Landing Camp   This basic hammock camp is located on the banks of the Burro Burro River, three miles from the eco-lodge. In a large clearing that has been cut into the dense jungle, there is one large open *benab* for hanging hammocks; a smaller adjacent *benab* has a table and cooking area where food is prepared over an open fire. Pit toilets are in the trees and any bathing is done in the river.

It's a basic set-up but the permanent structures provide good shelter for anybody wishing to experience a night camping in the jungle without roughing it too much. Staying overnight at the camp also allows visitors to experience night walks through the jungle and late evening and very early morning canoe trips on the river, when the animals and birds are most active.

What to see and do   Most casual visits to Surama consist of some or all of a few core activities: a village tour, hike up Surama Mountain and a dugout canoe trip on the Burro Burro River. Depending on your level of fitness and the availability of transportation, all can be done in a couple of days.

More adventurous visitors may want to enquire about longer trips that involve expanding upon some of the typical offered activities. Longer treks can be arranged through the Pakaraima Mountains and extended boat trips along the Burro Burro are also a possibility.

Birdwatching and wildlife spotting are inherent in most of the activities below. For birders, if you're lucky, guide Ron Allicock (see page 59) will be home when you visit Surama. His keen eyes and ears will increase your chances of getting a good look at the harpy eagle, bronzy jacamar, zigzag heron, and the elusive rufous-winged ground-cuckoo. He alos tells a good story.

Anytime you're in the trees, be sure to also ask your guide to talk about the forest's medicinal plants.

Village tour Most visits usually begin with a tour of Surama. While most houses are scattered all over the savanna with plenty of roaming space between neighbours, Surama's main buildings are located fairly close together.

During the tour, visitors are taken to the modest health centre, the primary school, the church, the community centre and a small shop, which sells some local crafts and some great homemade hot sauce. A few homes are also visited where locals display the process of turning raw cassava into one of the many food staples, such as farine, cassareep, or cassava bread.

Surama Mountain This hike is often advertised as a gentle climb, but those looking to climb to the top should not expect anything to be described as gentle. This hike entails a roughly one-hour exposed walk across the savannas followed by a climb up the Surama Mountain trail, which at the end – where it's at its steepest – entails scrambling up, over and around small rocks and boulders.

Because the walk through the savanna means being exposed to the intense sun, the trip often begins by leaving before sunrise, but it should be noted that the return trip involves plenty of direct sun. In the afternoon the walk to Surama Mountain will be in the sun, but the return trip will be just before dusk. This hike becomes much easier with a form of transportation as you can drive through the savanna to the trailhead at the edge of the forest.

It can take anywhere from 30 to 60 minutes to hike to the 750ft-high overlook on Surama Mountain. The trail, which starts out with a relatively gradual climb and grows steeper towards the end, winds through primary and secondary forest that often provides sightings of many bird, mammal, primate and reptile species. How much you see will depend on how quickly you are hiking and what you ask your guide to point out (sometimes they will only identify creatures such as snakes and tarantulas if you ask them to).

The motivation behind climbing the trail doesn't fully reveal itself until the end when a vista of Surama valley and the surrounding Pakaraima Mountains comes into view. Screeching macaws and unseen howler monkeys are often the only noises interrupting the silence.

From the eco-lodge, the return trip to Surama Mountain takes anywhere from three to five hours depending on how quickly you walk and how much time you take exploring the forest (birdwatchers could take much longer). The hike can be a bit of a challenge (especially after or during rains) but any pains induced by burning lungs or throbbing thighs will likely be erased by the view.

Burro Burro River Paddling a dugout canoe on the river is a trip that shouldn't be missed on any visit to Surama. From the eco-lodge, the Burro Burro River and the Carahaa Landing Camp are a relatively flat three-mile walk on a wide trail through the forest. During the dry season it's possible to drive a 4x4 vehicle to the river's edge; during the rainy season you should be prepared to get a bit wet walking across some of the creeks on the trail.

From the camp there are more trails to explore the surrounding jungle for birds and animals, but the main purpose of your journey (unless you are staying overnight at the camp) should be to get on the river.

Best done in the early morning or late afternoon when forest activity is at its greatest, the silence of the canoes on the river provides a much greater opportunity to spot birds and wildlife. To the north is Iwokrama Forest so the area is rich with wildlife, including giant river otters, howler monkeys, spider monkeys, jaguar, harpy eagles, peccary, tayra, macaws, herons, kingfishers, anhingas and many more depending on your luck.

Depending on the season, it's also possible to ask your guide to bring along a handline for fishing. If the time of year is right, gather some kokorite palm nuts and have your guide chop them open to get at the grub living inside. Besides being a sweet snack, they also make great bait for the many piranha, catfish and himarra found in the river.

Harpy eagle nest With harpy eagle nests, there is no guarantee of how long it will remain active, but at the time of writing, Surama had been having excellent luck with one located nearby their village. From the main road, it is a flat, one-hour hike in to the base of the Brazilian cedar tree whose top holds an impressively large nest for an equally impressive bird. Ask for the current status of the nest at Surama.

Extended river and trekking trips Most hikes and river trips are completed in the span of a morning or afternoon, but for visitors who would like to have a bit more of a challenging hike or want to see more of the river, it's possible to extend trips to an entire day or several days. Surama maintains several hammock camps in the forest surrounding their village and overnight stays in the bush always prove memorable.

Day treks from the eco-lodge are often to locations further in the Pakaraima Mountains. Depending on the season and year, destinations (if there are any) vary from hard-to-reach ponds and clear water creeks to cock-of-the-rock *leks* and harpy eagle nests (if the latter is active, it is an outing that should not be missed). Ask the local guides for ideas on all-day hikes.

Two recommended satellite camps that Surama has built outside of their village include Rock Landing on the Burro Burro River and Caronparo Landing, which is an excellent place to see poison dart frogs.

Spending an entire day in a dugout canoe can be a bit hard on the back and the bum so longer boat trips are best combined with a hike through some otherwise inaccessible forest. A good option is to be in the boat in the early morning and late afternoon, and retreat to the trees when the sun is hottest.

Longer trips involving camping overnight will take more planning and are to be undertaken only by those with the necessary equipment. You must also be willing to hang a hammock in the middle of the jungle. The guides at Surama are excellent and know the surrounding mountains and jungles intimately and can lead you wherever you desire. If you don't have the necessary kit but would like to venture out on a longer trek, contact Bushmasters (see page 59) for assistance in organising it.

Jungle Survival Training Surama works with the tour operator Bushmasters (see page 59) in their jungle survival course. The course is the best way to learn extensive jungle knowledge and skills (finding water, fishing, hunting, building a shelter, machete skills, starting a fire) from Surama's expert guides. The course culminates with a couple of nights alone in the forest to see how well you listened.

ROCK VIEW LODGE (☎ 645 9675; e info@rockviewlodge.com; www.rockviewlodge.com) In many ways, Rock View Lodge serves as the main hub for tourism in the North Rupununi. Just over half a mile (1km) off the main road, Rock View has a central location between Annai and Rupertee villages. The lodge is located on the edge of the savanna, where the Pakaraima Mountain foothills begin to rise to the north. The location is idyllic and the accommodation has been built to match.

The original Rock View ranch house was built in the 1950s with plans to host weary cowboys and ranchers involved in moving cattle from the Rupununi to the coast. In the late 1960s another family took it over and began raising cattle.

Rock View went through an early phase of glory when the Dakota flight would land on the nearby airstrip. The Dakota flight came in from the coast to pick up beef, tobacco and peanuts, and people from miles around would gather at the Dakota bar to gossip and talk about political problems that may have helped fuel the Rupununi Uprising in 1969.

In 1992, Colin Edwards, a gregarious Englishman with a vision, bought Rock View in order to fulfil a dream of building an environmentally friendly lodge and working farm that also benefits surrounding communities.

Colin started with arid and rundown ranching lands and has created an oasis in the savanna. Gardens flourish, cattle graze freely, flowering and fruit trees abound and numerous jobs have been created for local community members.

Getting there and away Rock View Lodge is easily accessed by road and air. Its central location is great for visiting locations throughout the North Rupununi and into Iwokrama, but keep in mind that without your own vehicle, the expenses of travel add up quickly. Explore all options for transportation around the area and try to plan trips so as to minimise overall travel costs.

By road The main Linden–Lethem road passes directly by the lodge. Rock View's Dakota bar used to serve as the main bus stop, but with the completion of the Oasis (see page 253) all Intraserv buses and minibuses stop 1km north of the lodge along the road.

See page 205 for detailed information on transportation options from Georgetown and Lethem, including Intraserv buses, minibuses and 4x4 rentals. See page 243 for information on local ground transportation options from locations such as Rock View Lodge, Bina Hill and Iwokrama.

When arriving by bus, depart at the Oasis Service Centre, from where you can either walk to Rock View or ground transportation can be provided to transfer you.

By air Annai's airstrip happens to be just 500m from Rock View, making arrival and departure by plane quite convenient. TGA has a scheduled flight seven days per week; for more information see *Getting there,* page 207. For groups, or those willing to pay for flexibility, chartered flights are also available to Rock View.

Where to stay (**$$$**; *FB* **$$$$**; *all-inclusive* **$$$$$**) Not only are the rooms at Rock View some of the most comfortable in the Rupununi, they also have a sense of style that can be a rarity in Guyana.

When surrounded by the grounds of Rock View, it's easy to forget the actual isolation of your location. There is no telephone contact (at least at the time of writing, although a cell tower is being constructed nearby), water comes from a deep well, most food is grown or reared locally and a diesel generator that rumbles for several hours each night produces the electricity. However with a beautiful swimming pool, an abundance of fresh fruits and vegetables, fans in the rooms, free WiFi, plenty of cold drinks, even ice machines, there is little to want for during your stay.

The eight rooms all have spacious bathrooms and showers (including hot water), comfortable beds covered in mosquito nets, desks and chairs and verandas with local cane furniture and hammocks. There are also plenty of little touches like fruit baskets and pitchers of iced water and fruit juice upon arrival as well as brochures and literature on the area. And thanks to an inverter system there is electricity provided 24 hours a day.

Meals are grand affairs where the family joins the guests to listen to Colin talk and feast on an assortment of meat and vegetable dishes (raised, caught or picked locally, of course) all influenced by Guyanese, Amerindian and Brazilian styles of cooking. There are often half a dozen types of fresh fruit juices to choose from as well.

COMMUNITY TOURISM

With assistance from Iwokrama, the North Rupununi District Development Board (NRDDB) was established in 1996 to give the Amerindian communities of the region a voice in dealing with Iwokrama and government agencies. The board has members from 16 villages of the North Rupununi District that participate in co-ordinating the endless educational, developmental, cultural and research programmes that take place in the region. The NRDDB has a seat on Iwokrama's International Board of Trustees and it is actively involved in making sure the activities of Iwokrama respect the protocols, customs and traditions of the indigenous communities.

Established in 2001, the Bina Hill Institute works with the NRDDB and their partners to help develop training, research and other related activities. This ranges from starting a local radio station (Radio Paiwomak FM 97.1) to overseeing fisheries' surveys on Arapaima.

Bina Hill and NRDDB carry out training in an effort to boost the knowledge of the local communities in several areas, including agriculture, horticulture, natural resource management, carpentry, mechanics, environmental work, masonry and sustainable business in timber, aquarium fish, medicinal plants and tourism.

And this is where it becomes more of an interest to visitors. With assistance provided by several donors, including Iwokrama and Conservation International, the NRDDB, through its North Rupununi Tourism Programme (NRTP) has been helping local villages to create their own community tourism product. All of these efforts look to Surama as a role model; some are more developed than others, but all have made important additions to tourism in the North Rupununi.

The community tourism efforts not only provide villages with much needed income, they also teach them the importance of conservation and sustainable land-use issues. For decades, locals have seen birds and animals as a source of income only when trapped for the wildlife export trade or killed for their meat. The fish in the rivers provide a necessary aspect of their diet but they have also been over-fished for money.

With tourism moving into the villages, people's mindsets are changing. Locals are realising that visitors from far away will pay money to do little more than look at flora and fauna in their natural habitat. Amerindian communities are beginning to see new value in their surroundings and are now starting to realise the importance of protecting what they have.

The system is far from perfect, of course. Tourism throughout Guyana is still developing; visitor numbers are relatively low. In some ways it's a benefit for those

Rock View offers several different lodging options, depending on your needs. The all-inclusive rates include your lodging, all meals, including drinks before dinner, use of the swimming pool and guided tours of Annai village and the Panorama Nature Trail.

The other rates, which allow for a breakdown of lodging, meals and activities' charges, work better for those who will be staying at Rock View while arranging trips to other nearby locations. Rock View also offers a discounted community development rate for volunteers, government employees, community development workers and the like; enquire upon booking.

For those looking to self-cater, cheaper meals and accommodation, including facilities for tents and hammocks, can be found just up the road at the Oasis Service Centre (see page 253).

who come to Guyana (places of pristine beauty are rare, the sense of having it to yourself is even more rare), but it's also a bane for local communities that hang hopes of salvation on the coat rack of tourism.

Workshops are attended, trails are cut, guides are trained, birds and mammals are identified and lodges are built, and yet still only limited numbers of visitors come. The 'build it and they will come' philosophy rarely works, and it becomes even more difficult in a country without a steady flow of tourists.

The established lodges in the Rupununi – Rock View, Karanambu, Dadanawa – have tourism largely figured out. They are all beautiful places with unique offerings. They should all be a part of any itinerary to Guyana, but so should one, two or even three of the smaller communities now getting into tourism.

You may not get as polished a product at such places, and you will have to put extra effort into planning and organising, but it's likely that any little kinks that occur will be nullified by the experience you'll have. And you'll be proving that ecotourism and conservation does pay off.

With the assistance of the NRDDB, Iwokrama, Conservation International and a few other donor agencies, several villages have been able to develop an ecotourism product as a way to generate income. Surama, which is the region's community tourism success story, is covered earlier in this chapter (see page 244), as it is much more established. Each village offers a unique tourism product so that there is no overlap, and competition for visitors is less.

The only daily form of communication most of the villages have is by radio, making it difficult for them to arrange trips. Email addresses are listed where applicable but response time can be delayed. Trips can be organised through the NRTP's tourism co-ordinator, who at the time of writing was **Alphonso Forde** (e alphonsoforde@yahoo.com). Another contact to use is the general email for the **Bina Hill Institute** (e binahill@yahoo.co.uk). However don't expect a prompt reply, or sometimes any reply. If after a few days there is no response to your query, email again with a sense of urgency. Don't be afraid to follow up daily until somebody has contacted you. Several of Guyana's tour operators (see page 58) and the Iwokrama International Centre (see page 224) can also assist in arranging trips to Guyana's community-run tourism projects.

Communication and transportation can be logistical nightmares in the Rupununi. There may be some frustration involved in organising a trip, but in the end, the trips normally go off just fine and you will be more than rewarded for your efforts by the unique experience.

Lodging is also available at the **Panorama Nature Trail Camp** (**$**; *FB* **$$**). The camp consists of one *benab* for hammocks and another for cooking and dining. It's a well-built camp and a great way to overnight in the forest without being very isolated. The views of sunset and sunrise are great, even from the unique pit toilet.

What to see and do Between the swimming pool, the sand volleyball court, Colin's eclectic library, the Dakota bar, the hammocks and the gardens, it's possible to happily pass an entire day without leaving Rock View. But there's a lot to do in the surrounding area that shouldn't be missed as well.

Rock View has a couple of trips built into their all-inclusive rates, and they will also arrange trips to other destinations around the North Rupununi. See the following sections of this chapter for tourism offerings of the villages near Rock View.

Rock View grounds The gardens and orchards that Colin has grown at Rock View are quite impressive, especially when you see pictures of what the land looked like when he bought it (ask to see the photo album). Horticulturalists will be pleased to find more than 40 species of fruit trees, at least six of flowering trees, roughly the same for palm trees and more than 15 species of flowering plants.

Over the years, Rock View has also managed to collect wild and tame orphaned animals that are kept in cages throughout the grounds. It's not like seeing the creatures in their natural habitat, but it does allow for a closer look than you'll get in the wild. Some species include paca, red-rumped agouti, red-footed tortoise, yellow-footed tortoise, yellow-spotted river turtle and matamata turtle.

Panorama Nature Trail (*US$5/person*) This fairly short nature trail makes a nice loop through the foothills of the Pakaraima Mountains and has a good variety of tree, bird and monkey species. It entails some uphill climbing but the trail is kept in great condition and there are handrails throughout. There are more than 100 tree species on the trail and several are marked with identity tags. The guides are good about pointing out different plant species and explaining their local usage. The trail isn't crawling with wildlife, but it's a good introduction to rainforest flora and fauna, and the views of the surrounding savannas are superb. There is also a cave on the trail where the curare poison was prepared in old clay pots, fragments of which can still be seen.

Horseriding (*half-day US$20/person*) The tame horses at Rock View may not provide the most exciting ride, but once you convince them to move, they provide good vehicles for sightseeing. Guests are also allowed to join the vaqueros to take the cows out to graze or round them up in the afternoon.

Bicycle riding (*US$20/day*) Bikes are also a great way to explore the areas outside of Rock View's grounds. For those who don't mind eating dust on the main road, bikes are the cheapest way to reach other villages for arranged tours or treks.

Annai village tour (*US$10/person*) See page 258 for information on this small Amerindian village located just behind Rock View. Tours organised through Rock View are not normally the elaborate cultural events sometimes offered by the village, but those aren't necessary to enjoy this beautiful village. Walking to the village in the early morning or late afternoon often provides great birdwatching opportunities.

Rupununi River There are two options for exploring the river – canoe (US$40/day) or aluminium boat (US$200/day, including motor and boatman; extra for fuel). River trips are ideal for birdwatchers, but can also include visits to oxbow lakes to see *Victoria amazonica* lilies, sport fishing or swimming from the sandbanks.

Remember that when going from Rock View to the river, guests must also pay for the vehicle transfer; ask to use the nearest landing at Kwatamang (US$30).

OASIS SERVICE CENTRE
Simply put, the Oasis is a Rupununi truck stop. Located on the main road, just after the road to Rock View and just before the turn to Annai, the Oasis roughly marks the halfway point between Lethem and the Kurupukari crossing at the Essequibo River.

The main building at the roadside stop features beautiful wallaba wood posts and clay tiles from Brazil and the restaurant serves all meals, including a hearty Brazilian-style barbecue of grilled meats and a range of side dishes. A variety of snacks and cold drinks is also available (**$$**).

Where to stay (*camping/hammock* **$**; *room* **$$**) To provide an option for travellers in need of a place to spend the night without all the frills, lodging was built at the Oasis. There is a *benab* with hooks for 11 hammocks and a patch of grass for pitching tents. Bathrooms and showers are in a separate building and are usually kept pretty clean.

There are also four rooms available. Built in a similar fashion to Rock View, they are all self-contained, have two beds, nice furnishings and verandas.

Package rates are also available that include meals at Rock View or the Oasis.

BINA HILL
While the small community of Bina Hill, located 5km east of Annai, has no real reason for tourists to visit, it does play an important role in the tourism, conservation and research efforts currently being undertaken in the North Rupununi, as it's home to the Bina Hill Institute and the North Rupununi District Development Board (NRDDB).

To facilitate the many workshops and training sessions that take place at Bina Hill, the Bina Hill Institute has two 4x4 pickups and there are a few basic *benabs* for guests. While Bina Hill does not regularly host tourists, the lodging is cheap (if not a bit out of the way) and they also have boats, bicycles, motorcycles and canoes available for hire.

Getting there and away Bina Hill is located just over half a mile (1km) off the main road, and 5km from Annai. Access to the area is by road or using the airstrip at Annai.

By road See pages 205 and 278 for detailed information on transportation options from Georgetown and Lethem, including Intraserv buses, minibuses and 4x4 rentals. See this chapter's earlier *Getting there* section on page 243 for information on local ground transportation in the region, including what is offered by Bina Hill.

When coming from Rock View or the Oasis, walking is a perfect way of moving about, as is renting a bike.

By air Annai's airstrip is just three miles (5km) away. TGA has a scheduled flight seven times per week; for more information see *Getting there* (page 207).

Where to stay Lodging at Bina Hill (**$**) is in unfinished traditional *benabs* that are little more than one-room clay brick buildings with cement floors and thatched roofs. Shared toilets and showers are in separate buildings; meals can be provided upon request (**$**). If you don't have your own hammock and mosquito net, they can be rented and are usually on sale in the small store that also sells a range of other basic necessities, drinks and snacks.

Hanging a hammock here is not as convenient as it is at the Oasis, but at Bina Hill it's cheaper, quieter and much more scenic. The newly built *benab* that is used to host meetings is great for late afternoon lounging.

There is also internet access available at the Bina Hill Institute (⊕ *08.00–17.00 Mon–Fri; US$3/hour*).

Contact If you are planning on visiting Bina Hill, advance notice should be given. Their vehicles should also be reserved with as much advance notice as possible. The office can be reached by email (℮ *binahill@yahoo.co.uk*); don't expect a prompt reply. From within Guyana, communication can be made via radio (most interior locations have one).

WOWETTA (℮ *bertiexavier@yahoo.com*) Wowetta is an Amerindian village with approximately 230 inhabitants of mixed Makushi and Arawak nations. The village of Wowetta is spread out along both sides of the main road on the northern edge of the Rupununi. When coming from the north, Wowetta is the first village after the thick forest abruptly ends and the savannas begin; from Rock View, to the south, it is a distance of 5½ miles (9km).

Like most villages in the area, daily life in Wowetta depends on subsistence farming and fishing, with cassava being the main staple. However, Wowetta now looks at its surroundings with different eyes, and thanks to a bright-orange bird, has launched an ecotourism product of its own.

Wowetta Kuwanaru Tours is a community-based project managed by a local tourism board. The village has constructed one of the best and easiest hiking trails through pristine forest that is teeming with bird and mammal species. The trail, which is ideal for birdwatching, leads to the nesting and *lekking* grounds of the Guianan cock-of-the-rock; with a healthy population of about 30 birds, visitors are almost guaranteed a sighting.

While most people normally take the trip in a morning or afternoon, it's also possible to overnight at an isolated hammock camp near the trail's end.

Getting there and away Wowetta is located on the main trail, making for easy access to the village. While it's possible to have an Intraserv or minibus drop you at the village, it's more likely that you will be visiting as part of a day trip from another destination.

See page 243 for information on local ground transportation options from locations such as Rock View Lodge, Bina Hill and Iwokrama. If you're prepared for a walk in the sun, Wowetta's proximity to Rock View Lodge and the Oasis makes a jaunt down the road a possibility. Bicycle rental from Rock View Lodge is also an option.

The closest airstrip is in Annai, 5½ miles (9km) to the south.

The nature trail begins roughly 2½ miles (4km) from the community centre in Wowetta, which is where you will meet your guide. With a vehicle it's possible to drive to the trailhead, otherwise it will entail a pleasant walk through the savanna.

Where to stay (*FB* **$$**, *inc guide & tour*) As mentioned earlier, most visitors to Wowetta undertake the trip as part of a day tour, but if you enjoy camping, the village has built a basic hammock shelter near the end of the trail.

There are plans of expanding the current camp to include a couple of cabins, a larger dining hall and a guide lodge. At the time of writing facilities were a rough wooden *benab* with tarpaulin roof, a small dining area and pit toilet. Hammocks and mosquito nets can be provided.

It's far from luxurious, but it provides good shelter and the camp's location is perfect for exploring the forest. The cock-of-the-rock lek is just 1.5km away, the mountain directly behind camp has views of the Iwokrama Mountains and Makarapan Mountain, and there's a pond nearby that is frequented by nocturnal animals seeking water.

What to see and do The main reason most visitors come to Wowetta's nature trail is because they want to see the Guianan cock-of-the-rock in its natural habitat. Few leave disappointed. And while seeing the spectacular orange bird set amongst the dark green forest and drab grey rocks is an incredible sight, the rainforest the trail cuts through offers up many more reasons to take this tour. Birdwatchers will be delighted to tick off several coveted species of birds from their lists.

The trail, from the beginning to the cock-of-the-rock *lek*, is roughly 6km (US$25/person, including guide, community fee and lunch). While it cuts through rolling mountains, it follows the valley floor and remains fairly flat throughout. There is a short incline towards the end, but overall the walk would be classified as long but easy. The return trip takes four to six hours, but could take slightly less or more depending on several factors. Birdwatchers will likely spend more time in the trees, while those just looking for an energetic hike will do it much faster. However, expect your guide to slow you down so he can transform the blur of green into a fascinating ecosystem.

The trail winds through pristine primary forest that holds an amazing diversity of wildlife. Red howler monkeys are often heard (if not seen), parrots, macaws, capuchin and spider monkeys feed from the ripe fruit of kokorit palms, agoutis scamper in the deadfall, leaf-cutter ants leave spotless trails through the cluttered forest floor.

Staying overnight at the camp will increase your chances of seeing some of the elusive and nocturnal mammals, but even during the day you will likely come across evidence of their existence: fresh peccary tracks; jaguar vomit (with the hair of a grey brocket deer); jaguar-claw marking on trees; cracked nuts remaining from an agouti feeding; tapir tracks; giant armadillo burrows. All would probably be missed if it weren't for the keen eyes of your guide.

Then there are the birds. A few of the species found include red-and-green macaws, long-tailed hermits, golden-handed manakin, thrush, black-faced hawk, toucanette, capuchinbird, purple-throated fruitcrow, red-necked woodpecker, black-throated antbird, white-plumed antbird, shrikes, wrens, buff-throated woodcreeper, white-crowned manakin, red-throated caracara, green oropendola, grey-winged trumpeter, black curassow, roufous-winged ground-cuckoo, and of course the Guianan cock-of-the-rock.

Guides often pepper sightings with tales of local folklore that explain the appearances, shapes or names of many birds and animals. They also point out the many local uses of the plants, trees and berries in the rainforest. The hike is also a perfect time for visitors to learn more about the culture of Guyana's indigenous people.

For those who have more time, either during the day or by spending a night, there is a trail leading to the top of Bamboo Mountain, providing fantastic vistas of the surrounding savannas and jungle-covered mountains. Keep your eyes open

10

for colourful poisonous dart frogs as well. There is a separate trail that also leads to Shocking Pond, which is a magnet for wildlife.

The best time to go on the trail is in the early morning and during the dry season. The cock-of-the-rock can be spotted during any of these months, but the males perform their mating dances from January to February; March is when the females incubate the chicks and April is when they typically hatch.

The advantage of visiting during the wet season is that many trees bear fruit, increasing the chances of seeing birds and mammals feeding.

ARANAPUTA The village of Aranaputa is unique in that it is state land that was identified by the government as being ideal for agricultural pursuits. The government encouraged people living along the coast to move to the Rupununi and start tobacco and peanut farms and rear cattle for beef. An airstrip was put in at Annai to help move the goods to the coast. As a result, the 450-odd current inhabitants comprise mostly Makushi Amerindians mixed with Afro- and Indo-Guyanese. Farming around the village continues today, but mainly on a relatively small scale.

The main ecotourism offering at Aranaputa is the Clarence Mountain Nature Trail and Cabin. The fairly steep trail climbs up the side of a mountain in the Pakaraima Mountain foothills, named for the man who first came up here to farm. The well-maintained trail has a resting *benab* at the halfway point with spectacular views and eventually leads to a cabin perched at 1,000ft. For those with enough energy, a rougher trail leads to a rocky outlook at 1,600ft with amazing views of the entire North Rupununi Savanna.

Getting there and away Aranaputa is located on the main road, three miles (5km) west of Rock View Lodge. Intraserv buses and minibuses pass the village, and will drop passengers on request.

See page 243 for information on local ground transport options from locations such as Rock View Lodge, Bina Hill and Iwokrama. The hike up Clarence Mountain is rigorous but if you're full of energy and staying nearby at Rock View Lodge, the Oasis or Bina Hill, it would be possible to walk. Renting a bike from Rock View is also an option.

Clarence Mountain sits a couple of kilometres behind the village, so the trek either begins from the main road or if you have 4x4 transport it's possible to drive to the trailhead.

 Where to stay (*FB $$, including guide & tour*) For visitors wishing to spend more time on the mountain, there is a hammock cabin that has been built at 1,000ft. The basic wood and thatch cabin can accommodate 12 persons in hammocks, although you'd get to know your neighbour well. A smaller building has a simple kitchen and covered dining area. Meals are prepared and provided and hammocks and nets are available. Two pit toilets are nearby and a spring provides a constant supply of cold fresh water for drinking and bucket baths.

The cabin is set in cleared area of land where Clarence used to farm. Some fruits and vegetables still grow in the area and are often used in the meals. The surrounding forest doesn't allow for the views found at the *benab* or further up on the rocks, but the jungle setting means there are more birds and other wildlife in the area.

The advantage of staying overnight means you can watch sunrise and sunset from the mountain, have more time for birdwatching and go on longer daytime and night-time treks in the maze of trails that begin near the cabin.

What to see and do The main activity at Aranaputa is hiking on the nature trail, but the village recently also began offering boat trips on the Rupununi River during the dry season.

Clarence Mountain Nature Trail (*US$30/person, including guide & lunch*)
This trail is steep, but it's a small price to pay for the views offered on top. The trip is best done by those who enjoy hiking and are in decent shape, but plenty of people who are not avid hikers complete the trip without problems. The trail is cleared regularly and kept free of debris and there are regular resting points along the way.

If you're capable of walking at a quick pace it takes about 30 minutes to reach the halfway *benab* and another 30 minutes to the cabin. The top of the mountain is another 20–30 minutes of quick walking. On a normal tour the walking is slow, the breaks are frequent, the times to enjoy the views are lengthy and the trip to the top takes three to four hours.

The trip can also be shortened to go just as high as the *benab*. This cuts the hike in half and only the views from the very top are better than those at the *benab*.

At roughly 400ft, the resting *benab* is literally built on the side of the mountain. On a clear day you can see Annai, Wowetta, Makarapan Mountain, the Kanuku and Pakaraima mountains, Surama Mountain, the Rupununi River and the vast savanna that lies between them all. The view is worth a trip in itself.

From here the trail continues to follow a dried creek bed and it involves manoeuvring around some rocks and small boulders. Closer to the cabin, the ground begins to level a bit and the trail passes through a grove of heliconias in all different colours.

Trees surround the cabin so the views from here are not as stunning as on the way up. However, the thatched shelters provide relief from the sun and on day trips lunch is served here.

The cabin sits at 1,000ft but it's possible to walk up another 600ft to a group of rocks on the mountaintop that provide one of the best views in the North Rupununi. The catch is that the trail onwards from the cabin isn't as well maintained and involves clambering over rocks and deadfall. There are handrails in sections but it's a steep climb that involves a series of natural steps formed by rocks. In the dry season the wood ticks on this section of the trail can be horrendous.

From the top there are views in all directions except immediately behind. This point is roughly four times higher than the first *benab*, and the views are that much more spectacular. Instead of looking upwards for soaring hawks and macaws, you get to look downwards. Going to the top is highly recommended for anybody who feels they can handle the hike.

Not far from the cabin there is a small swampy area with a natural salt lick that attracts many species of animals. There is also a series of nature trails that branch out all over the mountain. If you will be spending the night or have an entire day to dedicate, you may want to spend some time further exploring the forest.

The guides at Aranaputa are not experts at identifying all the species of birds, but unless you're a keen birdwatcher you should be pleased enough with the birds and animals that they do point out.

Mammals that are seen with some regularity in the area include tapirs, peccaries, jaguars (often only their territory markings), spider, capuchin, squirrel and howler monkeys. Those bright tropical birds – toucans, parrots, macaws – are also regulars on the mountain, as are many other species of birds. Another creature of interest is the orange-and-black poison dart frog, of which there is a healthy population under the cabin.

Rupununi River trip Looking to expand its offerings to visitors, Aranaputa village recently began running trips on the Rupununi River. These are mainly scenic journeys during which visitors can also try their hand at fishing (a good chance to catch a piranha). Offered only during the dry season, there are plenty of sandbanks for sunbathing and swimming and the low waters also make it more likely that you'll spot giant river otters, giant river turtles and black caiman. The birdwatching along the Rupununi River is also excellent.

The best time to schedule a trip is in the early morning or late afternoon, when the birds and river life are more active. As this is a new tourism offering, at the time of writing prices were still being set.

Peanut butter factory The Rupununi has long been seen as offering ideal conditions for growing peanuts, and if it weren't for the expense involved in transporting them to the coast, it would surely be a larger agricultural industry than it is now. However, peanut farming is an activity that has been revisited many times over the years as a way for local residents to earn income and so there are peanut farms scattered around the North Rupununi.

Aranaputa is home to a small factory that processes the peanuts into natural peanut butter. If you're in the area and have an extra hour, the tour is worth a visit see a fairly traditional process of making peanut butter, which is also delicious and usually for sale.

ANNAI The central, hilltop location of Annai is the perfect setting for the role it plays in the region. The small Amerindian village of approximately 420 Makushi residents is home to the regional administrative compound, which has a health centre, police station, guesthouse and administration offices. However, even with this government outpost, Annai is still a very traditional village.

The thatched-roof houses are mainly made of clay bricks and they are built close together along the top of the hill. It's a direct contrast to the sprawling villages located on the flatlands of the savannas, and it also makes the entire village much more accessible to visitors.

Instead of offering mountain hikes and nature-based tours to visitors, Annai has developed a cultural tourism product that gives visitors an insight into the traditional lifestyle of the indigenous population.

Getting there and away Annai village is located just over a mile (2km) south of the main road. Intraserv buses and minibuses stop at the Oasis (see page 253), which is very near the Annai access road and within walking distance of the village.

See page 243 for information on local ground transportation options from locations such as Rock View Lodge, Bina Hill and Iwokrama. Rock View Lodge is located just on the edge of Annai village, at the bottom of the hill. From Rock View, walking, renting a bike or riding a horse, are all options for getting to Annai.

TGA has regularly scheduled trips to and from Annai (see page 207).

Where to stay Annai has a basic guesthouse (**$**), but with Rock View Lodge (see page 248) so close by, it's rare for outside visitors to stay in the village. The guesthouse essentially provides a shelter and bed; the shared toilets and showers are behind the building. Simple meals are prepared on request.

Staying in Annai can provide an interesting insight into village life, but in regard to the cultural tourism product, there is no real advantage to staying overnight in Annai.

What to see and do Annai has created a tourism product, which gives visitors a chance to experience the history and culture of the Makushi Amerindians through a village tour, traditional dances and local crafts. Annai's idyllic hilltop setting provides a perfect panoramic backdrop to the tour (US$20, including US$5 village fee).

On an ideal tour this is how it will happen: guests begin by meeting a village council member who may or may not be their guide for the village tour. The village tour takes guests in a loop around the village; like daily life, it focuses on cassava.

You view a cassava garden before visiting several houses to see the different stages of cassava processing; one house will be grating cassava, another straining and yet another cooking. The final house will have some cassava bread or farine available for sampling. Maybe one or two houses will also be demonstrating the spinning of cotton or the weaving of hammocks.

After the village tour, guests are led to the widest *benab* in Guyana (Georgetown's Umana Yana is taller), which was built for the 2006 Amerindian Heritage Celebration that Annai hosted. (How long Annai will hold onto this claim is anybody's guess, as the building of Guyana's largest *benab* now seems to be synonymous with hosting the annual heritage celebration.)

The *benab* is a beautiful structure and it's here where visitors are treated to cultural skits or dances, usually performed by children. After the show, locally made crafts are set out for visitors to purchase.

That is how the perfect visit will play out. Keep in mind that your chances of getting perfection are slim. If you are only a couple of people, it's less likely that as much effort will be put into organising the houses and skits. But regardless of what your visit entails, Annai is a beautiful village and just getting a chance to walk around and talk to some of the locals, will be enough for most. Sometimes uncontrived is best.

All visits to Annai must be arranged in advance, either with Rock View or with the NRDDB. If you'd like to visit Annai without all the pre-planned cultural activities, a guide can be arranged for a simple tour.

RUPERTEE This small Makushi village has a population of roughly 240 inhabitants. Subsistence farming is relied upon in daily life, although a number of villagers are employed at the adjacent Rock View Lodge and Oasis. The village of Rupertee consists of widely spaced houses, a small community centre and a resource centre where wooden crafts are made and sold.

The villagers of Rupertee have long depended on the endemic species of the paurine tree (*Centrolobium paraense*) for building houses, furniture and crafts. The wood is coveted because it's extremely hard and durable, making it ideal for construction purposes, and it also has a beautiful yellow heart, which is desired for handicrafts. The oily wood is also favoured as firewood. Unfortunately, the desirable aspects of paurine didn't work in its own favour, as the villagers were slowly decimating the local tree population.

In an effort to protect the paurine tree, the community began a conservation project to help promote sustainable harvesting of the wood. To create an ecotourism product around this, the community also built a nature trail leading up the mountain where the trees grow.

Getting there and away Rupertee is located along the main road, just 2km north of Annai village and 1km north of Rock View Lodge. Intraserv buses and minibuses stop at the Oasis (see page 253), just in front of the Rupertee community centre, which is where the tours begin.

See page 243 for information on local ground transportation options from locations such as Rock View Lodge, Bina Hill and Iwokrama. Rupertee is located just behind Rock View Lodge, from where walking, renting a bike or riding a horse are all good options of transport.

Where to stay At the time of writing, Rupertee did not have any established guesthouses or hammock *benabs*, although if visitors are really interested in spending the night, arrangements can always be made for a hammock.

However, with Rock View Lodge and the Oasis both within 1km of the village, good lodging options are plentiful. Rupertee village is not a destination in itself, and most visitors will do the hike as a short afternoon activity while staying nearby.

What to see and do The reason to visit Rupertee is to walk up the Uncle John Nature Trail (US$20, including guide). The start of the trail is located a few kilometres from the community centre; reaching it entails a beautiful 45-minute walk through the savanna or, with a 4x4 vehicle, a short drive across it.

On the path heading to or from the trailhead there are two landmarks to note. The first is a massive silk cotton tree that in the recent past was reportedly possessed by a bad spirit. The tree was making loud noises; it sounded like a tractor was trapped inside it. Not wanting a bad spirit to take up residence in their village, a group of local men gathered their bows and shot the tree full of arrows. The spirit left, but more than 50 valuable, hand-carved arrows still line the tree.

Closer to the trailhead is a reminder of a more distant past. There are a couple of large rocks with round dimples on their flat surfaces. The indentations were made from past inhabitants who used the stones to sharpen their tools and arrow points. Tourism isn't as established at Rupertee as it is in Aranaputa or Wowetta, and this shows most obviously in the state of the nature trail. It's a good trail that follows a fairly gentle slope up the side of the mountain, but a lack of regular use and maintenance can leave it full of deadfall and other obstacles. The deadfall itself isn't too hard to walk over or around, but rotting trees are often full of ant colonies and wood ticks, which rapidly move from their home to your legs when passing.

The trail passes through secondary forest, which at times seems to be worn out from overuse. Many trees along the way have labels announcing the common, scientific and Makushi name of the species, but there is a strange lack of emphasis put on the paurine tree.

It is present in all forms of growth, from the incredibly hard, thorn-covered seeds to saplings and adult trees, but the organised planting scheme one might expect is lacking. Judging by the low number of the trees seen on the trail, the conservation project is much needed.

The highlight of the trip comes in the views that are found from the top. The hike up the 600ft mountain takes roughly 45 minutes and the view to the north is of the Pakaraima Mountains, Surama valley and the Burro Burro River.

The secondary forest doesn't have an extremely rich diversity of birds and wildlife, but with luck you'll see capuchin, spider or red howler monkeys and perhaps some white-lipped peccaries. Birds include blue-crowned motmot, green oropendola, several species of macaws, parrots, woodcreepers, trogans and a tree full of nesting yellow-rumped caciques.

REWA (e *rovinalvin@gmail.com* or *rudolphedwards@yahoo.com; www.rewaguyana. com)* Located at the confluence of the Rewa and Rupununi rivers, Rewa village is a small community of roughly 250 inhabitants. It's more isolated than other tourism destinations in the north – it's accessed by a two- to five-hour boat ride (depending on water levels) or 2½-hour bum-jarring motorcycle ride – but it also has one of the most beautiful settings and equals Surama for a destination for adventurous tourists.

Being located on two of Guyana's most diverse rivers and in the heart of the Rupununi wetlands, as well as being surrounded by pristine rainforest, Rewa is a great destination for ecotourists looking to get off Guyana's beaten path.

The Rewa River is renowned for the excellent wildlife viewing. The area offers visitors one of the greatest chances of seeing many of Guyana's great mammals, including jaguar, ocelot, tapir, capybara, brocket deer, giant armadillo, peccaries and seven different monkey species. In the rivers there are healthy populations of giant river otters, black and spectacled caiman and giant river turtles.

The primary forest that lines the Rewa's banks also provides for good birdwatching. Sightings of scarlet macaws, tiger herons, bat falcons, kingfishers, great black hawks and several species of parrots and cotingas are common. Harpy eagles are also sometimes seen flying overhead.

Fish life in the rivers is also rich. Peacock bass, pacu, piranha, payara and several large species of catfish can be caught with relative ease. In the ox-bow lakes and ponds, of which there are many along the Rewa, there is a relatively healthy population of arapaima, the world's largest scaled freshwater fish.

Besides attracting tourists to the area, the rich biodiversity of the Rewa River has long attracted researchers and organisations intent on helping the village to conserve its natural surroundings. There are currently a couple of conservation projects revolving around giant river turtles and arapaima. Villagers are learning to fish, hunt and log in a sustainable manner. Through ecotourism they see the value in keeping many of their species alive.

Unfortunately the rich diversity of the area is also attracting the attention of companies who seek to make money in different avenues. Oil exploration is ongoing not far from Rewa village and timber concessions are being granted in the surrounding forests. It's another case of conflicting progress, but for now Rewa, the surrounding wetlands and the forested rivers remain pristine locations for tourism.

Tourism Thanks to a community grant provided by Conservation International, Rewa was able to build an eco-lodge to host visitors. Activities offered include a community tour and are otherwise mainly nature based and include rainforest, mountain and savanna treks and river trips.

Community-based trips to Rewa can be organised through the village directly (see email address above), the North Rupununi Tourism Programme (NRTP; see page 250), and some tour operators like Wilderness Explorers (see page 59). Bushmasters (see page 251) also runs longer treks around the Rewa area.

Those looking to go on a longer and much more adventurous river expedition to the Rewa River head should contact Ashley Holland (see page 58) or Duane de Freitas at Rupununi Trails (see page 59); both are excellent river guides with itineraries to the area. They also cater trips to the desires of clients.

Getting there and away Rewa can be accessed by boat along the Rupununi River or by going overland on a rough trail that at the time of writing was only wide enough for motorcycles and bicycles.

By river Boats usually leave for Rewa from Kwatamang Landing near Annai (see page 258) on a journey that varies from about two to five hours, depending on water levels. Boat hire through the NRTP is US$125 return.

By road Getting to Rewa using the overland route is via a rough and narrow path best traversed on motorcycles and bicycles, and only passable during the dry season. Through the NRTP, you can hire a motorcycle and driver for US$40 per day. The 2½-hour journey winds over rutted savanna lands, loose gravel, deep sand and into muddy and pot-holed jungle paths. It can be trying on the most calloused of posteriors.

Those who never take the easy route can hire a bicycle (US$10/day) and pedal the trail like the locals do. This should be done only by those confident with their physical ability and you should always hire a local guide to show you the way.

With the oil exploration near Rewa it is only a matter of time before the access road is repaired to a condition allowing vehicle traffic to pass. Enquire with the NRTP for updates on the possibility of driving into Rewa.

By air The closest airstrip to Rewa is in Apoteri, some 20 miles further up the Rewa River. No scheduled flights go to Apoteri; access would entail chartering a plane and then organising a boat to Rewa from Apoteri (easily done in the village).

Otherwise fly to Annai on the scheduled TGA flight (see page 184) and arrange transportation from there.

Where to stay (*FB* **$$$$**) Accommodation at Rewa is at the eco-lodge, which consists of two *benabs*, each with two separate rooms, and three new self-contained cabins. The four rooms in the *benabs* each have two beds and share separate toilets, sinks and showers, which are a few steps across the grass. The new cabins have two beds and en-suite bathrooms, which at the time of writing have almost been completed and will soon have running water. There is also one large *benab* that is used as the kitchen and dining hall. The eco-lodge is surrounded by forest and situated on a hill with beautiful views of the river. Breakfast at the outdoor tables on the bank of the river makes for a serene start to the day.

Some of the trekking and river-based trips also involve camping along riverbanks, in the savannas or in the jungle. Hammocks and nets are provided.

Meals are provided either at the eco-lodge or on the trail or river, depending on your activities.

What to see and do Rewa is a destination for nature lovers, travellers who want to get out and explore the rivers and jungles of the area. A village tour can be part of a visit, but it's a long journey just for a village tour. The real sites involve a bit of travel from the village and eco-lodge, but all trips are full of amazing scenery and plenty of bird and wildlife watching opportunities.

Any trips listed below that involve overnight stays are all-inclusive tours; meaning lodging, meals, two guides, boat captain and any necessary transportation are included. Prices vary depending on number of people; contact Rewa or a local tour operator for pricing. All the areas listed below can be visited on shorter or longer trips catered to visitors' wishes.

Village tour Each visit to Rewa includes a tour of the community to visit the mostly Makushi population. The village is located a short ten-minute walk from the lodge. If the Tuschao, or village captain, is around you'll likely also meet him. It's a good time to talk to the locals about the conservation projects they are currently involved in and experience different aspects of their daily lives. If you're lucky, the tour will include a presentation at the school by the children in the local wildlife club.

Awarmie tour This tour begins with a 40-minute boat ride to the base of Awarmie Mountain, a few miles from the eco-lodge. The Awarmie Mountain area has much importance for locals as this is where they have their sustenance farms, and they also do much of their hunting and fishing in the area.

There is a good path cut up to the top of the mountain, but the climb can be steep in places (it's more of a scramble up a steep rock at the start) and should be done by those confident with their level of fitness. On the top there are expansive views of the surrounding forests and winding rivers. It is one of the best jungle vistas in Guyana and well worth the effort.

The village has also built a *benab* on the top that can be used for overnight camping with hammocks, although that would entail lugging your gear up. Depending on your level of fitness, the hike takes around two hours.

Grass Pond tour This trip starts with a short boat ride up the Rewa River to a landing where you begin an easy 15-minute hike to Grass Pond. Many that visit this 3km-long ox-bow lake cite it as one of the most beautiful and serene places they experienced in Guyana. The trip is often planned around sunset so visitors can take a dugout canoe ride while watching the flower of the *Victoria amazonica* lilies bloom. The pond is also home to a healthy population of arapaima; birdwatchers won't be disappointed either.

Seawall The seawall is the local name for a rock formation that lines the bank of the Rewa River. It's a popular spot for fishing, and the sandbanks in the area are where giant river turtles lay their eggs. It's also the perfect setting to enjoy some sundowners while trying your luck at catching a piranha on a hand line. Caiman are found here, too, sometimes.

Makarapan tour Makarapan Mountain is seen as a main focal point for the North Rupununi. The 3,000ft peak can be seen for miles around and can be used for pinpointing other locations in relation to it.

From Rewa it's possible to do an overnight trip in which you climb to the top of the peak and camp in the savannas. On the first day you trek for four hours through rainforest and savanna lands until reaching the base of Makarapan. That afternoon is spent exploring the savannas and wildlife spotting and birdwatching. The next day is a five- or six-hour, tiring trek to the top of the mountain.

Makarapan is visited rarely so it provides a good opportunity to see many mammal and bird species, including Guianan cock-of-the-rock and harpy eagle. There are several species of monkeys on the trail.

Bat Creek tour This is a canoe trip up Bat Creek, a small inlet off the Rewa River. The area is rich in mammals, birds and aquatic species. The trip, during which you spend three nights camping along ponds, is geared towards sport fishers, but it can be catered to fit any activities including nature walks, birdwatching and nature photography.

Rewa River tour An extended trip that spans four days and three nights exploring the Rewa River. Two days are spent travelling upriver, stopping at ponds and falls along the way, and then two days are spent slowly drifting down the Rewa back to the eco-lodge.

While this trip doesn't reach the most isolated parts of the Rewa River, it still provides excellent wildlife spotting and birdwatching. In the dry season giant river turtles nest along the riverbanks, giant river otters, black and spectacled caiman are plentiful and there's a healthy population of jaguars, tapirs, peccaries, labba, monkeys, capybara and giant armadillo. The area is also good for sport fishing, and while you can't catch them, the ponds have high numbers of arapaima.

When pushing further up the Rewa River, with Ashley Holland or Rupununi Trails (see *Tour operators*, page 56), you venture into an area that is rarely accessed by man, and the wildlife here shows little fear of human presence. There is a 90% chance of seeing jaguars, peccaries, tapirs and the like and the animals often laze around and stare at passing boats with a certain indifference. This trip is also ideal for avid fishermen. It's a rugged trip heading a step beyond remote, but for those who can rough it out, it's a trip into the most archetypal jungle.

Sportfishing The waters around Rewa have long been known to locals as being excellent for fishing, and the community is now working on developing a new sustainable tourism enterprise: catch-and-release sportfishing. Small numbers of anglers have been coming from Europe and North America to fish the legendary waters of Rewa for giant, toothy fish and the sought-after peacock bass. In 2011, a study began to monitor the effects of catch-and-release fishing on protected arapaima, the world's largest scaled freshwater fish. In the future, you may be able to pack a fly rod for your visit to Rewa and reel in a fish up to 7ft long. For more on fishing in Guyana, see page 27.

KARANAMBU LODGE Karanambu (e *reservations@karanambulodge.com*; *www.karanambulodge.com*) is one of Guyana's true tourism highlights. It's a place steeped in local history, extremely rich in nature and very much in tune with the local surroundings. In more recent years it has become widely known for owner Diane McTurk's work rehabilitating wild, orphaned giant river otters. Her unique passion has caught the attention of many film crews, including those from the BBC and National Geographic, and provides an interesting backdrop to any visit to Karanambu.

Actually, it was a need to fund Diane's ever-expanding work that gave rise to Karanambu Lodge being opened as an eco-tourism destination. However what was once the driving force and backbone of tourism at Karanambu is now only a fraction of the whole, as Karanambu's sights have expanded.

In 1997, the Karanambu Trust was formed and a private protected area was established for the conservation and protection of Karanambu's 125 square miles of unique habitats, and endless flora and fauna. At the time of writing, Salvador and Andrea de Caires were managing and looking after the daily operations at Karanambu, allowing Diane to focus her attention on the otters.

History Karanambu Ranch dates back to 1927 when Tiny McTurk moved with his wife to the Rupununi and set up a balata collection station. Tiny was a pioneer and knew how to live off the land by hunting and fishing, rearing livestock and growing crops. They're qualities that are still respected and necessary for modern life in the Rupununi.

However, Tiny was also an amateur naturalist and conservationist, learning from the indigenous population around him. Tiny also created the long history of hospitality at Karanambu, hosting such notables as Gerald Durrell, Michael Swan and David Attenborough.

Rearing cattle and the brisk balata trade supported the ranch, but in the early 1970s the market fell out of the Rupununi cattle trade and by the 1980s synthetic rubbers had replaced the demand for balata. What there was of the local economy all but collapsed.

In need of a way to support their families, many local indigenous men left for nearby Brazil or began selling animals and birds to the wildlife export trade. Diane, Tiny's daughter, who was running the ranch by now, saw the devastation this was having on the local population of the giant river otter and she began caring for orphans. It was also at this time that Diane had come to find herself in control of the ranch. In need of a means of support, she turned to the hospitality industry.

Karanambu Trust (*www.karanambutrust.org*) In 1997 the McTurk family established the Karanambu Trust as a private charity. It's mission is to 'ensure the sustainable use of the Karanambu Wetlands through wildlife and habitat conservation, research and education in partnership with local communities.'

With Diane as the visionary behind the trust, special emphasis is placed on the giant river otter, but their conservation and research efforts are much broader than the beloved water dogs.

Karanambu is currently working towards becoming Guyana's first private protected area while striving to meet goals that include conserving the rare and biologically important wildlife of the Karanambu Wetlands; conduct and support research and apply the results to conservation and sustainable development; and support the sustainable use of Karanambu through ecotourism and other activities consistent with conservation.

The trust also focuses on providing different forms of education to indigenous people to foster social and economic development to help them become financially independent.

Volunteers are always needed; positions range from Orphan Otter Keper to Conservation Biologist. For more information and contact info, visit their website.

Tourism A visit to Karanambu largely revolves around nature, which is here in abundance, while being treated like a member of the family. There are some 300 species of birds (bearded tachuri, jabiru stork, agami heron among them), a plethora of aquatic species (eg: arapaima, lukanani) and numerous plants (eg: orchids, the amazing *Victoria amazonica*). The area is also rife with mammals (capybara, bearded saki, red howler, giant anteaters, tapir, giant river otter), reptiles (black and spectacled caiman, snakes, iguana) and two dozen species of bats. It's dizzying and stunningly beautiful.

Being a part of the Rupununi wetlands, the surroundings at Karanambu vary wildly between the wet and dry seasons. Most visitors will want to come during the dry season, when the bugs are at their fewest and the animals are at their greatest. However, the rainy season is a magical time in the Rupununi and holds many perks for visitors, such as boating right up to nesting water birds in the oxbow lakes.

Getting there and away Karanambu is located in the northern Rupununi, 12 miles from the main road and 62 miles from Lethem.

Karanambu can be reached by air, land or river. Air travel is obviously the most convenient; the ease of travel by land and river varies between dry and wet seasons.

When not flying return from Georgetown, Karanambu can be easily reached from other locations within the Rupununi, such as Rock View, Surama or Iwokrama. When travelling within the Rupununi consider using both land and river forms of transportation. From the main road, head in via land and come out via river (or vice versa). This way you get to experience the bumpy, yet scenic, ride over the savannas (which is also where you may get to see giant anteaters and oversized termite mounds) and the smooth river journey filled with bird and wildlife.

By air Karanambu's main airstrip is located a short distance from the main lodge; guests are greeted upon landing and transportation is provided to/from the airstrip. TGA has a scheduled flight seven times per week; for more information see page 84. Groups, or those on unlimited budgets, can also arrange chartered flights to Karanambu.

By road See pages 205 and 278 for detailed information on transportation options from Georgetown and Lethem, including Intraserv buses, minibuses and 4x4 rentals. See page 243 for information on local ground transportation options from locations such as Rock View Lodge, Bina Hill and Iwokrama.
Karanambu is 12 miles (at the nearest point) from the main road. While that may not sound far, access is via crisscrossing trails of varying condition; travel takes roughly one hour during the dry season. For those who are very adverse to bumpy, off-road driving conditions in ageing vehicles, going in by river may be a better option, but for most, an overland savanna drive should perhaps be part of any itinerary to Guyana.

Bus When arriving in the Rupununi by bus, you should depart at the Oasis (see page 253), or be dropped along the main road and Karanambu can arrange transportation from there.
To combine bus travel with river travel, leave the bus at the Oasis Service Centre and arrange (preferably in advance) transportation to Ginep Landing.

4x4 If arriving in a hired or personal vehicle, and you or the driver aren't sure of the way, make sure to get explicit directions or have somebody from Karanambu meet your party on the main road to lead you in. It's incredibly easy to become lost in the maze of trails that cross the savanna.
Karanambu offers road transfers from Lethem (US$250; 3hrs).

By river From the Rupununi, it's possible to finish your journey by boat on the Rupununi River. The trip begins at Ginep Landing (13 miles (21km) from Annai), and takes roughly two hours to reach Karanambu. It's a beautiful stretch of river, great for birdwatching and animal spotting, including giant river otters and black caiman. It's also a much smoother ride than taking the rough trail.
Boat transfers to/from Ginep Landing can be arranged through Karanambu (one-way US$180) or the highly recommended river guide Ashley Holland (US$180; see page 58), when he's available.

🏠 **Where to stay** The wide majority of visitors to Karanambu will stay at the main lodge, but a night or two spent camping in the bush can also be arranged.

Karanambu Lodge (*FB, inc two guided tours per day, limited bar & transfer to/from airstrip;* **$$$$**) is set amongst a large gravel clearing in the middle of the savanna, with the river a few minutes' walk away. There are six guest cabins, the main house, an otter house, a Karanambu Trust house, a staff house, volunteer house, and several storage and maintenance buildings. All are built in a traditional manner.
Guest lodging at Karanambu is provided in traditional Amerindian-style clay brick and thatched-roof cabins that can accommodate two singles or one

double. The design is traditional Rupununi style, with floors of bare cement and the walls are built separately from the roof, leaving the upper part of the cabins open to the outside.

However, the six cabins are also filled with unexpected touches. All have spacious bathrooms and showers, complete with a full range of toiletry items, and the main rooms have bookshelves, large desks and a host of mosquito repellent and anti-itching creams. Each cabin also has a covered veranda with hammock and all beds have mosquito nets, a necessity considering their open designs.

The accommodation is very comfortable, but guests must consider their surroundings and realise that there may be uninvited houseguests. Lizards may scurry up the walls, spiders hide in corners, mosquitoes buzz the nets and bats rustle in the thatch. All are relatively harmless, and some can be removed upon request.

Bath water is pumped up from the river, drinking water is provided, electricity is generated from 18.00 to 22.00 nightly and complimentary laundry is provided.

There is also now Wi-Fi access in the main lodge and a small computer room that is available to guests during certain hours.

Meals Breakfast, lunch and dinner are enjoyed family-style in the main ranch house. They are multi-course affairs that work creatively with fruit and vegetables primarily grown on site. Meats, including organic beef from the ranch and fresh fish from the river, are always served alongside a vegetarian entrée. Mealtime is held around the large table that Diane's father made to her mother's exact specifications and they are peppered with stories from the Rupununi's pioneer days.

Bush camps (FB $$$$$) Camping trips along the river and the ox-bow lakes can also be arranged. Lodging is a hammock and mosquito net, bathrooms are in the woods and meals are prepared over an open fire. Normally, camping is done only on fishing trips, but spending a night in the jungle with local bushmen is a learning experience for anybody.

What to see and do Karanambu consists of 125 isolated and pristine square miles of stunning natural beauty. The lands include a variety of habitats, including savannas, wetlands, rivers, ox-bow lakes, marshy ponds, riparian forest and 40 miles of the Rupununi River. And through a series of rivers, creeks, roadways and hiking trails it all becomes incredibly accessible, and it often seems too archetypal to be real.

All activities offered at Karanambu are designed to give visitors a chance to experience the many faces of the protected lands. Every visitor to Karanambu should try to include a trip to the savannas, a hike through the forest and a couple of river excursions. For many, the last will be the highlight.

Included in Karanambu Lodge's all-inclusive rates are two guided trips per day. Trips are either on the river by boat, on the savannas by Land Rover or to the nearby ponds by walking trails (during the wet season most walking trips become boating trips). Barring unfortunate weather, one trip usually begins in the very early morning and the other in the late afternoon. Meals, feeding the orphaned giant river otters, swimming in the river, perusing Diane's books and resting in a hammock often take up the time between trips.

Birdwatching, observing wildlife, photography and learning about the habitats and the life forms found therein are inherent in every trip. To ensure that the guests get the experience they came for, specific trips or itineraries are often sorted out during mealtimes with the helpful guidance of the guides.

Boat trips It's from the comfort of a boat that you're likely to see the highest concentration of wildlife at Karanambu. Each trip starts at Karanambu's landing on the Rupununi River and heads to a destination of a pond, a creek, an ox-bow lake up or down river. Each has its own highlight, be it a specific bird, higher number of monkeys, or the *Victoria amazonica*, and all are idyllic.

The afternoon trips involve snacks and drinks (Diane's famous rum punch) while watching the sunset, the moonrise or the *Victoria amazonica* open. The boat ride back to Karanambu is often in the dark, when large spotting torches are used to seek out nocturnal creatures along the riverbanks, including black caiman, capybara, snakes, fish-eating bats, roosting birds, agouti and other mammals, including – if you are very lucky – jaguar.

Each trip varies with the season. Water levels can rise and fall 20–30ft between wet and dry seasons, meaning that some pure boating trips in July will involve some walking in December.

On these trips even non-birdwatchers will likely be converted by the diversity of birdlife. Binoculars are a great accessory but it seems that the birds are so close they only serve to block out the other surroundings.

A few examples of destinations include:

Taraquoi This is a small inlet that is best visited from September to December for a spectacle of birds. A few of the birds you have a chance of seeing include agami, boat-billed, tiger and black-capped herons, rufescents, anhingas and cormorants, ringed and Amazon kingfishers. There are often giant river otter holts around this area and capybaras are sometimes spotted on the banks.

Mobai Pond At 1½ miles long, this is the largest pond in Karanambu. In the dry season you walk for the last five to ten minutes to benches on the shore; when the water levels are high you boat right into the ponds. This stunning pond is covered with *Victoria amazonica* lilies, on which you can watch wattled jacanas nest. There are also good chances of seeing striated and agami herons, red-and-green macaws, black caracaras, purple gallinules and brown capuchin, squirrel and red howler monkeys.

Simoni Lakes This is the trip that puts Karanambu's beauty on display. On the perfect day, a deep blue sky, dotted with puffy white clouds will linger over the palm trees and gnarled and exposed mangrove roots that line the shores. Squirrel, brown capuchin and brown-bearded saki monkeys will rustle the trees, green-and-roufous kingfishers will skim the water and a jabiru stork will have made an appearance on the river. All will be seen in double as the calm black water reflects the entire scene. Before leaving, the full moon will rise over the horizon and the Amazonica lilies will open, and on the return trip snakes, bats, caiman and capybara will be seen. Wildlife co-operation can't be guaranteed, but the beauty can surely be counted on.

Crane Pond This is a site of sprawling beauty, the poster child for wetlands preservation. The water is mostly green with *Victoria amazonica*, reeds and water hyacinth. In the evening, the surrounding trees are filled with roosting herons and egrets. Wattled jacanas are regulars and this is the only pond where the black-capped donacobius is found. While watching the Amazonica open, caiman often glide through the water and arapaima fish provide the background music with strange belching noises as they come up for air.

Savanna trips Taking a 4x4 trip through the savannas can provide a nice change from being on the water all the time. If you're lucky you'll spot a giant anteater or crab-eating fox, and birdwatchers may see some additional species, including white-faced and black-bellied whistling ducks, vermilion flycatchers, bi-coloured wren, maguari storks, burrowing owl, Brazilian teal, bearded tachuri, blue-backed manakin and snail kite. In the wet season there also some good places to see several orchid species.

Walking trips From Karanambu, the most popular trip is the three-mile walk to Honey Ponds (although this is a boat trip in the wet season). This loop takes roughly two hours and it's a good way to get up close to the trees to allow your guide to point out different features of the forest. The ponds are a good place to see the *Victoria amazonica* lilies with their flowers still open in the morning, with caiman lurking amongst them. You also have a chance of spotting turtles, white-faced and squirrel monkeys, Finsch's euphonia, pied water-tyrants and channel-billed toucans.

Around Karanambu

For an extra fee, additional trips can be arranged from Karanambu. These include fishing, visiting nearby Amerindian villages, extended savanna trips, camping and fishing.

Savanna trip If you will be flying to and from Karanambu, you may want to think about organising a driving tour through the savannas. (If you will be arriving via the road, the savanna tour will be inherent in your travels.) This is the best way to see the termite mounds (some tower well over 6ft in height) and see the part of Guyana that resembles Africa's plains. A savanna trip could also be part of a visit to nearby villages.

Amerindian villages Kwaimatta is a very small Amerindian village located just six miles from Karanambu. The community welcomes visitors to experience their traditional lifestyle.

Visits to Yupukari village (see page 270) can also be arranged from Karanambu. It's possible to organise a day tour of the village or an overnight stay at the Caiman House (see page 270). Depending on their schedule, the caiman researchers will also pick Karanambu guests up in a boat to join them for a night of caiman catching (see page 272).

Camping trips See page 267 for information on Karanambu's bush camps. The lodging is rustic, but the surroundings are beautiful. Camping is most commonly joined with extended fishing trips to the Simoni Lakes or the Mapari Rapids.

Fishing The rivers and ponds within Karanambu's land have long been a fishing haven for visitors from throughout Guyana and overseas, as well as, and more importantly, for the local Amerindians who rely on fish as a staple of their diet. Fishing trips can be arranged for novices (to experience hooking a piranha) or more serious sport fishers.

Some of the more common species found in the waters around Karanambu include lukanani (peacock bass), tiger fish, arawana and piranha. (For more information on fishing in Guyana, see page 27.)

Novice fishing trips typically entail bringing a hand line or fishing rod along on the normal boat excursions, but it's also possible to join one of Karanambu's fishermen on their daily outings to catch fish for the lodge and for the otters.

More avid fishermen will want to arrange a boat, driver and fishing guide. Most fishing is done at Simoni Lakes. To maximise the amount of prime fishing time you get every day, overnight camps can be set up along Simoni. Guests must bring all tackle.

YUPUKARI (e *info@rupununilearners.org; www.rupununilearners.org*)Yupukari is a small Amerindian village in the northern savannas with a population of roughly 500 (mostly) Makushi inhabitants. The village is situated on a hill, about one mile from the Rupununi River; from the outskirts of the village there are stunning views of the Kanuku and Pakaraima mountain ranges. It's a very traditional village reflecting lifestyles that have changed little in decades. Most of the houses are built of handmade clay bricks and topped with thatched roofs, cooking is done over open flame, bullock carts are a common means of transportation and when the pump isn't working, water has to be lugged from the river. Tourism to the village is still a relatively new thing and while the villagers are very friendly and open, they are also quite shy and curious about outsiders.

With Karanambu being about one hour away (either by land or river), tourism is far from new to this general area of Guyana, but thanks to the Rupununi Learners Foundation (RLF; a US-based nonprofit organisation) and the Rupununi Learners International (RLI; a Guyanese nonprofit organisation) and the Caiman House Field Station, it has descended upon Yupukari village quite rapidly in the past several years, along with growth in development projects, new jobs and a strong conservation ethic.

Caiman House Field Station Caiman House was built several years ago in Yupukari by Americans Peter Taylor and Alice Layton, who came so Peter – a keeper and supervisor at the Bronx and St. Louis zoos for nearly 20 years – could conduct an ongoing field study on Black caiman (*Melanosuchus niger*), the largest member of the alligator family and a species that is listed by CITES as Appendix I: endangered (for more information on black caiman see page 40). Black caiman are severely depleted in nearly all their former range, but are found in abundance in the waters of the Rupununi River.

The ongoing field study, which is now entirely run by community members, is an attempt to gain an understanding of the black caiman's ecological role, as well as its context within local communities. By basing the study in a local village, and using local residents to run it, it will hopefully instil a better understanding of the caiman's importance in the local ecosystem. The study itself, and the healthy population of caiman it is finding, has generated a sustainable ecotourism business for the community.

The black caiman research is what will draw most visitors to the region. Guests are invited to join the caiman research crew in a night of caiman capturing. It's a bit like having a job with a National Geographic crew.

Rupununi Learners International (RLI) Peter's (now ex-) wife, Alice Layton, is not one to sit still. While Peter was absorbed in caiman studies she was tackling social issues that plague most Amerindian communities in the Rupununi. Believing that the basis of change is built on education, Alice established the RLI and set about improving Yupukari's schools. In a short time she built two libraries in the primary school, one in the nursery school and then built a two-storey public library next to Caiman House.

The public library has hundreds of books, several laptop computers and internet access, in a village where most live without electricity and running water. In the region of 6,500 books have been brought to Yupukari, reaching the 200-odd children who come from miles around to attend school here.

RLI also established the Yupukari Crafters, a furniture business that uses traditional craft skills to make functional furniture items that can be sold to generate needed income for the villagers. More men are able to stay at home with their families instead of leaving to find work in mining or timber.

Getting there and away Yupukari can be accessed via the Rupununi River or overland roads through the savannas. The village is located just 16 miles south of Karanambu, the site of the nearest airstrip. It would be foolish to come to Yupukari without also visiting Karanambu, and combination visits are common. A popular trip organised through Caiman House has guests fly into Karanambu for lunch, transfer to Yupukari by boat, spend the night and then transfer back to Karanambu by 4x4 vehicle the next day.

By road See page 207 for detailed information on transportation options from Georgetown and Lethem, including Intraserv buses, minibuses and 4x4 rentals. See page 243 for information on local ground transportation options from locations such as Rock View Lodge, Bina Hill and Surama.

During the dry season, travel by road between Yupukari and Karanambu takes 45–60 minutes; from Karanambu to the main Linden–Lethem road is about another hour. For those who are averse to bumpy, off-road driving conditions in ageing vehicles, going in by river may be a better option. Road transfers to/from Karanambu are US$90 one-way.

By river Yupukari can also be accessed by using the Rupununi River. To or from Karanambu the boat trip takes roughly 30 minutes; from Karanambu to Ginep Landing (13 miles (21km) from Annai), it's another 1½–2 hours. It's an incredibly scenic trip with plentiful birdwatching and animal spotting.

Boat transfers to/from Karanambu are US$90; from Yupukari to Ginep Landing costs US$200.

By air Weekly scheduled flights with TGA can land at the Karanambu airstrip; for more information see page 207. Chartered flights are also an option (see page 84).

Where to stay Lodging options abound at the **Caiman House Field Station** (*FB* **$$$$**, *hammock* **$$**) and adjacent Guest House and to be in such a remote and beautiful Amerindian village and be staying in a lodge that never stops bustling with activity – be it YouTube videos or captured snakes – is a surreal experience.

Caiman House has quickly become the focal point of the village, especially for kids who plop into sofas and crowd around wireless laptop computers to watch movies, surf the internet or play video games against kids in other parts of the world; at times it feels like a Starbucks in the middle of nowhere.

The field station provides a home base for researchers and volunteers, and visitors share the public area with them and their laptops, books and research gadgets that are scattered around one end of the main room. Caiman House has something of a hostel feel to it, with chairs grouped around a coffee table, a central kitchen that everyone makes use of, and a large dining table at the far end. People come and go or, if the weather's poor, lounge around in hammocks.

The main accommodation is in the Guest House at the bottom of the garden, where there are four self-contained rooms, each sleeping two and comfortably furnished with locally made furniture and traditional arts and crafts. The en-suite shower rooms and toilets work well. A second-floor balcony provides sweeping views of the surrounding forest.

The field station has additional rooms that are mainly used for volunteers and researchers, but may not be up to the standards expected by most travellers. Unfortunately, at the time of writing, the two-level tower room had been deemed unfit for guests due to the large population of bats calling it home.

For those sticking to a budget, there is also a covered *benab* in the garden that has space for hammocks, which are available.

Meals can either be self-catered or prepared (with the absence of stores, unless you are carrying your own supplies, self-catering isn't an option).

It's also possible to stay at Karanambu and visit either Yupukari village on a day trip or join the caiman researchers for a night of capturing caiman.

What to see and do With a hilltop perch offering scenic vistas and the Rupununi River providing amazing flora and fauna, Yupukari village is in an idyllic location. A village tour takes a couple of hours, but then you should plan on spending the rest of your time on or around the river.

Caimaning (*US$60/person*) Creating a verb from the noun seems to be the only appropriate way to summarise the act of joining the caiman crew in their field research. This takes nocturnal wildlife spotting to the next level.

The team typically heads out around 18.00 and boards boats to ply up and down the Rupununi River in search of black caiman. When one is spotted, an attempt is made to put a noose over its large jaws. If it's a successful capture, the caiman will start to thrash about in self-defence. It's then run up and down the river with the boat in an attempt to tire it out.

Once it's deemed tired it's brought to the nearest sandbank, the mouth is taped shut and the research begins. It's sexed, sized, weighed, tagged and marked. It is truly a rare experience that also features everything from the snake in the tree to the spider in the sand to the beetle in the bush.

The crew often stays out all night capturing as many caiman as they can; guests can choose to return whenever they desire as they have a separate boat, but plan on a late night. During the trip you're likely to see much more than just black caiman, such as spectacled caiman, nocturnal bird species, bats, snakes and various mammals.

If it's the right season, during the day guests can also examine caiman nests and check the eggs while the mother looks on from the water. Why she doesn't attack seems a bit of a mystery, so participate at your own risk.

It's important to note that during the rainy season (roughly May through August), the river levels are typically too high to go on the caiman trip. Caimaning makes the trip to Yupukari worth it for most visitors, but when it cannot be offered, some visitors may find it best to spend the extra night at a different location already on their itinerary.

Village tour (*US$15*) On the Yupukari village tour, guests get to see some local homes, perhaps see cassava being processed, visit the local woodshop, primary schools, church and meet locals. The guide will also take you to the outskirts of town where the views are the best.

You can also expand your walk around the village to include nearby hiking trails, swimming in the river and night walks to look for snakes, frogs and other nocturnal creatures.

Boat tours As Yupukari is also on the Rupununi River, there is much the same birdwatching and wildlife spotting that is available in Karanambu. Locals have dugout canoes that can be rented with a guide for a nominal fee; they are the perfect vessels for exploring some great ponds in the area. A recommended trip is paddling through flooded forest from Awarikru Lake to the Rupununi River.

Yupukari has many guides that are excellent on the river and it's possible to rent a boat for a morning or afternoon (US$35/person) and look for birds, caiman and otters.

Ashley Holland, a local river guide (see page 58), also lives in Yupukari. If he isn't off on one of his epic river trips see if he's available to give a boat tour during the early morning or afternoon. He's an excellent birder, fisherman and overall naturalist with an explorer's personality. He knows the surroundings well.

THE KANUKU MOUNTAINS

According to Conservation International (CI), the Kanuku Mountains support the highest biodiversity in Guyana and are one of the last remaining pristine Amazonian habitats. This helps to explain why it is such a *rich forest*, as its name means in the local Makushi dialect.

The mountain range, which rises out of the Rupununi Savanna in southwestern Guyana, sustains more than 50% of Guyana's avifauna and at least 70% of the country's mammal species. Rare and endangered species include the giant river otter, black caiman, harpy eagle, jaguar, giant river turtle, giant armadillo, giant anteater and the arapaima fish. Surveys have concluded that the area supports at least 6,000 different kinds of plants and some 2,300 different animals.

This high biodiversity stems from the variety of habitats – at elevations ranging from 150 to 900m – that are found on and around the Kanukus. Near the base there are savannas, gallery forests (forests along streams and rivers) and semi-deciduous forests. Mid-level areas are mostly evergreen forests and higher levels are montane evergreen forests. The peaks have sparse vegetation and elfin forests (forests stunted by strong winds).

Eighteen indigenous communities – mostly Makushi in the north and Wapishana in the south – live at the foot of the mountains; all depend on the Kanukus to supply them with daily sustenance, whether it's through agriculture, fishing, hunting or a source of water. Because of this, the locals recognise the importance of protecting the mountains and all that they support. Thanks to much lobbying on the part of CI, the Kanuku Mountains have been chosen as one of two pilot projects in the Guyana Protected Area Systems (see box text, page 197).

With nearly no development outside of the Amerindian communities, pressure from humans on the Kanuku Mountains remains relatively low and allows the mountains to remain in a pristine state.

Tourism infrastructure remains limited in and around the Kanuku Mountains, but there are a few good options for visitors who wish to explore this area of Guyana. The Maipaima Eco-Lodge at Nappi (see page 275) is the best lodging and provides easy access to a network of trails through the mountains. Bushmasters (see page 59) and Rupununi Trails (see page 59) also offer longer treks and boat excursions through the area. Rupununi Trails has a well-located hammock camp in the Kanukus – Mapari Wilderness Camp – that is recommended for those willing to camp.

NAPPI (e *guyfredericks@wildrupununi.com*; *www.wildrupununi.com*) Nappi is a small but spread-out Amerindian village in the southern end of the north Rupununi Savannas, 20 miles from Lethem. The Makushi village is built along the savannas that run up against the foothills of the Kanuku Mountains. The surroundings are superb, the villagers are friendly and the village now has an isolated eco-lodge deep in the rainforests at the base of the Kanuku Mountains. In the past Nappi was known mainly to outside visitors as being the source of intricate balata crafts, but the village is now a top-notch ecotourism destination in Guyana.

The community of Nappi has long depended on sustenance farming, fishing and hunting for their daily survival. In order to make money, many men leave the village to find work in mining or timber concessions in Guyana, or go to nearby Brazil in search of jobs. With the species-rich Kanuku Mountains at their doorstep, many villagers also depended on the (often illegal) wildlife trade as a source of income.

The expert huntsmen used their skills to capture a range of mammals and birds; the amount they sold them for was a tiny fraction of what the animals would receive at their destinations in North America, Europe or elsewhere. The wildlife trade is an old business in Guyana, but it is also not a sustainable one. Villagers are aware of this and are open to new ways to generate income from their surroundings.

With the help of Foster Parrots Ltd (*www.fosterparrots.com*), a US-based non-profit parrot rescue, adoption and sanctuary organisation, Nappi is now looking to ecotourism as an alternative means of income.

Project Guyana In 2004, members of Foster Parrots began talking with Amerindian communities in Guyana about protecting the local parrot and wildlife population through an ecotourism project. Their talks led them to the like-minded Shirley Melville, an Arawak Amerindian living in Lethem, and she introduced them to the village of Nappi.

Nappi embraced the idea of ecotourism as a means of income for the village and worked out an agreement with Foster Parrots. Nappi agreed to declare 250 square miles (144,000 acres) of tribal territory, and all the wildlife found within, as protected from foreign exploitation. Foster Parrots raised funds to build an eco-lodge within these protected lands, which is entirely community run, with all profits going directly to Nappi. Foster Parrots also assists by acting as an impromptu tour operator to bring visitors to the area.

Project Guyana also focuses on the preservation of Amerindian culture, by encouraging villagers to embrace their cultural arts and ceremonial activities that are being passed down from generation to generation with less frequency. Traditional Makushi culture is an important aspect of every visit to Nappi.

It's an ambitious project that deserves full support. The problem is that with Guyana's low tourism numbers, monetary returns are far from immediate, especially compared with the gains reaped from exploiting the forest. The only way for this to truly succeed is by having visitors. And with Nappi providing an entryway into the Kanuku Mountains, there is little reason intrepid visitors won't be coming.

Getting there and away Nappi is accessed by road. The village is 20 miles (32km) from Lethem, which also has the nearest airport. From Lethem, part of the trip is on the main Linden–Lethem road and the remainder is on a trail that is kept in good condition in the dry season, but can get a bit rough during the wettest months.

The eco-lodge is located six miles (10km) from Nappi centre. A good 4x4 vehicle can drive the rough access road or visitors can hike in. During the rainy season the road floods and the only way in is by walking, and often through water.

Advance notice should be provided for all visits to Nappi, which can be arranged through the email above or one of the following contacts. Shirley Melville can be reached at her New Kanuku Bar in Lethem (see page 282) or on email (e *shirleyjmelville@yahoo.com*). Local tour operators Wilderness Explorers and Bushmasters (see page 59) also organise trips to the Nappi eco-lodge and to destinations deeper in the Kanuku Mountains. Bushmasters offers a horse trail ride to Nappi's lodge, followed by a trek to Jordan Falls where you camp and abseil down the falls. Trips can also be organised with the help of Foster Parrots (see page 58).

By road Nappi is best accessed from Lethem. During the dry season, travel by road between the two locations takes 45 minutes to one hour (add another hour for travel to the eco-lodge); it can be longer in the rainy season. Trips to Nappi, including transportation, can be organised through Shirley Melville (see above). Otherwise see page 280 for information on how to hire a vehicle in Lethem. To hire a truck from Lethem to the eco-lodge is around US$175. Nappi can also arrange transport via motorbike.

If you will be arriving in your own vehicle, the trail to Nappi is signposted from the main road. Check with Shirley or another local for more specific directions.

By air TGA has weekly scheduled flights from Georgetown to Lethem; for more information see page 207. Chartered flights are also an option.

Where to stay
Maipaima Eco-Lodge (*6 rooms;* e *egbertfredericks@wildrupununi.com; www. wildrupununi.com; FB* **$$$$**) is the main accommodation at Nappi. The lodge is roughly six miles (10km) from the village, at the base of the Kanuku Mountains and surrounded by pristine primary forest. The beautiful lodge is built next to the Maipaima creek in a large opening in the trees that was once used for farming. There is one main round *benab*, which acts as a lounge/dining area, and four

BALATA

Balata is a natural latex found in the bulletwood tree (*Manilkara bidentata*), a species of tree that can reach heights of more than 120ft (40m) with a base diameter of nearly 10ft (3m). Balata is collected by 'balata bleeders' who tap the trees by scoring their trunks with diagonal slashes, in a manner similar to how rubber and molasses are collected. Each tree can be bled yearly and produces up to 9lb of the sticky resin, which is collected in bags or buckets placed at the base of the tree.

Amerindians have long used the resin to make such items as domestic utensils, water vessels and balls, and when European settlers 'discovered' the useful material, they created a large demand for balata. For nearly a century starting in the 1800s, the balata trade was booming in Guyana, but with the discovery of synthetic rubbers, the trade began to diminish by the 1970s.

Today, a handful of Amerindian artisans continue to use balata in the making of crafts. The artisans re-warm the sun-dried balata in hot water to make it pliable. After adding colourful dyes, the balata is shaped into vessels, animals, birds, human figures, traditional village scenes, chess sets and just about anything else that is requested.

additional buildings used for lodging. All buildings are built in a traditional manner with wood and thatch and sit on stilts; two are connected to the main *benab* via an elevated walkway.

Two of the *benabs* have two bedrooms and two individual *benabs* (still under construction at the time of writing) all have two beds, mosquito nets, verandas and private bathrooms. The main *benab* has some chairs, stools, couches and tables for lounging and eating some of the Rupununi's finest and freshest meals. The accommodation is basic but very comfortable given the isolated location. Extra perks include binoculars and bird and mammal guides and a generator for limited electricity (key for recharging batteries). Extra hammocks can also be hung in the *benab*.

The best thing about the lodge is the location deep in the rainforest. The Maipaima Creek runs along the treeline and there is excellent bird and mammal watching directly from the lodge and within short distances on the numerous trails that emanate from here. Paca, Brazilian tapir, jaguar, several species of monkeys and dozens of birds have been spotted at or from the lodge.

Nappi also has satellite camps in locations throughout the surrounding forest. While the lodging at these will be rustic – hammocks, bathing in streams, pit or no toilets, cooking over an open fire – they will allow more adventurous guests to use the eco-lodge as a base while taking longer treks through the mountains.

What to see and do The star attraction of the Nappi eco-lodge is the access it provides to the Kanuku Mountains (see box, page 273), with particular emphasis on Jordan Falls. The Kanukus remain one of Guyana's most pristine habitats, largely because they are so inaccessible. With an abundance of wildlife, waterfalls and unexplored terrain, they are a haven for ecotourism. Tourism to Nappi has only recently started and the forests are constantly being explored for new sites of interests and new destinations and trails pop up with regularity. If you come with a particular interest – harpy eagle, macaws, cock-of-the-rock, mammals, waterfalls, etc – ask your guides which trails would be best.

Most activities undertaken while staying at the eco-lodge involve getting out and exploring the surrounding rainforest, but a stay wouldn't be complete without a village tour to see the balata artisans at work.

Village tour This is usually given upon arrival at Nappi. With stops at the school, church and perhaps a house or two, it's typical of most Amerindian village tours, with one exception. Nappi is the site of many balata craftsmen, the most famous being George Tancredo, who has been carving figures and traditional Amerindian scenes from latex for more than 40 years.

There are a handful of artists working in the village; at one point they were all concentrated at the craft centre, which was built with assistance from Conservation International. Unfortunately, due to money issues the craft centre site is empty (at the time of writing) and the artists work from their homes, using open flames, old pots and traditional tools to practise their trade.

Visitors should note that while Nappi provides a unique opportunity to see the artists at work, actual crafts are not always available to buy. Most of the artists work to fill orders (both local and international) and aren't able to create a bank of stock items. The balata crafts are, however, widely sold throughout Guyana and orders can always be placed with the artists themselves.

Treks The hiking trails in the area are quickly becoming endless and vary from short one- or two-hour jaunts to several days or weeks. When you have a good local guide outfitted with a machete, the possibilities are nearly endless. Keep in mind that during the rainy season all bets are off regarding the conditions of trails, as some, including the access trail to the lodge, are drowned in two to four feet of water.

From the eco-lodge there are a series of shorter trails that can be done in the morning or late afternoon when the birdwatching, animal spotting and nature photography are at their peak. Some lead to ancient petroglyphs, some to *lekking* grounds or bird or mammal feeding areas. Longer trails can take you to unexplored waterfalls and harpy eagle nesting grounds.

Nappi Falls These falls are located 2½ miles (4km) from the village on a well-worn trail (the site is frequently used by villagers for bathing and washing). It's an easy walk to the falls which are good for swimming.

Jordan Falls At some 900ft these are spectacular falls, although they are in a series of steep steps and not one long drop. Located 8 miles (13km) from the lodge, they are not easily accessed but a satellite camp has been built at their base so the return journey doesn't have to be made in one day. The arduous hike takes roughly five hours, goes up and down many hills, crosses slippery rocks and leads you through flowing water on many occassions, but it's definitely one of the more spectacular areas around Nappi, if not in all of Guyana. Unless you're incredibly averse to sleeping in a hammock, overnighting next to the falls shouldn't be missed. It also allows for a more leisurely hike that can include more time to spot birds (including white bellbird) and wildlife. At the falls, meals are enjoyed on the open rocks where the stargazing is superb. If you're fit and enjoy a good trek, Jordan Falls is not to be missed.

LETHEM

Thanks to a new bridge between Guyana and Brazil, Lethem is quickly changing from a small frontier town to a boomtown. Lethem's population is roughly 3,000, but if you add in people from the nearby communities, it becomes nearer 8,000. It's a good number of people for these parts but it feels much smaller and everybody seems to know everybody else. When a vehicle drives by, people turn their heads to see who it is, who they're with and where they're going. Not much goes unnoticed.

Being on the border of Brazil adds another interesting dimension; Brazilian influence is everywhere. Brazil is seen in the dress, the food, the music and the beer. Lethem and the Rupununi have always fancied themselves removed from the rest of Guyana. Letting a foreign culture seep into daily life creates a unique identity.

Even with the touches of modernisation, Lethem is still far removed from the present. It's dusty and dirty and people still saddle up their horses to come into town. People leave the bar early some nights not because they have to be up early for work, but because they need to search the savannas for their horse that has been misplaced. They only hope it hasn't been stolen by rustlers.

This strange, but charming in its own right, little town in a forgotten part of South America acts as the administrative capital for the entire Rupununi region. Lethem is where people come from outlying communities to get their supplies for the week, month or longer. There's a police station, a hospital, immigration offices and some government outposts. Once a month a judge and a couple of lawyers fly down from Georgetown so court can be held. The jail is adjacent to the police station – a small boxy building with little barred windows.

Lethem is not far off from the Wild West of old. Ranchers still beat up policemen, cattle rustling is a common occurrence and the buildings across from the airstrip

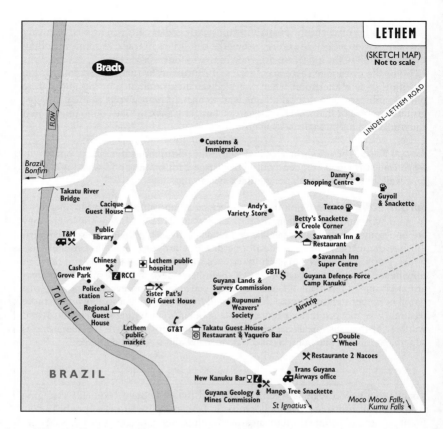

still have bullet holes and burn marks from when a group of ranchers tried to secede from Guyana in 1969 (see box, page 279). The army came in with force and stopped the rebel ranchers, but a certain outlaw spirit still survives more than 40 years later.

Readers should keep in mind that after the 2008 opening of the Takatu River Bridge, Lethem has seen a boom in commercial growth. This section includes an extensive listing of hotels, restaurants and shops in Lethem, but many new arrivals will likely arrive on the scene as this edition remains in print. However even as Lethem continues to spread geographically, it's still a small enough town for visitors to quickly find any new options.

GETTING THERE AND AWAY This section covers transportation from Lethem north to Georgetown and also informs visitors how to hire vehicles for transportation to sites around Lethem and further south. Transportation options for many of the Rupununi's major tourism destinations are covered in their relevant sections. For more detailed information on travelling south from Georgetown to Lethem, see page 205.

By air
Scheduled flights TGA (see page 84) has regularly scheduled flights between Georgetown's Ogle Airport and Lethem. They leave Lethem at 12.30 and 15.00, on Monday, Wednesday, Friday and Sunday and at 09.30 and 15.00 on Tuesday,

Thursday and Saturday. See page 207 for more details, including other destinations served on the route and pricing.

Air Services Limited (see page 84) also has scheduled flights between Ogle Airport and Lethem. They leave Lethem on Monday, Wednesday and Friday at 09.00. See page 207 for more details.

Chartered flights It's not cheap to charter an entire plane, but if you have a big enough group it can become more affordable. For a list of airlines in Guyana see page 84.

By road More detail on the options listed below is covered on page 205. For information on private vehicle hire around North Rupununi, see page 243.

RUPUNUNI UPRISING

The Rupununi Uprising is the name given to the events which began on 1 January 1969, when a group of large ranch owners from the Rupununi declared that the Rupununi district had seceded from Guyana. With support offered by many Amerindian ranch hands, they informed the government of Guyana that they would be setting up their own government to oversee the 'Republic of the Rupununi'.

The revolt began when a group of the ranchers attacked Lethem, taking over the police station using guns and a bazooka. The rebels also took over many of the surrounding Amerindian villages and blocked off most of the airstrips in an effort to cut off easy access to and from the rest of Guyana. Five policemen and two civilians were killed, and numerous government buildings were destroyed.

The Guyana Defence Force in Georgetown was notified of the uprising via radio and promptly responded. Under fire from the ranchers, they were able to land at an airstrip at Manari Ranch, the only one in the area that hadn't been blocked off. Less than a day later, forces made their way 5 miles south to Lethem, and the rebels quickly fled. Many ranchers eventually went over the borders to neighbouring Brazil and Venezuela.

It is widely believed that one of the main reasons for the uprising was because the group of ranchers were unhappy with the results of the (rigged) election that took place just a few weeks earlier in Guyana, which returned the People's National Congress (PNC) to power.

The Guyana government said that their investigations of the incident showed that Venezuela had a hand in organising and supporting the revolt, providing training and weapons to the rebels. Venezuela denied these claims.

In the months following, government forces set about controlling the situation with what has since been described as excessive force. The entire Rupununi region was effectively shut down to all but those who lived there. The army's punishment took the form of largely destroying the area's cattle industry. Cattle trade infrastructure was burnt down along with much of the grasslands on which the cows fed. The government also confiscated much of the area's cattle and havoc was wreaked at many of the Amerindian villages.

The Rupununi was never quite able to recover from the damage the uprising caused to the cattle industry, but a small outlaw attitude still prevails.

Intraserv bus At the time of writing the service between Lethem and Georgetown has been cancelled until interior road conditions improve. It may or may not resume so check with the booking agent in an office across from the airstrip (☏ *772 2202*), near the New Kanuku Bar (formerly Don & Shirley's).

Minibus Vans heading to Georgetown depart from T&M Restaurant (☏ *643 5156*) at 13.00 and 18.00, provided there are enough passengers. The cost to Georgetown is US$50. If the van is not full they will take passengers to locations along the way for a lesser charge.

_4x4_ Hiring a vehicle from Lethem is quite easy, as just about anybody who owns a truck or 4x4 vehicle will take on passengers for the right amount of money.

The best places to ask are at the New Kanuku Bar (see page 282) or the Savannah Inn (see below). You'll be able to meet somebody with whatever form of transport you're after, including bikes and horses. Prices for vehicle hire vary wildly with the cost of petrol, distance, destination and road conditions. To get a rough idea, figure on US$2–3 per mile.

WHERE TO STAY

Savannah Inn (13 rooms) ☏ 772 2035; e Linda@savannahguyana.com; www.savannahguyana.com. Lethem's priciest hotel is good for those seeking privacy in individual, but small, self-contained cottages with AC, TV & mini-fridge. Also have 5 small self-contained rooms off the dining area that can be noisy & often carry the scent of meals. All rooms have 2 beds. Staff vary from aloof to friendly & location is a bit out for those without transport, but free airport pick-up offered. **$$**

Takatu Guest House (21 rooms) ☏ 772 2034; e morsha_j@hotmail.com. The smallest rooms here are fan-cooled & have strange shower/toilet cubicles that make them self-contained. A slight upgrade gives you AC & hot/cold water, a bit more space but similar bathrooms. Next rate gives you breezier upstairs rooms that are spacious, have normal bathrooms, TV, fridge & less dust. One more upgrade gets you a nice king bed & even more space. All are kept pretty clean. Those on a tight budget can stay in the large hammock *benab* behind the guesthouse. For very little you can rent a section (privacy given by tarpaulins) & locker; hammocks & nets also available. Toilets & showers are shared. The garden also has space for tents.

Restaurant & newly built bar also on site. Service friendly when you can harness it. At the time of writing, the hotel was constructing a new building that will likely double the number of rooms. **$–$$**

Ori Guest House (6 rooms) ☏ 772 2033. This new guest house owned by Sister Pat and Peter is a tidy cement home located in the centre of town. The clean rooms have AC & bathrooms & meals are served in the gazebo in the well-manicured garden. **$$**

Cacique Guest House (7 rooms) ☏ 772 2083. Friendly guesthouse in middle of town has clean & basic self-contained rooms with fans & nets; one room has AC. Small porch & living room with TV for lounging & spacious dining room serves all meals (**$**) on request. **$**, *AC* **$$**

Regional Guest House (10 rooms) ☏ 772 2020. Often overlooked, this large wooden guesthouse is the best bargain for your money. Most of the tidy rooms are self-contained, 1 has AC & all have plenty of space with vaulted ceilings, mosquito nets, fans, desks & bureaux. Situated on a hilltop, there are great views of Lethem & surroundings from the large upper-level veranda. The meals (**$$**) & friendly staff are some of the best in town. **$**

WHERE TO EAT Keep in mind that while many restaurants in Lethem advertise long opening hours they often depend on the amount of business on any given day. Don't be surprised to show up two hours before closing time to find the doors shut; it's just the way things work in this small town.

✕ Savannah Inn Restaurant ☏772 2035; ⏰ daily, meals served upon request. With advance notice open to non-guests for meals. Serves range of Creole dishes, but daily menu is typically limited to 1 or 2 items. $$$

✕ T&M Restaurant ☏643 5156 / 671 7777; ⏰ 08.00–20.00 daily. This Brazilian-influenced restaurant is tucked away on the edge of town but does good business due to the minibuses that arrive & depart from here. Menu is typical selection of meats & side dishes, but sometimes have buffet of many choices. Worth visiting for the Brazilian ice cream. $$$

✕ Regional Guest House ☏772 2020; ⏰ daily, meals served upon request. With advance notice, non-guests can order lunch & dinner at this basic guesthouse. The home-cooked meals are hearty & some of the best in town. $$

✕ Takatu Guest House Restaurant ☏772 2034; ⏰ 06.30–22.00 daily. Small dining room has large b/fast menu & a range of sandwiches, soups, steak, chicken & fish offered for lunch & dinner. Service can be slow & aloof, but usually friendly. $$

✕ Betty's Snackette & Creole Corner ⏰ 07.00–19.00 Sun–Fri. Small & friendly snackette behind Texaco patrol station serving fresh juice, pastries, bread & a changing menu of typical Creole dishes. $

✕ Chinese Restaurant ☏772 2132; ⏰ 08.00–17.00 daily. Calling this a restaurant may be pushing it, but small shop does sell one meal: chicken fried rice. $

✕ Guyoil Snackette ⏰ 10.00–22.00 daily. Another small snackette serving the usual mix of fried chicken, chips, burgers, curries, drinks, snacks & fresh-baked goods. $

✕ Mango Tree Snackette ⏰ 09.30–14.00 Mon–Sat. Located opposite the TGA/Intraserv office is this simple food stand where Mark sells the best homemade burgers in town. Usually has roti & curry as well. Come early as he often sells out over lunch. $

✕ Restaurante 2 Naçoes (The Brazilian) ⏰ 10.00–23.00 Sun–Fri. Located just across from the airstrip, this casual indoor/outdoor Brazilian restaurant/bar is Lethem's unofficial gathering spot. The food centres around grilled meats (chicken, beef or pork) served on a stick; rice, salad, beans or other sides can be added for more complete meal; come before 20.00 for best selection of food. Good place to drink beer, meet locals & ask around for any trip-planning advice should you have questions. $

✕ Sister Pat's ⏰ 06.00–20.00 daily. Nondescript café & bakery that serves excellent fresh breads, cookies, buns, coffee, cold drinks & odds & ends like fried chicken or curries. Located near the original GBTI. $

ENTERTAINMENT AND NIGHTLIFE Nightlife in Lethem is about what you'd expect in a small frontier town – pretty quiet. On most nights people gather at **The Brazilian** near the airstrip to swap gossip and down Brazilian beer. **New Kanuku Bar** (previously called Don & Shirley's), not far away, is also a popular gathering spot and the place to head if you need transportation or information for travelling through the Rupununi. The Takatu Guest House recently built the new **Vaquero Bar** that serves drinks daily and offers karaoke on some nights. And the **Double Wheel**, a rundown bar across from the airstrip, has a long history of alcohol-tinged memories. It's typically open on weekends.

SHOPPING As strange as it sounds, people from Brazil flock to Lethem on the weekends to do their shopping. Even stranger is that they often come to buy goods that were imported from Brazil in the first place. But here Brazilians can come and shop without paying taxes. And after the Takatu River Bridge opened in 2008, the amount of trade – and shopping Brazilians – has only increased. What exists now are several shops selling much the same goods, few of which will likely be of interest to the average traveller.

Most of the shops listed below sell a variety of cold drinks, spirits, beer, snacks, dried and tinned goods, toiletries, motor oil, random vehicle parts, electronics and Brazilian shoes and sandals. When this varies, or if there is something of particular interest to travellers, it's noted in individual entries.

Andy's Variety Store ☏772 2225; ⏱ 06.00–20.00 daily. Lethem's true 'everything' store. Besides the usual goods, there's a large selection of fruits, vegetables, Brazilian sausage & other grocery items. Also sell Brazilian & small nylon hammocks good for camping.

Danny's Shopping Centre ⏱ 09.00–12.00 & 13.00–18.00 Mon–Sat, 09.00–12.00 Sun

Lethem Public Market ⏱ 07.30–17.00 Mon–Sat. Lethem's attempt at starting a public market hasn't quite caught on. A few stalls sell random goods & food.

Rupununi Weaver's Society ☏772 2092; ✉ rweavers@gol.net.gy; www.gol.net.gy/rweavers. ⏱ 08.00–16.30 Mon–Fri. Outlet shop selling the famous Wapishana hammock,

hand-woven from specially cultivated cotton. Also sells baskets, jewellery, balata figurines & has indigenous museum with small selection of artefacts on display.

Savannah Inn Super Centre ☏772 2035; ⏱ 08.00–17.00 Mon–Sat. Lethem's first version of a big-box store. Adds large appliances & more clothes to otherwise typical goods. Also has some supplies useful to those in need of basic camping equipment.

Shirley's Airport Shop & New Kanuku Bar ☏669 4513; ⏱ 08.00–23.00 daily. Basic staples & small selection of Amerindian crafts, including balata from Nappi . Also the unofficial information spot for travellers.

OTHER PRACTICALITIES This section covers local services that visitors may require while in Lethem.

Bank

$ GBTI ☏772 2241; ⏱ 08.00–13.00 Mon–Fri. Lethem's first bank exchanges foreign currency & travellers' cheques A new branch, located on the main road leading into town was under construction during writing & will have an ATM.

Communications
Post
✉ **Lethem Post Office** ☏772 2014; ⏱ 07.00–16.00 Mon–Fri, 07.00–11.00 Sat

Email and internet Computers and internet access are offered to the public at the Takatu Guest House (see page 280). Cost is roughly US$2.50/hr to browse. Also offer printing and scanning.

Hospital

Lethem Public Hospital ☏772 2206. Not the ideal place to head to for medical attention, but will do for minor injuries or illnesses. If it's more serious you'll probably want to be evacuated to the coast.

Tourist information At the time of writing, tourist information was found on a largely ad hoc basis. Locals realise that Lethem is not so much a destination itself, but is more of a hub for travellers looking to branch out further into the Rupununi. As a result, many people living in Lethem have gone into freelance work of offering their vehicle, motorbike, horse, or whatever it may be, for hire. There are many unofficial guides and drivers in the area as well.

The unstructured nature of tourism in the area is fitting. The best way for outsiders to figure it out is to simply ask around town for whatever it is that you may need, but the best place to start is at **New Kanuku Bar** (previously Don & Shirley's; see above) near the airport. It's the unofficial official place to gather information on everything from trekking guides to vehicle hire.

At the time of writing the **Rupununi Chamber of Commerce & Industry (RCCI)** (*Block A Takatu Dr;* ☏ *772 2213;* ✉ *rcciguyana@yahoo.com;* ⏱ *08.00–16.00*

Mon–Fri) had big plans to add some structure to tourism around the area. And if they accomplish all they plan to, it could add some welcome change, and certainly make planning trips easier for visitors.

Their new location across from the police station is meant to be a one-stop shop for visitors, as it will house a tourist information centre. The Guyana Tourism Authority will have a desk there to provide visitors with information on local accommodation, guides and trips throughout the Rupununi (and Guyana). They even plan to provide information on travels to Brazil and Venezuela.

WHAT TO SEE AND DO There is little to do or see in Lethem proper. Most visitors will come here on their way to or from somewhere else. But if you're going to be around for a day or two there are a few good options for day trips and afternoon or morning activities.

For the activities below that are within Amerindian villages (the falls and cashew factory) visitors need to get permission from the Tuschao in St Ignatius village. The village is accustomed to visitors exploring the area, but it's a necessary courtesy. You also need to pay a village fee to the Tuschao (*US$5/person*). If you are with a guide or local, they will know where to go, otherwise the Tuschao's house can be located by asking anybody once you cross the bridge from Lethem and arrive at St Ignatius.

The Moco Moco and Kumu falls can be difficult to find, but anybody from the area will be able to direct you. The best thing is to hire a vehicle and/or guide from Lethem or St Ignatius; the Tuschao should be able to find a good guide (if there is no agreed-upon fee, don't forget to tip them (US$5–10) for their time).

Moco Moco Falls Located at the base of the Kanuku Mountains, about 20km or 30 minutes' drive from Lethem, are these falls that were once harnessed for hydro-electric power. In 1999, the People's Republic of China built a hydro-power station here to provide power to Lethem and the surrounding villages. Unfortunately, in 2003, after heavy rains there were several landslides that damaged the site and it has sat in disrepair ever since.

But the creek, with its huge boulders and deep swimming holes, makes for a great day trip from Lethem. For the best swimming, from the old station, cross the creek and follow the left side up until you see a large pool surrounded by large rocks. The site is unfortunately marked by spray-painted names on the rocks.

The entire area is great for exploring and it's also located within the forest so you'll likely see some birds and wildlife about. To explore further, and actually see the falls, you can climb the 975 steps that lead up the mountainside; they begin just behind the old station. It's not the safest trek up – the stairs are in poor condition and some were washed away in the landslide – but the view of the savannas from the top is beautiful.

In the past there has been talk of building a small lodge at the base of the falls, and while it's questionable as to whether it will ever be done, it's something worth checking into (try asking at the Savanna Inn).

Kumu Falls About 30 minutes south of Lethem is Kumu. It's a beautiful Amerindian village of traditional homes widely spread out over the savannas, with the Kanuku Mountains looming behind. The setting is worth a visit in itself, but the village also provides good access to the Kanuku Mountains. With a 4x4 vehicle, you can drive a rough path nearly to Kumu Creek and a trailhead in the Kanuku foothills.

From here, a quick walk takes you to Kumu Creek and a large opening where the village has built a basic hammock shelter for those who wish to spend the night. It's a beautiful setting: open savannas at the base of the mountains, with pristine jungle just a short walk away.

Another five-minute walk through the forest leads to Kumu Falls. The falls have a drop of about 15–20ft; the falling water and pool make a natural jacuzzi. When you are within the jungle here it seems a long way from the dusty and hot streets of Lethem.

This area is also the starting point for the hike up to Schomburgk's Peak (see page 284), which looms overhead.

St Ignatius Just across the bridge heading south from Lethem, over the Moco Moco Creek, is the Amerindian village of St Ignatius. The village is of interest to visitors who want to see the cashew nut processing plant and explore some of the smaller satellite villages in the area. When going to the village, it's necessary to visit the Tuschao and pay a village fee. This can be done at his house, which is easily found by asking anybody on the street.

Rupununi Natural Cashew Enterprise (*St Ignatius;* ⊕ *08.30–12.00 & 13.00– 16.30 Mon–Fri, 08.00–12.00 Sat*) Don't mind the fancy name, this is a simple cashew and peanut roasting and processing plant run by the Helping Hands Women's Group, a community-run project. The cashew factory, as it is commonly called, uses cashews and peanuts that have been locally grown in the Rupununi. Depending on the timing of your visit, you can see different stages of the process, including roasting, cracking, drying and processing. You'll leave with a new appreciation for the work that goes into making a cashew edible. Peanuts, cashews, cookies, trail mix, cashew butter and peanut butter that are made on site are also for sale.

Horse rentals The locally based tour operators, Bushmasters (e *amazon@ bushmasters.co.uk*; see page 59), has horses available for rent (US$10) and will also arrange a local guide (US$10) to take guests around the surrounding savannas. With enough advance notice, longer day or multi-day trips can be arranged to destinations further off, including to Nappi village or other nearby villages and jungles.

Brazil If Brazil doesn't figure in to your overall travel plans, you may want to think about heading there for a day trip. The small town of Bonfim is just across the river and very easily accessible, even by foot. From there it's possible to get a taxi or bus for the two-hour journey to Boa Vista, a medium-sized city with good shopping and restaurants. It's an easy way to get a dose of real Brazilian culture.

Before leaving Guyana you must visit immigration to have your passport stamped. It's also necessary to visit the immigration office in Bonfim upon arrival. There are plenty of taxis waiting on the opposite side of the bridge for transportation. Make sure you have any necessary visas and be sure to get stamped back in upon arriving in Guyana again – even if your trip was just for a day.

SCHOMBURGK'S PEAK Towering above the village of Kumu is Schomburgk's Peak, an imposing mountain with a large rock face on the peak; the view from the top was one of Schomburgk's famed 12 views.

The trek to the top starts two miles (3km) from the centre of Kumu, and while the trail is kept in good condition it is very steep in parts and not an easy journey. Depending on your level of fitness, it takes three to five hours to reach the top, with an ascent of more than 3,000ft. From the top, Lethem is laid out below and the savanna stretches into the invisible distance.

Fit trekkers can go up and down in a day with light packs, but there are good places to hang a hammock and there's plenty to see along the trail if you have the extra time provided by spending a night.

Interested parties need written permission from the Tuschao of St Ignatius or the senior councillor in Kumu village. You must pay a village entry fee (US$5/person) and will also need to hire a guide. Michael is widely regarded as the best guide in the area. No surname is required; just ask in Kumu or St Ignatius for Michael to guide you up Schomburgk's Peak.

Michael knows of several routes to the top, enabling you to make a sort of loop out of the trip. He is very keyed into his surroundings and is a keen bird and wildlife spotter.

Guide fees are roughly US$20 per day. You will need to have all necessary kit, food and water. If you need transportation it can be arranged in Lethem (US$25); be sure to arrange a pick-up time and get a back-up phone number.

SPECIAL EVENTS Lethem is home to a couple of yearly events that have become the reason for people from the coast to pile into their 4x4 vehicles and head to the Rupununi. It's a coming together of Brazilian and Guyanese cultures, of the coastlanders and the savanna dwellers. It's always used as the perfect excuse for a drink-up.

Rupununi Rodeo
Every Easter weekend Lethem becomes a destination for travellers from throughout Guyana and northern Brazil. The small town is transformed. Buses to and from town are booked, flights fill up weeks in advance and the Linden–Lethem trail becomes like an actual highway. Lodges are filled to capacity, hammocks are strung throughout town and tough guys from Georgetown preen and primp their 4x4s so they can drive up and down Lethem's dusty streets. And then there are the vaqueros, wild horses and angry steers.

The Rupununi Rodeo began as a form of entertainment brought to Guyana by the American Ben Hart. He ended up in Guyana's Rupununi after work ran out on the Madeira Mamore railway in the Amazonian forest. He married locally and on weekends held impromptu rodeos to see who had the best ranching skills. The event caught on and it's now an annual event run by local ranchers in the area.

The festivities unofficially begin on Good Friday night when there is a party at Macedo's Texaco petrol station. Everybody in town gathers around the gas pumps to smoke cigarettes, drink Guyanese rum and Brazilian beer and eat meat on a stick. It's a surreal scene complete with Georgetown politicians, scantily clad Brazilian women, drunken foreign volunteers and plenty of locals. It's a fitting start to rodeo weekend.

On Saturday and Sunday the events move to the rodeo grounds. The best vaqueros come from ranches around the Rupununi and Brazil to test their skills at wild bull riding and horseriding, horse racing, steer roping, wild cow milking, barrel races, bucking bronco and more.

But this isn't like a typical rodeo. Most of the vaqueros are barefoot, many of the cowboys are Amerindians and if any of the spectators are feeling particularly confident in their skills, they can sign up for an event.

At the grounds there are stalls selling food, drinks and local crafts. After the sun goes down, the music is turned up loud and people continue the drinking that likely started early in the day.

Dadanawa Ranch, which supplies many of the steers and horses, offers a trail-riding trip where guests can join the vaqueros as they move the cattle and horses from the ranch to Lethem (see page 286).

Rupununi Expo This event takes place the third weekend in November and is an exposition of the Rupununi lifestyle to showcase the culture, crafts and heritage of the area. Taking place at the rodeo grounds, the expo is actually much like the rodeo without the horses and bulls.

There is loud music, dancing, drinking and a pageant or two with some local communities performing skits. Everybody from the area gathers around to swap the local gossip; for outsiders it's great people-watching.

Organisation varies from year to year, but what could be a great opportunity for local Amerindian villages to exhibit their local crafts and sell their produce seems to be more of a showcase for those with money, largely government organisations and large donor agencies.

Within the exhibits you can learn about Guyana's forestry sector, see maps of land plots with the Lands and Surveys Commission, see Guyana's agricultural exports (most of which are grown along the coast), learn of the dangers of HIV or donate blood with the Red Cross. Thankfully a couple of local villages manage to display their crafts, but the separation of the Georgetown-based government and the villagers and locals that make the Rupununi what it is, is painfully evident.

Another interesting insight into local culture comes through the heavy presence of Brazilian music, beer, rum and cuisine. Brazilian culture, disconnected Guyanese government bodies and overshadowed locals unfortunately give a startling insight into life in the Rupununi.

The Rupununi Expo, at least in its current incarnation, is interesting to visit if you happen to be in the area, but is nothing to plan your trip around.

SOUTH RUPUNUNI

South Rupununi remains overlooked by most visitors to Guyana, and if you ask those who call it home, many will say they're glad. That doesn't mean they don't welcome visitors with the same genuine hospitality (indeed the doors here are often thrown open wider and with a bit more flair), it's just that they like being a bit off the radar; like they're in the know on a well-kept secret.

That this area of Guyana remains largely off the tourism trail is because access can be a bit trickier, although from Lethem, getting to Dadanawa Ranch – the area's main tourism destination – is about as easy and equally time-consuming as going to Karanambu Lodge in the north. It just seems further since the main road ends in Lethem.

Unless you know somebody who knows somebody, visiting this area will likely be through Dadanawa, which is actually the ideal way to experience the south. The ranch holds a long history and your hosts are the people who know this area of Guyana the best. From Dadanawa it's possible to explore the furthest reaches of Guyana, although sticking close to the ranch is good enough for most.

Another way to experience the Rupununi's cowboy history is to go on a trail ride with the local vaqueros. This is possible through Dadanawa, and Bushmasters also offers trips that entail exploring the south on the back of a horse.

Either way you do it, if it's at all possible (or affordable) you should make your way south. It's just a little bit different here. Once the main Lethem–Linden road gets paved, this area of Guyana will certainly prove to be more valuable than ever.

DADANAWA Dadanawa (e *defreitasduane@yahoo.com*; *www.rupununitrails.com*) has a long and rich history in Guyana. At one point in time Dadanawa held the claim of being the world's largest cattle ranch; fast forward a bit and the ranch was used as a home base for the filming of several episodes of Mutual of Omaha's *Wild Kingdom*, one of television's first wildlife shows. Stan Brock, one of the show's hosts and one-time manager of Dadanawa, captured America's attention by wrestling giant anacondas in waters where black caiman and piranha lurked, and where jaguars were often spotted along the banks.

Today little has changed; it is a place where the past lives on in the present. There are still some 6,000 cattle that openly roam the 1,700 square miles; Dadanawa still holds the title of being Guyana's largest cattle ranch. The ranch is also a favourite of wildlife film crews and it has served as a temporary home base for many scientists and researchers over the years. The wrestling of anacondas still happens from time to time as well.

Dadanawa is first and foremost a working ranch. Barefoot vaqueros frequently head out on cattle drives to round up steers and wild horses. Talk often lands on the problem with cattle rustlers coming in from the south. Vaqueros must also protect the cattle from jaguars and puma known to poach from the herd.

Sounds of a working ranch fill the air – sheep baa, kids laugh, roosters crow, motorcycles rev, pigs snort, frustrated men pound on engines, horses whinny and cattle moo. But then there are also sounds of the tropical forest – macaws screech overhead, small songbirds sing, beetles scream, monkeys scamper in the trees. And it all, somehow, comes together in beautiful harmony.

Dadanawa is a place where visitors can join vaqueros on an overnight ride to round up cattle one day and birdwatch the next, seeing as many as 80 different species in a few hours around the ranch. You can see the age-old process of tanning leathers and watch vaqueros attempt to tame wild horses one afternoon and then leave the next morning for some of Guyana's most remote terrain, with some of Guyana's best and most knowledgeable guides to lead you.

At Dadanawa, guests interact with the locals, the family and the history and are always treated as old family friends. Not because that's part of the routine but just because that's how life is. Dadanawa is a place rich in textures, from the people and lifestyles to the weathered woods and worn vehicles, and guests are invited to a place where time seems to have stood still, while still gracefully moving forward. An oxymoron surely, but it should be welcome in today's modern world.

History Dadanawa, which gets its name from the Wapishana Amerindian name of a nearby mountain, *Dadinauwau*, means 'spirit of the giant macaw hill'. The ranch traces its beginnings to c1865 when it was a small trading post with a few hundred cattle. In the late 1880s, the trading post and cattle were sold to a Mr Melville, who had come to Guyana from Barbados in search of gold. He settled for cattle, until 1919 when the entire ranch was sold to a group of investors known as the Rupununi Development Company.

The Rupununi Development Company focused on expanding the cattle business and over the following years, cattle multiplied and soon it was the world's largest cattle ranch, and also one of the most remote.

Cattle were transported from Dadanawa to the coast via the Rupununi cattle trail, on an epic cattle drive that covered hundreds of miles of savanna lands and jungle-covered mountains. Vaqueros drove the cattle to Surama, where they were handed on to another group of vaqueros. From here they went northwards, through the forests and to a pontoon crossing at Kurupukari. After getting the cattle to the other side of the Essequibo River they were marched northwards, eventually reaching the coast where they were once again fattened up before being sent off to market. (The current Linden–Lethem road follows some of the same path as the old cattle trail.)

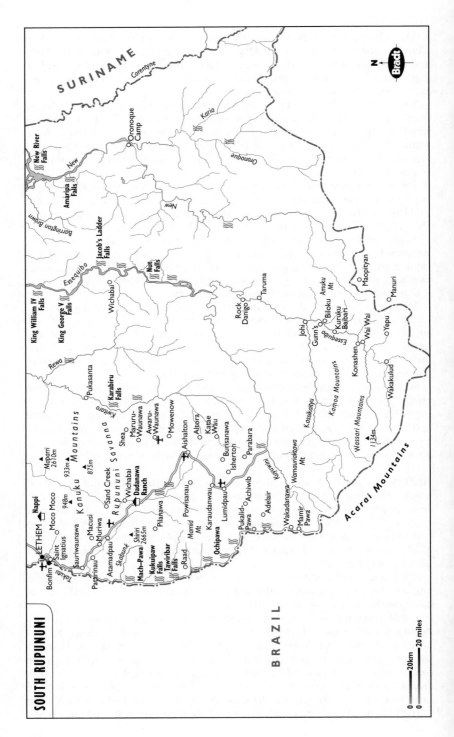

SOUTH RUPUNUNI

In the early 1970s, after the quashed Rupununi Uprising (see page 279), the cattle industry declined greatly, and with more and more cattle being reared on the coast, ranching became less profitable in the remote Rupununi. But the business didn't stop entirely. Dadanawa's remote and sprawling lands are ideal for rearing free-range cattle, but the location of the ranch has also been long known for pursuits outside of ranching.

Dadanawa is located on the Rupununi River and just south of the Kanuku Mountains; both are highly regarded for their wide diversity, and large populations, of bird and wildlife species. Dadanawa has had a long tradition of working with scientific institutions. During his time on the ranch, Stan Brock worked with various museums and science- and research-related organisations that built a strong base of knowledge of the surrounding natural environment; while cowboys chased down stray cows, researchers studied the flora and fauna.

And today this is still much how the ranch works. The Rupununi Development Company still maintains control over Dadanawa, vaqueros are still seen riding through the savannas cracking whips, scientists come to spend weeks studying one or two different species and Duane de Freitas, the current general manager, effortlessly slides between the two worlds, as comfortable in the cattle pen as he is in the middle of the jungle.

Tourism Due to its location in the South Rupununi, Dadanawa is often regarded as being one of Guyana's more remote tourism destinations. And in many ways it is. But instead of this being a factor in people choosing *not* to visit Dadanawa, the location should really be a deciding point in trying to add the ranch to your itinerary.

Granted, Dadanawa isn't for everybody. It has a rugged feel to it. The vehicles are mostly all aged Land Rovers that often spend as much time getting repaired as being driven. The guesthouses are weathered wooden structures on stilts. The general store is decorated with ancient machine parts, animal skulls and jaguar skins. But everything is perfectly fitting. It would be hard to imagine a fancy new lodge or shiny new truck on the grounds.

Visiting Dadanawa offers an insight into a true ranching life that hasn't let go. In a way time has stood still here partially because change isn't necessary (or desired) and partially because the isolation of location won't allow time to march forward.

Visitors should allow for at least a few days at Dadanawa, but it would be easy enough to spend weeks. The main grounds of the ranch can easily be explored for a day, slipping in and out of a hammock to wander over to the corral, the store, the tannery, the river, the mechanic shop or to the main house to see Duane's pictures and videos.

Then you branch out. Go on an overnight round up with the vaqueros, climb Shea Rock, birdwatch at the bush islands, camp in the savannas, trek through the Kanuku Mountains, canoe down the river or head out on an extended river expedition. Dadanawa is home base for exploring further throughout the southern savannas. And the knowledge of the guides is extensive. They are very tuned in and it quickly becomes obvious why so many researchers and scientists pass through here.

Rupununi Trails This is Duane's tourism offshoot that uses the combined forces of several Rupununi ranches to allow visitors the greatest opportunity to explore the least accessible parts of Guyana. Rupununi Trails caters to a niche market seeking specialised trips that focus on adventure, scientific research, birdwatching, sport fishing, and/or nature.

Most trips are longer, typically one to three weeks, and involve all the hardships of travelling through very remote jungles and savannas. Options include canoe trips, trail rides, boat trips to Maparri (in the Kanuku Mountains) and the Rewa River head. The Wai Wai Amerindians of southern Guyana have also given Rupununi Trails the exclusive right to take a limited number of people on an exploration of their 2,300-square-mile territory. For the truly adventurous, the rainforest expedition offers the chance to explore some of Guyana's most remote and pristine terrain with its most isolated Amerindian tribe.

Getting there and away Dadanawa can be reached by land, river or air. Since no scheduled flights stop at Dadanawa's airstrip, flying involves the costly option of chartering a plane. Coming in by river is for the more adventurous and can be done only in the wet season. The road, which is a beautiful trail through the savannas, is the most common way of getting to Dadanawa.

By air Chartered planes can be organised for trips to Dadanawa. For more information on planes that offer charters in Guyana, see page 84.

By road Dadanawa is most easily accessed from Lethem. For information on getting to Lethem, see page 278.

Dadanawa is located 50 miles (85km) southeast from Lethem. In the dry season the trip along the bumpy road takes roughly three hours. In the wet season, road conditions change dramatically and the trip can take several additional hours.

Dadanawa can organise transportation to or from locations throughout the Rupununi. During the dry season they charge US$3 per mile; in the rainy season, when driving is much harder on vehicles and drivers, the charge is US$4 per mile (prices can fluctuate with cost of fuel). These prices hold for both transfers and for longer day trips from the ranch.

Within this structure, costing varies slightly. For transfers guests may pay for the mileage each way; pick-up in Lethem would be US$150 and drop-off would be an additional US$150. But when going on trips that start and return at the ranch, guests are required to pay only the mileage for one way. Shea Rock, for example, is 30 miles away; the cost of transportation would be US$90, not US$180.

To further complicate the issue, if Dadanawa is already planning on going into Lethem for supplies, guests can go along for the ride and pay US$30 per person.

Transportation arrangements can also be made in Lethem for rates that are similar or slightly less. If you will be driving your own vehicle, Sandy or Duane can organise a guide to help direct you from Lethem. Unless you know which trail leads where, without a local there's a good chance you'll end up lost in the savannas.

When coming from Lethem, Dadanawa is on the opposite side of the Rupununi River. During the driest months, it's possible to drive right through; for the wet season months there is a hobbled collection of wooden planks and oil barrels that acts as a pontoon to transfer vehicles.

By river In the wet season, it's possible to arrive at Dadanawa via the Rupununi River. However, this is unlikely for most as it would involve a long river expedition from a location such as Karanambu to the north. For more information on extended river trips, see above.

Where to stay (*FB, inc limited activities* **$$$$**) Accommodation rates at Dadanawa are all inclusive of the following: three meals, local juices and rum, laundry services and guided trips within seven miles of the main ranch, including birdwatching, horseriding, canoe and boat trips (dependent on water levels) and drives to nearby mountains. Trips further out incur extra fees.

Dadanawa Ranch proper is built on 300 acres and is a collection of weathered buildings that are at ease with the surroundings. There are two main wooden guesthouses that sit on stilts and have high, vaulted ceilings. The lodging is basic but comfortable. The five rooms all have a similar set-up with private bathrooms, two single beds covered in crisp white linens and mosquito nets. All rooms have easy access to wide verandas hung with hammocks and stunning views of the rolling hills in the distance.

Much of ranch is wired for electricity, but the generator hasn't been fixed since it broke (it's quieter that way). At night, battery-powered lanterns light the rooms and for those needing to charge the batteries of computer or cameras, there is a small generator at the main house.

The meals are reflective of the ranch: large family-style portions, usually involving the local organic beef, and prepared with an influence of styles, from Amerindian to international. Special diets are also catered for.

Evenings – before and after dinner – often involve listening to the locals tell tales of their exploits over beverages on the veranda.

Also note that the inclusive rates do not include bottled water. Water is from a deep well and has reportedly never given anybody a weak stomach. For those wanting to be cautious, bottled water can be purchased, or pack purifying tablets.

Camping trips can also be arranged while you are at Dadanawa. These vary from slinging a hammock by the riverside, sleeping with the vaqueros and cattle in the savanna or pitching a tent at the base of a mountain. It's only the location that changes; all rates, meals, etc remain the same.

What to see and do Whether you go for the ranching or the birdwatching, activity options at Dadanawa are often limited only by personal time and budgets.

The ranch A good part of one day should be set aside to spend exploring the main grounds of the ranch. You can visit the **corral** and watch the local vaqueros do everything from taming wild horses to branding steers. At the **tannery**, see the traditional process of tanning anything from leather to fish skin. The **mechanic shop**, which demonstrates the philosophy of 'everything will be of use someday', is an entirely different history lesson. The **ranch store** sells a hotchpotch of supplies, food, drinks and random parts; it's also a local gathering place. And the main house, where Duane and Sandy live, is surrounded by a Land Rover graveyard and a small collection of animals that have all come to Dadanawa with their own stories. Ask Duane to see some of his photographs and amazing video footage shot in the surroundings (it may be your only chance to see video of an anaconda eating a boa constrictor that had just eaten an iguana).

Round up Dadanawa welcomes visitors to participate in the daily life of a vaquero. Guests aren't expected to tame their own wild horse, plait their own lasso and build their own saddle like the locals, but you can ride along on a round up.

Trips are catered to the riding ability of visitors. More experienced riders can help chase down cattle, while novice riders can hang back with the cattle that have already been rounded up and be an observer. A typical trip entails one seven-hour day of riding, a night spent at a cowboy camp and then returning the next day with the cattle. Trips can be shortened or lengthened.

Branding and castrating of animals takes place at the end of September through March; this is when most of the round ups take place.

Horseriding For those not interested in trying to keep up with the vaqueros, more casual horseback rides can be taken around the grounds. Length and destination of the trips are largely up to guests.

Canoe and boat trips Depending on the water level, short trips in canoes and boats can be taken to see ancient petroglyphs carved in stones along the river. Bird and animal watching often become part of this trip by default. The petroglyphs can also be accessed by land during the dry season.

Birdwatching The area in proximity to Dadanawa is home to more than 400 species of birds. With the help of a local guide, it's not uncommon to tick off some 80 species of birds around the main ranch grounds in a few hours. Near the lodge there is a good mix of savanna birds and waterbirds, as the Rupununi River runs within sight and there are a series of ponds just behind the guesthouse that attract many birds.

KONASHEN

Konashen – literally *God's Country* – is the name given to an area of the Amerindian Wai Wai lands of southern Guyana. One of Guyana's most remote areas, it can only be reached via light aircraft or a day-long jungle trek. But even with its isolation, the area doesn't (or won't forever) remain out of the reach of those seeking to expand their logging, mining and wildlife trapping interests.

Seeking to protect their lands, the Wai Wai community of Konashen asked the government of Guyana to provide them with the title to their traditional lands. Once that was secured, the community asked Conservation International Guyana (CI) to help them protect their now officially-recognised lands. In 2004, a partnership between the Wai Wai residents of the Konashen district and CI was formalised and a Community Owned Conservation Area was established to protect the nearly one million acres of largely intact pristine rainforest.

In 2006, CI carried out a rapid assessment programme (RAP) of Konashen and found it to be home to an amazing range of biodiversity. The RAP identified 318 species of bird from 50 different families, more than 100 species of fish and many of Guyana's greatest animals and birds, such as healthy populations of jaguars, harpy eagles, Guianan cock-of-the-rock and scarlet macaw.

The local residents of Konashen are now taking a proactive role towards conserving their forests. Many residents once relied on the wildlife trade to generate income, but it has since been stopped. And CI has been working with the Wai Wai communities to develop new forms of sustainable development, such as ecotourism and craft projects, so that the men don't have to leave and work in logging and mining camps.

Tourism to the area is extremely limited and very much in the developmental phase. For the most hardy travellers, Rupununi Trails (see page 59) offers trips to Wai Wai country that combine boats, trekking and aircraft to access the area.

By branching out and exploring the vast surroundings by Land Rover or boat you have the possibility of seeing a harpy eagle nest, jabiru storks, roosting yellow-crowned parrots, Guianan cock-of-the-rock *leks*, and the rare red siskin, a population of which was recently found in the forested mountains not far off (see *Birds*, page 41). Based at Dadanawa, the South Rupununi Conservation Society is currently creating a monitoring and management plan for the rare bird.

Nature photography Over the years, Dadanawa has attracted at least as many photographers – both video and print – as researchers. Photography is inherent in all the above activities but if you are a specialist or want to capture one certain bird or mammal, trips can be catered to meet your needs. One of Duane's many hats is that of amateur photographer, combined with being an expert guide and great naturalist – you're sure to come away with good images.

Shea There are several small Amerindian communities around Dadanawa and visiting them is a good way to explore the south savannas. Birdwatching, hiking and looking for animals can all be incorporated into the trip. Perhaps the most popular village to visit is Shea.

Shea is 30 miles from Dadanawa, a 4x4 journey of 1½ –2 hours in the dry season. The village itself is a typical Wapishana community: traditional clay brick and thatch houses are widely spaced over a large area of the savanna. The focal point is Shea Rock, which towers over the flat surroundings. An easy 20–30-minute hike up leads to the top of the flat rock.

From here you can see the Kanuku Mountains stretching off in the distance; famed Bottle Mountain is in one direction and Shiriri Mountain is in the other. The views are stunning.

For those who want to spend a night at Shea, Marjorie takes guests at her house. Accommodation is traditional and simple. There is space to hang a hammock or put a tent in her dirt yard. It's a great opportunity to experience a traditional Amerindian lifestyle and can be organised with Dadanawa.

Appendix

FURTHER INFORMATION

A selection of the following books was chosen by Longitude (New York); the titles they have available for purchase can be easily sourced from www.longitudebooks.com.

BOOKS
History and background

Abrams, Ovid *Metegee: The History and Culture of Guyana* Ashanti Books, 1997. In-depth background on Guyana.

Adamson, Alan H *Sugar Without Slaves: The Political Economy of British Guiana, 1838-1904* Yale University Press, 1972.

Balkaran, Lal *Bibliography of Guyana and Guyanese Writers, 1596-2004* LBA Publications, 2004. An extensive list of 820 authors and 1300 titles.

Bisnauth, Dale *The East Indian Immigrant Society in British Guiana* Peepal Tree Press, 1996.

Bisnauth, Dale *Settlement of Indians in Guyana, 1890-1930* Peepal Tree Press, 2001.

Benjamin, Joel, Kallicharan, Lakshimi, McDonald, Ian and Seawar, Lloyd *They Came in Ships: An Anthology of Indo-Guyanese Prose and Poetry* Peepal Tree Press, 1997.

Braveboy-Wagner, Jacqueline Ann *The Venezuela-Guyana Border Dispute* Westview Press, 1984

Brett, William Henry *Legends and Myths of the Aboriginal Indian of British Guiana* Kessinger Publishing, 2003.

Burrowes, Reynold A *The Wild Coast: An Account of Politics in Guyana* Schenkman, 1984.

Burnett, D Graham *Masters of All They Surveyed: Exploration, Geography, and a British El Dorado* University of Chicago Press, 2001. A lively, well-illustrated account of the 19th-century exploration, mapping and British Imperial adventures in what is now Guyana.

Costa, Emilia Viotti *Crowns of Glory, Tears of Blood: The Demerara Slave Rebellion of 1823* Oxford University Press, 1994.

de Angelis, Gina *Jonestown Massacre: Tragic End of a Cult* Enslow Publishers, 2002.

de Barros, Juanita *Order and Place in a Colonial City: Patterns of Struggle and Resistance in Georgetown, British Guiana, 1889-1924* McGill-Queens, 2003.

Gibson, Kean *Cycle of Racial Oppression in Guyana* University Press of America, 2003.

Hall, John R *Gone from the Promised Land: Jonestown as American Cultural History* Transaction Publishers, 2001.

Hollett, David *Passage from India to El Dorado: Guyana and the Great Migration* Fairleigh Dickinson University Press, 1999.

Jagan, Cheddi *A New Global Human Order* Harpy, 1999. A collection of speeches and writings by the folk hero and late president.

Jagan, Cheddi *West on Trial, My Fight for Guyana's Freedom* International, 1972.

Jagan, Cheddi *Forbidden Freedom: The Story of British Guiana* Penguin Publishing, 1999.

Menezes, Mary Noel (Editor) *The Amerindians in Guyana 1803–1873, A Documentary History* Routledge, 1979. This collection of early accounts is an invaluable introduction to the customs, beliefs and history of the Amerindians in Guyana.

Mangru, Basdeo (Editor) *The Elusive El Dorado, Essays on the Indian Experience in Guyana* Rowman & Littlefield, 2005. This collection of eight scholarly essays brings to a general audience the history of East Indians in British Guiana.

Naipaul, V S *The Middle Passage, The Caribbean Revisited* Vintage Books, 2002. Novelist and travel writer Naipaul tackles the history of the Caribbean and northern South America in this incisive portrait.

Odeen, Ishmael *Amerindian Legends of Guyana* Artex Publishing, 1995. Folk heroes, myths, traditions and legends of the first inhabitants of Guyana.

Rabe, Stephen *U.S. Intervention in British Guiana: A Cold War Story* University of North Carolina Press, 2006. Rabe presents convincing evidence of a covert intervention by the CIA in British Guiana between 1953 and 1969, intended to unseat Cheddi Jagan.

Raleigh, Walter, Sir *The Discovery of Guiana, With Related Documents* St Martin's Press, 2007. First published in 1859, this fascinating report includes a chapter on British Guiana.

Stephenson, Denice *Dear People: Remembering Jonestown* Heyday Books, 2005. The story of Jonestown told through letters, oral histories, journal entries and other personal accounts.

Young, Alma, and Perry Mars (Editors) *Caribbean Labor and Politics: Legacies of Cheddi Jagan and Michael Manley* Wayne State University Press, 2004. This collection of scholarly articles celebrates the life, times and legacy of two pivotal leaders, who died on the same day, 6 March 1997.

Travel literature and memoirs

Bernard, Deryck *Going Home and Other Tales from Guyana* Macmillan, 2002. These stories of boyhood days capture the flavour of growing up in British Guiana.

Brock, Stan *All the Cowboys Were Indians* Synergy South, 1999. Personal account of Stan Brock's many years spent at Dadanawa Ranch, from Amazonian bush pilot to vaquero.

Durrell, Gerald *Three Singles to Adventure* Penguin Books, 1969. Tale of Durrell's adventure in Guyana to capture live species for science.

Gimlette, John *Wild Coast: Travels on South America's Untamed Edge* Profile Books, 2011. Gimlette's masterfully written book that is part travel memoir and part history tells of his entertaining journey through the three Guianas.

Herman, Marc *Searching for El Dorado, A Journey in the South American Rainforest on the Tail of the World's Largest Gold Rush* Vintage Books, 2004. This dramatic journalistic account of the lives and fortunes of gold miners in the forests of Guyana combines interviews with independent prospectors, Herman's own travels through the region and a hard-hitting report on international mining corporations.

Layton, Deborah *Seductive Poison: A Jonestown Survivor's Story of Life and Death in the People's Temple* Anchor, 1999. A moving account of Jonestown from the inside.

Plotkin, Mark *Tales of a Shaman's Apprentice* Penguin Putnam, 1994. Plotkin recounts his work documenting the use of medicinal plants among remote tribes in the northwest Amazon of Suriname, Venezuela, Guyana and French Guiana. The book is a portrait of people and their environment, a tale of adventure and, most of all, a moving example of science in the service of preservation.

Schomburgk, Robert *Travels in British Guiana, 1840–1844* Many editions (but rare). Schomburgk's seminal account of his travels in Guiana between 1835 and 1844 on behalf of the Royal Geographical Society is especially interesting for its depiction of the Amerindian peoples.

Swan, Michael *British Guiana: The Land of Six Peoples* HMSO, 1957.

Swan, Michael *The Marches of El Dorado: British Guiana, Brazil, Venezuela* Cape, 1958.

Waterton, Charles *Wanderings in South America* Book Jungle, 2007. A reprint of the observations and travels of the early 19th-century naturalist in Guyana.

Waugh, Evelyn *Waugh Abroad, Collected Travel Writing* Everyman's Library, 2003. The collected travel writing of the peripatetic Waugh, including *92 Days*, the account of a comically miserable stint in British Guiana in the 1930s.

Young, Matthew French *Guyana: The Lost Eldorado, My Fifty Years in the Guyanese Wilds* Peepal Tree Press, 1998. An account of a white Guyanese Scotsman's time in the Guyanese bush.

Natural history

Attenborough, David *Zoo Quest to Guiana*, Pan Books, 1958. A classic photo book based on the popular nature documentary television series.

Beebe, William *Edge of the Jungle* Cooper Square Press, 2001. Originally published in 1921, a collection of 12 essays on the Amazon and its ecology and wildlife from the past director of the New York Zoological Society's research centre in Guyana.

Caufield, Catherine *In the Rainforest, Report from a Strange, Beautiful, Imperiled World* University of California Press, 1984. Caufield deftly combines good basic information on the ecology of the world's rainforests, a report on thorny conservation issues and a sympathetic treatment of indigenous inhabitants through masterly prose.

Forsyth, Adrian and Ken Miyata *Tropical Nature* Scribner, 1984. A lively portrait of the rainforest as seen by two thoughtful field biologists and told through 17 essays introducing the habitats, ecology, plants and animals of the Central and South American rainforest.

Gibbs, Allan and Barron, Christopher *Geology of the Guyana Shield* Oxford University Press, 1993.

Kyte, Cwolde *Caribbean Medicine Forward to Eden: A Source Book on the Healing Modalities of Guyana, the Caribbean and the Americas* Center for Sacred Healing Arts Publishing Co, 1988.

McConnell, Ro *Land of Waters: The South American Rainforest and Savannah* Book Guild Publishing, 2000. Based on six years of studying Guyana's ecosystems, flora, fauna and Amerindians.

Guides

Braun, Michael J, Finch, Davis W, Robbins, Mark B and Schmidt, Brian K *A Field Checklist of the Birds of Guyana, 2nd Ed* Smithsonian Institution, Washington DC, 2007. Most recent list with 814 species, colour map and information on habitat.

Doyle, Chris *Cruising Guide to Trinidad and Tobago plus Barbados and Guyana* (3rd ed) Chris Doyle Publishing, 2006. Recently updated sailing guide includes short section on Guyana, focused on the Essequibo River.

Eisenberg, John F *Mammals of the Neotropics, The Northern Neotropics Vol. 1* University of Chicago Press, 1989. A comprehensive overview of the mammals of the northern neotropics.

Emmons, L H *Neotropical Rainforest Mammals, A Field Guide*. University of Chicago Press, 1997. An illustrated guide to the mammals of the New World tropics, compact enough to slip into your daypack, with 29 colour plates illustrating more than 200 species.

Hilty, Steven *A Guide to the Birds of Venezuela* Princeton University Press, 2002. The classic South American bird guide, revised and expanded by Steve Hilty. A bit hefty for a field guide, but still an essential reference to over 1,400 bird species and the bible for birdwatching in Guyana.

Kricher, J C *A Neotropical Companion* Princeton University Press, 1999. A tropical primer aimed at the motivated general reader. From plants and animals to birds and bugs, it's all here in this wonderfully written primer on the ecology, habitats, plants and animals of Central and South America.

Lentino, Miguel, Restall, Robin and Rodner, Clemencia *Birds of Northern South America: An Identification Guide, Vol 1: Species Account* Yale University Press, 2006. In-depth information on species, including habitats, vocalisation, nomenclature and taxonomy.

Lord, Rexford D *Mammals of South America* Johns Hopkins University Press, 2007. An authoritative, illustrated overview of the mammals of South America, featuring 252 photographs.

Matthews, Downs, and Kevin Schafer (Photographer) *Beneath the Canopy, Wildlife of the Latin American Rain Forest* Chronicle Books, 1999. Portraits of the birds, mammals, reptiles and other elusive animals of the neotropic rainforest.

Restall, Robin, Rodner, Clemencia and Williams, Roger *Birds of Northern South America, Vol. 2: Field Guide* Yale University Press, 2006. This comprehensive field guide, featuring an astounding 6,400 paintings and 2,308 maps covers all the birds from Ecuador to French Guiana.

Photo books

Ali, Arif *Guyana* Hansib Publications, 2008. A large-format photo and text book that provides a good overview of the complete Guyana, from history and travel to business and education.

Bish, Renee, Oxford, Pete and Watkins, Graham *Rupununi: Rediscovering a Lost World* Earth in Focus Editions, 2010. An outstanding book using words and stunning photographs to show the underappreciated North Rupununi to the world.

Dunn, Katherine *Guyana* Twin Palms Publishers, 1996. Photography book with light text.

Fiction

Bhattacharya, Rahul *The Sly Company of People Who Care* Farrar, Straus & Giroux, 2011. This wonderful debut novel, which is based on the author's year spent living in Guyana, brings the culture, landscape and people of Guyana to life.

Kempadoo, Oonya *Buxton Spice* Beacon Press, 2004. This semi-autobiographical novel captures the culture and flavour of Guyana, and the tensions between the racially mixed East Indian and Afro-Caribbean inhabitants of fictional Tamarind Grove.

Kempadoo, Peter Lauchmonen *Guyana Boy* Peepal Tree Press, 2002. The hierarchical world of a colonised Guyana sugar plantation, as seen through the eyes of a child.

Melville, Pauline *The Ventriloquist's Tale* Bloomsbury USA, 1999. A fine novel which explores the nature and culture of post-colonial Guyana.

Health

Wilson-Howarth, Dr Jane, and Ellis, Dr Matthew *Your Child Abroad: A Travel Health Guide* Bradt Travel Guides, 2005

Wilson-Howarth, Dr Jane, *Bugs, Bites & Bowels* Cadogan, 2006

Children

Henderson, James D and Temple, Bob *Guyana, Discovering South America.* Perseus, 2003. This illustrated primer for ages 10–14 covers the geography, history, economy, politics, people and culture of Guyana.

Morrison, Marion *Guyana: Enchantment of the World* Children's Press, 2003. Describing the geography, history, culture, religion and people of Guyana.

Maps
Guyana Lands and Surveys Commission (*www.lands.gov.gy*) offer a range of city, regional and country maps as well as a detailed digital gazetteer for sale, some of which served as source maps for this guidebook.

ITMB *Guyana Map* ITMB. A colourful, detailed travel map of Guyana, which served as the source for many of the maps used in this guidebook.

FILMS

A Dream for Guyana's Natural Heritage Conservation International, 1998. Short documentary introducing Guyana's pristine biodiversity while outlining the importance of protecting it.

Herzog, Werner *The White Diamond* Fox, 2005. Documentary about one man's quest to build a prototype airship to float over the rainforest canopy around Kaieteur Falls.

Kanuku, Mountains of Life Conservation International, 2005. Short documentary on the flora, fauna and people found in the Kanuku Mountains.

Lost Land of the Jaguar BBC, 2008. Three-part BBC documentary about an international team of explorers, scientists and film makers discovering the plants and animals of Guyana.

Nelson, Stanley *Jonestown: The Life and Death of People's Temple* Firelight Media, 2006. Most recent documentary on the People's Temple, with never-before-seen footage and interviews with past members.

Rettig, Neil *Flight of the Harpy Eagle* National Geographic Society Explorer, 1993. Documentary on the protection and preservation of the harpy eagle, filmed in Guyana.

NEWSPAPERS

Guyana Chronicle (*www.guyanachronicle.com*)
Guyana Times (*www.guyanatimesgy.com*)
Kaieteur News (*www.kaieteurnews.com*)
Stabroek News (*www.stabroeknews.com*)

WEBSITES
General information

Explore Guyana (*www.exploreguyana.org*), the website for the Tourism and Hospitality Association of Guyana, includes tourism information and a digital version of the annual tourism magazine *Explore Guyana*.

Government Information Agency (*www.gina.gov.gy*) catalogues news with a favourable slant towards the ruling party.

Guyana Consulate (*www.guyanaconsulate.com*) is Toronto based with info on tourism, export products, government and consulate services.

Guyana News and Information (*www.guyana.org*) has links to current news, history, photographs, tourism, government agencies and more.

Guyana Office for Investment (*www.goinvest.gov.gy*) provides detailed information for those interested in investing in or exporting from Guyana.

Guyana Online (*www.guyana.com*) is a general site with news, events, recipes and history.

Guyana Outpost (*www.guyanaoutpost.com*) is another general Guyana site with news, proverbs, recipes, photos and books for sale.

Guyana Portal (*www.guyana.cc*) organises links to an array of topics, including arts, business, entertainment, government, news, culture, sports and tourism.

Guyana Tourism Authority (*www.guyana-tourism.com*) has an extensive, if not a bit cluttered, website with info on all things Guyana, from booking tours to history.

Land of Six Peoples (*www.landofsixpeoples.com*) has endless articles on dozens of topics from sports and health to festivals and environment.

Office of the President (*www.op.gov.gy*) has information on past and present activities of the president and government, including archived speeches.

Natural history

Biological Diversity of the Guiana Shield (*www.mnh.si.edu/biodiversity/bdg/*) is a Smithsonian Institution project; website has info on the programme, researchers and studies. Also has link to online version of *A Field Checklist of the Birds of Guyana*.

Guiana Shield Initiative (*www.guianashield.org*) is a project seeking to set up a sustainable financial mechanism to conserve the ecosystems of the Guiana Shield.

Guiana Shield Media Project (*www.gsmp.org*) has information, videos and photos on the biodiversity of the Guiana Shield.

Guyana Birding (*www.guyanabirding.com*) provides in-depth information for twitchers, including trip reports, checklists, newsletters, media resources and travel info.

Guyana Marine Turtle Conservation Society (*www.gmtcs.org*) includes a wealth of information related to the society and the turtles they protect.

Guyana.travel (*www.guyana.travel*) has information on Guyana's ecotourism offerings, including extensive photo collections.

Iwokrama International Centre for Rain Forest Conservation and Development (*www. iwokrama.org*) runs a very extensive website with information on research, tourism, sustainable forestry, flora and fauna and climate change.

Rupununi (*www.rupununi.org*) provides an extensive look at the Rupununi Savanna and features beautiful photographs; counterpart to book of same name (see page 298).

Arts

Guyana-Gyal (*http://sapodilla.blogspot.com*) is a blog with stories of life in Guyana told through beautiful, poetic Creolese.

Guyana Journal (*www.guyanajournal.com*) online site of journal that has well-written accounts of Guyana issues past and present.

Guyana National Library (*www.natlib.gov.gy*) website has basic information on their services, activities and collections.

Radio Guyana (*www.radiogy.com*) broadcasts Guyanese and Caribbean news and music from London.

WIN A FREE BRADT GUIDE

READER QUESTIONNAIRE

**Send in your completed questionnaire and enter our monthly draw
for the chance to win a Bradt guide of your choice.**

To take up our special reader offer of 40% off, please visit our website at
www.bradtguides.com/freeguide or answer the questions below and return to us
with the order form overleaf.

(Forms may be posted or faxed to us.)

Have you used any other Bradt guides? If so, which titles? . . . .
. . . .

What other publishers' travel guides do you use regularly? . . . .
. . . .

Where did you buy this guidebook? . . . .

What was the main purpose of your trip to Guyana (or for what other reason did
you read our guide)? eg: holiday/business/charity . . . .
. . . .

How long did you travel for? (circle one)

weekend/long weekend   1–2 weeks   3–4 weeks   4 weeks plus

Which countries did you visit in connection with this trip? . . . .
. . . .

Did you travel with a tour operator?' If so, which one? . . . .
. . . .

What other destinations would you like to see covered by a Bradt guide?
. . . .

If you could make one improvement to this guide, what would it be?
. . . .

Age (circle relevant category) 16–25   26–45   46–60   60+

Male/Female (delete as appropriate)

Home country . . . .

Please send us any comments about this guide (or others on our list).

. . . .
. . . .
. . . .

Bradt Travel Guides
IDC House, The Vale, Chalfont St Peter, Bucks SL9 9RZ, UK
✆ +44 (0)1753 893444 **f** +44 (0)1753 892333
e info@bradtguides.com
www.bradtguides.com

TAKE 40% OFF YOUR NEXT BRADT GUIDE!
Order Form

To take advantage of this special offer visit www.bradtguides.com/freeguide and enter our monthly giveaway, or fill in the order form below, complete the questionnaire overleaf and send it to Bradt Travel Guides by post or fax.

Please send me one copy of the following guide at 40% off the UK retail price

No	Title	Retail price	40% price
1	....	....	....

Please send the following additional guides at full UK retail price

No	Title	Retail price	Total
...	....	....	....
...	....	....	....
...	....	....	....

Sub total ....

Post & packing ....

(Free shipping UK, £1 per book Europe, £3 per book rest of world)

Total ....

Name ....

Address ....

Tel ....   Email ....

☐ I enclose a cheque for £........ made payable to Bradt Travel Guides Ltd

☐ I would like to pay by credit card. Number: ....

Expiry date: ... / .... 3-digit security code (on reverse of card) .....

Issue no (debit cards only) .....

☐ Please sign me up to Bradt's monthly enewsletter, Bradtpackers' News.

☐ I would be happy for you to use my name and comments in Bradt marketing material.

Send your order on this form, with the completed questionnaire, to:

Bradt Travel Guides
IDC House, The Vale, Chalfont St Peter, Bucks SL9 9RZ, UK
☎ +44 (0)1753 893444   f +44 (0)1753 892333
e info@bradtguides.com   www.bradtguides.com

Bradt Travel Guides

Africa

Access Africa: Safaris for People with Limited Mobility	£16.99
Africa Overland	£16.99
Algeria	£15.99
Angola	£17.99
Botswana	£16.99
Burkina Faso	£17.99
Cameroon	£15.99
Cape Verde	£15.99
Congo	£15.99
Eritrea	£15.99
Ethiopia	£16.99
Ghana	£15.99
Kenya Highlights	£15.99
Madagascar	£16.99
Malawi	£15.99
Mali	£14.99
Mauritius, Rodrigues & Réunion	£15.99
Mozambique	£15.99
Namibia	£15.99
Niger	£14.99
Nigeria	£17.99
North Africa: Roman Coast	£15.99
Rwanda	£15.99
São Tomé & Príncipe	£14.99
Seychelles	£14.99
Sierra Leone	£16.99
Sudan	£15.99
Tanzania, Northern	£14.99
Tanzania	£17.99
Uganda	£16.99
Zambia	£17.99
Zanzibar	£14.99
Zimbabwe	£15.99

The Americas and the Caribbean

Alaska	£15.99
Amazon Highlights	£15.99
Amazon, The	£14.99
Argentina	£16.99
Bahia	£14.99
Cayman Islands	£14.99
Colombia	£16.99
Dominica	£15.99
Grenada, Carriacou & Petite Martinique	£14.99
Guyana	£15.99
Nova Scotia	£14.99
Panama	£14.99
Paraguay	£15.99
Turks & Caicos Islands	£14.99
Uruguay	£15.99
USA by Rail	£14.99
Venezuela	£16.99
Yukon	£14.99

British Isles

Britain from the Rails	£14.99
Eccentric Britain	£15.99
Eccentric London	£13.99
Slow: Cotswolds	£14.99
Slow: Devon & Exmoor	£14.99
Slow: Norfolk & Suffolk	£14.99
Slow: North Yorkshire	£14.99
Slow: Sussex & South Downs National Park	£14.99

Europe

Abruzzo	£14.99
Albania	£15.99
Azores	£14.99
Baltic Cities	£14.99
Belarus	£15.99
Bosnia & Herzegovina	£14.99
Bratislava	£9.99
Budapest	£9.99
Cork	£6.99
Croatia	£13.99
Cross-Channel France: Nord-Pas de Calais	£13.99
Cyprus see North Cyprus	
Dresden	£7.99
Estonia	£14.99
Faroe Islands	£15.99
Georgia	£15.99
Greece: The Peloponnese	£14.99
Helsinki	£7.99
Hungary	£15.99
Iceland	£15.99
Kosovo	£15.99
Lapland	£13.99
Latvia	£13.99
Lille	£9.99
Lithuania	£14.99
Luxembourg	£13.99
Macedonia	£15.99
Malta & Gozo	£12.99
Montenegro	£14.99
North Cyprus	£12.99
Riga	£6.99
Serbia	£15.99
Slovakia	£14.99
Slovenia	£13.99
Spitsbergen	£16.99
Switzerland Without a Car	£14.99
Transylvania	£14.99
Ukraine	£15.99
Zagreb	£6.99

Middle East, Asia and Australasia

Armenia	£15.99
Bangladesh	£15.99
Borneo	£17.99
Eastern Turkey	£16.99
Georgia	£15.99
Iran	£15.99
Iraq: Then & Now	£15.99
Israel	£15.99
Kazakhstan	£15.99
Kyrgyzstan	£16.99
Lake Baikal	£15.99
Maldives	£15.99
Mongolia	£16.99
North Korea	£14.99
Oman	£15.99
Shangri-La: A Travel Guide to the Himalayan Dream	£14.99
Sri Lanka	£15.99
Syria	£15.99
Taiwan	£16.99
Tibet	£13.99
Yemen	£14.99

Wildlife

Antarctica: Guide to the Wildlife	£15.99
Arctic: Guide to Coastal Wildlife	£15.99
Australian Wildlife	£14.99
Central & Eastern European Wildlife	£15.99
Chinese Wildlife	£16.99
East African Wildlife	£19.99
Galápagos Wildlife	£16.99
Madagascar Wildlife	£16.99
New Zealand Wildlife	£14.99
North Atlantic Wildlife	£16.99
Pantanal Wildlife	£16.99
Peruvian Wildlife	£15.99
Southern African Wildlife	£19.99
Sri Lankan Wildlife	£15.99

Pictorials and other guides

100 Alien Invaders	£16.99
100 Animals to See Before They Die	£16.99
100 Bizarre Animals	£16.99
Eccentric Australia	£12.99
Northern Lights	£6.99
Tips on Tipping	£6.99
Wildlife and Conservation Volunteering: The Complete Guide	£13.99

303

Index

Page numbers in **bold** indicate major entries; those in *italics* indicate maps